# HEALTH
# SERVICES
# MANAGEMENT

ELEVENTH EDITION

# HEALTH SERVICES MANAGEMENT

## A Case Study Approach

Ann Scheck McAlearney
Anthony R. Kovner

AUPHA

Health Administration Press, Chicago, Illinois

Association of University Programs in Health Administration, Washington, DC

**Library of Congress Cataloging-in-Publication Data**
Names: McAlearney, Ann Scheck, editor. | Kovner, Anthony R.
Title: Health services management : a case study approach / [edited by] Ann Scheck McAlearney and Anthony R. Kovner.
Description: Eleventh edition. | Chicago, Illinois : Health Administration Press ; Washington, DC : Association of University Programs in Health Administration, [2017] | Includes bibliographical references and index.
Identifiers: LCCN 2017022337 (print) | LCCN 2017015158 (ebook) | ISBN 9781567939101 (eBook 13) | ISBN 9781567939118 (Xml) | ISBN 9781567939125 (Epub) | ISBN 9781567939132 (Mobi) | ISBN 9781567939095 (print : alk. paper)
Subjects: LCSH: Health services administration—Case studies.
Classification: LCC RA971 (print) | LCC RA971 .H434 2017 (ebook) | DDC 362.1—dc23
LC record available at https://lccn.loc.gov/2017022337

The paper used in this publication meets the minimum requirements of American National Standard for Information Sciences—Permanence of Paper for Printed Library Materials, ANSI Z39.48-1984. ∞™

Acquisitions editor: Jennette McClain; Project manager: Michael Noren; Cover designer: James Slate; Layout: Cepheus Edmondson

Found an error or a typo? We want to know! Please e-mail it to hapbooks@ache.org, mentioning the book's title and putting "Book Error" in the subject line.

For photocopying and copyright information, please contact Copyright Clearance Center at www.copyright.com or at (978) 750-8400.

Health Administration Press
A division of the Foundation of the American
   College of Healthcare Executives
One North Franklin Street, Suite 1700
Chicago, IL 60606-3529
(312) 424-2800

Association of University Programs
   in Health Administration
1730 M Street, NW
Suite 407
Washington, DC 20036
(202) 763-7283

*Ann would like to thank her husband, John, and daughter, Fiona, for their love, support, and patience while she completed this project.*

*Ann would also like to thank and acknowledge her mother, Carol, and the memory of her father, Tim, for serving as positive role models in management as well as in everyday life.*

*Tony would like to thank his wife, Chris, and daughters, Sarah and Anna, for their love and support.*

*Tony would also like to thank Ann Scheck McAlearney for her partnership and direction of this latest edition of the book.*

*This book is dedicated to our students, past, present, and future, who have to make sense out of the healthcare organizational predicament, find their own way, and take ownership of their careers.*

Ann Scheck McAlearney
Tony Kovner

# CONTENTS

## Part III: Organizational Design

**Part VI: Accountability**

# PREFACE TO THE ELEVENTH EDITION

**H**ealth Services Management: A Case Study Approach is distinctive in its overview of management and organizational behavior theory. The six parts of the book are arranged according to a framework that first examines those areas of work over which managers have the greatest control—the manager herself and control systems. The book next covers areas over which managers have a good deal of control (at least over the short run)—organizational design and professional integration. The book concludes with those areas of work over which managers have less control—adaptation, including implementation of strategy, and accountability. Throughout, the book's focus is on the case method approach to teaching healthcare management, with an additional emphasis on the use of evidence in management practice. The cases in this book take place in a variety of organizations, including a faculty practice, an accountable care organization, a small rural hospital, a patient-centered medical home, a multihospital health system, a county health center, a medical group, an academic medical center, a home health organization, an ambulatory care center, and a number of community hospitals.

We wrote and edited *Health Services Management: A Case Study Approach* with the idea that it would be used as a stand-alone textbook, but it can also be used as a complement to other textbooks. By presenting cases, commentary, and suggestions for additional readings in a single book, we have aimed to (1) reduce expense for the student, (2) facilitate course use with other textbooks, and (3) take advantage of the availability of the readings on the Internet (meaning that the readings themselves do not have to be reproduced in the book). We have included in this book a set of tips to help students effectively and efficiently search the literature of health services management.

Through the 11 editions of this text and the now 39 years of writing these books, some things have not changed. One constant has been the desire to point students to readings that build on good evidence rather than just opinion. At first, this goal was challenging because of the lack of literature; now, choosing from among so many good articles is difficult. A second constant has been our goal to link theory with practice—to build a bridge between the social science literature and the actual work of improvement. Third, the text has always been divided into six sections—focusing on the role of the manager, control, organizational design, professional integration, adaptation, and accountability—each with a commentary. That structure continues with this eleventh edition.

We welcome dialogue with our readers and can be reached via e-mail:

Ann Scheck McAlearney      mcalearney.1@osu.edu
Anthony R. Kovner      anthony.kovner@nyu.edu

---

## Instructor Resources

This book's Instructor Resources include an instructor's manual with answers to case questions and approaches for discussing key topics in each part.

For the most up-to-date information about this book and its Instructor Resources, go to ache.org/HAP and browse for the book's title or author name.

This book's Instructor Resources are available to instructors who adopt this book for use in their course. For access information, please e-mail hapbooks@ache.org.

# REFLECTIONS ON THE ELEVENTH EDITION

*Anthony R. Kovner*

These reflections are intended to provide a frame for my editing of this book with Ann Scheck McAlearney. They draw from my experience of having worked at two major research universities as a health services management educator for 50 years.

## Context

Now in my eightieth year, I have been part of health services management since 1957, when I graduated from college, and I have taught at the Robert F. Wagner School of Public Service at New York University (NYU Wagner) for 35 years. One observation from more recent years is that the younger generation of millennials does not seem to pay as much attention to the past as people of my own generation did. A feeling is present today that "we can always look it up"—which wasn't the case 50 years ago.

But "looking it up" involves knowing where and how to look something up, making the right decisions to answer an appropriately framed research question, weighing the valid and reliable evidence, and understanding what needs to take place to implement a solution. Lacking experience, the prospective manager often is at a loss to explain why managers don't implement what might seem to be an obvious solution to a management challenge.

## Beginnings

The first edition of *Health Services Management*, published in 1978, was edited by Duncan Neuhauser and me. At the time, I was chief executive officer (CEO) of Newcomb Hospital in Vineland, New Jersey, and Duncan was associate professor of health services administration at the Harvard School of Public Health.

In the foreword for that first edition, Gerald Katz, then president of St. Christopher's Hospital for Children in Philadelphia, suggested that "today's health services manager faces unprecedented challenges, demands and opportunities. Never before has there been such focus on management. . . . With the challenges come new opportunities to make our institutions perform responsibly and at a high level of achievement." Katz, if he were still alive, could easily write the same foreword today.

Duncan and I noted in the preface of the first edition that our text was conceptualized in the Task Force on Organization and Administration, appointed by Gary Filerman of the Association of University Programs in Health Administration (AUPHA). We presented our Task Force report in 1974. As of 1978, many of the programs for which we developed the book had no courses in health services management.

## The First Edition

The 566 pages of the first edition were organized, after an introduction, into six sets of readings: (1) "The Role of the Manager," (2) "Organizational Design," (3) "Control," (4) "Physician Integration," (5) "Adaptation," and (6) "Accountability," followed by an annotated bibliography. As coeditors, Duncan and I introduced each set of readings with several pages of comments. The topics ranged from areas over which managers have the most control (the role of the manager) to areas over which managers have much less control (accountability to those who provide the organization with resources).

Most of the readings from the first edition have been forgotten, although many can still be read with profit today. One such reading is "The Gouverneur Health Services Program: An Historical View" by Harold L. Light and Howard J. Brown. Light and Brown were the leaders of one of the first neighborhood health centers funded by the Office of Economic Opportunity in the 1960s; these neighborhood health centers were the forerunners of accountable care organizations. (I worked at Gouverneur subsequently as the administrator.) A second highly recommended reading from the first edition is "The Notion of Hospital Incentives," by Robert M. Sigmond, a quest for the yet-to-be-found holy grail of "pay-for-performance."

## Changes in the Teaching of Health Services Management

The history of health administration (HA) education is largely unfamiliar to most HA faculty, as well as to students, but the subsequent editions of this book have reflected constant changes in the field. This eleventh edition remains a valuable source of information about the diverse circumstances and challenges faced by health services managers across a wide range of organizations; however, the book in its current form is primarily a casebook, rather than a collection of readings. The need for such a casebook has increased over time, with the industry becoming so large, the vocabulary so specialized, and the reimbursement so complex. Relationships between managers and clinicians have changed rapidly, yet relationships between HA faculty and managers haven't changed nearly so quickly. This gap has created a muddle between the competencies typically developed by managers in HA programs and the reality of what managers actually do. In 2017, the way we teach managers is perhaps in greater need for change than it was when we prepared the first edition more than 35 years ago.

## My Own Perspective

My perspective on health services management stems from my background. My father was the co-owner of a group of small for-profit hospitals in New York City. My doctoral work in hospital organization of nursing units was carried out under the direction of an eminent sociologist, Charles Perrow, who was interested in the technology of work as the independent variable and the organization of the workers as the dependent variable. My work experience was dominated by three jobs—as manager of the Gouverneur Health Services Program; as CEO of the Newcomb Hospital; and as a faculty member and director of the health policy and management program at NYU Wagner, a master of public administration (MPA) program. Over the past 20 years, my research has focused on governance of nonprofit hospitals and on evidence-based management as a way of improving managerial decision making.

Fictionalized accounts of many of the management challenges that I faced during my career are included in my books *Health Care Management in Mind: Eight Careers* (Springer, 2000) and *Evidence-Based Management in Healthcare: Principles, Cases, and Perspectives* (Health Administration Press, 2017; coedited with Thomas D'Aunno). In addition, many of the case studies in this book are based on my own work situations. They include the following:

- Case 2: "The Associate Director and the Controllers"
- Case 3, Part 1: "What More Evidence Do You Need?"
- Case 16: "Financial Reporting to the Board"
- Case 34: "The Complaining Doctor and Ambulatory Care"
- Case 35: "Doctors and the Capital Budget"
- Case 51: "Letter to the CEO"
- Case 52: "Whose Hospital?"

## Going Forward

Performance improvement for health services organizations depends heavily on metrics and accountability. Do the managers of these organizations develop and sustain metrics that are related to a limited number of performance indicators? How are health services managers accountable to various organizational stakeholders for achieving performance targets that are continuously improving? And what are the consequences to managers and to organizations of not meeting targets as negotiated with stakeholders?

## Goodbye

I do not expect to work on the twelfth edition of this casebook. Thanks to our publishers at AUPHA and Health Administration Press. Thanks to my coeditors, Ann Scheck McAlearney and Duncan Neuhauser. Thanks to the case study writers and the authors of the readings. Thanks to the students and alumni of HA programs.

# INTRODUCTION TO THE CASE STUDY APPROACH

# A SHORT HISTORY OF THE CASE METHOD OF TEACHING

*Karen Schachter Weingrod and Duncan Neuhauser*

Teaching by example is no doubt as old as the first parent and child. In medicine, it surely started with a healer, the first apprentice, and a patient. But when university education in medicine started about 800 years ago, it focused instead on abstract principles and scholastic reasoning, largely removed from practicality. Medical theories, often dealing with the "four humours," likely had little bearing on actual disease processes. Then, in the late 1700s in France, medical education moved into hospitals or "the clinic," where patients in large numbers could be observed, autopsies performed, and the physiological state linked back to the patients' signs and symptoms (Foucault 1973). This shift represented an early step away from the abstract medical theorizing that had become the norm.

Education in law had also emphasized the abstract, conveyed through erudite lectures. University instruction built theoretical constructs and was logically well reasoned. The professor spoke, and the student memorized and recited without much opportunity for practical experience or discussion. This had become the standard by the late 1850s.

The case method of teaching, which can be traced to Harvard University, represented a striking change from this approach. Perhaps it is not surprising that this change occurred in the United States rather than in Europe, considering the American inclinations toward democratic equality, practicality, and positivism, and the lack of interest in classic abstract theorizing.

This change started in 1870 when the president of Harvard University, Charles William Eliot, appointed the obscure lawyer Christopher Columbus Langdell as dean of the Harvard Law School. Langdell believed law to be a science. In his own words: "Law considered as a science, consists of certain principles or doctrines. To have such a mastery of these as to be able to apply them with constant faculty and certainty to the ever-tangled skein of human affairs, is what constitutes a good lawyer; and hence to acquire that mastery should be the business of every earnest student of the law" (Langdell 1871, vi).

The specimens needed for the study of Langdell's science of law were judicial opinions as recorded in books and stored in libraries. He accepted the science of law, but he turned the learning process back to front. Instead of giving a lecture that would define a principle of law and give supporting examples of judicial opinions, he gave the students the judicial opinions without the principle and, through a Socratic dialogue, extracted from the students in the classroom the principles that would make sense out of the cases. The student role became active rather than passive, as students were subjected to rigorous questioning of the case material. They were asked to defend their judgments and to confess to error when their judgments were illogical. Although this dialectic was carried on by the professor and one or two students at a time, all the students learned and were on the edge of their seats, fearing or hoping they would be called on next. The law school style that evolved has put the student under public pressure to reason quickly, clearly, and coherently in a way that is valuable in the courtroom or during negotiation. After a discouraging start, Langdell attracted such able instructors as Oliver Wendell Holmes Jr. They carried the day, and now the case method of teaching is nearly universal in American law schools.

Application of the case method of teaching to medicine also has roots at Harvard. Walter B. Cannon, a medical student of the class of 1901, shared a room with Harry Bigelow, a third-year law student. Cannon was struck by the excitement with which Bigelow and his classmates debated the issues in the cases they were reading; the energy contrasted sharply with the passivity of Cannon's medical school lectures.

In 1900, discussing the value of the case method in medicine, Harvard president Charles Eliot (1900, 557) described the earlier medical education as follows:

> I think it was thirty-five years ago that I was a lecturer at the Harvard Medical School for one winter; at that time lectures began in the school at eight o'clock in the morning and went on steadily till two o'clock—six mortal hours, one after the other of lectures, without a question from the professor, without the possibility of an observation by the student, none whatever, just the lecture to be listened to, and possibly taken notes of. Some of the students could hardly write.

In December 1899, Cannon persuaded one of his instructors, G. L. Walton, to present a case from his private practice in written form as an experiment. Walton printed a sheet with the patient's history and allowed the students a week to study it. The lively discussion that ensued in class made Walton an immediate convert (Benison, Barger, and Wolfe 1987). Other faculty soon followed, including Richard C. Cabot.

Through the case method, medical students would learn to judge and interpret clinical data, to estimate the value of evidence, and to recognize the gaps in their knowledge—something that straight lecturing could never reveal. The case method of teaching allowed students to throw off passivity in the lecture hall and integrate their knowledge of anatomy, physiology, pathology, and therapeutics into a unified mode of thought.

As a student, Cannon (1900a, 1900b) wrote two articles about the case method for the *Boston Medical and Surgical Journal* (later to become *The New England Journal of Medicine*), and he sent one of these papers to the famous clinician and professor Dr. William Osler of Johns Hopkins University. Osler replied: "I have long held that the only possible way of teaching students the subject of medicine is by personal daily contact with cases, which they study not only once or twice, but follow systematically" (Benison, Barger, and Wolfe 1987). If a written medical case was interesting, a real live patient in the classroom could be memorable. Osler regularly introduced patients to his class and asked students to interview and examine patients and discuss medical problems. He would regularly send students to the library and laboratory to seek answers and report back to the rest of the class (Chesney 1958). This is ideal teaching. Osler's students worshipped him, but with today's division of labor in medicine between basic science and clinical medicine, such a synthesis is close to impossible.

The May 24, 1900, issue of the *Boston Medical and Surgical Journal* was devoted to articles and comments by Eliot, Cannon, Cabot, and others about the case method of teaching. In some ways, this journal issue remains the best general discussion of the case method available. The approach was adopted rapidly at other medical schools, and books of written cases quickly followed in neurology (1902), surgery (1904), and orthopedic surgery (1905) (Benison, Barger, and Wolfe 1987).

Cannon went on to a distinguished career in medical research. Cabot joined the medical staff of the Massachusetts General Hospital and in 1906 published his first book of cases. (He also introduced the first social worker into a hospital[1] [Benison, Barger, and Wolfe 1987].) Cabot was concerned about the undesirable separation of clinical physicians and pathologists; too many diagnoses were turning out to be false at autopsy. To remedy this, he began to hold his case exercises with students, house officers, and visitors.

Cabot's clinical/pathological conferences took on a stereotypical style and eventually were adopted in teaching hospitals throughout the world. First, the patient's history, symptoms, and test results would be described. Then an invited specialist would discuss the case, suggest an explanation, and give a diagnosis. Finally, the pathologist would present the autopsy or pathological diagnosis, and questions would follow to elaborate points.

In 1915, Cabot sent written copies of his cases to interested physicians as "at home case method exercises." These became so popular that in 1923 the *Boston Medical and Surgical Journal* began to publish one per issue, starting in October 1923. This journal has since changed its name to *The New England Journal of Medicine*, but the "Cabot Case Records" still appear with each issue.

A look at a current *New England Journal of Medicine* case will show how much the case method has changed since Langdell's original concept. The student or house officer is no longer asked to discuss the case; rather, it is the expert who puts her reputation on the line. She has the opportunity to demonstrate wisdom, but she can also be refuted in front of a large audience. Although every physician in the audience probably makes mental diagnoses, the case presentation has become a passive affair, like a lecture.

Cabot left the Massachusetts General Hospital to head the social relations (sociology, psychology, and cultural anthropology) department at Harvard. He brought the case method with him, but it disappeared from use at Harvard by the time of his death in 1939 (Buck 1965). The social scientists at that time were concerned with theory building, hypothesis testing, and research methodology; to such "unapplied" pure scientists, perhaps the case method was considered primitive.

In 1908, the Harvard Business School was created as a department of the Graduate School of Arts and Sciences. It was initially criticized as merely a school for "successful money-making." Early on, an effort was made to teach through the use of written problems involving situations faced by actual business executives, presented in sufficient factual detail to enable students to develop their own decisions. The school's first book of cases, on marketing, was published in 1922 by Melvin T. Copeland.[2] Today, nearly every class in the Harvard Business School is taught by the case method.

Unlike the law school, where cases come directly from judicial decisions (sometimes abbreviated by the instructor), and the medical school, where the patient is the basis for the case, the business faculty and their aides must enter organizations to collect and compile material. This latter mode of selection offers substantial editorial latitude. Here more than elsewhere, the case writer's vision, or lack of it, defines the content of the case.

Unlike a pathologist's autopsy diagnosis, a business case is not designed to have a right answer. In fact, one usually never knows whether the business in question lives or dies. Rather, the cases are written in a way that splits a large class (up to 80 students) into factions. The best cases are those that create divergent opinions; the professor becomes more an orchestra leader than a source of truth. The professor's opinion or answer may never be made explicit. Following a discussion, a student's question related to what really happened or what should have been done may be answered, "I don't know" or "I think the key issues were picked up in the case discussion." Such hesitancy on the part of the instructor is often desirable. To praise or condemn a particular faction in the classroom can discourage future discussions.

William Ellet (2007, 13) defines a business school case as describing a real situation with three characteristics: "A significant business issue or issues, sufficient information on which to base conclusions, and no stated conclusions." A good case allows the reader to construct conclusions, filter out irrelevant information, furnish missing information through inference, and combine evidence from different parts of the case to support the conclusions.

The class atmosphere in a business school is likely to be less pressured than in a law school. Like a good surgeon, a good lawyer must often think very quickly, but unlike the surgeon, the lawyer must demonstrate his thinking verbally and publicly. He must persuade by the power of his logic rather than by force of authority. Business and management are different. Key managerial decisions—What business are we in? Who are our customers? Where should we be ten years from now?—may take months or even years to answer.

The fact that the business manager's time frame reduces the pressure for immediate answers makes management education different from physician education in other ways. Physicians are required to absorb countless facts on anatomy, disease symptoms, and drug side effects. Confronted with 20 patients a day, the physician often has no time, even with the convenience of the Internet, to consult references. The manager has a longer time horizon for decision making in business. Therefore, managerial education focuses more on problem-solving techniques than does standard medical education.

Not all business schools have endorsed the case method of teaching. Some schools focus on teaching the "science" of economics, human behavior, and operations research, with faculty emphasizing theory building, hypothesis testing, statistical methodology, and the social sciences. Some business schools use about half social sciences and half case method. Each school, typically, is convinced that its teaching philosophy is best. Conceptually, the debate can be broken into two aspects: active versus passive learning, and science versus professionalism.

There is little question that active student involvement in learning is better than passive listening to lectures. The case method is one of many approaches to increasing student participation. Student-written reports are another form of active learning.

Academic science is not overly concerned with the practical problems of the world, but professionals are, and professional education should be. The lawyer, physician, and manager cannot wait for perfect knowledge; they have to make decisions in the face of uncertainty. Science can help with these decisions to varying degrees. To the extent that scientific theories have the power to predict and explain, they can be used by professionals. In the jargon of statistics: The higher the percentage of variance explained, the more useful the scientific theory, the smaller the role for clinical or professional judgment, and the lesser the role for case method teaching as opposed to, for example, mathematical problem solving.

It can be argued that the professional will always be working at the frontier of the limits of scientific prediction. When science is the perfect predictor, then often the problem is solved, or the application is delegated to computers or technicians, or, as in some branches of engineering, professional skills focus on the manipulation of accurate but complex mathematical equations.

Scientific medicine now understands smallpox so well that it is no longer a major public health threat. Physicians spend most of their time on problems that are not solved: cancer, heart disease, or the common complaints of living that bring most people to doctors. In healthcare management, the budget cycle, personnel position control, sterile operating room environment, and maintenance of the business office ledgers are handled routinely by organizational members and usually do not consume the attention of the chief executive officer. In law, the known formulations become the "boilerplate" of contracts.

The debate between business schools over the use of cases illustrates differences in belief in the power of the social sciences in the business environment. Teaching modes related to science and judgment will always be in uneasy balance with each other, shifting with time and place. Innovative medical schools have moved away from the scientific lectures of the preclinical years and toward a case problem-solving mode. On the other side of the coin, a quiet revolution is being waged in clinical reasoning. The principles of statistics, epidemiology, and economics, filtered through the techniques of decision analysis, cost-effectiveness analysis, computer modeling, and artificial intelligence, are making the "Cabot Case Record" approach obsolete for clinical reasoning. Scientific methods of clinical reasoning are beginning to replace aspects of professional or clinical judgment in medicine (Barnes, Christensen, and Hansen 1994).

This does not mean that the professional aspect of medicine will be eliminated by computer-based science. Rather, the frontiers, the unknown areas calling for professional judgment, will shift to new areas, such as the development of socioemotional rapport with patients—what used to be called "the bedside manner."[3]

The cases that make up this book are derived from the business school style of case teaching. As such, they do not have answers. The cases can be used to apply management concepts to practical problems; however, these concepts (*scientific theory* seems too strong a term to apply to them) generally will not yield the one "right" answer. They all leave much room for debate.

## Notes

1. Although not the first hospital-based social worker to work with Cabot, his best-known social worker colleague was Walter Cannon's sister, Ida Cannon.

2. For more on the history of the case method of teaching managers, see Roy Penchansky's *Health Services Administration: Policy Cases and the Case Method* (Harvard University Press, 1968), 395–453.

3. A proposal to increase the problem-solving content of medical education is found in the Association of American Medical Colleges' *Graduate Medical Education: Proposals for the Eighties* (AAMC, 1980). This material is also reprinted as a supplement in *Journal of Medical Education* 56, no. 9 (September 1981), part 2.

## References

Barnes, L. B., C. R. Christensen, and A. J. Hansen. 1994. *Teaching and the Case Method*, 3rd ed. Boston: Harvard Business School Press.

Benison, S., A. C. Barger, and E. L. Wolfe. 1987. *Walter B. Cannon: The Life and Times of a Young Scientist*. Cambridge, MA: Harvard University Press.

Buck, P. (ed.). 1965. *The Social Sciences at Harvard*. Boston: Harvard University Press.

Cannon, W. B. 1900a. "The Case Method of Teaching Systematic Medicare." *Boston Medical and Surgical Journal* 142 (2): 31–36.

———. 1900b. "The Case System in Medicine." *Boston Medical and Surgical Journal* 142 (22): 563–64.

Chesney, A. M. 1958. *The Johns Hopkins Hospital and the Johns Hopkins University School of Medicine, Vol. 2, 1893–1905*. Baltimore, MD: Johns Hopkins Press.

Eliot, C. 1900. "The Inductive Method Applied to Medicine." *Boston Medical and Surgical Journal* 142 (22): 557–558.

Ellet, W. 2007. *The Case Study Handbook*. Boston: Harvard Business School Press.

Foucault, M. 1973. *The Birth of the Clinic*. New York: Vintage.

Langdell, C. C. 1871. *A Selection of Cases on the Law of Contracts*. Boston: Little, Brown & Co.

# LEARNING THROUGH THE CASE METHOD

*Anthony R. Kovner*

**A** "case" is a description of a situation or problem facing a manager that requires analysis, a decision, and a course of action. A decision may be to delay a decision, and a planned course of action may be to take no action. A case takes place in time, and it must have an issue. As McNair says, "There must be a question of what somebody should do, what somebody should have done, who is to blame for the situation, what is the best decision to be made under the circumstances" (Towl 1969, 67). A case includes only selected details about a situation; it represents selection by the case writer.

The case method involves class discussion that is guided by a teacher so that students can diagnose and define important problems in a situation, acquire competence in developing useful alternatives to respond to such problems, and improve judgment in selecting action alternatives. Students learn to diagnose constraints and opportunities faced by a manager in implementation and to overcome constraints such as limited time and dollars.

As Ellet (2007, 16) points out, "You have to read a case actively and construct your own meaning." Students should consider what the situation is, what the manager has to know about the situation, and what the manager's working hypothesis is. Can the problem be defined differently? What's the biggest downside of the recommended decision? Has the student been objective and thorough about the evaluative findings that do not jibe with the overall assessment?

Students often have difficulty adjusting to a classroom without an authority figure, without lectures from which to take notes, and in which little information is offered by the teacher, at least until the class discussion has ended. Some students find it irritating to have to listen to their peers when they are paying to learn what the teacher has to say. But students must learn to take responsibility for their own view of a case, to develop an argument that they can explain, and to listen to others who disagree. Students should speak up early and learn to be good participants. When students go to the classroom, they should be familiar with the information in the case, have a conclusion about the main issue, have evidence explaining why their conclusion is reasonable, and show that they have thought about other conclusions. It is suggested that students spend at least two hours preparing for case discussion.

In a case course, students are often asked to adopt the perspectives of certain characters in the case, to play certain roles. To deny someone or persuade someone requires an understanding of the needs and perceptions of others. Role-playing can promote a better understanding of viewpoints that might otherwise seem irrational. Students can better understand their own values and underlying assumptions when their opinions are challenged by peers and teachers.

To conclude, understanding what a case is not, and what the case method cannot teach, is important. Cases are not real life—they present only part of a situation. Writing or communicating a case may be as difficult as or more difficult than evaluating someone else's written case. Like many a consultant, the student will never see the results—what would have happened if the case participants had followed his advice.

Some aspects of management can be learned only by managing. How else can one understand when someone says one thing but means another? How else can one judge whether to confront or oppose a member of the ruling coalition when that member's behavior appears to threaten the long-range interests of the organization? Students and managers have to form and adopt their own value systems and make their own decisions. A case course can give students a better understanding of the nature of the role they will be playing as managers—an understanding that will help them manage the best they can.

## References

Ellet, W. 2007. *The Case Study Handbook*. Boston: Harvard Business School Press.

Towl, R. 1969. *To Study Administration*. Boston: Harvard Graduate School of Business Administration.

# SEARCHING THE LITERATURE OF HEALTH SERVICES MANAGEMENT

*Alison Aldrich*

**M**any of the journal articles referenced in this text are available online through your college or university library. Knowing how to find and use journal articles and other scholarly literature is critical to your academic and professional success. The following tips will help you conduct more effective and efficient literature searches:

1. Use your college or university library's homepage as a starting point. Although many full-text articles can be found with a Google search, many more are only accessible to paid subscribers. Starting at your library's homepage will identify you as someone who has access to the university's paid subscriptions in addition to materials that are freely available online. If you are conducting your literature searches from off campus, look for an off-campus sign-in option on your library's homepage and enter your university credentials before beginning your search.

2. If you know exactly which article you are seeking and you have the full bibliographic citation (author, title, year, volume, etc.), look for a list of electronic journals and search for the title of the journal, not the title of the article. When you find it, look for the appropriate volume/year and page numbers, or search within that journal for the article title you need. If you do not find an electronic journals link, search in the library catalog by journal title.

3. If you want to look for all articles on a topic, you will need to search in a database. Your library likely subscribes to many article databases that are specialized for different fields of study. PubMed, for example, is a comprehensive database of journal literature in the biomedical sciences. On your library's website, look for a list of databases with descriptions. The librarians at your institution may also have prepared online subject guides (also called research guides or pathfinders) for various subject

areas such as business or social science. These subject guides will point you to the best databases to search for articles in that subject.

4. Familiarize yourself with the services your library offers for retrieving full-text articles when they are not readily available online. Most college and university libraries offer an interlibrary loan or document delivery service whereby you can request articles even if they are not included in the university's subscriptions. Many libraries offer this service at no charge for students, faculty, and staff.

5. Meet with a librarian. The librarians at your institution can assist you in developing search strategies to help you thoroughly explore your topic of interest. They can recommend sources and search terms that you may not have considered. They may also be able to recommend citation management tools that will help you keep your references organized as you prepare papers and presentations.

# OVERVIEW

*Anthony R. Kovner*

> Why do we do what we do?
> How do we know it works?
> How can we do it better?
> —*John Bingham, Twin Falls, Idaho*

This casebook is about management, and management is about managers. Yet, the boundaries of management are not clear. As managers, we bring our full selves to work. And, of course, we bring ourselves as managers back home. Most importantly, in terms of success at work and at home, we manage ourselves or fail to manage ourselves according to our view of the world, our track record of performance, and our hopes and fears for the future.

We focus on the work managers do and how they talk about management. Thinking about how managers function, what they want, and how they achieve their goals is critical to improving performance. A key to success is being able to act reflectively in the present. Managers do learn from the past, and by planning creatively for the future. But managers learn by doing, not by talking about what they are going to do. If managers reflect too long about what they are going to do, they will often act too late. People want answers. Reflecting takes only a moment before doing or saying something. Ask, "Is what I am about to do or say going to be good for me?" We define what's "good for me" as the right action, which can mean something quite different with the benefit of hindsight. Managers do not always act based on what is good for them or for the organization, but they can often reflect in advance and then alter what they are going to do or say, or not say anything at all. Helping another person, not taking the credit, being charitable, or showing gratefulness may or may not be the right action depending on context. The right action will involve achieving one's own and organizational goals, subject to situational and other constraints.

## The Healthcare Sector

Healthcare is a large sector of the economy, and its boundaries are often fuzzy. From one point of view, health is everything, from swimming to sex; from another perspective, health is nothing, since we are dying every day. Patients and their families have strong feelings about at least some of the healthcare services they receive—notably life-or-death services such as those provided by emergency departments. But many health services are not measurable in terms of their outcomes. Most Americans do not pay for the majority of their healthcare expenses themselves. Rather, the expenses are paid for by private and public insurance.

The Institute for Healthcare Improvement (IHI) describes a framework known as the "Triple Aim" for healthcare organizations (HCOs). It focuses on providing the best care (improving the patient experience) for the whole population at the lowest cost (IHI 2017); however, such goals can raise questions and controversy when applied at the organizational level. What priority does improving the patient experience have when the patient isn't going to pay for his care? Why should patients contain costs? What is involved in improving the health of the population? Do such efforts include financially penalizing patients for bad health behaviors such as smoking, poor diet, lack of sleep, and lack of exercise? Broadly stated, the goals of the Triple Aim may not be realistic for many HCOs, nor for the job descriptions of most managers. But the aims can be specified as follows: to improve patient experiences that patients are willing to pay for, to increase costs only where there is adequate reimbursement, and to help patients change their health behaviors so that health outcomes may be improved.

Numerous stakeholders are involved in HCOs: owners, managers, clinicians, consumers and taxpayers, pharmaceutical and insurance companies, payers, and regulatory and accrediting organizations. Often, powerful stakeholders do not agree. In a sense, for the manager, there is no such thing as "the organization"—only powerful groups within and without, whose leaders seek to control organizational decision making.

## Levels and Issues

Current and prospective employers examine a manager's track record. What individuals have done in the past is the best guide to what they will do in the future. Assessing the skills and experience that managers have is relevant to learning what skills and experience managers need to carry out the demands of a new or a current job. Each job has its demands, its constraints that limit what the manager can do, and a range of choices associated with the position.

Managers can change demands, constraints, and choices over time. Managers generally have a larger scope for choice than do other workers.

As in past editions, we have organized this textbook into six parts that parallel the levels of work over which managers have influence. Managers' influence at these six levels ranges from greater to lesser: They have the greatest influence over themselves and the least influence over the external environment. We describe the least controllable level as *accountability* within the context of the general environment. At this level, managers influence those who supply the HCO with inputs to which the HCO adds value, and suppliers and others buy or use the value-added goods and services. The levels, issues, and degree to which the manager can influence activities are shown in the accompanying exhibit.

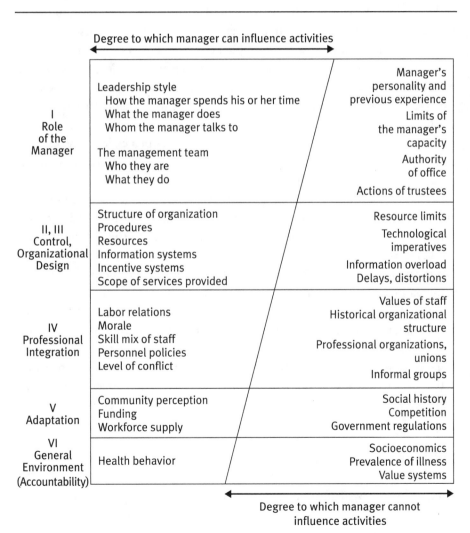

**EXHIBIT**
Examples of Issues and Challenges Associated with Different Levels of the Organization

Degree to which manager can influence activities

**I Role of the Manager**

Leadership style
How the manager spends his or her time
What the manager does
Whom the manager talks to

The management team
Who they are
What they do

Manager's personality and previous experience
Limits of the manager's capacity
Authority of office
Actions of trustees

**II, III Control, Organizational Design**

Structure of organization
Procedures
Resources
Information systems
Incentive systems
Scope of services provided

Resource limits
Technological imperatives
Information overload
Delays, distortions

**IV Professional Integration**

Labor relations
Morale
Skill mix of staff
Personnel policies
Level of conflict

Values of staff
Historical organizational structure
Professional organizations, unions
Informal groups

**V Adaptation**

Community perception
Funding
Workforce supply

Social history
Competition
Government regulations

**VI General Environment (Accountability)**

Health behavior

Socioeconomics
Prevalence of illness
Value systems

Degree to which manager cannot influence activities

Part I of this book, "The Role of the Manager," concerns the immediate context within which managers work and the way managers spend their time. The importance of judgment, the kinds of challenges managers face, and the opportunities and constraints managers choose to respond to in implementing change and sustaining organizational performance are all emphasized. At this first level, managers have the greatest influence on how they work with whom, on what activities they perform in what order and priority, and on how they spend their time.

In parts II and III, "Control" and "Organizational Design," managers rely on others to get things done, using formal rules and hierarchy, budgets, information systems, and other forms of control and evaluation. Managers attempt to structure and monitor activities to varying extents to achieve organizational objectives. Managers are limited in these efforts by resource availability and political acceptability. Structural changes and control systems are not error-free, need to be changed over time, and can be expensive, both in terms of money and time spent in implementation and system maintenance.

Organizational stakeholders respond to management initiatives by independent action, resistance, or cooperation. A distinctive element in HCOs in part IV, "Professional Integration," is the degree to which clinician activities can be aligned with organizational goals. Clinicians are subject, to varying degrees, to external reference and representing bodies such as professional associations and trade unions. Achieving these organizations' buy-in is often essential to organizational goal achievement and managerial effectiveness.

Managers adapt to changes in the organization's internal circumstances and to the organization's specific external environment, as discussed in part V, "Adaptation." Finally, managers must be accountable to the communities or publics served, as discussed in part VI, "Accountability." The environments that healthcare professionals face are constantly changing, and the pace of change is increasing. Managers must adapt to change, or their organizations will not survive at current levels of effectiveness. Managers may have influence on legislation, regulation and third-party financing, and community perceptions, particularly when they are constituents of effective lobbying and public relations organizations, such as hospital associations. On the other hand, many of the activities of external stakeholders cannot be effectively controlled by managers and HCOs or their representatives, nor should they be in a democratic society.

## Evidence-Based Management

Evidence-based management aims to do the right things right. Barends, Rousseau, and Briner (2014) define *evidence-based practice* as "making decisions through the conscientious, explicit and judicious use of the best available evidence from multiple sources to increase the likelihood of a favorable outcome." The evidence-based approach has six steps: (1) framing a question that can be answered, (2) obtaining the evidence, (3) validating the evidence, (4) adapting the evidence to local organizational circumstances, (5) determining whether the organization can act based on the evidence, and (6) determining whether the evidence is adequate to take appropriate action.

All the cases in this book can be examined using this evidence-based approach. In reality, however, few of them are, usually because the manager has not framed an answerable question or gathered the available evidence from scientific, organizational, experiential, and stakeholder sources. Often, a manager will consider a problem and decide on an action—increasing emergency department waiting space, for instance—and then look for evidence to justify the chosen action. A manager taking an evidence-based approach, on the other hand, might begin by asking, "What are the reasons for crowding in the emergency department?" By framing this question and seeking out appropriate evidence, she might find that the department can ameliorate bottlenecks in the discharge process, and thus reduce patient wait times without investing capital to increase space.

## Skills and Competencies

Professional education is rapidly moving toward requiring students to demonstrate specific competencies rather than merely requiring them to learn about defined topics or functions. Programs in healthcare management, to be accredited, are required to specify competencies and show how these competencies are met. The process occurs whether the program is located in a school of business, school of public health, or other school, and these other schools typically have their own accreditation requirements as well.

Programs are required to cover the following content areas in healthcare management: population health, policy formation, program implementation and evaluation, organizational behavior, management, operations management, human resources management, information management, governance, leadership, communication skills, statistics, economics, marketing, financial management, ethics, strategy, quality improvement, and professional skills development.

These programs will vary in how they cover the material. For example, the Robert F. Wagner School of Public Service at New York University (NYU Wagner) specifies five competencies for managers: (1) leadership; (2) process and quality management; (3) health policy; (4) critical decision making; and (5) communication, networking, and continuous learning. Course competencies are then specified as well. Competencies addressed in NYU Wagner's basic management course, for instance, include the following:

- The ability to examine and synthesize data used in information systems and apply evidence-based management principles for use in organizational analysis, problem solving, and strategic decision making
- The ability to measure, monitor, and improve safety, quality, access, and system and care delivery processes in HCOs

Despite the emphasis on competencies, we still lack scientific data that link students' demonstration of these competencies to success in healthcare management jobs. In addition, vast differences exist in the competency sets required for different managerial jobs, from managing community advocacy to managing information systems to managing operations and quality improvement.

Competencies can be used to analyze organizations as well as managers. Management theorists have generalized that having a distinctive competency, rather than trying to be all things to all people, pays off for organizations. Ways that organizations can make themselves distinctive include providing the lowest-cost service, providing the most comprehensive service, and providing niche services (e.g., "Our hospital provides the highest-quality eye care on the Eastern Seaboard").

## Metrics and Accountability

Increasingly, HCOs are being held accountable for meeting the goals of the Triple Aim, and organizations must align their definition and measurement of the Triple Aim with the perspectives and expectations of various organizational stakeholders. Organizations set their own goals to meet these expectations, and stakeholders can justifiably raise questions about the appropriateness and difficulty of the chosen metrics and about the fairness in determining whether the organization has met the metrics. Additional questions can then be raised concerning the acceptability of organizational changes, either in metrics or performance, in response to stakeholder feedback. Still more questions can be raised about how much weight each stakeholder group should have in voicing its concerns (especially when views differ among stakeholders) and whether each stakeholder's measurement and voicing of feedback are representative of the constituents the stakeholder claims to represent.

## Conclusion

This overview has set forth at least four ways of looking at managers in HCOs, and all are linked to various parts of this book. The first way focuses on the degree of influence the manager has, from greater to lesser. The second considers the extent to which the manager uses an evidence-based approach, making decisions based on the best available evidence. The third involves viewing organizations and their managers in terms of industry performance norms and benchmarked performances of similar organizations and their managers. The fourth focuses on the metrics used to measure performance and the mechanisms of accountability used to respond to stakeholder concerns. Readers are encouraged to consider each of these perspectives as they develop their own views on the cases and commentaries that follow.

## References

Barends, E., D. M. Rousseau, and R. B. Briner. 2014. *Evidence-Based Management: The Basic Principles.* Center for Evidence-Based Management. Accessed January 20, 2017. www.cebma.org/wp-content/uploads/Evidence-Based-Practice-The-Basic-Principles.pdf.

Institute for Healthcare Improvement (IHI). 2017. "IHI Triple Aim Initiative." Accessed January 20. www.ihi.org/offerings/Initiatives/TripleAim/Pages/default.aspx.

## Recommended Readings

Kenney, C. 2011. *Transforming Health Care: Virginia Mason Medical Center's Pursuit of the Perfect Patient Experience.* New York: Productivity Press.

Knickman, J. R., and A. R. Kovner. 2015. *Health Care Delivery in the United States,* 11th ed. New York: Springer.

Rousseau, D. M. (ed.). 2012. *The Oxford Handbook of Evidence-Based Management.* New York: Oxford University Press.

White, K. W., and J. R. Griffith. 2016. *The Well-Managed Healthcare Organization,* 8th ed. Chicago: Health Administration Press.

# THE ROLE OF THE MANAGER

A leader is best
When people barely know that he exists
Not so good when people obey
And acclaim him,
Worst when they despise him.
Fail to honor people,
They fail to honor you;
But of a good leader, who talks little,
When his work is done, his aim fulfilled,
They will say, "we did this ourselves."

—*Lao Tzu*

# COMMENTARY

**M**anagers work with others to achieve organizational goals. The aspect of this work that they have the greatest control over is their own behavior in relation to their work with others. The cases presented in part I of this book all deal with aspects of the manager's role. This role is determined by what the organization expects the manager to do. Managers do what they are supposed to do, what they want to do, and what they can do.

These cases deal with the following topics: hiring a new manager, firing an existing manager, making decisions as a management team, developing the manager's own career, scoping out a managerial job after the manager has already accepted it, setting priorities for starting out on a management job, recognizing the manager's influence on employee morale, handling conflict among those reporting to the manager, and evaluating performance before promoting a worker to manager.

## What Do Healthcare Managers Do?

Managers of healthcare organizations (HCOs) confront reality, develop agendas and networks, and strategize. They work with and react to other managers. Because they generally lack ownership of the firm, healthcare managers are often risk averse. They worry about their own survival as well as goal attainment. They negotiate trade-offs between improving patient care or keeping it from deteriorating, breaking even financially or operating at a profit, and controlling clinician dissatisfaction or engaging clinicians in the organization's mission.

Healthcare managers address a variety of challenges. Purchasers demand low prices, documented quality, and responsive services, and competition—whether from existing or new organizations—may be increasing. HCOs primarily provide medical care, yet a growing emphasis has been placed on efforts to improve population health—whether or not such efforts contribute to the bottom line or have been scientifically validated.

Clinicians may regard managers primarily as "support staff," and they may consider working with managers or meeting at a manager's direction a waste of time relative to the important work of providing patient care. They may view the manager's important work as "relating the organization to its environment" or "coordinating processes of care to achieve measurable objectives."

Reasonable people may differ—and they often do—over the extent to which medical care and population health are measurable.

The work of healthcare managers varies by type of organization, as well as by level within the organization. HCO types include academic medical centers, neighborhood health centers, small community hospitals, large public hospitals, visiting nurse services, accountable care organizations serving Medicaid recipients, Veterans Health Administration hospital networks, and health departments, among others. These organizations can be for-profit, not-for-profit, or governmental; large or small; rural, suburban, or urban; financially strong or struggling. The managers of these organizations face different challenges and have different capabilities in responding to these challenges or to market opportunities.

## Expectations for Managerial Performance

The healthcare manager's work is being transformed by evolutions in information availability and performance expectations. Managers are expected to lead or colead quality improvement efforts while also implementing initiatives to generate increased revenue. They are expected to maintain costs and increase value relative to costs while also managing relationships with important stakeholder groups. Many managers must strive to meet these expectations while lacking resources that are central to providing high-quality care. Greater performance expectations are being placed on managers in the face of limitations on what HCOs can charge for their services, even though costs often increase at a faster rate.

Managers should ask themselves: Who are the key stakeholders affecting goal achievement? What do these stakeholders expect? How satisfied are they with current performance? Managerial interventions should always be financially and politically feasible. Managers should know where the money is going to come from before they suggest an initiative, and they should know where the buy-in must come from to achieve a successful implementation.

Managers should reflect on what they plan to accomplish over the next 12 months, and they should determine whose support they need to achieve these goals. Every manager should consider her resume as her lifeline and keep it current. She should ask herself: What results did I achieve last year? What results will I achieve this year that show a convincing track record of accomplishment?

Managers, on average, spend six years in their positions. They should consider themselves independent contractors in charge of their own careers, and they should not accept a position without an exit strategy. They should determine in advance the conditions under which they would no longer be willing to work in the position, and they should know what steps to take once that decision has been made.

## Thinking Strategically About the Job

Managers should understand the flexibility of their position. Each managerial job has three characteristics: (1) the demands that the manager must actively carry out; (2) the constraints on the position, or those activities that the manager is not allowed to carry out; and (3) the available options or choices about how the manager is going to spend his time and attention (Stewart and Fondas 1992). Managers should reflect on how they can strengthen relationships with the people on whom they depend for goal achievement; managing oneself is essential for this purpose.

Goleman (1998) stresses the importance of emotional intelligence (EI) for management success. He suggests that EI can be learned and that it is more important than IQ and advanced technical skills. The five components of EI are as follows:

- Self-awareness (how managers see themselves being seen by others)
- Self-regulation (thinking before speaking)
- Motivation (the drive to achieve results)
- Empathy (seeing others as they see themselves)
- Social skills (listening and responding)

Another way to think about EI centers on the skills of interaction that enable the manager to hear what people are saying, understand what they are not saying, and adjust what she is saying based on how she sees her message being received by the people she is talking to.

Barends, Rousseau, and Briner (2014) have written extensively on managerial decision making, emphasizing the need for managers to make decisions based on the best evidence available from multiple sources. This process includes the following steps:

- Translating a practical issue or problem into an answerable question
- Systematically searching for and retrieving the evidence
- Critically judging the trustworthiness and relevance of the evidence
- Weighing and pulling together the evidence
- Incorporating the evidence into the decision-making process
- Evaluating the outcome of the decision made

Self-evaluation—reflection on one's skills and experience in terms of the job—is key. McCall, Lombardo, and Morrison (1988) have suggested the following framework for management development:

- Find out about shortcomings.
- Accept responsibility for shortcomings, which may result from a lack of knowledge, skills, or experience, or from personality, limited ability, or being a situational misfit.
- Decide what to do about the shortcomings accordingly. Either build new strengths, anticipate situations, compensate, or change yourself.

Obviously, the manager should also do an assessment of strengths and consider how to take advantage of and build upon strengths. Such an assessment can help ensure a good fit between the job the manager has or seeks and the manager's own skills and experience.

## Conclusion

The work of HCOs continues to be standardized, even in the face of new technology, as organizations become larger and work is increasingly contracted out. The world of large and complex HCOs has led to the specialization of managers in areas such as operations, marketing, strategy, knowledge management, internal auditing, compliance, and human resources, among others. Many of these functional specialists and managers have not been trained in healthcare prior to being employed in HCOs. Meanwhile, physicians are increasingly becoming organizational employees, either in their own organizations or as part of large hospitals and health systems. The challenge of interdisciplinary teams largely remains to be solved, as healthcare professionals are trained and organized separately but then expected to work seamlessly together in the delivery of care at the unit or organizational level. Increasingly, metrics and accountability are the order of the day. Each manager must manage his own narrative about whether he is doing well in his job and how he can improve his and his organization's performance.

## Discussion Questions

1. How can managers assess the metrics and accountability for effective performance?
2. How is healthcare management similar or dissimilar to management in general?

3. What can a manager do to successfully move from one managerial position to another?

4. What are the obstacles to managerial self-improvement, and how can these best be overcome?

## References

Barends, E., D. M. Rousseau, and R. B. Briner. 2014. *Evidence-Based Management: The Basic Principles.* Center for Evidence-Based Management. Accessed January 24, 2017. www.cebma.org/wp-content/uploads/Evidence-Based-Practice-The-Basic-Principles.pdf.

Goleman, D. 1998. "What Makes a Leader?" *Harvard Business Review* 76 (6): 93–102.

McCall, M. W., M. M. Lombardo, and A. M. Morrison. 1988. *The Lessons of Experience: How Successful Executives Develop on the Job.* Lexington, MA: Lexington Books.

Stewart, R., and N. Fondas. 1992. "How Managers Can Think Strategically About Their Jobs." *Journal of Management Development* 11 (7): 10–17.

## Recommended Readings

Arndt, M., and B. Bigelow. 2007. "Hospital Administration in the Early 1900s: Visions for the Future and the Reality of Daily Practice." *Journal of Healthcare Management* 52 (1): 34–48.

Barends, E., B. Janssen, and W. Ten Have. 2014. "Effect of Change Intervention: What Kind of Science Do We Really Have?" *Journal of Applied Behavioral Science* 50 (1): 5–27.

Berry, L. L., and K. D. Seltman. 2008. *Management Lessons from Mayo Clinic.* New York: McGraw-Hill.

Bock, L. 2015. "Why Everyone Hates Performance Management, and What We Decided to Do About It." In *Work Rules! Insights from Inside Google That Will Transform How You Live and Lead*, 150–77. New York: Hachette Book Group.

Christensen, C. M. 2010. "How Will You Measure Your Life?" *Harvard Business Review* 88 (7–8): 46–51.

Gabarro, J. J., and J. R. Kotter. 2005. "Managing Your Boss." *Harvard Business Review* 83 (1): 5–12.

Gilmartin, M. J., and T. A. D'Aunno. 2007. "Leadership Research in Healthcare: A Review and a Roadmap." *Academy of Management Annals* 1: 387–438.

Griffith, J. R. 1993. *The Moral Challenges of Healthcare Management.* Chicago: Health Administration Press.

Griffith, J. R., and K. R. White. 2005. "The Revolution in Hospital Management." *Journal of Healthcare Management* 50 (3): 170–90.

Institute of Medicine. 2001. *Crossing the Quality Chasm: A New Health System for the 21st Century*. Washington, DC: National Academies Press.

Kovner, A. R. 2000. *Healthcare Management in Mind: Eight Careers*. New York: Springer.

———. 1987. "The Work of Effective CEOs in Four Large Health Organizations." *Hospital & Health Services Administration* 32 (3): 285–305.

Lee, T. H., and J. J. Mongan. 2009. *Chaos and Organization in Health Care*. Cambridge, MA: MIT Press.

McAlearney, A. S. 2008. "Using Leadership Development Programs to Improve Quality and Efficiency in Healthcare." *Journal of Healthcare Management* 53 (5): 319–31.

———. 2006. "Leadership Development in Healthcare Organizations: A Qualitative Study." *Journal of Organizational Behavior* 27 (7): 967–82.

Pfeffer, J. 2015. "Take Care of Yourself." In *Leadership BS*, 171–92. New York: Harper.

Studer, Q. 2004. *Hardwiring Excellence*. Gulf Breeze, FL: Fire Starter Publishing.

White, K. R., and J. R. Griffith. 2016. "Cultural Leadership." In *The Well-Managed Healthcare Organization*, 8th ed., 45–73. Chicago: Health Administration Press.

# THE CASES

**M**anagers often have a great deal of difficulty making decisions. Hiring decisions are a key challenge, but even more important are the continuous evaluation and motivation of subordinates and colleagues, many of whom may have been hired by a manager's predecessors. If associates do not perform at an expected level of competence, what are the supervisor's options? What are the manager's options if she disagrees with her own boss's expectations or evaluation? If the boss does not fire or transfer an ineffective manager being evaluated, the boss's own effectiveness may suffer because he might not be supported in his efforts to implement strategy or negotiate organizational politics. Removing an ineffective manager may be difficult because the ineffective manager might be loyal, because searching for and training a new manager costs time and money, and because the boss knows that a new hire's performance may not be as anticipated.

The manager's job is often a lonely one, and important decisions often involve personal as well as organizational risks and benefits. In Case 1, titled "The Search Begins for the Next Faculty Practice Administrator for the Department of Surgery," the weighing of risks and benefits is different for Dr. Eric Francis, the chair of surgery, than it is for Bonnie Goldsmith, the faculty practice administrator, or for Goldsmith's eventual successor. Similarly, in Case 2, "The Associate Director and the Controllers," the stakes of the game are higher for Jim Joel, the ambulatory care manager, and Percy Oram, the controller, than for Milton Schlitz, the medical center director of finance, and Dr. Miller Harrang, the chief executive officer of the ambulatory care program.

Why must Joel decide to do anything at all? In Case 1, Dr. Francis *must* choose a new faculty practice administrator. But in Case 2, Joel can choose to not get involved and allow Harrang and Schlitz to deal with the consequences of Oram's ineffectiveness. How much should it matter to Joel whether Oram remains on the job, so long as Joel can protect his own job? On the other hand, Joel is paid to manage, not to observe or protect himself.

Managers often search for evidence to validate their intuition, and their intuition is often limited by systematic bias, such as confirmation bias, which involves settling on an opinion and arranging evidence to support that opinion. Politics intrudes, further complicating matters, in Case 3, Part 1, titled "What More Evidence Do You Need?" The question remains, "How does one make decisions based on the best available evidence?" Is Sally's approach to evidence-based decision making the right one, or necessary? What are the stakes for Sally, the medical director, and Mark, the CEO? How should one confront the point of view of "if the wagon isn't broken, don't fix it"?

Good management generally makes a difference to the patient, as well as to the organization's ruling coalition. How much of a difference is open to question. But who will look after the manager's interest if she doesn't look after it herself? This is the first rule of managerial survival. Looking after one's own interest does not mean that the manager should close her office door, read reports, and tell subordinates what to do. Instead, there are opportunities to strategically plan one's professional development, as considered in Case 4 and Case 5, titled "Now What?" and "What Then?"

Healthcare managers often face tremendous pressures from government to move in certain directions, as well as resistance from physicians who do not wish to move one step farther than what is required by law. How much value do managers add to performance? Not much, according to Pfeffer and Salancik (1978), who argue that the contribution of managers accounts for only about 10 percent of the variance in organizational performance, and who agree with the sportscaster cliché that "managers are hired to be fired." An increasing amount of evidence, however, indicates that managers *do* make a difference in organizational performance, if only because they play a key role in obtaining the resources necessary for organizational survival and growth.

Even if the healthcare manager can never meet all the expectations of key organizational stakeholders, he can at least be seen as taking stakeholder interests into account in policy formulation and implementation. This requires regular communication, which takes valuable time. What makes for an effective healthcare manager? Effectiveness depends on perceptions of various stakeholders, as well as performance and motivation. Sometimes—as in Case 6, "Facing Reality in a New Job"—the right move for a manager may be looking for another job.

Clearly, managers must acquire information, learn skills, and have values consistent with the organizational context and its ruling coalition. Deciding what actions to take after receiving disquieting information is not always easy. Similarly, the realities faced by new managers in cases 7 through 10—titled "The First Day," "Managing Volunteers in the Hospital," "Conflict in the Office," and "Annual Performance Evaluation"—all involve challenges in managing expectations as well as in job performance.

Evaluating managerial effectiveness or contribution carries a cost. Some pertinent information might not be available at a reasonable cost. Reliance on measurement may divert attention inappropriately away from what is easily measured. Evaluating managers, like management itself, involves judgment, which in Ray Brown's (1969) phrase is "knowledge ripened by experience."

For management students, case discussions are an excellent way of obtaining safe experience in forming managerial judgments.

## References

Brown, R. 1969. *Judgment in Administration*. New York: McGraw-Hill.

Pfeffer, J., and G. R. Salancik. 1978. *The External Control of Organizations*. New York: Harper & Row.

# ▌CASE 1

# The Search Begins for the Next Faculty Practice Administrator for the Department of Surgery

*David M. Kaplan*

## Background

Wise Medical Center (WMC) is regarded as one of the largest and best-managed hospitals in Eastern City. The CEO, Dr. Chris Dante, was appointed in 2001. He has elevated the medical center from the depths of financial despair to becoming one of the most successful in the country. His philosophy has been one of growth and investment in new faculty, clinical programs, research, and teaching programs. Dr. Dante also worked to replace nearly all the department chairs.

The Department of Surgery is one of WMC's largest departments. Dr. Eric Francis, who is the chair of surgery, is a vascular surgeon, world-renowned for his ability to treat aortic aneurysms, but also regarded as a savvy businessman. The faculty practice in the department has been in place since 2002, when Dr. Francis took over as chair and Donald Matthews joined him as the administrator. Dr. Francis and Mr. Matthews developed a tremendous partnership and significantly expanded the department. Specifically, they recruited more than 30 faculty and increased total faculty practice revenue by more than 150 percent. In 2006, the department earned more than $40 million in physician receipts for the first time in its history.

Dr. Francis has been praised for his leadership skills, his business intelligence, and his loyalty to his faculty and staff. This loyalty, however, sometimes inhibits his ability to make tough decisions regarding less-productive faculty, such as reducing their salaries or moving them out of the institution. Both the department and the medical center face increasing financial pressures as the state and federal government look to reduce funding for Medicare, Medicaid, and other related programs. Dr. Dante and others are trying to determine the most effective response to these increased financial pressures.

Donald Matthews left his role as the administrator for WMC's Department of Surgery in 2006 to move to a chief operating officer position at Lakeshore Medical Center, another local medical center. WMC quickly worked to replace him with a strong administrator to enable continued leadership. After a series of interviews with many qualified candidates, the decision was made to hire Bonnie Goldsmith, who had been previously working as the vice president of surgical services at Rochester Medical Center. Since joining WMC, Bonnie has been a very effective administrator, helping to achieve the goals of increasing volume, improving room utilization, and ensuring that the department was financially solvent (see exhibit 1.1). Her extensive experience and connections with a surgery department made her an ideal candidate to quickly transition into the role and provide seamless leadership at WMC.

In the decade following Bonnie's hiring, a number of changes affected WMC and its market (see exhibits 1.2 and 1.3). In early 2016, WMC merged with two of its former competitors, Lakeshore Medical Center and Western Medical Center, to form Wise Health System (WHS). The merger was led by the WMC CEO, Dr. Dante, who had been looking to solidify market share and create a competitive accountable care organization (ACO) in the region. Dr. Dante continued to thrive in his role as CEO and was determined to

**EXHIBIT 1.1**
WMC Surgery Suites Billing and Collections, Fiscal Year 2016

| Month | Billings | Collections | Contractual Allowances | Gross Collection Rate | Net Collection Rate |
|---|---|---|---|---|---|
| January | $13,578,644 | $4,616,739 | $8,826,119 | 34% | 97% |
| February | $12,635,841 | $4,548,903 | $7,707,863 | 36% | 92% |
| March | $13,549,632 | $4,742,371 | $8,400,772 | 35% | 92% |
| April | $13,021,645 | $4,687,792 | $7,812,987 | 36% | 90% |
| May | $12,547,302 | $4,391,556 | $7,653,854 | 35% | 90% |
| June | $13,699,356 | $5,068,762 | $8,356,607 | 37% | 95% |
| July | $13,693,691 | $4,792,792 | $8,490,088 | 35% | 92% |
| August | $13,698,652 | $4,794,528 | $8,630,151 | 35% | 95% |
| September | $13,478,699 | $4,852,332 | $8,087,219 | 36% | 90% |
| October | $13,586,985 | $5,027,184 | $8,423,931 | 37% | 97% |
| November | $13,652,966 | $4,778,538 | $8,464,839 | 35% | 92% |
| December | $13,678,592 | $4,924,293 | $8,617,513 | 36% | 97% |
| **Total** | **$160,822,005** | **$57,225,790** | **$99,471,943** | **36%** | **93%** |

| Item | 2006 | 2016 |
|------|------|------|
| Total number of providers | 100 | 225 |
| Total number of provider sessions | 1,000 | 3,210 |
| Total number of visits | 15,450 | 31,679 |
| Revenue | $40,967,788 | $57,225,790 |
| Expenses | $39,568,745 | $56,359,784 |
| **Net profit/(loss)** | **$1,399,043** | **$866,006** |

**EXHIBIT 1.2**
WMC Department of Surgery Comparison, 2006 and 2016

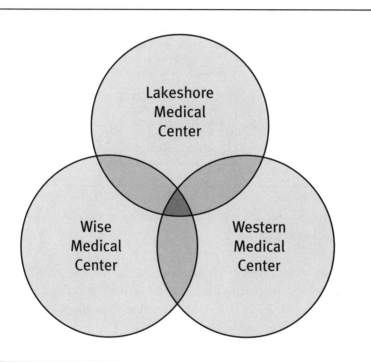

**EXHIBIT 1.3**
Merger to Form Wise Health System

create one of the largest population health programs in the country. As part of the merger, clinical service lines, including a new Surgical Service Line, were developed to help streamline operations and create efficiencies and cost savings across the newly merged entity.

Dr. Francis, still the chair of surgery at WMC, became the clinical leader of the new system-level Surgical Service Line. Meanwhile, Donald Matthews, who had been the chief operating officer at Lakeshore Medical Center, became the service line's administrative leader. Thus, the change reunited Dr. Francis with his former administrator. The arrangement is illustrated in exhibit 1.4.

The WHS merger announcement happened to roughly coincide with the birth of Bonnie Goldsmith's second son. Within a few months of the

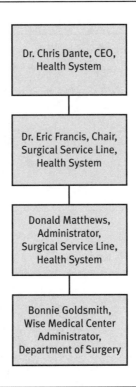

announcement, Bonnie informed Dr. Francis that she would be leaving her post. Their dialogue follows:

**Bonnie:** Dr. Francis, I have really enjoyed working for you and the Medical Center for the past ten years. Having started in this role as a young 27-year-old, I feel that I've been able to work closely with you to achieve all the things we set out to do. I hope you feel the same. It is bittersweet that I am leaving this position.

**Dr. Francis:** Bonnie, I must admit that when I first interviewed you, I wasn't quite sure about your commitment or abilities in this role. However, from the minute you arrived, you have proven me wrong. You have been an absolute pleasure to work with, and yes, I do believe we have accomplished all we set out to do and then some. I will be very sad to see you go. But of course, I only want the best for you and your family.

   Also, I am very appreciative that you will be working closely with Donald to help identify and screen new candidates. As you know, Donald was made the COO overseeing the newly merged Surgical Service Line across the campuses, which should help us since he is familiar with our department.

**Bonnie:** Yes, of course. I have already been working with Donald to accomplish this, and we have identified a handful of highly qualified candidates. We will perform the initial screening of these candidates and give you our recommendations. The only question we have is, with Donald in the mix, what is the ideal type of candidate you have in mind? For example, do you want a full-fledged administrator or more of an operational or financial person instead? We will need some guidance on this from you.

**Dr. Francis:** Great. I'm glad to hear you are already working together to identify this individual. I think it is best for you and Donald to make a recommendation, and once I meet the candidates, I will weigh in with my thoughts. I do think that we need to consider a candidate who can relate to our very diverse patient population. For us to continue our success, we must be able to connect with the communities that we serve, and this role will be instrumental to ensuring that connection occurs.

After compiling the extensive job description (see exhibit 1.5), Bonnie and Donald scheduled several meetings to screen resumes. They have reached agreement about four candidates to be interviewed over the next four weeks. The four candidates are Bradon Roberts, Maria Santiago, Narris Sun, and Ashley Jones.

Bradon Roberts is a master's-trained candidate who is currently employed as the practice director for a large multispecialty practice in Westchester, New York. Maria Santiago is the department administrator for urology at the University of Toledo Medical School, and she is looking to relocate to the area. Narris Sun is the finance director for the Department of Obstetrics and Gynecology at Western Medical Center, and he has a master's degree as well. Finally, Ashley Jones is a nurse director for a large ambulatory surgery suite within WMC, and she is looking for career growth.

Donald recorded each interview to share with Dr. Francis as he had done in the past. The following is a recap of each candidate's discussions with Donald and Bonnie:

### Bradon Roberts

**Bonnie:** Good afternoon, Mr. Roberts. Thank you for making time for our interview today. Allow me to introduce myself. I am Bonnie Goldsmith, and I am the current administrator for surgery at Wise Medical Center.

**Donald:** Yes, thanks for coming in today. My name is Donald Matthews, and I am the chief operating officer for the newly merged Surgical

Service Line. Also, I used to have Bonnie's job prior to moving into the COO role.

**Bonnie:** So please tell us about yourself. What interested you in this position?

**Bradon:** As my resume shows, I've been in healthcare for the past seven years. I started my career as a front-desk receptionist and have worked my way up to my current role as the director of operations for a 50-physician multispecialty practice in Westchester, New York. I have a staff of about 12 people, some of whom handle various operational tasks such as front-end registration and some of whom are medical assistants. Though I enjoy my current job, I feel like I am ready for a change, and this seems like a tremendous growth opportunity.

**Donald:** What skills do you feel you would contribute to this position in the Department of Surgery?

**Bradon:** Given my experience, I believe I can contribute immediately. I have strong interpersonal skills and relate well to physicians. I understand how practices flow, as well as the operational needs that must be addressed. I have been responsible for my operational budgets and can effectively track and monitor these budgets for any variances or opportunities for improvement. Lastly, I am an expert recruiter for staff such as medical assistants, who tend to have high turnover rates.

**Bonnie:** Given that the role of a department administrator tends to be very wide in scope, do you have any experience in managing academic teaching or research efforts?

**Bradon:** Honestly, no, as most of my role has been operational in nature within what is essentially a large private practice. That said, I did study those topics in my master's program and would be fully equipped to learn how to manage these critical areas.

**Donald:** Are there any questions that you would like to ask us about this role?

**Bradon:** Sure. I have a couple of questions. First, how soon are you looking to make a decision about this role? Also, what would the ideal candidate for this role look like to you?

**Bonnie:** We are looking to identify someone for this role within the next two weeks. My last day here at Wise will probably be in about three months, so we want to develop a solid transition plan. I will defer to Donald to answer your second question.

**Donald:** Ideally, this candidate would have a strong operational and/or financial background. The person should have strong interpersonal skills as you've mentioned, and he or she should have some exposure to the various other facets of the job, such as teaching and research, and a strong record of successful accomplishments.

**Bradon:** That sounds great. Well, thank you both for your time today.

**Bonnie:** Absolutely. We appreciate you coming today, and we will be in touch very shortly.

### *Maria Santiago*

**Donald:** Nice to meet you, Maria. We really appreciate you making your way all the way from Ohio today. Let's jump right in. Why are you looking to relocate to Eastern City?

**Maria:** It's kind of a long story, but the abbreviated version is that my parents retired to Eastern City a few years ago and they are now a bit older and frail. I need to be closer to help them, so I made the decision to relocate to the area.

**Bonnie:** That is really nice of you! They are lucky to have you as a daughter. So how long have you been in healthcare?

**Maria:** I graduated from college about 12 years ago, and I started working in healthcare as a physician biller immediately. I have had some great mentors throughout the years who have helped me to grow into my current department administrator role.

**Donald:** Can you describe a typical day in your current position?

**Maria:** Well, as I am sure you both know, every single day is different for an administrator. Aside from putting out the fire of the moment, we have the traditional issues such as putting together business plans, recruiting faculty, ensuring the finances are in good shape, managing the revenue cycle, and monitoring practice operations. The key is putting together a great team that can assist with handling each of these aspects on a daily basis.

**Bonnie:** I totally agree. It's nice to hear from someone who can relate to the role. So what about this role is attractive to you?

**Maria:** Given that I need to relocate, this role seemed very similar to the role I have had in Ohio, so I assumed it would be a good fit. I am not looking for a larger role than my current position, so I am comfortable with a comparable position in a new place.

**Donald:** What is your time frame to relocate?

**Maria:** I am hoping to move within the next two months. I already gave my current employer notice that I need to make this move, so they are aware and have already started to search for my replacement. How does that work for your timing? Also, why is this position becoming vacant?

**Bonnie:** Well, I am actually leaving my position here to raise my family. I've really enjoyed my time here, and Dr. Francis is amazing to work with. I just need to focus on my family's needs for a while. I am hoping to leave WMC within the next three months, so your timing would work well.

**Donald:** We wish Bonnie would stay in her current role. She has been a real asset to the organization. Maria, let me ask you a very challenging question, given your experience. Have you ever worked in a merged entity with a complex matrix leadership table? If not, how do you think this might fit your personality?

**Maria:** Honestly, I have never worked in a merged entity, but I have worked in academic medicine, and academic medicine seems to always have a complex table of organization. Who would I be reporting to in this role?

**Donald:** You would be reporting to both me and Dr. Francis in this position, but you would be working with other surgery administrators at the other hospitals as well. This would include at least two other individuals.

**Maria:** Will I get to meet these other administrators, and Dr. Francis?

**Bonnie:** Once we finish our initial interviews, we will be asking Dr. Francis to meet with a finalist. He will be making the final determination. I'm not sure about meeting the other administrators until after Dr. Francis makes his decision, but it might be a good idea.

**Donald:** It was a real pleasure meeting you today. Thank you again for making the trip to see us. We will be in touch shortly, as we would like to make a decision as soon as possible.

**Maria:** Great. Well, here is my card. Please feel free to contact me any time with questions you might have. I look forward to hearing from you both very soon.

### Narris Sun

**Donald:** Mr. Sun, thank you for coming in today. I see that you are currently working within the health system. Tell us about your current role, please.

**Narris:** Forgive me, but my English is not that good. I am originally from China. I am actually a doctor and went to medical school in China. I came to the United States to make a better life for my wife and me. Since I have been here, I went to get my MPA, and I have really focused on finance. I have been in my current role for about one year, but I have been in other financial roles at Western Medical Center over the past six years.

**Bonnie:** Sounds very impressive. Out of curiosity, why not try and reestablish your medical training here in the US?

**Narris:** Honestly, I am 42 years old, and I feel that at this point I would have to invest more time than I can give. I am very happy focused on the finances of a department, and I wish to help run a department like surgery.

**Donald:** It seems like you are very motivated to succeed at whatever role you are performing. It also seems like you really like finance. Have you thought about the other aspects of a department administrator role?

**Narris:** I am indeed aware of the demands of the administrator role. I work very closely with the department administrator in my current role.

So I often help not only with the finances but also with other areas such as the faculty practice operations, research dollars, and teaching. I also help with monitoring faculty effort and other special projects such as construction, employee recognition, and so on.

**Bonnie:** Well, it sure seems like the department is getting a lot of use from you. Why would you be looking to leave, especially after such a short time?

**Narris:** While I am happy in my current role, I saw this opportunity and feel that, given my background and experience, I would do very well in this role. I feel that my life experiences will allow me to accomplish great things in surgery.

**Donald:** Great to hear. What questions do you have for us?

**Narris:** What are the goals you would want a person in this position to achieve to gauge success?

**Bonnie:** We would want the person to ensure that the department continues to meet the goal of a 2.5 percent positive operating margin. We would want to increase overall volume by 5 percent and overall revenue by 5 percent as well. We need to ensure that our patient satisfaction is 90 percent or higher when compared to national benchmarks. That is just to name a few.

**Narris:** OK, this is very helpful to know. What do you envision are the next steps in this process?

**Donald:** We have a few more candidates to meet, and then we will identify a finalist to meet with Dr. Francis, the chair of surgery. Hopefully, we will be able to hire the individual quickly after that interview.

**Bonnie:** Thank you for coming in today. We will certainly be in touch shortly.

**Narris:** Thank you very much. I really enjoyed our discussion.

### Ashley Jones

**Bonnie:** Welcome, Ms. Jones. We're so glad to see you. I must admit I was a bit surprised you were interested in this position. I always thought you were interested in becoming a perioperative director for the hospital.

**Ashley:** I honestly would love a role like that, but those seem very difficult to obtain. Also, I have been in my current position for seven years and am ready for a change. I believe my skill sets as a nurse director have prepared me to perform many different roles clinically and administratively.

**Donald:** Glad to hear that you are so well trained. What would be your priorities as the administrator for surgery? Also, won't you miss the clinical side of things?

**Ashley:** First, yes, I would most certainly miss the clinical side of things, but if it means advancement for me, I would make the shift. As for the priorities, I would take my lead from Dr. Francis. I am very close to Dr. Francis, as I often handle his cases in the ambulatory surgery suites.

**Bonnie:** Ashley, you and I have worked together for years, but I am wondering if you really understand my role. In a few words, can you describe the role?

**Ashley:** Sure. Your role is very chaotic, and it deals mostly with the surgeons and the finances of the department. That would include the day-to-day finances and the billing, all of which I handle now for the ambulatory surgery suites; so this would be very similar but on a slightly larger scale. Dealing with physician recruitment would be a new aspect for me.

**Donald:** Well, we certainly appreciate your honesty. No question you've done a great job managing your surgery suites, as the numbers reflect. How would you describe your management style?

**Ashley:** As Bonnie can attest, I am a very direct, honest, and no-nonsense manager. I am fair, but I don't accept poor performance. As a nurse, my license is on the line every single day, and I can't let anything fall through the cracks. I would apply the same philosophy in this role.

**Bonnie:** No question, you are no-nonsense. We've certainly had our share of encounters together over the years. Do you have any questions for us?

**Ashley:** No, I don't really have any questions. I feel like I have a good sense of this role after working with Bonnie for the past ten years. I look forward to hearing from you soon.

**Donald:** Thank you, Ashley. We will get back with you shortly.

Following these interviews, both Donald and Bonnie met with Dr. Francis to review the recordings and discuss the candidates.

**Bonnie:** Dr. Francis, now that we have reviewed the candidates, we were hoping to seek your guidance on the candidate you found most impressive and would like to meet in person.

**Dr. Francis:** Bonnie, I trust you and Donald will select the most talented candidate for me to meet. It would be unfair for me to weigh in, since you both actually met these folks. But just to reiterate what I am looking for in this role: someone who provides an appreciation for diversity in the community; a person with strong business acumen; an effective communicator with patients, staff, and faculty; and a strong leader whom people will want to follow.

**Donald:** I recall we had a very similar conversation when I left here ten years ago—funny how things seem to repeat themselves. No problem. We would be happy to select the finalist for you to meet, and we'll be sure that our final selection has these characteristics.

**Donald:** I must say, it is great to be back working with surgery again.

**Dr. Francis:** Donald, we are glad to have you back in the fold. It is great to have someone familiar with our department in such a high-level position.

**Bonnie:** It is certainly comforting to know that at least Donald will be here to help with this transition. Dr. Francis, please give us a week, and we will pick the finalist for you to meet.

---

**ADMINISTRATOR, DEPARTMENT OF SURGERY**

PRIMARY DUTIES AND RESPONSIBILITIES:
- Understand the current culture and direction of the Wise Health System department of surgery.
- Aid in the development of an overall strategic vision for the departments/ divisions that are in line with institutional expectations and those of the Wise Health System chair of surgery.
- Work with WHS chair of surgery to outline a 30-, 60-, 90-, and 180-day plan to implement the strategic vision, as well as long-term plans for continued assessment of progress against the plan outline.
- Develop relationships with faculty, staff, and leadership teams across the WHS institutions.
- Define and implement organizational/governance structure across the institutional departments of surgery as envisioned by the WHS chair of surgery.
- Participate on all institutional committees and various task forces as assigned by institutional leadership.
- Represent the Department of Surgery at all institutional meetings and meetings with various affiliate organizations (e.g., Queens Hospital Center, Elmhurst Hospital Center).
- Work closely with other surgery department chairs, senior leaders, and other administrators to develop new programs and continue strategic planning.
- Define the management team, organizational structure, and key role players for the WHS and the member departments.

Faculty:
- Develop faculty recruitment business plans and offer letters as required by the WHS chair.
- Develop retention plans for faculty as necessary.
- Assist in the development of innovative faculty compensation structures to help recruit and retain faculty.
- Develop and implement key physician monitoring processes and reports to track productivity and outcomes.
- Develop and maintain a robust faculty database to record key progress toward outcomes using data points as outlined by the system chair and senior leadership.

*(continued)*

**EXHIBIT 1.5**
Job Description for Administrator, Department of Surgery

**EXHIBIT 1.5**
Job
Description for
Administrator,
Department of
Surgery
*(continued)*

Financial:
- Evaluate current financial status and conduct a comprehensive review of all accounts and departmental financial activity across WHS departments of surgery.
- Develop an understanding of departmental and institutional funds flows.
- Actively manage and oversee all departmental financial activity.
- Assume responsibility for compiling and managing all aspects related to the departmental budgets.
- Implement a mechanism to track and monitor physician profitability (e.g., physician P/Ls).
- Ensure overall department profitability across WHS.
- Develop financial and business plans for existing and new programs.
- Meet regularly with surgery department chairs and administrator(s) to review financial performance of all divisions and faculty members.
- Develop plans to meet with faculty and staff to provide necessary financial information as required, or as deemed necessary.
- Oversee all billing/collections (revenue cycle) performance across the network departments, some of which will be in partnership with the WHS Central Business Office (CBO).
- Develop the finance team and structures at a corporate level and at each member institution if required.
- Implement standardized financial processes across the member departments as well as detailed financial reports.

Operations:
- Gain understanding of current-state operational processes and develop proposed future-state recommendations to help standardize across the WHS hospitals/departments.
- Develop operational team structure across the WHS facilities.
- Assume responsibility for all day-to-day operational activities within the surgery departments across WHS.
- Ensure that all aspects related to staffing, equipment, supplies, and facilities are managed appropriately in all WHS locations.
- Oversee all practice-related staff and management on a day-to-day basis.
- Work to develop operational improvements and enhancements throughout the WHS surgery department locations to allow for more efficient operation, including additional patient volume.
- Implement oversight of all clinical activities and ensure adherence to policies and procedures by faculty.
- Develop metrics to measure faculty productivity, and develop a process to track the metrics on a regular basis.
- Aid in the development and enhancement of new initiatives and programs, physician recruitment, etc.
- Design and implement staffing models with approval of the WHS chair of surgery.
- Evaluate volume and throughput for all clinical aspects (e.g., outpatient, inpatient, surgical services, etc.).

**EXHIBIT 1.5**
Job
Description for
Administrator,
Department of
Surgery
*(continued)*

- Oversee supply chain aspects related to clinical activities.
- Ensure that all clinical activities are compliant and follow the standards set forth by the institution and oversight bodies.
- Oversee all day-to-day revenue cycle (billing/collections) operations, including front, middle, and back end. This also includes overseeing out-sourced operations and aspects related to the WHS CBO.
- Work closely with the WHS chair of surgery to ensure that the supply chain is managed effectively.
- Assist in the oversight of the ambulatory surgery operating rooms within the department's purview across the system.

Academic:
- Work with the program director and the WHS chair of surgery to manage the surgical education program within each network hospital.
- Help to ensure Residency Review Committee (RRC) and Accreditation Council for Graduate Medical Education (ACGME) compliance for all residency and fellowship programs.
- Work with institutional leadership to define educational policies, distribution of trainees, etc.
- Oversee and manage all finances related to the academic program; negotiate with the institution to provide additional residency and fellowship funding.
- Work closely with affiliate institutions to ensure adherence to RRC and ACGME standards.

Research:
- Work with the WHS chair of surgery to define research infrastructure and support current research endeavors (clinical and basic research projects) across the network.
- Define the research management team in conjunction with the vice chair of research for the departments of surgery across the WHS network.
- Outline the funding for clinical trials, health services research, and basic research.
- Assume responsibility for all financial activity as it relates to research activities.
- Link the department's clinical research with other clinical initiatives in other departments.
- Develop a robust research database across the various hospitals/departments in the WHS network.

Quality:
- Aid in the development and oversight of the quality program for the network departments.
- Develop understanding of quality metrics currently in use, including the methodology for data collection at each of the participating network institutions.
- Work with MDs and RNs to continually refine and improve quality data, as well as to improve data collection methods.

*(continued)*

EXHIBIT 1.5
Job
Description for
Administrator,
Department of
Surgery
*(continued)*

- Aid in the development and maintenance of the detailed National Surgical Quality Improvement Program (NSQIP) and work to implement the program in conjunction with hospital quality departments.
- Establish a customer service committee to monitor and track customer service and quality initiatives within the department.
- Develop a robust committee and continuous quality improvement (CQI) process for patient satisfaction and quality across the WHS network hospitals / surgery departments.

Managed Care:
- Review the current managed care structure and contracts for each of the network departments of surgery.
- Gather necessary information to justify higher rates, review current billing data to evaluate proper payment as per current contracts, and renegotiate as required.

Philanthropy:
- Review current philanthropic sources and the way dollars have been directed within each network department.
- Work with the WHS chair of surgery, the development office, and senior leadership to develop a strategy regarding philanthropy.
- Work directly with physicians, donors, and the development office to obtain additional philanthropic support for each network department.

Facilities:
- Map out all current facilities, service locations, square footage, and costs (both direct and indirect), by program and by usage.
- Work with the WHS chair of surgery to define a vision for future facility requirements, including expansion, program growth, etc.
- Develop a phased plan to achieve strategic vision for growth, including economic and operational impacts.
- Provide day-to-day oversight of all construction projects and ensure that all projects remain Joint Commission (or other accredited body) and Department of Health compliant.
- Obtain approval on all phasing, transitions, and moves, working closely with the School of Medicine and individual hospital facilities, as well as any outside contractors; then assume responsibility to ensure execution of the process.

Information Technology (IT):
- Understand all current department IT infrastructures, including equipment, interface with School of Medicine and hospital IT, staffing, etc.
- Develop a needs assessment for the department and faculty/staff.
- Identify areas of opportunity to use technology to create efficiencies.
- Work to implement electronic medical record (EMR) use and reduce paper use across the system's hospitals/departments.

**EXHIBIT 1.5**
Job
Description for
Administrator,
Department of
Surgery
*(continued)*

- Assess intranet and web presence and outline a strategy to enhance and integrate across the departments of surgery in the health system.
- Facilitate initiatives to develop automated performance metrics to enhance efficient means to track faculty activity across entities in the network.
- Develop collaborative efforts across departments and areas to facilitate IT solutions to improve patient flow and outcome data.

REQUIREMENTS:
Candidate must have at least 7–10 years of progressive leadership experience in a healthcare setting. Specifically, the ideal candidate should have experience working in an academic medical center, a faculty practice, a hospital, or consulting over the span of his/her career. Candidate should also have experience running a surgical department or another large academic department. Candidate should have an advanced degree such as an MBA, MPA, MPH, MHA, or a master's in nursing or social work.

## Case Questions

1. What has changed in the Department of Surgery in the last ten years?
2. How should diversity be taken into consideration as a separate factor in evaluating the four candidates?
3. What role should the departing administrator play in the selection of her successor?
4. What should the chief of surgery be looking for in the new administrator?
5. What are the pros and cons of each of the four candidates?
6. Whom would you recommend Dr. Francis choose for the position and why?

# CASE 2

# The Associate Director and the Controllers

*Anthony R. Kovner*

Fortunately for Jim Joel, he didn't lose his temper often. Otherwise, he might not have been able to function as associate director of the Morris Healthcare Program of the Haas Medical Center (HMC) (see exhibit 2.1). But now, he had become so enraged at the Morris program controller, Percy

**EXHIBIT 2.1**
Organization
Chart: Haas
Medical Center

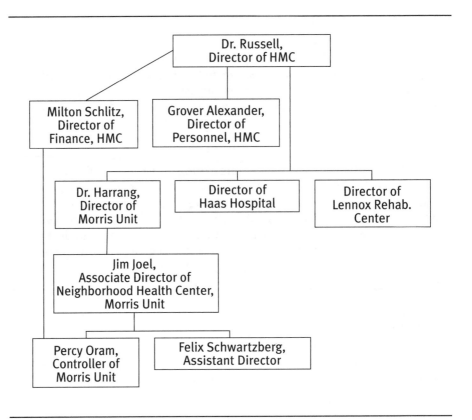

Oram, that he had to concentrate hard to keep from yelling. Joel had just been informed by Felix Schwartzberg, an assistant director, that the accounting department was not collecting cash from the billing assistants in the family health units as previously agreed. Unfortunately, Oram did not usually keep Joel informed of his actions. But in any case, Joel knew his own reaction was excessive—an aspiring health services executive did not throw a tantrum, which is what he now felt like doing.

Joel was 30 years old, ambitious, and a recent graduate from Ivy University's master of healthcare administration program. Before returning to school, he had worked as a registered representative on Wall Street, where he had found the work remunerative but uninteresting. The director of the Ivy program, Dr. Leon Russell, had assumed the post of director of the Haas Medical Center three years ago. Joel, one of his best students, asked to join Russell toward the end of that year, and he was hired shortly thereafter as an assistant hospital administrator. The Haas Medical Center is located in New York City and comprises three large programs: the Haas Hospital, the Lennox Rehabilitation Center, and the Morris Healthcare Program. The hospital and the rehabilitation center are owned by the Haas Medical Center, but the Morris

Healthcare Program is operated by the Haas Medical Center under contract with the city of New York and is located in a city-owned facility.

Russell had been impressed with his former student's drive and promise and had originally created a job for Joel—half-time as a staff assistant at Haas Hospital and half-time as an evaluator at the Morris unit, where new methods of delivering ambulatory medical care were being developed and demonstrated. Eventually, Russell offered Joel the position of associate director of the Morris unit. The director of the Morris unit was Dr. Miller Harrang, a 45-year-old physician.

Joel felt ambivalent regarding Russell's offer. He knew he would take the position, even before requesting a night to think it over, but at the same time he had certain reservations. Joel enjoyed his work at the hospital. He had submitted an in-depth plan for increasing the efficiency of the operating room, which had been enthusiastically accepted by the medical staff executive committee, and he was just starting an evaluation of patient transport in the hospital. His key interest was in implementing the findings from his master's thesis on nurse staffing. Joel believed that by assigning rooms to patients on the basis of their nursing needs, one-third fewer registered nurses would be required. Joel wished to be director of a large general hospital within ten years. He wasn't sure how working at the Morris unit would advance him toward that goal, nor how comfortable he would feel working in a facility serving the poor in a low-income section of the city.

After taking the job, however, Joel found that he liked working at the Morris unit immensely. Morris was rapidly expanding—in the past year, the number of physician visits had increased 25 percent to 215,000. Through a generous grant from the Office of Economic Opportunity (OEO), the budget had increased from $15 million to $25 million. There was so much to do, and Joel worked 65 to 70 hours a week. He liked Harrang and the others who worked at Morris. The atmosphere was busy and informal, a nice change of pace from Haas Hospital, where things happened more slowly. Dramatic change was the norm at Morris, whether it was conversion of the medical and pediatric clinics to family health units, or confrontations with a community health council resulting in increased participation in policymaking by the poor.

There was no formal division of responsibility between Harrang and Joel. Harrang spent most of his time in community relations (time-consuming and frustrating), in individual conversations with members of the medical staff at Morris, and in working out problems with Haas Hospital. Harrang also took responsibility for certain medical units such as the emergency room, obstetrics/gynecology, and psychiatry. Joel's primary responsibility lay in the area of staff activities such as finance, personnel, and purchasing. He also supervised several departments or units, including laboratory, X-ray, pharmacy, dental, housekeeping, and maintenance. Responsibility for the family health units was shared by the two top administrators.

Before Harrang became director, the Morris unit had been run as a unit independent of Haas Hospital. The unit was decentralized, with departments such as laboratory and internal medicine handling their own personnel and often their own purchasing. It was Russell's wish to create a more integrated medical center, and Joel saw an important part of his job as creating staff departments (such as personnel and purchasing) and upgrading these functions with the help of medical center experts.

When Joel arrived, the controller's department consisted of four individuals: Bill Connor, the controller, who promptly resigned (Joel had never met this individual but had been told that Connor had personal problems of an unspecified nature); Peter Stavrogin, an industrious bookkeeper, who was a 55-year-old Eastern European refugee with a limited knowledge of English; a payroll clerk; and a secretary. This was the staff for an organization of more than 400 employees that was funded by five different agencies under five different contracts. The accounting department had heavy personnel responsibilities as well, at least as far as payroll was concerned, because no personnel department as such existed. One of the first things Joel did was hire Connor's replacement. In doing so—and to conform with Russell's policy of operating as an integrated medical center—Joel enlisted the help of medical center staff: Milton Schlitz, the director of financial affairs, and Grover Alexander, the director of personnel. Alexander volunteered to place the job advertisements and check the references of applicants for the controller position, and Schlitz suggested that he screen the applicants. The best three or four candidates would then be reviewed by Joel and Harrang who, between them, would select the new controller. Joel was pleased with this arrangement, although he thought the recommended salary for the position was too low. He agreed to go along, however, based on the recommendations of Alexander and Schlitz, who both had considerably more experience in these matters.

However, because of what Schlitz and Alexander considered a shortage of qualified accountants, and because of the undesirable location of Morris, they found only two prospective applicants. Albert Fodor, a 55-year-old certified public accountant (CPA) with no hospital experience but good references, was the obvious first choice, and he was hired as Morris's new controller. Fodor was pleasant and industrious. It took him six months to learn the job, but he then resigned, claiming that the tremendous pressure and workload were too great for a man of his years. The payroll clerk also resigned at this time to move to a higher-paying job at another hospital.

During the next three months, Joel employed three new billing clerks as well as a personnel assistant and a purchasing agent. Most of the accounting department's work, which would have been done by the controller, was performed by Joel, who handled the budgetary aspects, while Stavrogin covered the accounting aspects. This system was unsatisfactory, however, because both felt Joel should spend less time troubleshooting financial problems and more time on the programmatic aspects of the job. Also, Joel wanted to conduct and supervise a variety of special studies for contract purposes and cost comparisons—an undertaking hardly feasible under the present setup.

So Joel went back to Schlitz and Alexander, insisting that the salary for the controller job be raised $3,000 per year because of the complexity of the job and the distance from Schlitz's direct supervision. Schlitz agreed reluctantly; he knew he would have to raise salaries or face morale problems in the accounting department at Haas Hospital.

After advertising the job extensively, Schlitz screened eight to ten candidates and sent three candidates to Joel and Harrang. Out of the three, Percy Oram seemed the best. Oram was 40 years old and, although not a CPA, had solid accounting experience in a medium-sized business firm. Oram had no hospital or healthcare experience, but Schlitz and Joel did not feel that such experience was necessary for the job—although, of course, they would have preferred it. Oram was well dressed and married with no children. He said he was interested in advancing himself in the expanding hospital field.

Joel explained the Fodor experience to Oram and emphasized the position's work pressures. Oram responded that he was looking for a job where he would have more autonomy, where he was in charge and responsible, and where he knew he would be rewarded (or blamed) based on his performance. Of course, he would like to spend a lot of time at first learning the ropes with Schlitz. Joel promised to let Oram know later that week if the job was his. Afterward, Joel and Harrang agreed that Oram was the best of the three candidates. However, Harrang had a vague feeling of unease—Oram seemed too good, too qualified for the job. Independently, Schlitz also agreed that Oram was the best of the three candidates. Alexander checked Oram's reference, who confirmed the high opinion of Schlitz and Joel. Oram was then offered the job as controller of the Morris unit, which he accepted.

From Joel's point of view, things went fairly well at first, perhaps because Joel was busy with other matters and because Oram was spending a lot of time at Haas Hospital with Schlitz. The first sign of trouble was the lateness of the monthly statement that Joel had instituted and required. The statement included detailed categories of departmental costs, comparing costs for this month, last month, and this month last year (Joel hoped eventually to compare costs with performance as well), as well as cumulative totals for this year. Joel had reviewed with Oram how he wanted the statement done (in what categories), with a cover sheet that would suggest the reasons for any large variances. Oram agreed to furnish such a report, but one month later, Joel still had not received it. When asked about the report, Oram said that he was too busy and that he was working on it.

When the statement finally did arrive on Joel's desk, it had no cover letter about variances, and large variances had been caused by sloppy accounting (items in one category last year, for instance, were in another this year, causing large discrepancies). Even some of the amounts were incorrect, such as salaries of certain individuals that had not been counted in the proper categories. Joel, patiently but with irritation, told Oram that this was not what he wanted. He explained why he wanted what he wanted, as well as when he wanted the report—15 days after the end of the month. Timeliness, Joel emphasized, was especially important because, although the city contract remained at the same sum every year, changes in the OEO budget had to be individually approved by Washington, and OEO funds had to be spent by the year's end. This meant a lot of shuffling had to be done (e.g., transfer of city positions because of increased salary costs to the OEO budget) based on correct information. Oram apologized and agreed to improve his performance.

At the same time, Joel had begun to hear complaints about Oram from other staff members. Linda Lee, the personnel assistant, and Felix Schwartzberg, the assistant director, complained about his rudeness, arrogance, and insensitivity to the poor—as evidenced by his repeated statements about "welfare chiselers." Such terminology was at odds with the philosophy of the unit. When changes in employee paychecks had to be made because of supervisory mistakes or because of inadequate notice concerning an employee's vacation, Oram reluctantly did the extra work. He warned those involved, without clearing it with Joel, that eventually checks would not be issued on this basis.

Joel had been approached by Oram two weeks previously about a personal matter. Oram explained that he had to come to work an hour and a half late twice a week because of an appointment with his psychiatrist. The psychiatrist was unable to see him before or after work, and Oram hoped Joel would be sympathetic. Oram was willing to stay late to make up the time. Joel said he wanted to think it over before responding, and he discussed Oram's situation with Schlitz and Harrang. They all agreed that they would have liked to have known this before Oram was hired, but that if the work was done and he made up the time, the arrangement would be permitted. It was agreed that Joel would check occasionally in the accounting office, which was located in a separate building a block away from the health services facility, to see if Oram was indeed putting in the extra time.

For about the next six months, Oram's performance remained essentially the same. The cover letters he provided were superficial, and the statements were late and often contained mistakes. (The statements did, however, eventually arrive and were eventually corrected.) The special studies requested of Oram were done late, and Joel often had to redo them. In checking on Oram, Joel never found him in the office after 5:00 p.m., though Joel did not check every day. The routine work of the accounting department was being done effectively, but this had been the case before the current situation with Oram, when no controller had been present. Oram had added another clerk, and Joel suspected that Stavrogin was still performing much of the supervisory work he had been doing prior to Oram's arrival. Joel was not happy. He discussed the situation with Harrang, who agreed that the statements were less than acceptable. Harrang told Joel to do as he liked but to clear his actions first with Schlitz.

Soon after, Joel went to Haas Hospital to discuss Oram with Schlitz. Schlitz, a CPA, had been controller of Haas Hospital, now Haas Medical Center, for 27 years. Schlitz was talkative (though often vague), hardworking, basically conservative, and oriented primarily to the needs of Haas Hospital rather than to the medical center at large (at least in Joel's opinion). This latter point was reflected in the allocation of overhead in the Morris contracts (administrative time allocated was greater than that actually provided) and in the high price of direct services, such as laboratory work, performed for Morris by the hospital. More important, Schlitz saw his job almost exclusively as worrying about "the bottom line"—whether the hospital or the Morris unit ran a deficit or broke even—rather than in terms of performance relative to costs. Nevertheless, Joel thought he had established a cordial relationship with Schlitz, and their discussion about Oram was indeed cordial for the most part. Schlitz agreed that Oram's performance left something to be desired. He was particularly unhappy about the time Oram put in. On the other hand, Schlitz felt that the Morris unit was in good financial shape and that there was nothing to worry about. In light of the experience with the previous controller, Fodor, Schlitz wondered if indeed they could find a better man for the salary. Schlitz suggested that they talk to Oram together but said that he would go along with whatever Joel wanted to do.

Acting on Schlitz's recommendation, Joel set up a meeting with Schlitz, Oram, and Harrang to discuss his dissatisfaction. During the course of the meeting, Joel admitted that the monthly statements were improving, but the improvement had occurred only after extensive prodding. Oram remarked that the reason for this meeting surprised him; he had thought, on the basis of previous meetings with Joel and Schlitz, that they were pleased with his work. He then asked to be included in more top-level policy meetings, as he felt that controllers should be part of the top management group. Oram said he felt isolated, in part because the accounting department was located in a separate building. Joel responded that he would welcome Oram's participation in policy meetings after the work of the accounting department had been sufficiently upgraded, and that Oram would be kept informed of and invited to all meetings that concerned his department.

Returning to the Morris facility, Joel discussed his perplexity with Harrang. Actually, he asserted, he did not understand what was going on. Oram never gave him what he wanted. He had no way of knowing how busy Oram actually was. Lately, Oram had said that he couldn't produce certain studies by the stipulated dates because he was busy doing work for Schlitz or attending meetings at the hospital with Schlitz and the controllers of the other units of the medical center.

Harrang replied that he believed that Schlitz was indeed responsible in part for Oram's lack of responsiveness. Schlitz had probably told Oram not to listen to Joel but to do what he, Schlitz, recommended, because Oram's salary and benefits were largely determined by Schlitz rather than by Joel. Schlitz did not want the accounting department at Morris to use more sophisticated techniques than the hospital because such practices would reflect badly on Schlitz. Moreover, Schlitz wanted his "own man" at the Morris unit so that the hospital benefited in all transactions with Morris (e.g., ensuring enough slack in the city budget to meet any contingency, with as many staff as possible switched to the OEO budget).

Joel had to agree with Harrang's observation. Yet Harrang had become increasingly bitter toward Russell over the last six months. This bitterness concerned a variety of matters, most specifically Harrang's salary. Harrang was working much harder than he had bargained for at Morris, and he didn't feel he was getting the money or the credit he deserved. Nevertheless, Joel did think that Schlitz might be part of the problem; he had never been particularly impressed with Schlitz.

Several weeks later, a new state regulation was passed requiring city agencies, if they were to collect under Medicaid, to make every effort to collect from people who, by state edict, could afford to pay. This regulation was in conflict with Morris's philosophy of providing free service to all who said they could not pay, and the professionals at Morris opposed the implementation of the policy. The professional staff felt that no special effort should be made to collect from those who had formerly received free services. Oram disagreed with this philosophy and said that Morris should make every effort to collect.

When implementing collections, Oram requested that the registration staff who were to collect the money be made part of his department, or that a separate cashier's office be set up on the first floor of the health facility. Otherwise, his department did not wish to be involved. Schwartzberg, the assistant director in charge of registration, argued that the registration staff should continue as part of the family health units because of other duties, that no space was available on the first floor for a cashier's office, and that it was not fair to make patients stand in two lines, as they would have to under Oram's arrangement, before seeing a health professional. Joel and Harrang sided with Schwartzberg and discussed with Oram a plan under which he would be responsible for the cash collection aspects of the registrar's work. It was agreed that Oram would devise, within a week, a plan for implementation. After two weeks, Schwartzberg reported to Joel that Oram had not devised a plan and was unwilling to cooperate with the plan Schwartzberg and the chief registrar had devised.

Joel pounded his desk. What concerned him was not so much this specific matter, which he knew he would resolve, but what to do in general with Oram. Joel was working Saturday mornings with a militant community group over next year's OEO budget, and he was still working 60 to 65 hours per week. He didn't think Oram's performance would improve unless Schlitz agreed with Joel's priorities and, even in that event, sufficient improvement was unlikely. On the other hand, Joel did not look forward to hiring a fourth controller in the two years he had worked at Morris. Moreover, the routine work of the accounting department was being performed to Schlitz's satisfaction. Joel decided to go for a walk by the river and make his decision.

## Case Questions

1. What is the problem from Joel's point of view? From Oram's point of view? From Schlitz's point of view? From Harrang's?
2. In what ways should Oram be accountable to Joel and Schlitz?
3. Given that Oram's performance is not acceptable to Joel, what options does Joel have to affect Oram's performance?
4. What do you recommend that Joel do now? Why?
5. What is the evidence that you used in making the above recommendation?

# CASE 3, PART 1
# What More Evidence Do You Need?

*Anthony R. Kovner*

Reprinted with permission from *Harvard Business Review*, May 1, 2010.

Sally Randolph rose from her swivel chair and walked over to the Norman Rockwell print hanging on her wall. A remnant from the days when she and Mark Wiley worked together as resident physicians, it showed a concerned young girl holding up her doll to a white-haired doctor, who was kindly "listening" to its heart.

She loved this image and what it stood for: medicine focused on people. Mark had caught a glimpse of the print in her locker back then, and he had liked it. She wondered what he'd think of it now.

They both still worked at American Medical Center (AMC), a $2 billion institution, but Mark was now CEO and Sally chief medical officer. The image of the e-mail he'd just sent—marked urgent with a red exclamation point and the subject line "Evidence-Based Management Seminar Cancelled"—blurred her vision. Apparently Mark's focus had shifted from patient care to profits.

## Middle Managers Versus Chiefs

"Hi, Dr. Randolph. Are you interruptible?"

Richard Lee stood with his fist against the door frame, as if he'd been knocking. She wondered how long he'd been there.

"Oh, sorry, Richard! Yes, of course. Come in."

She walked back behind her desk and motioned for Richard to take the seat across from her. "What's up?"

Richard was one of 36 participants in the Evidence-Based Management (EBMgmt) seminar Sally had run for the past year with Harry Bradshaw, a professor at Lucas Business School. Every other month, clinicians and managers had met in teams of six and used EBMgmt to tackle the management challenges facing AMC.

Last month, Sally had presented a series of recommendations from the seminar, including those from Richard's team, to Mark and the medical chiefs. AMC clearly needed to improve the delivery and coordination of patient care, and the seminar participants had identified a structural reorganization as the best way to accomplish this. Despite all the proof, though, the chiefs didn't think that pursuing these improvements was as important as their research and teaching. Without their support—or Mark's—the recommendations never got off the ground.

Now Mark was asking seminar participants to serve as middle managers on task forces he was creating to carry out a new strategic plan. Everyone at AMC, he had written in the e-mail, could learn a lot from the participants about the importance of basing decisions on sound evidence. Sally couldn't help thinking, though, that Mark didn't really seem to respect EBMgmt when he rejected the recommendations that resulted from it.

"I just read the e-mail from Mark, and I'm really frustrated," Richard said. "Making us middle managers on these task forces won't change how anyone works. The medical chiefs weren't receptive to our recommendations, and they certainly won't like it if we start telling them how to make decisions. It seems like we can't get anywhere with evidence-based management in this organization."

Sally couldn't argue with him. Richard's team had tirelessly followed the evidence-based approach: translating management challenges into research questions, answering those questions with the best literature out there, and conducting pilot studies to support the interventions they proposed to senior management.

"I know, Richard," Sally sighed. "It's hard to imagine decisions ever getting made differently around here. If the chiefs weren't wowed by evidence-based management when Harry and I were selling it, all of you middle managers on the task forces will have an even harder time getting them on board. I'll talk to Mark, but I can't make any promises."

She thought of Mark's e-mail and how it seemed his focus had shifted from EBMgmt to Centers of Excellence, which he clearly considered to be the centerpiece of his new strategic plan. These would be run by the chiefs, and with this new responsibility—and power—Sally worried they'd have even less tolerance for change.

"Thanks, Sally. I appreciate it," Richard said as he stood to leave.

"We'll see how it goes," Sally said. She thought to herself, "Don't thank me yet."

## Running Out of Options

Deciding to make her morning run six miles instead of three, Sally began a second loop around the lake. She always entered a sort of Zen state after 30 minutes, and today she needed all the clarity she could get.

She knew AMC historically broke even financially, and chatter among senior management was that Mark had received clear direction from the board to focus on "not losing money." One way to boost the center's financial results was to increase patient volume, which surely was behind Mark's new strategic plan.

Centers of Excellence attracted more patients, and more patients equaled bigger profits—in most circumstances. Sally couldn't help but think that Mark had missed one crucial fact: 90% of AMC's current patients were low income, and their health care was paid for by Medicare or Medicaid. The chances of the new centers attracting enough higher-income patients to make up for the no-pay patients were slim, especially considering the nicer facilities that already existed in wealthier neighborhoods.

Shaking out her arms on a downhill stretch, she wondered if it was possible to salvage the situation. Perhaps if evidence-based management were part of the new strategic plan, the data would eventually tell the story the EBMgmt team had been trying to tell for some time.

Before she approached Mark, she decided, she'd check in with Harry. He had co-run the seminar, after all, and might have ideas of his own.

## A Patient Approach

"Have you tried the stir fry?" Sally asked.

Sally and Harry maneuvered around the Lucas Business students in the dining hall. It was a beautiful day—April like it is only in Virginia—and many students were taking their lunches out to the quad. One of them recognized

Harry as her professor, giving him a polite smile as she passed with her cell pressed to her ear.

"The stir fry is good, but beware the hot sauce," Harry responded.

They found a seat at a corner table, and Sally laid out the situation, emphasizing her worry about Mark's new direction, which left the fate of EBMgmt in the hands of a few relatively junior managers.

"Sally," he went on, "I've worked with Mark for 16 years. I know him, and I know AMC. My advice is to start small. There's no proof that evidence-based management has a high ROI. Limit your efforts to your jurisdiction, to quality and safety, and prove the effectiveness of the approach there before trying to sell Mark on structural change."

"But, Harry, Mark's focus on Centers of Excellence is a big step in the wrong direction," Sally said.

"Believe me, I wish the seminar hadn't been cancelled. And I completely agree it's a bad idea to leave it to the middle managers to enlighten the chiefs. At this point, though, there's not enough support for restructuring."

Back in her office, Sally pondered Harry's advice. Trying to show modest results in her own area would take months or years, and all the while AMC would be pouring resources into a misguided plan to increase profits and moving further away from better patient care.

True, the consequences of not having a seamless delivery system weren't always dire—one patient receiving a cold meal wasn't the end of the world. But it was unacceptable when a high-risk patient had trouble scheduling a crucial follow-up visit or when a patient missed several doses of medication because of miscommunication.

Doing what was right to improve the patient experience was increasingly complex, but every indicator suggested a seamless delivery system was the solution. If the organization seriously committed to using evidence for making better management decisions, maybe everything else would fall into place. Fostering that sort of commitment would require leadership from the top. And what better way to begin that process than as part of a new strategic plan?

## Proof of Evidence

Back home, Sally plopped down on the couch, mentally exhausted. Her husband walked in minutes later with their small dog, Penny, who was excited and straining to be let off her leash.

"How's it going?" Joe asked.

She let out a big sigh and recapped her conversation with Harry.

"I can accept that there's no appetite for a restructuring, but creating these Centers of Excellence shows a complete lack of interest in using evidence to make smart decisions. Mark needs to do more than pay lip service to promoting the 'great skills' we learned in the seminar."

"Well, maybe Harry has a point," Joe said, unlacing his shoes. "We have all the evidence we need that the U.S. health care system is not sustainable. Our costs are too high, quality is too uneven, and millions of people can't even get care. Still, that hasn't resulted in the right changes. Proving the value of evidence-based management is going to be tough."

Sally's look told him that wasn't the reaction she wanted.

"But why do I need to prove its value first?" she asked. "Is there a known positive ROI for top-down decision making? For decisions based on anecdotes and gut reactions?"

Joe didn't have the answers, but he did have the ingredients to make a killer baked ziti. As Sally watched him walk to the kitchen, Penny pitter-pattering behind, she thought about the odds of changing Mark's mind. At most institutions, it would be career suicide to confront the CEO about flaws in his strategic plan. But Mark had recruited Sally for this position. If she played up the potential cost savings of EBMgmt, she might have a chance.

Unfortunately, as Harry pointed out, scientific proof of evidence-based management's positive ROI did not exist—yet. She'd be taking a gamble by advocating for it so strongly. On the other hand, if they committed to Mark's plan as is, they might never make any improvements at all in patient care.

## Commentaries
### 1. Sally needs to argue for using data to make every decision at AMC.

*Jeffrey Pfeffer, professor at the Stanford Graduate School of Business*

Sally Randolph hasn't done the best job promoting organizational change, but it's not too late. First, she needs to create a much greater sense of urgency. Slow change often equals no change. That's because "slow" gives people the opportunity to put off action. It's the deadline effect (people work harder as a deadline approaches) in reverse. The fact that the EBMgmt seminar produced nothing tangible after one year means that talk has substituted for action.

Second, she must help the medical chiefs understand what's in it for them. If American Medical Center is like most other hospitals, it suffers from quality problems that expose it to financial difficulties, because Medicare and private insurers won't pay for care necessitated by treatment-induced issues such as infections. The medical chiefs should be alerted to initiatives such as the Institute for Healthcare Improvement's 5 Million Lives project, intended to reduce incidents of medical harm, and they need to see data on preventable deaths from the Institute of Medicine. The medical chiefs also need updates on AMC's own cost and medical outcomes performance, which Sally can assemble in frequent reports distributed widely throughout the medical center. In short, Sally needs to remind the chiefs that they have obligations to patients, not just to research and teaching—something that is easy to lose sight of in an academic medical center.

Third, Sally needs to spend much more time with Mark Wiley. He suffers from the "program du jour" disease—going from one thing, evidence-based management, to another, Centers of Excellence, apparently just to try something new. Quality and other organizational change initiatives often fail because of the short attention spans of senior leaders and the consequent tendency of people further down the ranks to wait until the latest program passes. Sally needs to explain that her work can yield improvements that will enhance not only AMC's financial results but also Wiley's stature as a hospital administrator.

Fourth, Sally needs to argue for using data to make every decision at AMC—even for creating Centers of Excellence. It sounds as if the incremental increase in patients may not be profitable, and the concept can easily be imitated. In contrast, evidence-based management results in process improvements that provide an enduring advantage. The value of EBMgmt doesn't need to be proven—its effects are in the studies on which it relies. Just as in medicine, if an organization implements something that has been shown to work, it will work in that organization, too.

Sally confronts the political realities of accomplishing organizational change. But she should be on her way to success if she shows people what's in it for them, provides information that builds a compelling case, creates a sense of urgency, highlights what other hospitals have done to improve, and argues that evidence should be used for guiding not just medical practice but administrative practice as well.

### 2. Managers could pilot the approach in pockets of the organization.

*David Fine, CEO of St. Luke's Episcopal Health System*

Mark Wiley's strategy to address profitability on the revenue side, through increased clinical volumes in Centers of Excellence, is commonplace. But this approach is not likely to generate the margins Wiley is hoping for unless the new centers radically change AMC's distribution of patients. AMC's Medicare and Medicaid payer mix is reported to be 90% of current patients. According to published reports from the American Hospital Association, 53% of hospitals receive Medicare payments less than cost, and 56% of hospitals receive Medicaid payments less than cost.

A more effective approach would be to focus on reducing costs associated with specific clinical outcomes through treatment protocols driven by best practices, supply chain standardization, simple strategies that decrease patient falls and reduce hospital-acquired infections, and other process improvements. The literature is replete with studies documenting the cost improvements that follow such interventions, all of which are illustrative of evidence-based management.

EBMgmt is a commitment to the use of informed decision making rather than instinct or precedent. Sally Randolph and at least one middle manager, Richard Lee, see the Centers of Excellence strategy as contrary to the culture promoted in the EBMgmt seminar. But there is little reason to conclude that evidence can play no role in establishing the centers. The EBMgmt partisans at AMC, acting through Sally, can help ensure that the centers are chosen and then financed on the basis of a realistic view of profit potential, ROI, community need, or other objective criteria.

Harry Bradshaw's encouragement of an incremental approach is wise. I have had the opportunity to manage as a disruptive innovator; this is easier from the CEO chair than from other places in the enterprise. If AMC is not ready to absorb EBMgmt across the board, some executives and middle managers could pilot the approach in pockets of the organization. Organizational politics at AMC need not impede the use of the best available scientific evidence. Those who aspire to adopt potentially transforming approaches don't have to wait until Mark designates lean management, Six Sigma, evidence-based management, or some other "state religion." I think a Randolph and Lee skunk works could do some good and certainly, in the spirit of Hippocrates, would do no harm.

# CASE 3, PART 2

## More Evidence—The Example of Inappropriate Admissions

*Alison M. Aldrich*

Julia Martin scrolled through some headlines while waiting for her morning coffee to brew. One story, from the local newspaper, raised her concern: "American Medical Center Facing Maximum Penalty for Medicare Readmissions."

Julia had been working as a hospital librarian at American Medical Center (AMC) for the past three years. In that time, she had made good progress expanding the number of electronic journals available to AMC clinicians, administrators, and staff, and she had been working with AMC's information technology staff to integrate links to clinical practice guidelines into the electronic medical record. She always received positive performance reviews from her supervisor, the hospital's director of continuing medical education. Despite these successes, Julia was concerned that she might lose her job. She knew that hospital librarians elsewhere were increasingly being laid off as administrators closed the libraries in an attempt to save money—because wasn't everything free on the Internet now? She knew that AMC was having some financial troubles, and this latest news about readmissions penalties was not good. Julia needed to do more to demonstrate the value of her services to AMC, but she was not sure what to do.

Later that afternoon, while Julia was at her desk in the library, puzzling over how best to spend her limited budget for updating textbooks, nurse manager Richard Lee walked in to check his e-mail on one of the computers.

"Hi, Richard! How is that falls pilot going?" Julia had worked with Richard several months back, identifying some systematic reviews of best practices for preventing falls in elderly inpatients.

"Hi, Julia! It's going really well, thanks for asking! The new fall risk signs we developed really seem to be helping. Falls on my unit are down 63 percent from a year ago. Thanks so much for your help on that project."

"You're welcome! It was such a pleasure working with you." And she meant it. Richard really seemed to understand evidence-based practice, and Julia could tell he was passionate about improving the quality of care his patients received.

Richard went back to his e-mail, sighing audibly a few moments later. "Did you see this *Times* story about the Medicare readmissions penalty?"

"I sure did. This has me really concerned. What are the chiefs planning to do about it? Have you heard anything?"

"They're not sure yet. I know Mark Wiley is really in crisis mode over it. He assigned Sally Randolph to head up a special task force. We're meeting next Tuesday at noon. Say, would you be able to attend? I think we could really benefit from having someone with your skills on board."

"Absolutely. Count me in!"

Julia got to work researching the reasons for hospital readmissions and ways to prevent them. She developed a comprehensive search strategy, thinking of alternate search terms to combine, and making use of advanced search tools such as MEDLINE and the Cochrane Library, as well as the open web. Once she had done what she felt was a comprehensive search, she started reviewing articles and assessing them for quality, taking notes on things such as research design, sample size, and potential applicability of the results to the situation at AMC. She selected ten sources that she felt provided the best evidence, then organized them into a summary table to present to the task force.

At the meeting, a resident physician in attendance expressed a concern that was on everyone's mind: "You know, a lot of the time readmissions just can't be helped. Complications happen! I would rather my patient come back to the hospital than not. Why should we be penalized for things that are beyond our control?"

Having reviewed the literature, Julia was able to add clarity to the discussion around avoidable versus unavoidable reasons for readmission. She spoke up: "That's true, doctor. A lot of readmissions can't be avoided, but some can. There is a growing body of research out there about how changing the way discharge procedures are managed, and providing better patient education at that point, can cut down on preventable readmissions. In fact, the Agency for Healthcare Research and Quality [AHRQ] put together a toolkit to help hospitals deal with this issue.[1]"

Julia connected her laptop to the conference room projector so everyone could view the AHRQ toolkit on the screen. The toolkit, along with the literature summary Julia had prepared, served as a good launch point for productive discussion. By the end of the meeting, the group had proposed several evidence-based policy changes they hoped would make a positive difference at AMC.

After the meeting, Sally approached Julia to express her appreciation.

"Julia, thanks so much for all of the research you did to prepare for this meeting. I'm really impressed! It makes so much sense to have an information professional involved in this process. I wish we'd thought of it sooner."

"You're welcome, Dr. Randolph. I know that, as busy physicians, you don't have a lot of time for in-depth research, but evidence-based practice is so important. As a librarian, it's my job to keep up with the latest information resources and advanced search techniques. I'm so glad I could use my expertise to help with this readmission issue!"

## Note

1. The AHRQ's Re-Engineered Discharge (RED) Toolkit is available at www.ahrq.gov/professionals/systems/hospital/red/toolkit/index. html.

## Case Questions (for Both Part 1 and Part 2)

1. As noted in the first part of the case, establishing a questioning culture is essential for effective evidence-based management practice. Sally, Richard, and others have made several attempts to influence the culture at AMC, some more successful than others. For example, they tried to establish regular evidence-based management workshops, and they implemented an evidence-based quality improvement project to reduce patient falls on Richard's unit. What more could they do to influence

the culture? What could they do specifically to encourage upper management to adopt a more evidence-based mind-set?

2. Many medical centers, particularly outside of academia, do not have professional librarians on staff. If you were an administrator at one of these institutions, what would be your strategy for conducting research and keeping up with the latest evidence in health services management?

3. Conduct a search for evidence about successful interventions to decrease inappropriate hospital readmissions. What do you find? What do you think about the evidence? What do you think about the search process?

# CASE 4
## Now What?

*Ann Scheck McAlearney*

**K**elly Carmon had been working at West Liberty Health System for four years, and she was starting to wonder about what was next for her career. She remembered her graduate school experience in health administration fondly, especially now that she had been in the same position for three full years since her first promotion. The excitement of learning new things and the terror of exams and presentations were seemingly distant memories. Instead, she felt stuck in her present job as manager of operations for the division of cardiology.

West Liberty Health System was a large, multihospital system located in a competitive Midwestern market. Though West Liberty was both large and doing fine financially, Carmon's expectation that she could grow and learn within the health system was not becoming a reality. She found that the real day-to-day existence of this operations management position was about as unglamorous as she could imagine, and she was unable to envision a promotion in her near future. Carmon had tried to continue to read and learn on the job, but there just wasn't enough time in the day. The firefighting of operations and real-time crises was always her first priority, and she was afraid that she would soon be unable to remember how to analyze the business case for a new venture or how to think strategically about just about anything.

As Carmon returned home at the end of the week, she decided things had to change. Even though West Liberty had seemed like a good and caring employer when she interviewed all those years ago, the company now seemed much better at talking about caring about employees than actually doing something about it. When Carmon looked back on the past three years, she realized that she had yet to successfully participate in any seminar or educational class offered by the health system because she could never seem to get away from her job. She also realized that she was not alone. Her friends in other departments had similar complaints, and they often felt that the only way they were able to take a break was to leave the country—but nobody had enough time or money to do that frequently.

At 25, Carmon was still single, but she was starting to feel that the time she was investing in her career was not paying off professionally—and it was certainly not helping her social life. Feeling burned out and disappointed, Carmon knew she needed to do something different, but she didn't know what. She wanted to take the educational programs West Liberty offered, but she needed to find some protected time. She also needed to figure out how to navigate the politics and chaos of West Liberty.

Carmon set up a meeting with her boss, Patricia Edwards, director of cardiology, to voice her concerns. Although she told Edwards that the reason for the meeting was "professional development," she wasn't sure that Edwards understood what Carmon meant; she also wasn't confident that Edwards would be able to provide the guidance Carmon sought. She had other mentors at West Liberty who had suggested different ways to develop herself professionally, but Carmon knew she had to get Edwards's support before she could reallocate her time to focus on her professional development.

In preparing for her meeting with Edwards, Carmon considered what information she should send to Edwards ahead of time and what she should leave for the actual meeting. Knowing Edwards hated to be caught off guard, Carmon decided to compile all of her preliminary planning ideas in a "for your eyes only" document that she could send a week in advance of the meeting. She knew Edwards's time was limited, but she wanted to make sure Edwards understood how important this issue was to her future at West Liberty. Carmon was dependent on Edwards's buy-in to help her achieve her professional development goals, and she felt that a personal professional development plan would provide a solid framework with which she could guide the discussion. Knowing her resume would be a good starting point, she decided to update it (see exhibit 4.1) before considering her next steps.

## Case Questions

1. What constraints does Carmon face within her position? What options does she have to overcome those constraints?
2. What can Carmon do in her present position to learn on the job?
3. What should Carmon do to prepare for the meeting with Edwards?
4. What should be part of Carmon's personal professional development plan?
5. What documents should Carmon bring or send in advance of the meeting?

**EXHIBIT 4.1**
Resume for
Kelly Carmon

# Kelly Carmon

4678A Weybridge Rd. East                                  Kelly.Carmon@email.com
Midwest City                                                        (987) 654-3210

## Experience

**West Liberty Health System**, Midwest City, State, *Operations Manager, Department of Cardiology*, October 2013–present
- Managed strategic operations projects that improved service to patients and increased revenues for Cardiology department
- Provided planning and operations assistance to department
- Facilitated consensus-building and decision-making
- Supervised statistical analyses of surveys to improve patient satisfaction

**West Liberty Health System**, Midwest City, State, *Administrative Coordinator, Department of Clinical Epidemiology*, May 2012–October 2013
- Developed, distributed, and collected quantitative survey on healthcare workers' perceptions and knowledge of isolation in relation to MRSA and *C. diff*
- Participated in Community Health Day and Public Health Farmers' Market

**Midwest University, School of Public Health**, Midwest City, State, *Student Research Assistant*, January 2011–May 2012
- Collected observational data on hand hygiene compliance at hospitals for infection prevention projects
- Reported monthly data for use in reports by CMS Partnership for Patients and participating hospitals
- Trained new hand hygiene auditors

**Eastern University Department of Anthropology**, Eastern City, State, *Research Assistant*, May 2009–May 2010
- Supported Dr. Fiona Bell's research on human adaptation to high-altitude hypoxia
- Analyzed videos to determine capillary measurements from stills of nomads and Eastern City community residents and compiled data into spreadsheets for statistical analysis

## Education

**Midwest University**, Midwest City, State, *Master of Health Administration* (May 2012)

**Eastern University**, Washington, DC, *Bachelor of Arts*, Anthropology and Sociology; Psychology minor; *cum laude* (May 2010) *Dean's High Honors — Provost's Special Scholarship Recipient*

## Skills

Proficient in Microsoft Office Suite; SPSS; ATLAS.ti - Versed in SAS; STATA

Proficient in Spanish

# CASE 5

# What Then?

*Ann Scheck McAlearney*

## Planning Her Professional Development

Kelly Carmon knew that the best approach to obtaining endorsement from her boss, Patricia Edwards, for her professional development was to devise a plan. By creating a formal plan, Carmon would be able to outline her professional development goals and build a case for why achievement of her goals would be important. Further, by developing a formal plan, Carmon would build the evidence case for her professional development, drawing from the available research literature she knew Edwards respected.

Though this process was difficult, it helped her to focus her own goals so she could be clear and compelling when she presented her case to Edwards. She focused on two- and five-year time horizons to keep herself from feeling completely overwhelmed. Knowing that the best goals were those that were measurable, Carmon outlined her professional development goals and their associated metrics as a starting point for her discussion with Edwards. This preliminary outline is presented in exhibit 5.1.

---

**EXHIBIT 5.1**
Professional
Development
Goals

***Two-Year Goals***
- Improvement in conflict management skills, reflected in improvement on Annual Performance Evaluation section of "Managing Conflict"
- Improvement in team-building skills, reflected in improvement in Annual Performance Evaluation section of "Building Professional Teams"
- Successful completion of cross-system project, involving collaboration outside Division of Cardiology
- Expansion of professional network to include at least two West Liberty executives
- Higher personal job satisfaction
- Promotion of at least one direct report to manager at West Liberty

***Three- to Five-Year Goals***
- Promotion to director at West Liberty
- By year three, Annual Performance Evaluation strong in all areas
- High job satisfaction of direct reports, reflected in Annual Employee Work–Life Survey
- Promotion of at least two direct reports to manager at West Liberty in years 3–5

---

# Focusing Professional Development Options

Once Carmon had outlined her goals, she saw that the next step in her professional development planning process was to highlight specific areas of development necessary for achieving her goals. Several areas jumped out at her in particular: (1) conflict management, (2) building professional teams, (3) internal networking, (4) cross-system collaboration, (5) leadership development, and (6) employee development.

Carmon recognized that Edwards, similar to many others, was a visual thinker. One tool Carmon knew of that might help both her and Edwards envision alternative professional development options was a scenario analysis exercise that described what success might look like if things did or did not go as planned. Carmon got herself a glass of iced tea and imagined how things might happen for good or bad, considering whether she was able to enlist the support and make the personal and behavioral changes she believed were necessary. Exhibit 5.2 shows how she envisioned these three scenarios for the two-year time horizon.

**EXHIBIT 5.2**
Scenario
Analysis of
Professional
Development
Achievements

### Scenario 1: Stormy Weather

Unable to enlist sufficient support for her own professional development, Carmon was forced to continue the development process on her own. She signed up for multiple class offerings through West Liberty's education division, but she was limited by both the course catalog and her own schedule. Though she successfully completed several online courses that introduced her to focused topics, her inability to get away from her job prevented her from completing any courses that required in-class sessions. The director of cardiology was supportive of Carmon's efforts but unable to provide additional resources for her to travel to off-site conferences or participate in courses that required time away from operations. Carmon's performance evaluations continued to be positive, but the director's comments consistently indicated room for improvement in her people skills. The director was particularly concerned about Carmon's ability to work with established nurses and her inability to create and sustain productive teams that involved clinicians. On Carmon's part, she remained frustrated about her lack of free time and about a seemingly endless career as a manager who would never be promoted. She started to look outside West Liberty for new positions but realized her lack of professional development had limited her job possibilities to lateral moves.

### Scenario 2: The Long and Winding Road

Though initially frustrated by her need to be continually available to meet her job's incessant demands, Carmon began to see windows of opportunity for her development. With her director's support, she was able to sign up for a new mentoring program at West Liberty, and she developed an interesting professional connection with the director of food services in the health system. This director had been at West Liberty for her entire career and was

**EXHIBIT 5.2**
Scenario
Analysis of
Professional
Development
Achievements
*(continued)*

able to provide advice about important topics such as negotiating the politics of the health system and using the performance evaluation process as
an opportunity for shameless self-promotion. As the director pointed out
to Carmon, West Liberty did not like to lose good people, so building one's
professional image as one of the "stars" of the system was an excellent first
step toward getting promoted. In addition, through her mentor, Carmon was
able to find a similarly minded manager of operations in food services who
was interested in learning more about West Liberty. With the help of both
directors, Carmon and her colleague negotiated a job switching arrangement
whereby the managers would spend two hours each day in the other's role
for a three-month period. During these three months, the managers also
agreed to have lunch together at least twice per week to ensure that they had
direct opportunities to coordinate with each other so that their job rotation
hours would not result in lost productivity for either department. Though the
job rotation itself did not directly lead to a promotion, this creative arrangement helped reduce Carmon's frustration with West Liberty, and it enabled
her to see opportunities throughout the system for the coming years.

### Scenario 3: Sunny Side of the Street
Carmon's meeting with the director went better than she could have hoped.
The director was in complete agreement about the need for Carmon to focus
on her professional development and offered to provide whatever resources
she could to help Carmon succeed. After reviewing Carmon's professional
development plan, the two agreed on a plan of attack for the coming year,
and they were able to identify two specific off-site conferences that were well
aligned with Carmon's need to develop her conflict management and negotiation skills. In the meantime, the director suggested that Carmon read several
books related to these topics, and she offered to serve as a sounding board
to discuss the books at a series of monthly lunches they would schedule. The
director also offered to recommend that Carmon be placed in the new program that was being developed at West Liberty for "high potentials," ensuring
that she would receive executive-level attention to her leadership development for the coming two years. At the end of the meeting, the director handed
Carmon a copy of one of her recommended books—*Crucial Conversations*, by
Kerry Patterson, Joseph Grenny, Ron McMillan, and Al Switzler (McGraw-Hill,
2002)—and the two agreed on a date for the first lunch meeting. Nine months
flew by, and at Carmon's annual performance evaluation meeting, she had
her next formal opportunity to discuss professional development with the
director. They agreed that the book discussion lunches were both productive
and fun, and they listed the next three books they would plan to read and discuss. They also spoke frankly about external courses Carmon had taken at a
recent professional meeting and about issues she faced in applying what she
had learned; this part of the discussion highlighted several opportunities for
Carmon to further develop her leadership skills and practice new behaviors.
Although the new West Liberty Leadership Development Program still had yet

*(continued)*

**EXHIBIT 5.2**
Scenario
Analysis of
Professional
Development
Achievements
*(continued)*

to begin, the director suggested that Carmon seek other leadership develop-ment opportunities within and outside the health system, to continue making progress toward her own professional development goals. In particular, the director recommended that Carmon enroll in a Center for Creative Leadership course focused specifically on leadership development for women, and she promised to provide Carmon with her full support to attend. Together, they laid out a plan for the next year and highlighted a possible promotion for Car-mon within the coming year as a goal toward which to strive.

## Advancing Her Plan

Carmon was dependent on Edwards's buy-in to help her advance in her pro-fessional development plan. However, she also knew that success ultimately depended on her own ability to achieve her two-year and three- to five-year goals.

## Case Questions

1. How has Carmon's analysis built or weakened her case for spending time away from operations to develop her professional skills?
2. What has to happen for Carmon to achieve her two-year and three- to five-year professional goals? What will lead to the best scenario, "Sunny Side of the Street," becoming a reality?
3. What should Carmon do if the meeting does not go well? What should she do if her plan does not work?
4. How much of professional development is one's personal responsibility, and how much is the responsibility of the employer?

# CASE 6

# Facing Reality in a New Job

*Adam Henick*

## The Urban Teaching Hospital System

The Urban Teaching Hospital System (UTHS) is a voluntary, not-for-profit organization that owns and operates six hospital campuses and a variety of off-campus ambulatory services in its metropolitan market. The main campus, however, is located in a city with a large population in a larger metropolitan area.

UTHS has annual revenues of over $2 billion and a profit margin averaging between 1 and 2 percent. The hospital system is affiliated with four medical schools, and more than 500 residents are trained annually throughout the system. However, none of UTHS's hospitals are the primary affiliate of the medical schools, and in many markets, UTHS hospitals compete with these medical schools' primary academic hospital partners.

Exhibit 6.1 shows some key operating statistics (rounded off) for UTHS last year.

Several of UTHS's hospitals have been in existence for more than 100 years. Many of the system's facilities are dated, and the system has very modest amounts of philanthropy, endowments, and research. Further, the metropolitan market served by UTHS is large and overbedded. Recruitment of physicians who have large practices and regional/national reputations could help UTHS bring new business to the system, but competition for such physicians is fierce. Overall physician compensation within UTHS's market has been bid up above national averages, even when factoring in the local cost-of-living differential.

## A New Vice President for Ambulatory Care

A new corporate vice president (VP) for ambulatory care has recently been recruited to help develop and implement strategies to expand the ambulatory care service line for the system. At this time, inpatient services represent approximately 75 percent of UTHS's operating revenues, and outpatient services represent the remaining 25 percent. In contrast, the national averages are hovering around 55/45 for the inpatient/outpatient revenue mix.

Each of the UTHS hospitals has vice presidents for ambulatory care who would report to this new corporate VP on a dotted line, with their primary

| | | |
|---|---|---|
| Certified beds | 2,700 | **EXHIBIT 6.1** Key Operating Statistics |
| Discharges | 124,000 | |
| Births | 12,000 | |
| Ambulatory visits | 1,400,000 | |
| Emergency department visits | 258,000 | |
| Operating room procedures | 77,000 | |
| Employed physicians | 1,400 | |
| Employees | 15,000 | |

reporting relationship remaining with the local hospital's chief operating officer (COO) or president. The new corporate VP would directly report to UTHS's COO and also have a dotted-line reporting relationship to the local hospital presidents and chief operating officers. This structure is commonly referred to as a *matrix relationship*.

David Harris, who has spent his entire career successfully managing ambulatory care services and physician practices, has been offered the position. During his recruitment, he had been told by UTHS's COO that all of ambulatory care would be removed from the authority of the local hospitals and placed into an enterprise under his responsibility. Although skeptical about the strategy, David did not voice any negative opinions about it during the recruitment process. The COO at UTHS had a reputation for getting what he wanted, and David did not see any upside in trying to change the COO's mind during the interview process.

After reviewing the UTHS financials prior to accepting the position, however, David was convinced that he would have limited capital to work with in attempting to develop a larger ambulatory care footprint. Lacking a strong balance sheet, and further limited by slim profit margins and a small amount of endowment, David knew capital resources would be scarce. His experience in other major healthcare systems suggested that, when push came to shove, ambulatory care was always last in line after all of the inpatient needs were funded. However, he had enjoyed maneuvering on this very narrow tightrope in his past positions, so these concerns did not scare him away from accepting the offer.

## Clarifying the Challenge Ahead

Once David came on board, he decided to spend the first 8 to 12 weeks visiting all of the hospitals and ambulatory care facilities and meeting with the hospitals' senior management, including the vice presidents for ambulatory care who would have new dotted-line reporting relationships to him. During these visits, David immediately found that, although many of the senior managers were warm and friendly, none of them were particularly interested in giving up responsibility for any of their ambulatory care enterprise, in spite of the edict from UTHS's COO. In some cases, managers directed overt hostility at David. At one hospital, the local vice president for ambulatory care refused to share any financial or operating performance information with David, under instructions from her hospital's president. In another hospital, the local vice president for ambulatory care refused to meet with David at all.

After visiting all the ambulatory care services throughout UTHS, David summarized what he had found:

1. Most of the facilities and services had been underfunded and undermanaged for years.
2. Meaningful financial and statistical information did not exist.
3. A direct ratio seemed to exist between the distance from the main campus and the managerial interest in the various ambulatory care service assets, especially the physician practices.
4. No one was evaluating the overall performance of the ambulatory care services, and because no ambulatory care strategy had been delineated, the services lacked data with which to benchmark performance or the appropriateness of each asset.

## Case Question

1. What would you recommend that David do, aside from beginning to look for another position?

# CASE 7
# The First Day

*Ann Scheck McAlearney*

Susan was both thrilled and terrified. Tomorrow was her first day as a manager. Having recently completed her master of health administration degree at a prestigious local university, she had conducted a thorough job search and been hired as the new manager of patient accounts at University Health System. She had had numerous interviews with various directors and other managers in the health system, as well as a lunch interview/meeting with six people who would report to her, but those interviews seemed very far away.

Susan wanted to make a good impression and get off to a positive start, yet she wasn't sure what to do first. She had learned the importance of listening in management, but she also knew she was the boss. Further, her own boss, the director of patient care services, had emphasized the importance of getting her employees to improve productivity at any cost. Susan had heard that, although her new direct reports were nice to one's face, they had a tendency to complain and scapegoat, which had led to the sudden departure of the previous manager of patient accounts. Susan was particularly nervous about being younger than all of her new employees. To quell her fears, she decided to make a list of what she wanted to accomplish in her first days and weeks on the job.

## Case Questions

1. Assume you are a friend of Susan's considering a similar position. What would you recommend that she put on the list?
2. How would you suggest that she prioritize her goals?

# CASE 8

# Managing Volunteers in the Hospital

*Kim Karels, Jennifer Lynn Hefner, and Ann Scheck McAlearney*

Hillbrook University is the first academic medical center in the United States to implement Hillbrook Bedside, a tablet-based inpatient medical portal. The portal provides hospitalized patients with instant access to test results, schedules, and educational materials, along with a feature for messaging the care team or requesting services. A research branch of the academic medical center has received national funding to study the portal's rollout, and results of the project will provide guidance for inpatient portal implementation in other hospitals. The four-year study will assess whether portal access increases patient efficacy for disease management, care team engagement, or patient use of a portal in the outpatient setting. The study is a randomized trial, and a key component is a patient education intervention designed to orient the patient to tablet and portal features, thus potentially increasing patient adoption of the technology.

Lauren Chacon was recently hired as the volunteer coordinator. In this role, she will oversee the staff of volunteers who will carry out the portal education intervention at the patient's bedside. The study team decided to use volunteers for this role because a volunteer staff is replicable at other health systems that may potentially implement this technology in the future but do not have grant funding to support staff salaries. Since the start of her employment three months ago, Chacon has been recruiting and training volunteers; she estimates that she will need 40 volunteers to work four-hour shifts at least once a week. Because hospitals are open around the clock, she will need to find volunteers who can work weekend and holiday shifts. Lauren needs volunteers not only who can agree to the time commitment but also who are fairly technologically savvy, have well-developed interpersonal skills, and can work with sick patients. Some of the patients they will have to work with have limited physical or cognitive abilities, and many are unfamiliar with advanced technology.

So far, Chacon has recruited and trained about 12 volunteers, and throughout the process, she has noted some unique managerial challenges. First, none of the volunteers are trained researchers. They have a lot of questions about the equitability of randomly assigning patients into groups receiving different educational interventions. Further, they have concerns about the inpatient portal itself, particularly with regard to the privacy of medical information. Chacon knows that, in order for the study to be successful, volunteers unfamiliar with research methods need to be able to understand and articulate to patients as succinctly as possible the process of randomization and the importance and potential of inpatient portals.

Chacon is also having difficulty motivating volunteers to commit the time and energy necessary to make this intervention successful. The volunteers need to have a lot of stamina, as a single intervention with a patient can take an hour and volunteers may have to walk around multiple hospitals to get from one patient to the next. Chacon worries about how she will motivate her staff not only to work long shifts, sometimes over the weekend, but also to be ambitious about visiting as many patients as possible during each shift. In overseeing this project, Chacon will learn valuable lessons about managing a volunteer workforce. The results will be useful to other medical centers replicating this intervention, as well as to any manager whose job description includes leading a volunteer staff in a dynamic, stressful hospital setting.

## Case Questions

1. What traditional managerial techniques for motivating paid employees would translate to motivating a volunteer staff? Would any traditional techniques not be suitable?
2. How might a manager engage her staff in a research project when the staff has had no prior research training?

# CASE 9
# Conflict in the Office

*Ramya Rao and Ann Scheck McAlearney*

Trisha Olsen has been an assistant director at Liberty Research Hospital for the past seven years. She currently manages eight people in the protocol department, which is responsible for ensuring that all research studies are compliant with research regulations and institutional review board requirements. Unfortunately, the protocol department has a reputation for high turnover rates, and many workers are rumored to have left because of how they were treated by their boss. However, two of the protocol specialists have been with the department for more than ten years, and these two special-ists have been promoted to team leaders within the past year.

Recently, the department changed its approach to quality control, requir-ing greater involvement and oversight by different employees. Whereas the former process required circulation of work only among the protocol specialists, workers now must circulate their work and have it reviewed by all coworkers, including team leaders. This new approach has introduced some tension within the department and raised issues about work quality that had not been raised in the past. Team leaders have become particularly critical of others' work, and they have also been unhappy when their own work has been returned to them with others' criticisms that needed to be addressed.

Yesterday, tension within the department was particularly high. Trisha was away at a meeting at the time, but apparently Stephanie, a protocol specialist, and Bella, a team leader, were overheard arguing about whether a comment should be made in a database about a minor change in the research protocol. The argument was heated enough that coworkers started to pay attention, and Trisha heard rumors about the incident after she returned from her meeting. To make matters worse, both Stephanie and Bella then e-mailed Trisha to describe the situation and give their points of view.

Trisha wasn't sure how to handle the situation. She knew that Bella had a history of getting into arguments with coworkers and could hold a grudge for months. The department would certainly suffer if the tension remained, and Trisha could not handle further turnover among protocol specialists.

## Case Questions

1. What should Trisha consider prior to addressing the conflict?
2. How can she help resolve the conflict?

## CASE 10
# Annual Performance Evaluation: Can You Coach Kindness?

*Ann Scheck McAlearney*

Bob Carter, RN, has been working at New Hope Hospital for six years, ever since he finished nursing school. He has always planned to become a manager at some point in his career, and it seems the opportunity might soon be available. As a floor nurse, Carter has earned the respect of his peers, never taking no for an answer and, in many cases, saving patients' lives with his solid clinical instincts. At this point, Carter has been working for two years as a case manager in the clinical case management department, where he has been involved in case management and discharge planning. He is considering applying for a promotion to manager of discharge planning, a newly vacated position in the same department. Carter is looking forward to his upcoming performance review with the director of clinical case management; he sees it as an opportunity to discuss this possible promotion.

Hannah Valen is the vice president of clinical operations, and the clinical case management department is one of her areas of responsibility. She is particularly concerned about the role of the department in ensuring appropriate discharge planning for all patients, especially in light of the heightened attention placed on discharge planning through the Centers for Medicare & Medicaid Services Core Measures Program.

You are the director of clinical case management, and you are eager to fill the vacant manager of discharge planning position. You know that any manager in the department must have a strong clinical background. You are also aware that this individual must have the ability to work well with others in process improvement activities that are necessary to strengthen discharge planning and clinical case management services throughout the hospital.

In reviewing Carter's file before his performance evaluation, you recall several issues that might affect your decision about his promotion. First, you are aware that Carter's attitude toward social workers within the department has been less than collegial. Your observations of his work style have suggested that he feels superior to the social workers, though you have not discussed this issue directly with him. Second, you are somewhat concerned about Carter's potential management style. Though he has yet to be tested as a manager, you have seen him verbally reprimand other nurses in front of other employees, which has frustrated some of his coworkers. On the positive side, however, you know that Carter has excellent clinical instincts. Further, though he may seem to have an air of superiority in interactions with some of his coworkers, his interactions with patients have been consistently outstanding. His ability to help patients manage challenging health issues and take responsibility for their care postdischarge has been noted several times. Your reflections about Carter's possible promotion have left you confused.

## Case Questions

1. What is the importance of clinical competence and patient focus relative to one's ability to work as a member of a clinical team in this department?

2. Do you want Carter to be a manager in your department?

3. Regardless of your decision on the possible promotion, what should you tell Carter to help him improve and develop his managerial skills?

4. If you have decided to recommend Carter for the promotion, what do you do now to help him succeed in a managerial role? If you have decided against the recommendation, what do you do to encourage his professional development within New Hope so he does not leave for a different job?

# CONTROL

The basic problem of service institutions is
not high cost, but lack of effectiveness.

*—Peter Drucker*

# COMMENTARY

In healthcare delivery, an effective system of control must monitor a variety of outcomes related to physical functioning (e.g., reduction in pain, ability to climb stairs) and physiological measures (e.g., blood pressure, cholesterol levels), as well as patient perceptions and satisfaction, professional judgment, and cost of care. The need to account for this wide range of factors has led to such concepts as the "value compass" and the "balanced scorecard" to guide control efforts.

A system of control comprises five elements:

1. *Goals and objectives.* For healthcare delivery, the goals and objectives emphasize meeting customer needs.
2. *Information.* An effective control system should gather information that can be used to measure performance.
3. *Performance evaluation.* Performance should be evaluated in relation to the goals and objectives. Did the customer get what she wanted?
4. *Expectations.* A control system should make clear what is expected. Was what the customer got good enough?
5. *Incentives.* Workers can be motivated by an internalized desire to do a good job or by external rewards. The desire to satisfy the customer and the desire to please the supervisor in hopes of a pay raise ideally go together without conflict; problems start, however, if a disconnect exists between satisfying the customer and satisfying the manager.

## Goals and Objectives

Mission, vision, values, goals, and objectives are widely used concepts, shown in exhibit II.1. In short, an organization might say that our mission is to meet the needs of our customers; our vision is to be the best; the values we live by are our religious beliefs; our goal is to survive this year; and our objective is to break even. Another example is provided in the exhibit.

A goal is a broadly stated intention or direction—to improve quality, for example, by lowering the infection rate. Organizational goals are determined by the preferences of individuals with power. Organizations are collectives of

**EXHIBIT II.1**
Organizational
Directions

| Concept | Definition | Example | Requirement |
|---------|-----------|---------|-------------|
| Mission | Reason for existing | To meet the primary healthcare needs in our town | System maintenance |
| Vision | What we hope to do | People will move to our town because our care is so good | Adaptive capability |
| Values | The philosophy that guides behavior | Mutual respect for both caregivers and care receivers | Values integration |
| Goal | An intention or direction | To open a new clinic this year | Goal attainment |
| Objective | A measurable intention | The new clinic will see 200 patients a week by the end of the year | Achievement of objective |

people and things brought together to achieve a common purpose, and they are created by individuals with similar goals. Goals provide organizational focus, establish a long-term framework for dealing with conflict, and encourage commitment from people who work in the organization. They are implemented by individuals working together on budgets, involve the allocation of functions, and may be influenced by the authority structure.

Imagine that an individual wants housing and food and health and entertainment, and this person decides he can do his best by working for pay as a nurse in a clinic. Nursing can be both a means to an end (providing a paycheck) and an end in itself (providing the satisfaction of helping people in a friendly work environment). The clinic's goal of good quality and reasonable cost assumes that this nurse continues to have an enjoyable job and a paycheck. The manager has the role of making this happen.

Organizations may have objectives to measure production, sales, profit, and quality. Unit or organizational objectives can be determined by reading formal goal statements or by observing what is happening in the organization. These observations may reveal shifts in resources or decision-making power among units or individuals, in the types of individuals leaving or being recruited to the organization, and in what the organization is not doing and what population it is not serving. Many large corporations expend a lot of effort in goal specification.

What happens if a healthcare organization does not specify objectives? The organization may lack focus in its programs, and it may be less likely to abandon products and services that are neither effective nor efficient. Powerful individuals and their short-term interests will tend to be favored over weaker individuals and long-term interests; the organization will be less adaptive to the environment; and it will have a greater tendency to retain the status quo.

Healthcare managers should determine their organization's operative objectives. Official goals may not always provide reliable guidelines for managerial behavior. When the people in power go against what a manager sees as the long-range interests of an organization, the manager should be careful, speaking out only if she is willing to pay the price and is certain about the facts.

## Information

Healthcare managers must obtain information for key product lines about volume of services, quality of care, service and production efficiency, market conditions, system maintenance, and the health status of the population served. They may use the following measures to assess performance: cost per case, cost per visit, cost per day, profit, fixed and variable costs, market share, capital expenditures as a percentage of sales, days of receivables and payables, top admitting physicians and their characteristics, staff turnover and overtime, sick time, and disability and fringe benefits costs. In addition, healthcare information systems are being expanded to include revenue by service line, budgeting and variance reporting, and clinical performance review. Computerized medical records are linked to cost and revenue data, concurrent review for quality of care, and final-product cost accounting for groups of similar patients at alternative levels of demand. Risk management relies on incident reports of untoward events, which are then aggregated and analyzed.

With the continuing investment in electronic medical records, required performance reporting, and standardized patient satisfaction surveys, healthcare is entering an era of information overload. Whereas management previously lacked data about quality of care, now it has more information than it can cope with. What measures should take priority? What are the key quality characteristics?

## Performance Evaluation

One of the problems with control systems is that they may measure the wrong thing. Another problem is that they may measure the right thing inaccurately. These issues are particularly relevant for outcomes measurement. The easiest response to information we do not like is to say the data are wrong. In a hostile, fearful environment, managers may feel that no information is accurate enough to be accepted. One of the important aspects of quality improvement (QI) is to create a climate free from fear, where data can be accepted for what they are, despite their limitations, and still be used to make improvements.

Increasingly, healthcare managers have access to performance data comparing their organizations to other similar ones. In the past, a nursing home board of directors may have simply believed without question that its care was outstanding; now, comparative data allow the board to actually see how the nursing home stacks up. The first step is for the organization to measure its care; for example, it can track the frequency of bed sores or the percentage of patients under physical restraint. The next step is to compare measures. Why are 15 percent of our patients under restraint while the statewide average is 8 percent? The third step is to make this information public on accessible websites. Examples of such sites include Nursing Home Compare (www.medicare.gov/nursinghomecompare) and Hospital Compare (www.medicare.gov/hospitalcompare), from the Centers for Medicare & Medicaid Services. Concurrent with these steps is a change from denial (e.g., claiming "our patients are sicker") and fear to a desire to improve. Managers at a nursing home with a high restraint rate can visit another similar nursing home with a low restraint rate to learn how to improve their own situation. This effort requires collecting performance data over time to track improvements. The process of systematic comparison to best-practice organizations is called *benchmarking*.

## Expectations

Medication errors—whether they involve the wrong medicine, the wrong dose, or the wrong time—occur frequently in hospitals. Although no clinic wants such errors to occur, clinics differ in the ways they approach the problem. What is the level of expectation for good performance? It could be "zero tolerance for error," or it could be that the clinic will make yearly improvements to continuously reduce its error rate. A clinic might assume, "Everyone has this problem, and we are no different"; alternatively, it might think, "We have the best nurses and physicians, so I am sure our error rates are lower than anyone else's." Performance expectations make a difference. Six Sigma is one method for reducing unwanted events.

## Incentives

How does the manager transform the individual worker's desire for a paycheck into a pursuit of organizational goals so that both individual and organizational aims are achieved together? Incentives are stimuli to affect performance. Adoption of incentives is usually based on the answers to the following questions: Does the incentive contribute to the desired results? Is the incentive acceptable to those workers whose behavior managers wish to influence? Could implementation of the incentives produce other dysfunctional consequences (e.g., rewards for cutting costs leading inadvertently to reduced quality of care)?

Organizations use both positive and negative incentives, and they can be monetary or nonmonetary. One of the underlying ideas of QI is that monetary incentives are often disruptive. The assumption is that people want to do a good job and that faulty systems—not the intentions or abilities of the employees—prevent that from happening. For instance, how can the admissions clerk rapidly process an admission if the computer has crashed? How can the dietary department provide hot food at the bedside when the patient is waiting in the X-ray department? QI calls for management to lead the effort in improving these systems. Monetary rewards for individuals, by contrast, may create rivalry rather than teamwork.

Improving care requires "just-in-time" data about key quality characteristics, as well as an observer who has the expertise to understand this information, whose job it is to improve care, and who is given the power to do so. For example, say the goal is to reduce the burden of asthma for children, measured by the number of school days missed because of asthma in a particular area. A just-in-time information system would show how many children missed school yesterday—not last year or even last month—and an asthma expert would be given the assignment to reduce this rate and the power to do something about it. Such a system would likely be effective, but there are too few examples of such management approaches in healthcare.

## Discussion Questions

1. For any healthcare organization, what are the most important things for the information system to measure?

2. Errors are frequent in healthcare, and they often have serious consequences. What steps would you recommend to reduce medical errors?

3. What is the role of senior management in promoting quality improvement?

4. What are the barriers to cost containment in healthcare organizations, and how can these barriers be overcome?

5. How much is too much control? How much is not enough?

## Recommended Readings

Batalden, P., and P. Stoltz. 1993. "Performance Improvement in Healthcare Organizations: A Framework for the Continued Improvement of Health Care." *The Joint Commission Journal of Quality Improvement* 19 (10): 424–52.

Berwick, D. M. 2005. "My Right Knee." *Annals of Internal Medicine* 142 (2): 121–25.

———. 2002. *Escape Fire: Lessons for the Future of Health Care*. New York: Commonwealth Fund.

Black, J., D. Miller, and J. Sensel. 2016. *Toyota Way to Healthcare Excellence: Increase Efficiency and Improve Quality with Lean*, 2nd ed. Chicago: Health Administration Press.

Bradley, E. H., E. S. Holmoe, J. A. Mattera, S. A. Roumanis, M. J. Radford, and H. M. Krumholz. 2003. "The Roles of Senior Management in Quality Improvement Efforts: What Are the Key Components?" *Journal of Healthcare Management* 48 (1): 15–28.

Curry, L. A., E. Spatz, E. Cherlin, J. W. Thompson, D. Berg, H. H. Ting, C. Decker, H. M. Krumholz, and E. H. Bradley. 2011. "What Distinguishes Top-Performing Hospitals in Acute Myocardial Infarction Mortality Rates? A Qualitative Study." *Annals of Internal Medicine* 154: 384–90.

Eisenberg, J. M. 1996. *Doctors' Decisions and the Cost of Medical Care*. Chicago: Health Administration Press.

Gawande, A. 2004. "The Bell Curve." *The New Yorker* December 6, 82–91.

Glandon, G. L., D. H. Smaltz, and D. J. Slovensky. 2013. *Information Systems for Healthcare Management*, 8th ed. Chicago: Health Administration Press.

Hefner, J. L., T. R. Huerta, A. S. McAlearney, B. Barash, T. Latimer, and S. Moffatt-Bruce. 2017. "Navigating a Ship with a Broken Compass: Evaluating Standard Algorithms to Measure Patient Safety." *Journal of the American Medical Informatics Association* 24 (2): 310–15.

Institute of Medicine. 2001. *Crossing the Quality Chasm: A New Health System for the 21st Century*. Washington, DC: National Academies Press.

James, B., and L. Savitz. 2011. "How Intermountain Trimmed Health Care Costs Through Robust Quality Improvement Efforts." *Health Affairs* 30 (6): 1185–91.

Jha, A. K., J. B. Perlin, K. W. Kizer, and R. A. Dudley. 2003. "Effect of the Transformation of the Veterans Affairs Healthcare System on the Quality of Care." *New England Journal of Medicine* 348 (22): 2218–27.

McAlearney, A. S., and J. Hefner. 2016. "Getting to Zero: Goal Commitment to Reduce Blood Stream Infections." *Medical Care Research and Review* 73 (4): 458–77.

McDonagh, K. J. 2006. "Hospital Governing Boards: A Study of Their Effectiveness in Relation to Organizational Performance." *Journal of Healthcare Management* 51 (6): 377–89.

McGlynn, E. A., S. M. Asch, J. Adams, J. Keesey, J. Hicks, A. DeCristofaro, and E. Kerr. 2003. "The Quality of Health Care Delivered to Adults in the United States." *New England Journal of Medicine* 348 (26): 2635–83.

Pointer, D. D., and E. Orlikoff. 2002. *Getting to Great: Principles of Health Care Organization Governance.* San Francisco: Jossey-Bass.

Richter, J., A. S. McAlearney, and M. Pennell. 2016. "The Influence of Organizational Factors on Patient Safety: Examining Successful Handoffs in Health Care." *Health Care Management Review* 41 (1): 32–41.

Rundall, T. G., P. F. Martelli, L. Arroyo, R. McCurdy, I. Graetz, E. B. Neuwirth, P. Curtis, J. Schmittdiel, M. Gibson, and J. Hsu. 2007. "The Informed Decisions Tool-Box: Tools for Knowledge Transfer and Performance Improvement." *Journal of Healthcare Management* 52 (5): 325–41.

Watts, B., R. Lawrence, D. Litaker, D. C. Aron, and D. Neuhauser. 2008. "Quality of Care by a Hypertension Expert: A Cautionary Tale for Pay-for-Performance Approaches." *Quality Management in Health Care* 17 (1): 35–46.

White, K. R., and J. R. Griffith. 2016. *The Well-Managed Healthcare Organization,* 8th ed. Chicago: Health Administration Press. (Chapter 13, "Financial Management," is particularly relevant to the topic of control.)

In addition, these five journals about quality and safety are well worth following:

- *American Journal of Medical Quality* (http://ajm.sagepub.com)
- *BMJ Quality & Safety* (www.qshc.bmj.com)
- *The Joint Commission Journal on Quality and Patient Safety* (www.jcrinc.com/the-joint-commission-journal-on-quality-and-patient-safety/)
- *Journal for Healthcare Quality* (http://journals.lww.com/jhqonline/)
- *Quality Management in Health Care* (www.qmhcjournal.com)

These three journals in healthcare management and finance cover topics relevant to control as well:

- *Journal of Healthcare Management* (www.ache.org/journals)
- *Journal of Health Care Finance* (www.healthfinancejournal.com)
- *Health Care Management Review* (http://journals.lww.com/hcmrjournal)

# THE CASES

How do hospitals and health systems continually improve? Healthcare organizations have many stakeholders—including patients and future patients, families, government, payers, insurers, employers, labor unions, professionals, and accreditation agencies—all of whom have an interest in the quality, safety, and cost of the care given. The challenge for management is to improve performance while meeting the needs of these multiple stakeholders.

Three recent trends with glacierlike power are contributing to a renewed focus on control and improvement. First is the development and acceptance of evidence-based medicine. How do we know the care we give is beneficial? The Cochrane Collaboration (www.cochrane.org) has now published more than 6,000 reviews, called Cochrane Reviews, summarizing the results of randomized clinical trials that demonstrate treatment effectiveness or the lack of it. Now that a greater degree of evidence-based agreement exists about what works, managers can more easily establish clinical guidelines for best-practice care and ask that those guidelines be followed. The second major force for change is the quality and safety movement, which encourages the use of best practices for all patients. The movement also produces disparity research focusing on groups that do not get such good care. The third force—and the most important in the long run—is the steady, relentless growth of computer capacity, combined with the declining cost of computing power. Although the first health management information technology applications were for insurance billing and finance, new information technologies have been implemented for clinical information.

The three longer case studies in this section demonstrate the process of control in different healthcare organizations. Case 11, "Moving the Needle," describes the implementation and results of a program designed to improve patient flow in a hospital, whereas Case 12, "Controlling Revolution Health," examines the issues management must face to address concerns about member complaints and vendor management for a growing organization. Case 13, "Reducing Healthcare-Associated Infections at Academic Medical Center," highlights the importance of focusing on people and high-performance work practices to improve patient safety and quality of care. These cases all demonstrate that we are moving from the absence of data to information overload.

The six shorter cases consider parallel issues, including the consideration of new metrics for hospital budgeting (Case 14, "Better Metrics for Financial

Management"), the introduction of new equipment designed to reduce staff injuries (Case 15, "Ergonomics in Practice"), the use of performance measurement concepts for a hospital board (Case 16, "Financial Reporting to the Board"), examination of handoffs from a hospital emergency department (Case 17, "Handoffs in Patient Care"), the challenges of managing clinical trials in an academic medical center (Case 18, "Chaos in the Clinical Trials Office"), and the introduction of new health information technologies (Case 19, "The Telemedicine Opportunity for Geneva Health System").

# CASE 11

# Moving the Needle: Managing Safe Patient Flow at Yale–New Haven Hospital

*Richard D'Aquila, Peter Follows, Michael J. Zaccagnino, and Anthony R. Kovner*

## Executive Summary

The purpose of this qualitative case study is to use the experience of Yale–New Haven Hospital (YNHH), a large academic medical center in New Haven, Connecticut, to help decision makers learn how to better manage safe patient flow. Hospitals today must make significant changes to cope with new developments under healthcare reform, including lower payments relative to higher costs of providing services. The process described in the case had important quality and financial consequences for a hospital that had been constrained by limited capacity.

What follows is a description of how YNHH's Safe Patient Flow (SPF) project achieved significant decreases in average lengths of stay and in waiting times for beds in the emergency department (ED) and in the postanesthesia care unit (PACU) during a period of considerable growth in hospital admissions. These improvements were accomplished in part through changes such as discharging patients earlier in the day, decreasing bed turnaround times, and improving patient job transportation turnaround times. YNHH improved safety, quality, patient and staff satisfaction, and efficiency—all while achieving significant positive financial results.

For more information about this case study, please contact Professor Kovner at anthony.kovner@nyu.edu.

# The Challenge: Implementing Significant Change Without a Crisis

How can a hospital ensure safe patient flow while improving safety, quality, patient and staff satisfaction, and financial health? How can a large academic medical center accommodate incremental admissions volume without adding positions? This case study suggests that positive results can be achieved through more effective management.

The SPF initiative at YNHH included the development of a system of green, yellow, and red indicators to communicate a patient's likely readiness for discharge the next day and to trigger steps in the discharge process. Green indicates that a patient is very likely to be discharged the next day; yellow indicates that a patient is clinically ready for discharge the next day but that this readiness is contingent on certain factors (e.g., pending laboratory results, the ability to tolerate a diet); and red indicates that a patient is not likely to be clinically ready for discharge the next day, or that an appropriate disposition is not available. The disposition requires that the interdisciplinary team be in close communication with one another regarding both clinical status and appropriate disposition resources. Some physicians opposed this change at first because they felt they needed to see their sickest patients first (rather than those patients who were most ready for discharge).

# Phases of Implementation

Implementation of the process change at YNHH had six phases: (1) creating the urgency for change, (2) framing the process properly, (3) ensuring proper staff support and systems, (4) engaging physicians, (5) building accountability and transparency, and (6) ensuring sustainability of change. We discuss these phases and conclude with lessons learned from the initiative.

## 1. Creating the Urgency for Change

At the start of implementation, YNHH had a backlog of patients, resulting in part from physician recruitment and program development that had temporarily outpaced facilities development (i.e., the opening of a new cancer center). Richard D'Aquila, the YNHH chief operating officer (COO), actively participated in and sponsored the SPF initiative; one of the key tasks was creating "a burning platform" for planning and implementing the change.

The associate chief of staff and vice president of performance management states:

In 2008, The Joint Commission said YNHH lacked an organized way of responding to capacity problems. I was the first director of bed management before I moved into my present job. The initiative was not so much about discharging patients faster as it was about getting the right patient into the right bed at the right time. The sickest patients were in the ED, and the critical staff to take care of them were waiting for them on the patient floors. The question was which patients should these physicians be seeing.

## 2. Framing the Process Properly

YNHH appointed a steering committee as the ultimate authority for decision making and hired Carpedia International, a consulting firm, to assist with the process. Nursing leadership conducted weekly meetings prior to steering committee meetings. Safety was the first priority; active management of organizational resources was the second. Frontline leaders and employees met daily to review schedules (typically in "huddles") and provide daily operating reports. Accountability was data driven relative to targets and time frames.

Prior to their engagement, Carpedia carried out an "opportunity analysis" to look for areas for particular gain, in terms of quantifiable financial results. This analysis took five consultants nearly three weeks to complete. Carpedia began by identifying and quantifying specifically what processes needed improvement. It next identified functional areas and support departments that would need to be involved. Support departments included transport, environmental services, admissions, and bed management. Outcomes were set for each area—for example, room turnover time for environmental services and turnover time for patient transportation. Carpedia identified the main database indicator as reduction of average length of stay (ALOS) from 5.23 to 5.02 days—primarily for adult medical and surgical patients.

Nurse directors quantified reasons for variances. Unit huddles were conducted three times a day for ten minutes each to review which patients were going home and which patients could go home if barriers were overcome (e.g., nursing home transfer, organizing rides home).

## 3. Ensuring Proper Staff Support and Systems

To assess YNHH's readiness to carry out the project, Carpedia's opportunity analysis set up targets and time frames relating to performance gaps in current processes. The seven-person operations support (OS) department provided consulting, behavior audit, support, and coaching. Execution controls were established to allow managers to monitor and prioritize assignments for both clinical and nonclinical managers. Daily operational supports gave a balanced set of key performance indicators, comparing actual to planned performance.

OS partnered with Carpedia, and four internal YNHH staff members were pulled out of their jobs to work with the six Carpedia consultants. Carpedia used the client's own performance data to describe current and desired states rather than relying solely on industry benchmarks.

One of the Carpedia consultants states:

> Carpedia spends 50 to 60 percent of its time in the preproposal phase, observing processes. This allows us to quantify "lost time." We can then play it back to the client so they can see what their employees are going through to get certain processes completed. We also observed the patient's experience through her eyes. We followed through an entire process for 20 patients and for 30 eight-hour employee shifts, observing managers, nurses, and physicians.

## 4. Engaging Physicians

YNHH augmented the Carpedia team (which lacked physicians and nurses) with a team of two physicians, one nurse, one pharmacist, and one financial analyst. Different service lines wanted to "own" their own beds. Centralized bed placement proved more effective in reducing waits for the PACU and for the ED.

For the first year, the associate chief of staff was chair of the steering committee. He explained to physicians that the basic premise of the initiative was to reduce crowding of the PACU and the ED by discharging patients earlier in the day. During this first year, when patients were admitted later in the day, house staff could not treat these patients promptly. These delays caused a poor match of resources, as house staff were needed for discharge summaries, prescription orders, and counsel on postdischarge care. The early discharge initiative was also in conflict with the scheduled teaching program because the house staff had educational responsibilities that might not be well timed with the need for early discharges. Under the SPF initiative, the discharge process begins the evening before the scheduled discharge. Residents huddle together and identify patients likely to leave and then work to facilitate earlier discharge by completing tasks such as notifying the family. Despite the challenges, success in reducing waiting times generated a cascade of support for the SPF initiative.

The associate chief of staff and medical director of hospitalist service comments:

> When physicians in the ED saw improvements in waiting times for beds, this was a motivator. . . . Now there was less delay in moving patients from interventional radiology, no cancelling of elective surgery cases, and more patients moving quickly through the system. ORs had been on hold because patients were sitting in the PACU. We now track all the waits. And we discharge every surgery patient to their floor of preference, such as oncological surgery, for more specialized care, post-op.

## 5. Building Accountability and Transparency

Carpedia met with the YNHH leadership team on a weekly basis. The steering committee navigated much of the work. Carpedia presented the work that had been done last week and what was going to be done in the next two weeks. Teams used a dashboard and targets, and they reviewed variances for identified performance measures. (See exhibit 11.1 for excerpts from the YNHH executive throughput scorecard, which tracks throughput for the week ending November 6, 2010.)

Units and departments reported to the steering committee, followed templates, and established desired outcomes. For example, 11:00 a.m. was set as the target discharge time because it was when the operating room, the PACU, and the ED got congested and when patients were waiting for treatment on the floors. The number of patients discharged by 3:00 p.m. was also measured. The goal was to increase the percentage of patients being discharged earlier rather than changing the hour of discharge for all patients. The median patient discharge time was moved from 3:00 p.m. to 1:30 p.m. Discharge is one of the hospital measures for the performance incentive program, common for all employees and managers and representing 80 percent of the annual performance bonus.

The COO, the steering committee, Carpedia, and OS pushed active management. The associate director of nursing comments:

> This was not just managing to meet targets, but holding the huddles three times daily, looking at the facility boards . . . so more patients were ready for earlier discharge. This meant actively managing physicians who were resistant and managing communications with families so they were better about rides. The tools we used included daily operating reports, variance reports, audit reports on methods changes, and weekly committee meetings.

## 6. Ensuring Sustainability of Change

The YNHH senior leadership management team has institutionalized regularly scheduled meetings to ensure accountability for results going forward as the organization tackles additional areas for improvement. One such area is an initiative for transforming patient care. YNHH nurses are now familiar with the Safe Patient Flow methodology and trust that the initiative will not primarily be a cost-cutting initiative ending with layoffs of nurses and nurse practice associates.

The associate director of nursing explains:

> The new transforming patient care initiative is about regulatory readiness, to take off the nurse's plate all the non-value-added tasks that nurses do so that nurses can focus on compliance, for example with more and better patient education. . . . We want 60 minutes of nurse time per shift for every patient. Nurses are on this new

**EXHIBIT 11.1**

Executive Throughput Scorecard, Week Ending November 6, 2010

| Area | Metric | Threshold (R1) | Target (R2) | Max (Stretch) | Last Week (Actual) | Direction (Last week compared to YTD performance) | YTD Performance | YTD Performance Compared to Target |
|---|---|---|---|---|---|---|---|---|
| | Surgery–11:00 a.m. discharges | 13.0% | 15.0% | 17.0% | 20.0% | Better | 17.0% | Above Max |
| | Surgery–Median discharge time (hour) | 13:57 | 13:42 | 13:27 | 13:55 | Better | 14:03 | Below Threshold |
| | Medicine–11:00 a.m. discharges | 19.0% | 19.5% | 20.0% | 22.0% | Same | 22.0% | Above Max |
| | Medicine–Median discharge time (hour) | 14:11 | 13:56 | 13:41 | 14:18 | Better | 14:30 | Below Threshold |
| | Oncology–11:00 a.m. discharges | 18.9% | 20.0% | 20.0% | 24.0% | Better | 13.0% | Below Threshold |
| | Oncology–Median discharge time (hour) | 13:50 | 13:40 | 13:30 | 13:52 | Better | 14:07 | Below Threshold |
| | Children's–11:00 a.m. discharges | 19.0% | 20.0% | 21.0% | 14.0% | Worse | 21.0% | Above Max |
| Patient Services | Children's–Median discharge time (hour) | 13:53 | 13:43 | 13:33 | 14:31 | Worse | 13:38 | ≥ Target Below Max |
| | OB–11:00 a.m. discharges | 13.4% | 15.0% | 17.0% | 8.0% | Worse | 11.0% | Below Threshold |
| | OB–Median discharge time (hour) | 12:23 | 12:08 | 11:53 | 12:33 | Worse | 12:24 | Below Threshold |
| | Psych–11:00 a.m. discharges | 31.0% | 35.0% | 37.0% | 37.0% | Better | 34.0% | ≥ Threshold, < Target |
| | Heart & Vascular–11:00 a.m. discharges | 24.0% | 24.5% | 25.5% | 22.0% | Worse | 26.0% | Above Max |
| | Heart & Vascular–Median discharge time (hour) | 13:41 | 13:26 | 13:11 | 13:17 | Better | 13:21 | ≥ Target, Below Max |
| | Hospitalwide–11:00 a.m. discharges | 19.0% | 20.1% | 21.1% | 19.0% | Same | 19.0% | ≥ Threshold, < Target |
| | Hospitalwide–Median discharge time (hour) | 13:41 | 13:27 | 13:17 | 13:31 | Better | 13:34 | ≥ Threshold, < Target |

and separate steering committee. The work is data driven, focusing on patient satisfaction; the support staff will support patient care, not nursing, but allow nurses
to do effective nursing.

## Results

The results achieved during a two-year period starting July 2008 are impressive indeed:

- ALOS decreased from 5.23 to 5.02 days, year to date through June
  2009.
- Length of stay in the ED for patients being admitted decreased by 25
  minutes, despite significant increases in ED volume.
- Percentage of discharges by 11:00 a.m. increased 50 percent, from 12
  to 18 percent on average.
- Median time of discharge decreased by 45 minutes.
- PACU length of stay decreased by approximately 25 minutes, and the
  percentage of "red phones" (an indication of a transfer delay out of the
  PACU) was further decreased by 8 percent in the past nine months.
- Bed turnaround time decreased by 35 minutes, on average, for "priority
  1" bed assignments (bed assignments that are higher priority because a
  patient is awaiting a bed).
- Patient transport time (i.e., transport turnaround time) remained within
  30 minutes, despite the addition of a new Cancer Hospital Pavilion.
  (Transport turnaround time has two components: the time needed to
  assign the transport job after it has been requested and the time needed
  to complete the transport, from when it is assigned to when it ends.)

## Lessons Learned

YNHH has achieved significant results in increasing throughput without
adding positions. Patients benefit by being in the right bed at the right time.
Often, management initiatives can be resisted by clinicians who have observed
past manager rhetoric as a facade for one-time efforts to cut costs, including
not filling vacant positions. To avoid this problem, YNHH senior leadership
was constantly engaged in articulating and rearticulating purpose. Data were
generated to show that patients were waiting less for needed treatments on the
floors as a result of new schedules and targeting. Success in reducing wait times
built support for changes in physician schedules. Transparency and accountability were accomplished largely through formation of a steering committee

with ultimate decision-making authority for the initiative. The steering committee was chaired by a respected physician, and half the members of the committee were physicians. Extra resources—obtained both externally from Carpedia and internally by temporarily reassigning key staff—were essential in implementing new methods that spanned many departments and involved major changes in schedules and workflow. Sustainability was ensured before the external and internal consulting services were withdrawn (although they are still available as needed). The purpose of the project was to provide safer care for the patients.

## Acknowledgments

The authors would like to acknowledge the contribution of Sandra Bacon, director, operations support, Yale–New Haven Hospital, for her contributions to the content of this case. Ms. Bacon, of course, had a great deal to do with the success of the actual project as well.

*Note*: Anthony R. Kovner wrote a first draft of this article as a consultant for Carpedia.

## Case Questions

Imagine you are Joe Miller, CEO at Jones Memorial Hospital, a 450-bed community hospital in Eastern City, and your administrative fellow, Timmy Fields, has just brought the YNHH case study to your attention. Your first response is to think of all the reasons you shouldn't do it. "Moving the Needle" is a big initiative. It will cost a lot and certainly be met with resistance. And where's the gain in it?

Besides, Jones Memorial is a community hospital, not an academic medical center. You don't need to build a new wing. The hospital is making money. You like the idea of shortening length of stay, but you think you are going to pass at this time. Maybe you will forward the case study to your chief medical officer, Dan Farber, and see what he thinks about it.

1. What would have to happen to change Joe Miller's response?
2. What adaptations to the initiative would have to be made at Jones Memorial Hospital to make it work?
3. What would be your response to this situation if you were at Medicare's Center for Innovation? In other words, would staff at Medicare's Center for Innovation think it would be a good idea to replicate and expand what YNHH is doing?

# CASE 12

# Controlling Revolution Health: Management Ownership

*Jacob Victory*

Rico started the meeting by saying, "I don't care that there are hundreds of new member complaints coming into the organization monthly. We have enrolled more than 400,000 members in this health plan. The ratio between the number of member complaints and total health plan membership is too small for me to consider."

Lester raised his right eyebrow and asked, "Shall I tell our chief regulator that our general manager of health plan operations thinks that an estimated 5,000 complaints—or possibly more—this year is peanuts?"

Grabbing his soda, Rico quickly got up and walked toward the door. "Not my problem," he snapped, before opening the door and leaving the room.

Lester followed Rico into the hallway.

"Look," said Rico softly, seeing Lester emerge. "I just don't have the time to solve your problems when I have a million of my own."

"But the way I see it," replied Lester, "is that your vendors are the cause of all of your and my problems. Many of our team members seem to be working more for the vendors than for the health plan. Moreover, many are doing everything—thus nothing is being done. Our days, and this chaos, are symptoms of the lack of standardized processes, the lack of responsiveness, and the lack of infrastructural authority in managing and monitoring these health plan vendors. We sit in endless meetings and yet only discuss the same problems again and again. We never solve anything, Rico. It has gotten so bad that we're now missing meetings just to avoid the issues."

Lester continued, "I got a call today from the head of the state's consumer advocacy division. He is irate that we seemingly have no control over our processes in health plan operations or over our vendors, and he has a lot of headaches from having heard from many of our members. He is receiving nasty calls and even harsher letters from these members. Provider groups are calling *him* out in medical society meetings—in public—and blaming him for *his* incompetence because we cannot solve claims payment issues or answer calls correctly. He actually noted that he has no confidence in any of Revolution Health's management team. He's already called our CEO and COO directly. After those calls, both pulled me into their offices and directed me to correct all issues. There is nothing like being asked to move mountain ranges!"

Rico looked at Lester and stated, "I have no additional resources to give you to resolve this. My folks are tied up, but I promise they are really trying to work with the vendors."

Lester sensed that perhaps Rico didn't fully understand that the health plan was being reactive instead of proactive. It was also possible that Rico did not see the bigger picture because he had little exposure to some of these significant corporate management issues. Yet it was clear to Lester that Rico's team was not focused on addressing the core issues or the root causes of the issues but instead was putting out one fire after the next.

Taking a slightly different tone, this time as a mentor, Lester patiently explained, "Rico, receiving calls from regulators is a big deal. Especially when they are annoyed or angry. To a regulator, receiving a complaint from a health plan member or a patient is not a good thing; to receive three complaints for the same reason from members is, in the eyes of the regulator, a huge problem. It may not sound big to you, but these folks can audit us, fine us, or, at the most extreme, close us down. We have to collectively pay attention to this in a unified and collaborative manner.

"Maybe it is our approach," Lester continued. "Your team is trying to fix the vendors' processes, which, because they are flawed, are driving the member and provider complaints. My team is answering questions and correcting the issues on a one-on-one basis after the issue has become red-hot. And I'm referring to the Escalations Unit, where members and providers write to our regulatory bodies with a huge number of complaints. They are feeling the burden grow weekly. Our call centers are overwhelmed. Call volumes are increasing, and we're receiving thousands of calls per day about the same key issues. It's as if we're reliving the same day over and over again."

"So what is the solution?" asked Rico.

"Ownership," was Lester's one-word reply.

Clearly, the task before them would require a lot of planning, organizing, and bringing internal and external staff together to reduce the number of complaints and to correct processes.

## Revolution Health: Founding and Structure

Revolution Health was founded by Ray Schwartz, a business mogul who had recently become the nation's tenth richest man, thanks to his real estate empire. He poured the profits from this enterprise into venture capital funds that he primarily controlled, mostly to fund other business lines from which he could procure more profits. Ray was also a generous benefactor and philanthropist in the medical industry, and he sought to "disrupt" and "revolutionize" healthcare. "It ain't working, and I'm going to fix it," he said after trying to navigate the healthcare system when his brother was faced with a serious and long-term medical issue. Through his powerful political connections and sheer influence within the state and federal governments, he was approved to develop an "affordable" health plan that was going to compete with the "big boy plans." He stated he was going to "teach them a thing or two about managing care."

Ray was angry that so many people were uninsured, and it hurt him to hear the sad stories about families going into bankruptcy because of the high cost of care and their inability to pay their medical bills. In response, he laid out initial start-up money from one of his venture capital funds and named his new health plan Revolution Health. It primarily aimed to cover people with low incomes or those who were members of the middle class.

A key feature of Revolution Health was its focus on the member. Ray named himself board chair and demanded that at least 60 percent of the board of directors be elected from the plan's membership. As he explained, "I want to see real folks get care, and I want to hear about it right from their mouths!"

*Affordable* was the key word for Revolution Health. When the initial management team came on board, they took that word literally and set the premiums for the plan's products as the least expensive in the marketplace. The interim CEO, who was hired only for the first six months to establish the basic mechanics of the health plan, was proud to have set Revolution's health plan premiums lower than those of the other health plans.

### Vendor Management Structure

The interim CEO and his staff had also signed five-year, air-tight management contracts with 13 vendors that would, respectively, administer all of the health plan's functions. These functions included member enrollment, billing and processing of member premiums, adjudication of provider claims and processing of payments, and pharmacy benefit and member identification card generation, among others. The enrollment and billing, claims adjudication, and pharmacy benefit management vendors were the largest of the vendors. The health plan was contracted to pay the vendors a total of $190 million to administer the health plan's functions—a sum that was likely 45 percent too high.

The vendors had a lot of shortfalls. First, they were scattered across the nation. One of the largest vendors was based in Chicago and was responsible for billing members (i.e., collecting members' monthly premiums) and for all enrollment functions, including production and generation of membership cards. The enrollment function was segmented into two parts. First, member enrollments came from insurance broker distribution channels. Brokers, for a commission paid by the health plan, would be the lead in promoting and selling health plans to individuals and small business owners. Second, because of the Affordable Care Act (ACA), individuals and small business groups now also had the option of purchasing health insurance through the marketplace, or the exchange, which "sold" health insurance and plans through a state or federal website.

This channel was newly developed, and although it increased the transparency of price and benefits for the consumer, it had major challenges related to technical problems. Key transaction issues included the tracking of who qualified for what health plan at which monthly subsidy (should a potential member qualify based on income levels) and the submission of enrollment data from the website to the exchange and then through the health plan selected for purchase.

The capture and processing of the files containing enrollment information were the responsibility of the Chicago-based vendor that Revolution Health had just hired. The vendor was a new subsidiary of a Japanese human resources management company and had little experience in the American health plan space. Like many other stakeholders and health plans, it had never worked with the newly developed websites through which individuals and small groups purchased health insurance under the ACA. At this point, the vendor did not have its operational policies and procedures clearly written, and the information systems the vendor used were antiquated.

Another vendor was responsible for claims payment, claims adjudication, and utilization management, and it was based in Dallas. Some people believe that the medical components of health plan operations—namely medical and utilization management—should never be outsourced. The plan's initial managers, however, disagreed with this approach and had chosen to outsource all functions.

Other vendors across the nation were responsible for preenrollment services, dental benefits, vision benefits, pharmacy benefit management, provider network management, and other functions. All of these vendors had their respective call centers that providers and members could call for general inquiries, issues, complaints, or follow-up. These call centers handled, in the plan's second year of operation, 250,000 calls per month. None of the vendors had ever worked together, and their systems were not integrated. Information was not easily shared between them, and their respective leaders did not actively engage with one another.

### Revolution Health Grand Opening and Projected Financials

With the first six months of planning about to come to a close, all members of the initial management team were putting final touches on their plans and assessing the vendors' abilities to meet the needs of the annual open enrollment period. The three-month period—during which new and existing members could purchase or renew health insurance for the coming year—would last from November through February.

For Revolution Health, the newness of many things was distinctive. Revolution Health was a new plan. The marketplace was new and run by the state. Consumers had never been able, until now, to compare and purchase health plans through a new and comprehensive website. Many of these projected consumers were people who had previously been uninsured—thus, they represented a new market segment that was able to purchase health insurance thanks to the ACA.

Indeed, the state in which Revolution Health operated had projected a total of 2.1 million uninsured individuals, about 35 percent of whom would qualify under the ACA to purchase insurance through the marketplace and receive subsidies. The others likely qualified for Medicaid coverage; this group represented a different population that could also newly purchase health plans through the marketplace, though Revolution Health was not licensed to sell a Medicaid managed care product. With all the changes in the market, Revolution Health had only several months to operationalize its core processes—processes that a majority of its competitors already had in place, given past history and experience—to serve the following year's membership.

The interim CEO and management team had thought it was going to be a slow and measured first year of operations. Their business plans, approved by the state and federal regulators, had projected 30,000 members at the end of the plan's first year of operations. By the third year, the business plan projected 45,000 members. Their financial statements projected a loss of $15 million in the plan's first year but estimated that Revolution Health would reach a financial break-even point in year three.

In reality, Revolution Health exceeded enrollment projections by the end of its first open enrollment period. The health plan surpassed its first year annual enrollment projections in its second week of operation, and by the sixth month of plan operations, membership stood at 145,000 members. New financial projections had the plan generating $1.6 billion in annual revenue in its first year. Projected losses in the health plan's first three years were now always in flux, as it would take up to four months to capture and analyze the claims the health plan paid its providers and to assess the plan's medical and administrative expenses (which, by law, had to account for over 90 percent of the health plan's expenses).

The first four months of operations were a whirlwind with a variety of crises to manage: systems backing up or shutting down because of the avalanche of consumer demand to purchase the plan's products; vendors lacking the system requirements, technology, or staff knowledge to administer the enrollment data that were passing back and forth from the state to the health plan at a sufficient pace; and a severe shortage of "bodies" to process the thousands of enrollment applications that were coming into the health plan. In its first three months of operations, Revolution Health had a corporate management staff of only 21 people in its central office to manage the vendor activities. It had to hire consultants and dozens of temporary staff to hand write and hand process member enrollment applications, because the existing systems were not able to process enrollments in such a massive volume. Of course, considering that Revolution Health was the least expensive health plan on the market and that hundreds of thousands of uninsured people were now mandated by the ACA to purchase health insurance, interim management should have anticipated the chaos that would likely ensue because of consumer demand.

With membership numbers soaring, the state and federal regulators were ecstatic. Some of the most powerful officials in the regulatory oversight bodies that had approved formation of the plan were secretly cheering for Revolution Health as it enrolled tens of thousands of the uninsured, amassing a significant market share almost overnight and creating a sharp thorn in the sides of the large for-profit health plans. Moreover, people in the member advocacy divisions of state regulatory bodies were thrilled that members had a seat in the boardroom of the new health plan. They wanted Revolution Health to thrive and help them address the healthcare system's myriad issues. When Revolution Health reached 400,000 members within its seventeenth month of operation and was projected to have $4.2 billion in annual revenue, regulators and the plan's management staff cheered. Revolution Health—in a very short while— had become the largest health plan of its kind and the largest health plan, by market share, on the marketplace.

## New Management

After the third week of the initial open enrollment period, the board of directors hired a full-time CEO, and the interim CEO retired to Arizona. The new CEO was a managed care expert with expertise in product development and marketing. When she came on board, she was shocked by the monthly premiums that Revolution Health was charging; she even made an in-person trip to meet with the regulators, noting that the premiums the plan had set for its first year of operations were too low and thus unsustainable. Nonetheless, because of plan and rate filing deadlines and governmental politics, the regulators did not allow her to increase the premiums.

Noticing other severe deficiencies in the vendor contracts (e.g., astronomical costs, no performance expectations) and the lack of management infrastructure, the new CEO quickly fired the interim COO and five other managers. She then brought on an ambitious new COO who immediately started hiring new executives. The new COO had charm and business savvy, but he was easily overwhelmed. Further, the multiple competing priorities required of a start-up health plan muddled his already short attention span. The CEO sought to remain involved in the operations but only marginally; she focused instead on developing a plan to tackle the political and regulatory issues facing healthcare reform initiatives, the marketplace, and nascent health plans competing with the "big boys."

### Table of Organization and Key Management

The new CEO and COO agreed to be thoughtful about developing an organizational chart. They wanted a streamlined infrastructure where quick decision making and collaboration were the foundation of management. Exhibit 12.1 shows Revolution Health's table of organization at the executive level.

As shown in the exhibit, the CEO had separate leads for operations, finance, human resources, legal and compliance, medical affairs, government and regulatory affairs, and commercial sales. These positions reflected the corporate divisions of Revolution Health; in time, these areas had 40 full-time employees.

The bulk of Revolution Health's staff were under the COO, who was responsible for an extraordinarily broad array of functions. The area of health plan operations included all the health plan vendor functions, from enrollment and billing to claims adjudication and payment to member identification card generation to fulfillment and broker services. Other key functions under the COO included market strategy, product development and management, member experience, information technology, data and analytics, and provider network and delivery systems management. Exhibit 12.2 shows the table of organization for the COO.

General managers at Revolution Health had the equivalent of a senior vice president role. Of the five divisions under the COO, two of them—health plan operations and marketing, product, and member experience—combined to represent 70 percent of the operations staff.

**EXHIBIT 12.1**
Executive-Level Table of Organization for Revolution Health

**EXHIBIT 12.2**
Table of Organization for Revolution Health COO

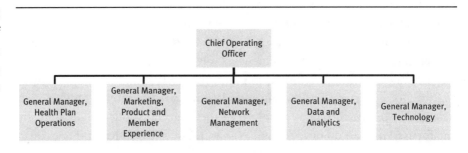

## Rico and Lester

In June of the plan's first year, the COO hired Enrico "Rico" Idol as the general manager of health plan operations. The following month, he hired Lester Molst as the general manager for marketing, product, and member experience. The two were the same age, but they had quite different personalities and approaches to management.

Rico's prior work experience was entirely with large local and national health plans. His background was in project management, but he had spent years dealing with the details and execution of health plan system workflows, business processes, and initiatives related to vendor management. Most recently, he had been focused especially on health plan member enrollment and billing functions, as well as annual enrollment initiatives. He was now responsible for the management of all Revolution Health vendors and their respective functions. Rico was noted for his nuanced, witty remarks. He was considered by many as "green" for the executive role of general manager, both because he had spent only 10 years in the workforce and because his last role was at the director level in a large local health plan. The COO took a risk hiring Rico but did so because of Rico's skill set in project management and his experience working with external vendors.

Unlike Rico, Lester had 21 years of work experience across a broad array of settings, including community and academic medical centers; home care; long-term care; managed long-term care; and, now, commercial insurance. Whereas Rico had only health plan project management experience, Lester had risen through the ranks quickly while working in a variety of functions. He had experience with strategic planning; building, implementing, improving, and managing clinical operations; leading healthcare reform initiatives, especially with innovative care models; leading performance improvement projects; and serving as the chief of staff for the CEO of a large parent company in the post-acute care space. Lester was known for the ease with which he managed and interacted with executive and frontline managers alike. He was well versed in working with noncompliant management staff and getting them on board and excited about performance improvement—specifically, focusing on standardized reporting and monitoring metrics. He was calm and business-minded, but he kept his eye on the objective at all times.

At Revolution Health, Lester was responsible for formulating and implementing the health plan's market strategy. He also was responsible for everything related to the member experience, including the development and management of the products (plans) sold to members; efforts to address member complaints, appeals, and grievances; and the call centers operated by the vendors. Lastly, he was responsible for developing a team to document all of the health plan's policies and procedures, with a particular focus on the contracted vendor functions. This latter role involved indirect oversight of Rico's role in managing the vendors, so Lester needed to have Rico on board. However, Rico and his team were not initially interested in working with Lester's team to document vendor processes.

### Core Issues

If you think of Revolution Health as an airplane, it flew high and fast, but its engine needed new parts and repairs. In the midst of building and flying this plane, Rico and Lester were inseparable, but they also knew how to push each other's buttons. Rico had to develop a strategy to make the vended operations model flow seamlessly so that its wheels could turn without effort. Lester, on the other hand, was never certain if Rico understood the difficulty of effectively managing the flow of work across the 13 vendors. As Lester considered the problems for Revolution Health, he noted four core issues:

1. Core vendor end-to-end processes were never documented. For instance, when Revolution Health asked, executives at the vendors were never able to provide documentation of their enrollment or claims adjudication processes. This lack of documentation not only put the organization at risk of being out of compliance with standard insurance law and practices, but it hampered performance improvement because no one knew the step-by-step processes involved. Moreover, while Lester was charged with building a department to codify the health plan's processes, Rico did not agree that such a task was needed. Instead, he dismissed the issue and stated that he would not allow his staff to partner with the vendors to document their processes.

2. Lester felt that Rico was defensive and had a distinct inclination to promote siloes within and among departments at Revolution Health. Lester knew that this tendency was deadly. Revolution Health was a new plan working in a completely vended model in a new marketplace; under such circumstances, a siloed model would prevent processes from being developed and operational initiatives from being carried forward across the various stakeholders. Rico's divisions would not share information about system breakdowns or incomplete processes, or even about mundane, day-to-day issues. Lester felt that Rico craved control over all operational divisions and, to maintain this control, was unwilling to share information.

3. The vended model was, at times, like a runaway train. The vendors did not take any initiative to work together. Instead, they relied on the overwhelmed staff at Revolution Health to lead the charge to inform, identify issues, develop workflows, and solve problems. When problems arose, the vendors sought answers from the health plan and offered neither suggestions nor solutions.

4. No standardized mechanism existed for running reports to show the root causes and volume of member complaints and issues. Lester was always the one who had back-of-envelope reports, but no one would systemically listen to his thoughts about the issues. The plan seemingly had no incentive to fix the problems, at least not in a standardized way.

Lester knew that Rico was tired of putting out operational fires at least five times a day. His entire existence seemed to be spent dealing with glitches, errors, and broken systems. Rico had grown weary of vendors that did not want to produce more than was required, and he had become testy toward others who threw more problems at him. Lester also had his share of problems. Even as he was overwhelmed by demands for growth and the need to develop the member experience strategy, he was also dealing with member—and, often, provider—grievances, complaints, calls, letters, and escalated, complex issues, most of which, he pointedly told his team members, were "caused by Rico's vendors."

The CEO and board members were also receiving member and provider letters and e-mails, and the COO continually sought updates about member issues. Lester knew that the real operational tasks across Lester's and Rico's departments were (1) to break down departmental silos and create a mechanism for information and issues to be shared more frequently and more publicly; (2) to get comfortable with the development of standardized reports to highlight process issues that were causing complaints; (3) to work collaboratively with the vendors to document the processes for which they were contracted and to monitor their performance in detail; and (4) to monitor complaints in a structured manner to get ahead of issues before they turned red-hot in the eyes of regulatory bodies.

## The Gathering

Lester's goal was to immediately set up a process to reduce the number of complaints that the health plan was receiving from members and providers. This was a multifaceted process with many steps that had to be taken both in tandem and in parallel with one another.

The first thing Lester did was devise a plan to bring the health plan decision makers together. He needed more than just Rico to help him. He made a list that included the divisional general managers and their directors responsible for network delivery, medical management, enrollment, claims, vendor management, member experience, and health plan policies and procedures. These individuals were invited to be part of a newly formed group called the Committee on Joint Services and Critical Operations. Lester and his staff wrote a formal charter for the committee, noting its chief objectives:

- Ensure executive-level focus on operational efficiency opportunities and critical issues.
- Prioritize and integrate the work of various work groups: Voice of the Member; Escalations; Operational Policy Implementation (to document and track the vendors' operational policies and procedures); and, as necessary, Health Plan Operations.
- Establish a centralized location for the sharing, evaluation, and analysis of ongoing operational efficiency efforts.
- Guide the operational focus toward the most critical operational initiatives in real time.
- Serve as the launching point for work plan development, implementation, and evaluation of opportunity initiatives.

The purpose of the committee was to institute a fundamental shift in the service experience for Revolution Health's members and providers. The committee was to have two basic goals. The first goal was to stabilize the receipt and handling of customer issues. To meet this goal, the committee would ensure the integration of major call centers via a robust oversight and service excellence model. A concurrent goal was to ensure the rapid resolution of emergent issues. Via multiple initiatives, the committee would proactively drive toward improved customer experience in conjunction with Revolution Health's vendor partners. Initiatives would focus on rapidly resolving customer issues while improving service excellence.

The committee was thus charged to perform the following activities to support both the management of operational services and critical alignment with operational areas:

- Define Revolution Health's principles of service excellence.
- Drive analysis to support efforts to identify issues, understand root causes, and determine service operations improvement opportunities.
- Determine key inputs to the member and provider experience (e.g., call center handling, claims processing times, access to provider networks).
- Identify and formalize rapid operational initiatives based on recurring findings from root cause analyses.
- Lead the development of cross-functional work plans for improvement initiatives.
- Engage vendor partners to ensure cross-enterprise alignment with broad-based corporate goals and priorities.

- Continue to facilitate the data analysis process for ongoing identification of opportunities with the greatest scope for improvement.
- Measure and evaluate the success of respective initiative implementations through key metrics (i.e., member service cost per member per month, number of phone calls per member, portion of concerns raised to regulatory levels).

Moreover, Lester wanted to be clear about what would make for a successful intervention. He made sure that the committee's charter clearly outlined what he called the Critical Success Factors (CSF), or the conditions necessary for success. The key CSFs proposed by Lester to ensure successful program development and implementation are as follows:

1. *Stakeholder participation.* Executive and external resources will be available for meetings and workshops to participate in strategic discussions and to provide input on key decisions.
2. *Executive sponsorship.* Executive leadership will be required to provide updates on key initiatives in other areas, including broad-based corporate goals and priorities.
3. *Performance reporting.* Executive-level performance reporting will occur regularly and, in as timely a manner as possible, facilitate program analysis and decision support.
4. *Internal committee coordination.* Executive leadership will have required access to key committee program leads and sponsors to ensure strategic direction alignment and achievement of operational efficiencies.
5. *Decision making.* Timely decision making will be enabled by clearly defined roles, accountability, and effective coordination.
6. *Seamless member experience.* The committee will have systematic mechanisms to create a user experience that is integrated from end to end.

This list was only the beginning of an attempt to set the "rules for engagement." Lester wanted to provide something that painted a compelling picture of the reality that he and Rico were facing with these challenging issues. He worked with the director of the Member Escalations Unit to run reports on the key complaints, both by complaint subject and by volume. Lester wanted to provide a list of only the most significant issues at the committee's first meeting, and he highlighted three high-level categories: billing and enrollment, claims, and provider network. He planned to be direct with the committee members and list the key complaints under each of the three categories. He also planned to present a chart (shown in exhibit 12.3) that would indicate the volume of each type of complaint.

**EXHIBIT 12.3**

List of Complaint Types and Volume (Over Three Months)

| Complaints (Q1 2015) | Complaint Volume | Percent of Total Complaints (by Section) |
|---|---|---|
| *Billing and Enrollment* | 2,350 | 100% |
| 1. **Reconciliation of enrollment** (e.g., ensuring enrollment data entered at enrollment match vendor data) | 1,100 | 47% |
| 2. **Open enrollment issues** (e.g., membership ID card generation; correct billing) | 760 | 32% |
| 3. **Premium refunds** (e.g., lateness in refunding members who overpaid) | 150 | 6% |
| 4. **Premium billing notices for members perceived to be in arrears** (e.g., payment tracking issues for members who have not paid) | 340 | 14% |
| *Claims* | 2,815 | 100% |
| 1. **Prompt payment of claims** (e.g., untimely payment of providers per contractual terms) | 1,900 | 67% |
| 2. **Accuracy** (e.g., inaccurate provider payments) | 360 | 13% |
| 3. **Out-of-network payments** (e.g., inaccurate payment of contractually determined rate) | 400 | 14% |
| 4. **Preventive coding vs. diagnostic coding** (e.g., inaccurate use of preventive and diagnostic codes causing payment issues) | 155 | 6% |
| *Provider Network* | 400 | 100% |
| 1. **Accuracy of provider network directory** (e.g., provider data incorrect in network directory) | 370 | 93% |
| 2. **Adequacy of provider network by geography** (e.g., inaccurate listing of providers by region) | 30 | 8% |
| **Total complaints (three areas)** | 5,565 | |

### Analyzing the Complaints

The analysis made clear that members had a significant number of complaints—more than 5,500 in the first quarter of the plan's first year of operation. If this trend continued, the plan was on track to receive 21,000 complaints per year; by comparison, the benchmark for a plan similar to Revolution Health was around 4,000 per year.

Across the core areas of billing and enrollment, claims, and provider network issues, a few specific areas accounted for the bulk of the complaints. First, member data inputted at enrollment did not match the data that vendors were using downstream. This issue was perplexing, as Revolution Health had to understand where enrollment information was changing in the process and why the changes were not reconciled. Moreover, a significant number of complaints related to the open enrollment period. Each complaint had to be fixed immediately; if not, the problems would escalate as new members continued to be enrolled in the plan.

Next, 67 percent of the first quarter's complaints in the claims category involved payments from the health plan to providers not being made on a timely basis. Providers were angry that they were not receiving their payments on the agreed-upon schedule. Furthermore, the lateness was costly for the health plan because it had to pay interest to the providers when the payments were late.

Lastly, the provider information listed in the health plan directory was often incorrect, according to 93 percent of the complaints in the provider network category. A large number of these complaints stemmed from instances in which a provider was listed as being in the plan's network when in actuality the provider was not. Such errors created payment problems for both providers and members, because if services were provided to a member and the provider was not in the plan's network, the member was fully responsible for paying the provider.

Having assembled the complaint data, Lester went one step further. He worked with his team to put together a more detailed chart that listed specific issues. This chart could then form the basis of a working exercise in which the committee could assign an accountable owner for each issue, rank the significance of the issue, assign next steps in developing a solution, and establish a work plan with a deadline to ensure that the solution is advanced and fully implemented on a timely basis (see exhibit 12.4). Lester noted that the list was still relatively broad but felt the approach was appropriate; broad issues would lead the accountable owners to probe and drill down on the problems, helping them to formulate solutions.

### Getting the Committee Started

Lester put the charts and the committee charter together with an agenda for the first committee meeting, and he scheduled weekly committee meetings for the next six months. He thought the issues were significant and broad enough in scope that the organization would need at least six months to develop solutions and implement work plans. For the first four meetings, he invited only the health plan's senior leaders; for all subsequent meetings, he invited a senior representative from each vendor as well. Lester knew that the first meetings would need to focus on obtaining management buy-in and commitment; subsequent meetings could then proceed as a whirlwind of displaying the dirty laundry to all stakeholders.

Lester wrote an e-mail of introduction, attached the charts and committee charter, hit the send button, and took a deep breath. He then exhaled and heard his phone ring, seemingly angrily. He recognized the number—it was the head of the consumer advocacy division within Revolution Health's chief state regulator. Lester took another deep breath before he answered the

**EXHIBIT 12.4**

Complaint Issue Listing, with Accountable Owners and Project Plan Deliverables

| Area | Process | Issue | Volume | Solution | Date Solution Due | Owner | Policies and Procedures Impacted | Project Status |
|------|---------|-------|--------|----------|-------------------|-------|----------------------------------|----------------|
| Member | Benefits administration | Inappropriate application of deductibles | | | | | | |
| Member | Billing | Billing changes not processed | | | | | | |
| Member | Billing | Disabled auto-payment | | | | | | |
| Member | Billing | Overpaid premium | | | | | | |
| Member | Billing | Payment incorrectly rejected | | | | | | |
| Member | Call center | Long wait / abandonment | | | | | | |
| Member | Call center | No callback | | | | | | |
| Member | Call center | Wrong information given | | | | | | |
| Member | Claims | Multiple copays | | | | | | |
| Member | Claims | Specialist-as-PCP copay policy | | | | | | |
| Member | Claims | Subrogation | | | | | | |
| Member | Enrollment | Member coverage incorrectly dropped when should not have been terminated | | | | | | |
| Member | Enrollment | Member not in system when they contact Revolution Health customer service | | | | | | |
| Member | Enrollment | Member told they are disenrolled nonpayment while plan collects premium | | | | | | |
| Member | Fulfillment | Mailing inaccuracies | | | | | | |
| Member | Fulfillment | No ID / incorrect ID / multiple ID | | | | | | |
| Member | Pharmacy | Pharmacy benefits / Art. 49 compliance | | | | | | |
| Provider | Claims | Duplicate claims editing logic | | | | | | |

# EXHIBIT 12.4
Complaint Issue Listing, with Accountable Owners and Project Plan Deliverables *(continued)*

| Area | Process | Issue | Volume | Solution | Date Solution Due | Owner | Policies and Procedures Impacted | Project Status |
|------|---------|-------|--------|----------|-------------------|-------|----------------------------------|----------------|
| Provider | Claims | Out-of-network ambulance | | | | | | |
| Provider | Claims | Paper claims reduction initiative | | | | | | |
| Provider | Claims | Balance billing | | | | | | |
| Provider | Claims | Claims adjudication | | | | | | |
| Provider | Claims | Preauthorization issue | | | | | | |
| Provider | Claims payment policy | Out-of-network ambulance billing | | | | | | |
| Provider | Claims payment policy | Timely filing administration | | | | | | |
| Provider | Claims: Prompt pay | Interest calculation and payment | | | | | | |
| Provider | Claims: Prompt pay | Not paying clean claims on time | | | | | | |
| Provider | Management | Lack of performance reporting | | | | | | |
| Provider | Management | Lack of periodic auditing | | | | | | |
| Provider | Provider data management | Provider appearing in directory as participating provider when provider is not in the network | | | | | | |
| Provider | Provider service | Call transfer issue from Vendor A to Vendor B | | | | | | |
| Provider | Provider service | Poor experience (inaccurate responses, etc.) | | | | | | |
| Provider | Provider service | Telephone abandonment rates | | | | | | |

phone. He readied himself for another earful from the regulator, but he was confident about how he would describe his plan to move forward and resolve the issues. His fingers were also crossed.

## Case Questions

1. How serious are the management challenges that Revolution Health faces?
2. How is Revolution Health responding to these challenges?
3. What are the main problems in its current adaptive methods?
4. What are the three most important short-term challenges about which Revolution Health can do something significant?
5. Detail possible responses to one of the challenges. Include a description of what will be necessary to bring about a successful implementation of that solution.

# CASE 13

# Reducing Healthcare-Associated Infections at Academic Medical Center: The Role of High-Performance Work Practices

*Julie Robbins and Ann Scheck McAlearney*

Late one Tuesday afternoon, Don Patterson, the CEO of Academic Medical Center (AMC), sat in his office putting the final touches on a board presentation. The presentation highlighted AMC's latest quality scores—and the scores were the best they had ever been at AMC. Patterson was particularly proud of these results because he had made a conscious effort over the past two years to make quality and patient safety top priorities for the organization.

Just as Patterson was about to leave for the day, his assistant stuck her head into his office. "I'm sorry to interrupt what you're doing," she began, "but I have the governor on the line. She wants to talk to you about AMC's infection rates."

As his assistant left, Patterson picked up the phone with confidence and asked, "Governor, what can I do for you?"

"Patterson," the governor answered, "I know you and your team at AMC are doing great work. You are an incredible resource for this state and the region. However, I am very concerned about central line–associated blood-stream infection [CLABSI] rates in your hospital."

As the governor continued, Patterson's confidence began to wane. She explained, "I just spoke to my health commissioner, Sally Slater. She had been at a national meeting where she learned that our state has the highest CLABSI rates in the country. Slater was surprised by this information, so she and her team further reviewed the data. They found that because AMC is the largest hospital in the state, AMC's CLABSI rates are a major contributor to our state's high CLABSI rates. That means that AMC's high infection rates have pulled our state's rankings to the bottom. This is absolutely unacceptable!"

Stunned but attempting to recover, Patterson interjected, "Governor, you must be mistaken. Our rates may be higher than those of other hospitals in the state, but that's because the patients we treat are much more complex and therefore much more prone to bloodstream infections. When we compare ourselves to our academic medical center peer institutions, we do as well as or better than they do with respect to CLABSI rates."

The governor sighed and stated, "Look, Patterson, that may be true. But I don't care about other academic medical centers. I care about my state, and I know you do, too. Also, my health commissioner tells me that there are some states—states that also have large medical centers—that have not had *any* CLABSI infections in the last year. So don't tell me that it can't be done. You need to fix this. We have enough problems in this state without becoming known for giving people infections when they come to our hospitals!"

After the call ended, Patterson knew he needed to do something, but he was still in shock about the governor's revelation. Given the lateness of the hour, he packed his briefcase, turned off his office lights, and walked toward the stairs to head home. He needed some time to think about how best to address the governor's concerns.

## AMC's Commitment to Quality

When Patterson was hired as AMC's CEO, he came into an already strong organization that was widely recognized for clinical excellence and that was routinely recognized as one of the country's best medical centers. Locally, AMC served as a hub for specialty and subspecialty services within the state and surrounding region—particularly for trauma, cardiac, neonatal, and other complex services. AMC had been a leader in quality, comparing favorably to its academic medical center peers across the country on key quality indicators.

Of course, Patterson recognized that there was always room for improvement, and he tried to do everything he could to ensure that patients at AMC got the best possible care, had good outcomes, and, most important, were not made worse during their stays. Like most healthcare leaders, Patterson was appalled by the national statistics showing that more than 98,000 people die every year from preventable medical errors in hospitals. He was thus motivated to set the ambitious organizational goal of making AMC the safest medical center in the country.

As part of this effort, Patterson hired an executive-level chief quality officer, Kristin Dempsey, MD, to lead the organization's ambitious quality and safety efforts. During her two-year tenure with AMC, Dempsey had helped the organization make significant progress toward improving safety, and she had developed a quality report card to track progress. Patterson shared the quality report card with the board of directors and reviewed the quality data at his monthly leadership meetings. He encouraged managers and staff to implement the changes necessary to make AMC the safest medical center in the country; he then held them accountable for results, celebrating successes along the way.

Given his personal commitment to quality and safety, Patterson was unsettled by the governor's phone call about AMC's CLABSI rates. Upon arriving at work the next day, he met with his executive team, told them about the call with the governor, and let them know, in no uncertain terms, that he expected them to improve the CLABSI rates. Specifically, he charged Dempsey with developing an aggressive CLABSI prevention plan within the week, and he told her that he intended to review the CLABSI rates and improvement progress at their biweekly updates.

## Could AMC Improve Its CLABSI Rates?

Like Patterson, Dempsey was upset by the governor's call and its implications. When she got back to her office, she asked her assistant to set up a meeting with the intensive care unit (ICU) leadership team. The ICU leadership team included Brigid King and Mary Hughes, the respective directors of the medical and surgical ICUs, and Dr. Brian Robinson, the medical director for both ICUs.

Although CLABSI rates had not been included on AMC's organizational-level quality report card, they had been tracked as unit-level indicators for the ICUs. Dempsey knew that AMC's CLABSI rates met the organization's standard of being within the top tenth percentile when compared with its academic medical center peers. Dempsey shared the view of others in the organization that some CLABSIs were virtually unavoidable—a regular part of the cost of doing business—for AMC's complex patient population.

At the unit level, ICU leaders had long recognized the importance of trying to minimize CLABSI rates and therefore had been tracking CLABSI rates as an important quality metric. In fact, several years earlier, the ICUs' rates had been out of line compared with the rates of ICUs in AMC's benchmark peer institutions, but the ICU team had implemented a coordinated effort to reduce them. This effort had been successful, and AMC's rates had dropped to an acceptable level and remained steady since then. In practice, the ICU team believed that, as long as CLABSI rates remained low and hit the benchmark targets, they had very little need to discuss CLABSIs at all.

When Dempsey met with the ICU leaders, she conveyed the concerns of both the governor and Patterson. She suggested that perhaps she and others in the room had gotten too complacent about CLABSIs and that their collective belief that some level of infection was inevitable might have been shortsighted.

Since her talk with Patterson earlier in the day, Dempsey had done some research on CLABSI prevention and learned that the clinical team at the Johns Hopkins Medical Center had virtually eliminated CLABSIs. Dempsey told the team about Johns Hopkins's success and said, "I know we have complex patients with many problems, and I certainly know that preventing infections may be difficult. Nonetheless, if Johns Hopkins, one of the nation's top medical centers, can do it, so can we!"

Even more compelling were findings from the state of Michigan. After launching a collaborative to implement the Johns Hopkins approach in hospitals across the state, Michigan hospitals had gone for more than a year without a CLABSI. After presenting these data to her team, Dempsey continued: "The Michigan experience demonstrates that it is possible to get to zero CLABSIs. I think that we here at AMC need to change our thinking. Rather than accept that infections are a cost of doing business and comparing ourselves to peers who may be stuck in the same way of thinking as we are, we need to aim higher and decide that we can get to zero CLABSIs too!"

Despite Dempsey's pep talk, not all members of the ICU team were in agreement. As Dr. Robinson started to explain why getting to zero would be impossible at AMC, Dempsey stopped him midsentence: "Look, I know it will be hard, and we can sit around and argue and grumble all day. However, I have a clear directive from Don Patterson. He has made a commitment to the governor and has charged me with turning this around. Based on the evidence I've just shared with you from other states and academic medical centers, I am convinced we can improve our CLABSI rates. Further, based on what I know about the quality of the leadership in this room and the level of commitment we have from the physicians and nurses in our ICUs, I don't see any reason why we can't eliminate CLABSIs from our hospital altogether. I have to give Patterson a plan by the end of the week explaining how we aim to address this issue, and I need your help to do it. I know that you all have already put a lot of effort into reducing CLABSI rates, so now I want you to build on those efforts to take our initiatives to the next level."

Brigid King, RN, was the first to respond: "I think we all know that, even though we have a good plan in place and have made some progress on the units, we could be more consistent and vigilant in our processes. We definitely have areas in which we could improve. None of us likes it when something we do or did gives our patient an infection. If we can change our practices to make sure that never happens, then we need to do it."

After some reflection, Dr. Robinson also appeared to come around: "I guess it's hard to argue. If Johns Hopkins can do it, why can't we?"

Dempsey, pleased with the responses from her team, forged ahead. "Great! I appreciate your support and commitment. Now, why don't the three of you work off-line to put together a plan for eliminating CLABSIs from our ICUs, and we can meet again next week?"

Leaving the meeting, Dempsey called Patterson to let him know that she had met with the ICU leaders and, as a result, could assure him that they were collectively committed to eliminating CLABSIs at AMC.

## Reinvigorating CLABSI-Prevention Efforts Through Management and Accountability
### Setting and Attaining CLABSI Prevention Goals

After meeting with the ICU leaders, Dempsey turned her attention to the CLABSI data. She knew that one of the keys to getting to zero would be to make sure that the ICU clinicians and staff were aware of their own unit's CLABSI rates and their ability to improve those rates. In the past, some ICU clinicians had grumbled about the way CLABSI rates were reported and tracked. She was concerned that her improvement initiative might get derailed if staff argued about the data.

For several years, AMC had used the state's CLABSI definition to calculate a rate that was expressed as the number of infections per 1,000 line days in the ICU. A few vocal physicians believed that this definition inflated the ICU CLABSI rates. Mostly they were concerned that the ICU could have infections counted against it if a patient received a central line in another department (e.g., the emergency department or surgery) and then developed a CLABSI shortly after arrival in the ICU. Not only did these physicians believe that this counting method overstated the ICU CLABSI rates, they also believed it improperly assigned responsibility for infections that were not really the ICU's fault, because the central line insertions had not been under the control of the ICU. Dempsey knew that the state's definition wasn't perfect, but she also knew that every definition had its own problems.

Dempsey pulled together a small group that included the most vocal ICU physicians, the ICU directors, and members of her own quality improvement department to develop an internal CLABSI report card that would include unit-level data. She opened the first meeting of this group by saying, "I know that the state's CLABSI definition is not perfect, but it is the best we've got. Since we have to use this definition to collect and report our data externally, I suggest that we use the same definition and data collection methods as the basis for our internal reporting and quality improvement efforts."

As expected, several of the physicians challenged the definition. Yet when they failed to provide a more suitable alternative, Dempsey redirected the conversation. She explained, "We need to focus all of our attention on getting our rates down. Even if these data aren't perfect, our CLABSI rates are unquestionably too high. Our goal is to get to zero infections—no matter how they get measured."

Dempsey continued, "Now that we have agreed that we need to use this standard definition, I think we need to talk about how we can use these data to focus our improvement efforts."

Several members of the group readily noted the importance of routinely disseminating data at the unit level so that frontline staff would know how many infections were occurring on their units. Mary Hughes, one of the ICU nurse managers, noted, "I sometimes review the ICU quality report that includes CLABSI rates at my staff meeting, and I then post the report in the break room. However, I don't spend much time on these reports, because I can see the nurses' eyes glaze over while I'm talking. I think it's hard for them to link data expressed as an infection rate back to individual patient care. I mean, what does two infections per 1,000 line days mean in terms of the patients that they're taking care of?"

King agreed: "My staff are passionate about providing the best care possible to their patients, but a unit-level rate does not mean much to them. I think it might be more meaningful if, instead of reporting out a rate, we tried to track the number of days without infections."

Dr. Robinson eagerly responded, "That's a great idea! Not only will the staff be able to relate to the number, but it will be expressed in a way that puts the emphasis on the positive—eliminating infections."

After a little more discussion, the group agreed that the quality department would produce reports indicating days without CLABSI infections for each unit every month. Leaders on each unit would then be expected to share these reports to enlist their staff in support of the AMC-wide goal of getting to zero infections. The group also decided that these unit-based reports, along with an aggregated report of days without infections across units, would be presented at the CLABSI work group's monthly meetings. Thus, reports indicating the standard CLABSI rates of infections per 1,000 line days would continue to be produced and reported to the ICU leadership team so that they could be tracked over time. Finally, the group agreed that Dempsey would present these reports and data to Patterson every month to ensure that the "Getting to Zero" campaign remained top of mind.

## Clinical Bundle Implementation

In her review of the CLABSI literature, Dempsey had found that prevention strategies were relatively straightforward from a clinical perspective. Clear protocols existed for inserting and maintaining central lines, but the challenge was making sure these protocols were consistently implemented. Proper protocol for central line insertion required the physician inserting the line to adhere to strict sterile precautions, such as wearing a gown and mask, using a full drape on the patient, and practicing hand hygiene. After insertion, central line maintenance protocols were more related to nursing care; they included a focus on timeliness of dressing changes, specific protocols for cleaning and accessing the line, and hand hygiene. Hospitals that had been most successful at eliminating CLABSIs had focused on helping physicians, nurses, and other staff to "do the right thing, every time," and on minimizing opportunities for error. Successful practices included use of standardized central line carts stocked with all the materials for sterile insertion; routine use of checklists; implementation of double checks, in which nurses can stop a physician from inserting a line if protocol is not being followed; and a universal emphasis on hand hygiene.

Dempsey asked her ICU leadership team whether AMC had been following these evidence-based protocols. All of them agreed that, although the AMC CLABSI prevention team had outlined guidelines for line insertion and maintenance, each unit had some flexibility as to how it implemented the practices. They all acknowledged that this approach may have led to too much variation in practice and potential confusion among staff.

Dr. Robinson explained, "Some of our physicians disagree with the evidence or have found areas of the literature that are less clear, and they do not want to change their practice. They say, 'I have been putting in central lines for 20 years without a problem, so why should I change now?' That said, most are willing to change if they find the evidence compelling, and if making the change is easy for them."

Hughes chimed in and noted, "Our nurses are willing to make changes if it's in the best interests of the patient, but they need to understand why the change is necessary and then have the resources they need to make the change effectively. Along those lines, these challenges are exacerbated when we have staff turnover or an influx of new nurses or residents who may have different approaches. Probably one of the issues we have is that we haven't been consistent in our education."

Dempsey responded: "We need to set a standard that is based on the best available evidence and make a decision that there will be one way to do things—the AMC Way. Then we need to make sure that our physicians and unit staff have what they need to do it that way. As leaders on the unit, you need to educate your staff about the AMC Way, emphasizing why it is important to patient care, and then hold them accountable for adhering to our standard. When any person on the unit is not adhering to our standard, any other person, regardless of rank, needs to feel that she can speak up to the individual directly, or to the attending or nurse manager, to inform her that the AMC standard has not been followed. In turn, when this happens, you, as leaders, need to support and reinforce the right behavior."

After a little more discussion, the group agreed to a three-point plan for improving the consistency of practice related to central line insertion and maintenance. First, they would convene a small group of frontline physicians and nurses to develop a single set of standards for line insertion and maintenance. These standards would become the AMC Way. Second, they agreed to each go back to their units, review operations, and speak to the staff to identify opportunities to support and hardwire consistent implementation of the standards. Finally, all four agreed that they would develop a systematic plan for communicating with and educating staff about the importance of infection prevention, the role of staff in preventing infections, and the AMC Way for central line insertion and maintenance.

Three weeks later, they had each worked with their respective teams to finalize standards and develop their CLABSI Prevention Plan. The next step was to roll it out on the units.

### CLABSI Prevention Plan Implementation

At the next medical ICU staff meeting, King announced the launching of a major CLABSI prevention effort on the unit. She told her staff that Patterson was upset about AMC's performance relative to other hospitals in the state, and he had challenged the ICUs to make improvements.

As she explained, "I recognize that our patient population is very sick, but I *know* we can do better. We have the best doctors and nursing staff in the state, so we should be the leaders, not the losers, in patient safety. I also know we have a lot of competing priorities, so I think we may have just taken our eye off the ball with regard to bloodstream infections. There are hospitals just like AMC that have completely eliminated CLABSIs, so I know we at AMC can too."

King unveiled a large poster proclaiming "____ Days Since Our Last Infection" across the top, with a space to write in the appropriate number. She noted, "We are going to put this poster in the hallway so that everyone can see it—physicians, staff, patients, and families. I am going to update it every day with a report of our current data. Unfortunately, we just had a CLABSI yesterday, so we are starting today at zero. But we can take it day by day, focusing on doing everything we can to make sure our patients don't get a CLABSI every single day, and the days will start to add up. Hopefully, someday we won't even need this poster because we will no longer get infections on this unit!"

King continued, "I have asked your colleague, Ann Dillard, who has been a nurse on this unit for ten years, to be our 'CLABSI Champion.' She has already been working with me and others on the ICU management team to develop a consistent set of evidence-based guidelines that will be our standard 'AMC Way' for inserting and maintaining central lines. Our goal is to have everyone do it the same way, every time, without error."

King further explained, "Ann has been working with unit champions from the other ICUs to develop a CLABSI training blitz for all ICU nurses for next Tuesday. Meanwhile, Dr. Robinson has developed a similar event for the attendings and residents. We also plan to incorporate detailed training about the AMC Way into our new nurse orientation, to make sure that anyone who comes to work on our unit learns how to work with central lines the right way, right from the start. Of course, if you have any questions or suggestions for improvement, do not hesitate to talk to Ann, Dr. Robinson, or me. We want your ideas about how we can do things better for our patients. And through all of this, the ICU leadership team will be tracking compliance with our central line insertion and maintenance protocols so that we can make sure we are doing it the right way every time."

### CLABSI Prevention: The First Year

Once all ICU staff were trained on the AMC Way and began to modify their practices, several important changes occurred (see exhibit 13.1).

First, the physicians started including the nurses in their daily patient rounds so that the nurses could report on the status of central lines (e.g., when the dressing was last changed and any problems) and the care team could decide whether a patient still needed a central line.

Second, the staff quickly realized that the central line carts, which were supposed to have all the materials needed for inserting a central line the AMC Way, were not consistently stocked. With the support of her manager and help from the process improvement department, Dillard convened a small group of residents and nurses to revamp the central line carts, and she specified processes for keeping them stocked. These newly organized carts made inserting the lines the right way every time easy, and the right materials were always available.

Finally, the small group that developed the central line carts continued to meet, and it morphed into a unit-based central line task team that worked with the AMC infection control division to conduct root cause analyses when infections did occur. As a result, the members of the team were empowered further to identify opportunities for improvement, solicit feedback about line insertion and maintenance processes from frontline staff, and serve as a general resource for their peers.

As unit staff became more aware of the importance of CLABSI prevention and better understood their practices related to these infections, they became increasingly committed to the goal of eliminating CLABSIs on the unit. As promised, King updated the "Days Since Our Last Infection" number on the poster every day, right outside the nurses' station for everyone to see. And fortunately, as the practice changes began to take hold, that number kept

**EXHIBIT 13.1**

Summary of Changes Made Involving AMC CLABSI-Prevention Initiatives

| Change Made | Before Initiative | After Initiative |
|---|---|---|
| CLABSI prevention goal setting | • Based on benchmark comparisons to like institutions<br>• Tracked as an ICU-based quality indicator | • Goal of zero infections based on experience of leading institutions<br>• Included as a top priority for organization-level quality report card |
| Clinical bundle implementation | • General guidelines adopted based on evidence-based practice, but unit- and/or physician-level variation permitted | • Consensus process to develop evidence-informed guidelines for "the AMC Way"<br>• Use of checklists to ensure bundle compliance every time<br>• Routine monitoring of bundle compliance |
| Clinical education | • Top-down approach in which nurse manager shares clinical changes associated with CLABSI prevention via staff meeting and/or in-servicing | • Staff-driven approach in which unit-based CLABSI champion was identified to participate in improvement efforts and support implementation; included communication and in-services to expand reach of training efforts<br>• Input from frontline nurses routinely obtained (e.g., regarding new products, changes in policies) |
| Reporting | • Unit-based reports of CLABSI rates (infections per 1,000 line days) shared at staff meetings | • Unit-based reports of days since the last infection visibly posted on the units<br>• Celebrations and recognition for meeting major milestones (e.g., one year since the last infection)<br>• Organization-level CLABSI data routinely shared with AMC leaders; public recognition of progress and accomplishments |
| Other initiatives | | • Interdisciplinary rounds to assess line necessity<br>• Standardized central line cart<br>• Unit-based CLABSI team<br>• Visible rewards and recognition for achievement |

getting larger and larger. First seven days, then ten, and then, eventually, the unit had gone more than a year since its last infection. Each major milestone was marked, and the contributions of the staff were recognized with a celebration. When the unit hit one full year without an infection, the ICU leaders threw a pizza party on the unit. In addition, a friendly rivalry—or competition—between the two adult and pediatric ICUs developed. When one of the units hit a major milestone in CLABSI prevention, the others were inspired to try to beat the record. As one pediatric nurse noted, "Of course we were happy when the adult ICU hit 50 days without an infection, but then we thought to ourselves, 'If they can do it, so can we.' We became even more committed to the work on our own unit."

The ICU managers and staff were also motivated by the fact that Patterson had added CLABSI rates as one of the three quality indicators on AMC's overall balanced scorecard. The balanced scorecard results were reported to the AMC board every quarter, and they served as the basis for both manager and staff performance bonuses. Further, Patterson presented the balanced scorecard results to the hospital leadership team every month. With every success, Patterson publicly recognized the ICU managers and staff for their efforts and praised them for their accomplishments. The ICU staff were both surprised and thrilled when Patterson showed up at their one-year celebration to personally thank them for their hard work.

## Case Questions

1. What leader behaviors were most important for reducing AMC's CLABSI rates? At the executive level? At the unit level?

2. How was information used to facilitate improvements in CLABSI rates?

3. As an administrator at AMC, what would you be concerned about in the coming year for CLABSI prevention? How about two years from now?

# CASE 14
## Better Metrics for Financial Management

*Terri Menser and Ann Scheck McAlearney*

Paul is a newly promoted chief financial officer of the Columbus City Health System (CCHS), a large, established urban health system. He has been with the organization for nearly two dozen years, and has seen the healthcare environment shift greatly over that time. Given all the changes that have taken place since the passage of the Affordable Care Act, Paul is concerned about his ability to present a clear picture of the CCHS financial situation to the board and to CCHS administrators. Not only is the reimbursement picture complicated due to the nature of third-party payments, but the introduction of financial incentives and penalties based on organizational performance has hampered his ability to develop a reliable budget or forecast hospital finances.

Given his promotion, Paul wonders whether he should use this transition as an opportunity to devise a better basis for the values estimated in the budget, along with accompanying metrics to monitor financial performance. New metrics might be able to account for penalties and more closely align with "worst-case scenario" income for the hospital, thus better preparing the institution if things do not go well. At the same time, Paul wonders how to best account for the unknown dollar amount that will be reimbursed for care given the shifting mix of payers and variability in negotiated rates.

Another concern involves the cost of tracking and reporting quality data. Since starting in his new position, Paul has tried to calculate the cost of the resources (e.g., additional labor) required to achieve the quality measures set by the Centers for Medicare & Medicaid Services (CMS), and he has found the amount of work to be daunting. He has found that CCHS currently reports more than 1,000 unique measures to 35 different organizations, reflecting the reporting burden common to many healthcare organizations (Murray et al. 2017). Paul understands the importance of population health and measuring quality, but he also knows that resources are limited. He is acutely aware of the financial constraints facing CCHS.

Paul thinks the time has come to improve the budget metrics so that CCHS will be better able to understand and report its financial picture. He does not consider any of these policy changes to be fleeting, and he believes they should be incorporated into the budgeting process. However, he is not sure how to do so. To get started with the process, Paul schedules a meeting with his analysts and asks them to come prepared to discuss how to improve their current budgeting process. $500,000 has been set aside for CCHS to invest in population health, which Paul believes will help the organization to reach some of the CMS quality measures. He has asked senior executives in each department to make recommendations on how best to spend the funds, bearing in mind how potential expenditures will affect the organization's bottom line.

## Case Questions

1. What are some of the issues Paul has identified with the current budget metrics? Are there other issues that should be considered?
2. What about the budget metrics can be improved? What cannot be controlled?

3. How can these new budget metrics be implemented, and who should be involved in rolling out the new metrics?

4. How could the list of metrics be shortened? Why would fewer metrics be a good idea?

5. How should the organization ensure that the metrics are regularly changed appropriately?

6. Provide a summary of your thoughts on how to best spend the funds set aside to improve the health of the population served by CCHS. Approach the issue from the perspective of a senior executive at the hospital.

## Reference

Murray, K. R., J. L. Hefner, A. S. McAlearney, A. VanBuren, T. R. Huerta, and S. Moffatt-Bruce. 2017. "The Quality Reporting Reality at a Large Academic Medical Center: Reporting 1600 Unique Measures to 49 Different Sources." *International Journal of Academic Medicine*. In press.

# CASE 15

# Ergonomics in Practice

*J. Mac Crawford and Ann Scheck McAlearney*

Riverlea Rehabilitation Hospital's administrators had recently begun to notice high levels of absenteeism, workers' compensation claims, and time off from work linked to back and other injuries suffered by workers. Staff were prone to injuries when patients lost their balance while being moved—especially when staff were required to use their own bodies to prevent patient falls. Patients, in turn, could be injured when staff were unable to secure patients due to an overwhelming physical load or because of preexisting injuries or deficits in staff members' physical strength. Tim Montana, the administrative director, expected that a new system of patient-lifting devices that was planned for installation at Riverlea could effectively reduce the number of workers' injuries and associated workers' compensation claims and absenteeism rates. The new system was expensive, but Montana believed the system's benefits would be worth the cost. Still, he wanted to make sure.

The new lift system had been designed so that patients could be placed in a harness and moved from a bed to a chair, the bathroom, or anywhere else in the room. It was meant to be used consistently; consistent use was apparently associated with reduced risk of injury to both staff and patients.

To prove that the new lift system helped address the injury problems reported by Riverlea nursing staff, Montana enlisted a team of researchers from the local school of public health. Montana wanted to be able to provide quantifiable evidence of the positive impact of the new system. During Montana's meeting with the team, Dr. Jason Terry, the lead environmental health services researcher, explained that the best approach to evaluating the impact of the lift system would be a longitudinal study of the health of Riverlea personnel. As Terry explained, the research team could first collect baseline information using existing injury data, and then it could supplement these data by collecting new information about work practices, shifts, and musculoskeletal symptoms among the target workers. After installation of the new lift system hospitalwide, the researchers could collect follow-up data to assess the system's efficacy.

Montana convinced the rest of Riverlea's administrative team that a research study was justified, and he approved the budget request to support the investigation. Baseline data were collected before the lift system was installed, and plans for the follow-up assessment were made. However, Montana observed the implementation and initial use of the lift system at Riverlea and became concerned about the process. He and his team had seen evidence that many staff members were using the devices incorrectly, were using them intermittently, or were not using them at all. Well aware that improper use of the system would bias any research data collection process, Montana decided to ask the engineering department to check whether the lift system was operating as planned. After a week of study, the engineering personnel reported to Montana that the lifts themselves were functioning properly.

Montana next asked individual staff members for their opinions about the lift system. After only a handful of conversations, Montana realized that people had plenty of opinions about the lift system, and most were negative. Staff appeared unconvinced about the value of the lift system, and they instead were delighted to tell Montana stories about how they had managed to "work around" the system to lift their patients in the "usual way." Montana still believed that the lift system could have a positive impact at Riverlea, but he knew that current use patterns were inconsistent and inappropriate. He knew he had to do something to intervene, but he didn't know where to start.

## Case Questions

1. What options does Montana now have to convince staff to use the new lift system consistently and properly?

2. Are there appropriate metrics and goals by which to evaluate the success of the lift system implementation? What metrics should be used to meet what goals? What is an appropriate timeline for meeting those goals?
3. What would be an appropriate role for a research team evaluating the impact of a new lift system?
4. Who should be accountable for correct adoption and use of the new lift system?
5. For a different organization considering the installation of a new lift system, what type of process would you propose to build staff support and buy-in for the system? Who would be the relevant stakeholders to include in planning for the new system's introduction?

# CASE 16
## Financial Reporting to the Board

*Anthony R. Kovner*

### Act I

At the December board meeting for Christian Health System, board member Sam Brown received the following 2008 Operating Budget Highlights from Larry Dolan, the chief financial officer:

**HOSPITAL 2008 OPERATING BUDGET HIGHLIGHTS**
- The surplus for 2008 is projected to be approximately $640,000.

*VOLUME*
- The budget is based on 28,000 inpatient discharges, or 76 discharges per day. This rate is 1.6 discharges a day higher than the hospital's projections for 2007 (74.4).
- The closing of Clark Hospital and the recruitment of new physicians are expected to produce the projected growth in discharges.
- Other hospital outpatient services (emergency, ambulatory surgery) are conservatively budgeted to continue at current volumes.

*REVENUE*
- Total revenue is budgeted to increase by 5.7 percent:
  - Net patient service revenue is projected to increase by 7.6 percent.

- Other revenue is budgeted to decrease by 17.8 percent, mostly due to the loss of one-time items such as donations, and a projected decrease in investment income.
- The reduction in investment income is a product of an anticipated decline in cash and investment balances due to amounts owed to Eastern State, pension payments, and capital purchases.
- New rates were included in the budget for Medicare, Medicaid, and other payers:
  - New Medicare rates included an inpatient increase of 1.5 percent. In the 2008 rate, the city wage index decreased.
  - Medicaid rates have been budgeted at the preliminary January 2008 issued rates, which include an adjusted trend factor of 1.88 percent.
- New negotiated rates for managed care are included in the revenue model by payer. The following are some examples of these increased rates:
  - Blue Cross: +6 percent
  - Aetna: +4 percent
  - Plan 1: +10 percent
  - Plan 2: +6 percent
  - United Medicaid: +15 percent, and Commercial: +3 percent
  - Plan 3: +5 percent
- Case-mix indexes for Medicare (1.43), Medicaid (1.38), and Plan 4 nonmaternity (1.22) are budgeted at the actual levels through October 2007.

## EXPENSES

- Total expenses are budgeted at 5.8 percent above projections of 2007 spending.
- This reflects the following:
  - The expansion of the available medical/surgical acute care beds by 16, with 8 beds as of January 1, 2008, and another 8 beds as of February 29, 2008, for a total increase of 16 beds.
  - The following contractual increases:
    - RN union: 3 percent, as of January 1, 2008
    - Technical and professional union: 3 percent as of January 1, 2008, and 3 percent as of December 1, 2008
    - Security guards union: 3 percent as of January 1, 2008
    - A 3 percent salary increase for nonunion staff as of April 1, 2008
  - Supplies and other expenses were increased for inflation at a rate of 3 percent.
- Other noteworthy expense changes included in the budget:
  - Benefits: an 11.8 percent increase from projected 2007 to 2008 as a function of the increased cost of union benefits and increases to nonunion healthcare benefits

— Physician contracted services: an 11.9 percent increase reflecting both changes in salaries and increased coverage (e.g., labor and delivery, 24/7 coverage)

— Bad debt: a decrease of 10.4 percent from projected 2007 to 2008 as a continuation of the "Stockamp Effect" and increases in charity care

# Act II

The day after the board meeting, Brown sent the following e-mail to Dolan:

To: Larry Dolan

From: Sam Brown

Re: Financial Reporting to the Board

1. The purpose of this memo is to improve the quality of financial reporting to the board so that the board can add more value to hospital performance.

2. This is not the first time I have expressed these concerns to you. I become especially frustrated around budget time. The board spends way too little time examining the budget.

3. I do not feel sufficiently informed about the choices that underlie financial performance despite 17 years of service on the board, including several years on the executive committee as chair of the performance committee and as vice chair of our Medicaid managed care plan.

4. I would like to see a plan and a commitment from you to do better.

**Questions That Came to Mind from Reading Your Distributed Materials and from Listening to Your Presentation**

- You made no report on last year's results in relation to what you had forecast when last year's budget was presented.

- There was no summary of or explanation of variance in the financials presented.

- What are the assumptions on which next year's budget is based? For example, what are the specifics regarding the impact on admissions of Clark Hospital's closing?

- How can we increase revenues?

- What are we doing to decrease rehospitalizations?

- What investments should we be considering to improve quality of care?

- How do our expenses compare with benchmark hospitals?

- Why can't we make greater improvements in our lengths of stay, and what would be the impact of such improvements on our operating financials?

- What is the relationship between our financials and our strategic plan?

- What is our community service budget? How do we spend these funds currently? How could we spend them better?
- You don't seem to be getting much help from the board with these matters. Is there a problem with leadership of the finance committee?
- What are our options for controlling the increase in health benefits each year?
- Where is the discussion about how Christian will meet its capital needs in the future?

# Act III

Two days after his e-mail, Brown received the following e-mail reply from Dolan:

Thanks for your thoughtful questions. Most of these issues are discussed in great detail by the finance committee. I think if you read some of the minutes from those meetings you could get a better sense of the issues that are discussed.

Regarding capital, as we have said at the past several board meetings, we are in the process of refinancing our housing complex. This effort will allow us to continue to operate the housing and allow us to continue providing existing subsidies to tenants, while at the same time draw significant funds from the refinancing. We are currently estimating approximately $30 million. In addition to this, we continue to explore with the state options for moving funds from our Medicaid managed care plan to Christian Health System. And as I mentioned last night, we are obtaining $5 million in TELP financing and $2.1 million in state ERDA financing. Additionally, we were able to come to final endorsement with HUD much faster than any facility in the region on our $87 million borrowing. So all in all, while the capital picture is not great, primarily due to the funding needed for our pension plan, I think we are doing better than most hospitals in the city that serve high proportions of Medicaid and uninsured patients.

I also think the finance staff works very closely with the program side of the house in trying to figure out new ways to fund productive, high-quality programs. Two examples of that were discussed last night: our relationship with University Hospital and our collaboration with the family health center on rehabilitation services. Our budget process is a "bottom-up" process, with detailed discussion at the cost center level, building up to cost groups, and then up to facility-wide discussion. In those discussions, we review old programs for viability and quality, and we consider new proposals that will enhance our strategic direction. It should also be noted that over the past four years we have met our budget targets and enhanced quality of care throughout the facility, while working in a fiscally restrained environment that has experienced reductions in both Medicaid and Medicare reimbursements that encompass approximately 75 percent of our patients.

I will continue to work with the finance committee and the board to make our financial presentations more meaningful.

## Case Questions

1. What are the strengths and weaknesses of Brown's e-mail about health system financial reporting?
2. What are the strengths and weaknesses of Dolan's response to Brown's e-mail?
3. How would you have responded to Brown's e-mail?
4. Why didn't Dolan respond as you would have?

# CASE 17

# Handoffs in Patient Care

*Brian Hilligoss*

Midwest University Medical Center (MUMC) is a highly specialized tertiary referral and trauma center affiliated with a major university in the Midwest. The main hospital is a 600-bed acute care facility that receives roughly 45,000 patient admissions each year, more than half of which come through the emergency department (ED).

When physicians in the ED decide to admit a patient, they complete an admission form in the electronic medical record (EMR), designating the service to which the patient is to be admitted. They also send a page to the admitting physician on that service. The admitting physician then calls the ED physician and takes a handoff over the telephone. During this handoff, the ED physician presents the patient's case, including some relevant medical history, information about the chief complaint, and how the patient has responded to care in the ED.

To a certain extent, the handoff signifies the transfer of responsibility for the patient from the ED to the inpatient service; however, this transfer can involve considerable ambiguity at times. Sometimes physicians on the inpatient services may feel that a patient would be better served by a different service. In such cases, they may redirect the admission to another service, and the ED physician must then make a handoff to that service.

## Boarding in the ED

Patients must often remain in the ED for some period after the handoff—a process known as "boarding"—until an inpatient bed is available and a transport tech can move the patient to the inpatient ward. Consequently, a kind of gray zone exists in which patients may receive less attention as staff incorrectly assume that someone else is looking after them.

This problem is exacerbated by the fact that boarded patients may be physically out of sight. After the handoff conversation has occurred, ED staff often move these patients into the hallways of the ED to make room for incoming patients. ED nurses and physicians, going about their duties caring for new, incoming patients, are physically removed from the hallways where the boarded patients wait. Meanwhile, the inpatient staff are even farther away. The MUMC ED is in the basement of the hospital, and most of the inpatient wards are in the tower on floors 4 through 11.

Because MUMC tends to operate at or near capacity, boarding is frequent, and patients often remain in the ED for six or more hours after the handoff. When shift changes occur in the ED or inpatient services during these times of boarding, the risk of a patient falling off someone's radar increases.

## A "New" Patient?

At 8:35 a.m. on a bleak February morning, Dr. Anita Henderson, a hospitalist, received an urgent page from a nurse. "Orders needed for Saunders. STAT. Nausea. In pain." Dr. Henderson was perplexed: She knew of no patient by the name of Saunders. She double-checked the paper list of patients she carried in her white coat. No Saunders. She looked at the whiteboard where her service lists the names of expected new patients. No Saunders. She asked several of her colleagues—other general internal medicine physicians on the hospitalist service—if they had a patient by the name of Saunders, but no one recognized the name.

Dr. Henderson had just begun her seven-day rotation on the hospitalist service that morning. Dr. Chris Clark had rotated off the service the prior afternoon, and now his patients were her responsibility. When she arrived at 7:00 a.m., Dr. Henderson had taken handoffs from the night float residents who had been cross-covering the patients during the night. They had reported two new admissions, but neither was named Saunders.

## Whose Patient Is This?

Dr. Henderson picked up the phone and called the nurse who had sent the page. The nurse reported that Mr. Saunders was a 61-year-old male with a history of smoking, emphysema, and diabetes. He had been admitted to the ED for shortness of breath and had just recently arrived on the general medicine floor. The nurse said that Mr. Saunders was complaining of pain and feeling nauseated. Dr. Henderson asked who was listed as the patient's attending physician. The nurse responded, "Dr. Chris Clark."

Hearing the nurse's concern regarding the patient's condition, Dr. Henderson laid aside for the time being any further questions about how this patient came to be on her service without her knowing or receiving some kind of handoff from another physician. She went to see the patient for herself.

After examining and interviewing Mr. Saunders, Dr. Henderson concluded that he had missed at least one dose of each of his several home medications because of his stay in the ED. He was somewhat dehydrated, his emphysema was flaring up, and he was clearly short of breath. He was also complaining of a "funny feeling in his heart." Dr. Henderson also learned that he had been down in the ED since the previous morning and had spent much of the afternoon and all of the night in a bed in a crowded hallway. She offered an apology to soothe the clearly irritated patient and wrote orders for his medications and for fluids.

Later, Dr. Henderson sat down and looked closely at the patient's electronic medical record. She found the name of the ED resident who had issued the admission orders the previous day and sent him a page asking him to call her. Twenty minutes later, Dr. Calvin Lee, a third-year resident in the MUMC ED, called Dr. Henderson.

**Dr. Henderson:** This is Anita Henderson.

**Dr. Lee:** Hi, Anita. It's Calvin Lee, returning your page.

**Dr. Henderson:** Hi, Calvin. Thanks for calling me back. I wanted to ask you about a patient by the name of Saunders. Did you admit him yesterday?

**Dr. Lee:** Saunders? Sounds familiar. We see so many.

**Dr. Henderson:** He says he came in yesterday morning with shortness of breath and maybe an irregular heartbeat. He has a history of smoking and emphysema.

**Dr. Lee:** Oh, my gosh! Yes! Did he end up on your service?

**Dr. Henderson:** Yes. He just arrived, and he's not doing well. I think he missed his medications and is dehydrated. Sounds like he was boarded overnight in the ED.

**Dr. Lee:** Could be. We were overflowing yesterday. Still super busy down here today. So, how can I help?

**Dr. Henderson:** Well, I just got a page from the floor nurse saying he was on my service and needed attention, but that was the first I heard of him. I'm trying to learn more about him and also find out where the ball got dropped.

**Dr. Lee:** Wow, nobody handed him off to you? And he's just getting to the floor now?

**Dr. Henderson:** Yes.

**Dr. Lee:** Well, that was a big ring-around-the-rosy yesterday! His EKG showed an irregular heart rhythm, so I called pulmonary because I thought the abnormal rhythm might be due to his emphysema. But pulmonary said, "Oh, no, no. We think they're two separate issues. Admit to cardiology to get the heart rate under control and we'll consult." But then, when I called cardiology and they heard about the emphysema, they were like, "No, no, no. This is a pulmonary problem, and the heart is just a side victim. This has nothing to do with us, and what are we going to do with this? And he's going to be on our service for four days recovering from emphysema, and this is ridiculous and this is not what we do." Oh my gosh! They went back and forth and had me call the hospitalist service—Dr. Clark, I think. I can't even remember how many phone calls there were. I finally told them to work it out and then call me back. But I guess they never did. When I left at 3:00 p.m., I handed the patient off to my colleague.

## Handoffs Within the ED

As the conversation continued, Dr. Henderson realized that the patient had been handed off several times in the ED—first when Dr. Lee's shift ended at 3:00 p.m., and then again at subsequent shift changes at 11:00 p.m. and 7:00 a.m. From experience Dr. Henderson knew that details about patient cases tend to get lost with multiple handoffs, particularly when patients have already been officially admitted and are being boarded in the ED.

Dr. Henderson learned that Dr. Lee had listed the hospitalist service as the admitting service in the EMR because, at the point when he issued the admission order, neither the pulmonary service nor the cardiology service seemed likely to take the patient, meaning that the hospitalist service would have to take him. (At MUMC, the hospitalist service is sometimes jokingly referred to as the "service of last resort" because they often receive patients whom no other service will accept.) Dr. Henderson knew that the EMR system requires an admitting service to be selected to start the admissions process. She also knew that because Dr. Clark was responsible for the admissions pager for the hospitalist service yesterday, the EMR system would have designated him as the attending by default.

Dr. Lee also said that when he handed the patient off to his colleague at the end of his shift, he had instructed her to update the EMR once the final decision on placement had been made and to update the involved services.

## Epilogue

Dr. Henderson cared for Mr. Saunders with consultations from physicians in the pulmonary and cardiology services and discharged him home after several days.

When Dr. Clark returned to work a few days later, Dr. Henderson asked him about the patient's case. Dr. Clark told her that, when he had left that evening, the issue about where the patient would go had not been settled, as the other services were waiting for results from additional tests. Dr. Clark said he notified the night float resident about Mr. Saunders and that the ED would call if the patient were going to be admitted to the hospitalist service.

## Case Questions

1. Multiple factors contributed to the problem. Identify as many distinct factors as you can.
2. Using your list of contributing factors from question 1, develop some strategies to reduce the likelihood of a recurrence.
3. Why do hospitals permit this handoff problem to continue?
4. As a hospital administrator, what would you do if this case had occurred in your hospital?

# ▌CASE 18
# Chaos in the Clinical Trials Office

*Alice Gaughan and Ann Scheck McAlearney*

Many cancer patients are waiting for treatment options to become available via clinical trials, but the start-up process of getting a trial active at a medical center and open for patient enrollment can be very lengthy. The process can delay patient treatment for weeks and sometimes months, and it leads to considerable frustration on the part of both treating physicians and the patients themselves.

Abrielle Grant, MS, is a protocol implementation coordinator in the Clinical Trials Office (CTO) at Please Hill Cancer Center, and her job responsibilities include overseeing the start-up process for new clinical trials. The start-up process has many parts that can take place concurrently, including four to six weeks of contract negotiations, eight to ten weeks of regulatory approvals, two weeks of treatment plan development, and two weeks of staff training. Abrielle has learned from staff members that the start-up process timeline is often delayed by such factors as problems with contract negotiations, pending approvals of regulatory requirements by the organization's Institutional Review Board, continual adjustments to treatment plans by clinical staff, and lack of adequate staffing in the CTO. Abrielle is sensitive to the concerns of staff members and eager to find ways to improve the process.

Abrielle reports directly to Jennifer Montgomery, the CTO manager, who insists the process can be accomplished more quickly. Ms. Montgomery encourages Abrielle to stick to a rigid timeline for the start-up process and suggests setting hard deadlines for CTO staff to complete their parts of the process. She believes the process could be completed within 14 weeks instead of the current average of 23 weeks. Ms. Montgomery has told Abrielle that she does not want to hear any excuses for delays in start-up and that she expects the 14-week goal to be met for all trials. She expects adherence to this time-line across all new trials, recognizing that it will involve at least 12 new trials opening each month.

To ensure adherence to her timeline, Ms. Montgomery implements a weekly conference call, led by Abrielle, during which CTO staff members are questioned about the status of trials in various stages of start-up. The initial calls are filled with staff members expressing concern about the timeline and describing the many challenges they face trying to open the trials on a timely basis. During the calls, however, Ms. Montgomery discourages discussion about the problems because she views them all as excuses. She insists that the 14-week timeline can be met. Abrielle becomes uncomfortable with the format of the call because she desperately wants to understand the problems so that she can help to identify solutions. CTO staff members participating in the calls share Abrielle's discomfort. Soon, afraid of negative feedback, some CTO staff members stop calling into the weekly conference calls or misrepresent the status of their tasks.

One of the CTO staff members affected by this issue is Victoria McDowell, a clinical research manager. Victoria confides in Abrielle, sharing that her clinical staff can't keep up with the work required for opening new trials in addition to the work required for already existing trials. Her staff's work involves educating and training clinical team members on trial details, obtaining consent from patients, serving as the main point of contact for patients, coordinating patient testing and treatment, adjusting treatment plans as new information is gathered, and addressing all adverse events. This workload leaves very little time for training clinical staff members about new trials; thus, the opening of new trials is often delayed. Victoria's staff members are stressed by the pressure to open more trials than they can handle. Adding to the challenges, a number of staff members quit over the next couple months, delaying the start-up of new trials even further.

You are the newly hired director of the CTO, and you are tasked with finding ways to improve and shorten the start-up process to make clinical trials available to patients as soon as possible. You know you will need buy-in from all team members and their input on process improvement opportunities to ensure that they can agree upon and achieve a reasonable start-up timeline for new trials. However, through conversations with various staff members, you have become concerned about the management approach of Ms. Montgomery and its impact on staff morale.

## Case Questions

1. Given what you have learned from staff members, what do you think are the biggest barriers to shortening the timeline for starting new clinical trials? Which of these barriers are under your control? What do you do about those?
2. What would you tell Ms. Montgomery about staff morale and its impact on productivity and employee retention? How can you coach Ms. Montgomery to work differently with CTO staff?

# CASE 19

# The Telemedicine Opportunity for Geneva Health System

*Ann Scheck McAlearney*

## Introduction

Geneva Health System (GHS) is a large academic medical center based in Longwood, a midsized metropolitan city in the Southwest. GHS is associated with the state university, and it includes three hospitals, a medical clinic facility, a medical research complex, and affiliated primary and specialty group practices spread throughout the region. Geneva University Hospital is the main hospital campus, with 500 inpatient beds and equipment and facilities that are considered state of the art. GHS is well known for its cancer and rehabilitation service lines, and it has recently expanded its cardiac service line in an attempt to keep up with increasing demand.

With strong clinical services lines and an excellent reputation, GHS is well positioned to expand its reach by developing telemedicine services. The GHS electronic health record (EHR) is fully operational, and telemedicine capabilities could be supported by the GHS information technology (IT) services division, but no one is convinced about this opportunity.

## Assessing the Situation

Dr. Dan Johnson has just been appointed CEO of GHS. He has come to the Longwood area after serving five years as CEO of a 200-bed community hospital. Johnson is a definite fan of EHR and electronic medical record (EMR) systems, and he is enthusiastic about the potential for telemedicine to increase the reach of GHS. In particular, he is aware of the opportunities to use telemedicine functionality to extend the reach of Geneva's physicians and enable them to communicate with and care for patients without requiring those patients to drive into the city.

Johnson's predecessor, Jeffrey Ash, retired after serving 20 years as GHS's CEO. He had been decidedly "old school" and had little interest in leading the charge to put Geneva on the telemedicine map. Even though he was aware that the use of telemedicine was expanding, Ash had no interest in pursuing this opportunity at Geneva.

Johnson is aware of the likely resistance he will face if he tries to introduce telemedicine capabilities at Geneva. He has followed some of the IT implementation literature and knows that common barriers to implementation, such as physician resistance to change, may present challenges. He also predicts resistance from the patient experience department, which is concerned about how telemedicine might affect patient satisfaction.

## A Hallway Conversation

As Johnson headed to the cafeteria for a cup of coffee, he was stopped in the corridor by Amy Chapman, who was leaving the patient experience department.

**Johnson:** Hi, Ms. Chapman. How is everything going in your department?

**Chapman:** Not well, Dr. Johnson. I heard a rumor that you were considering developing telemedicine services at Geneva, and that makes me very concerned.

**Johnson:** Well, Ms. Chapman, nothing has been decided yet, but there is a strong push to introduce telemedicine to better serve our patients in rural and outlying areas, and we don't want to be left behind.

**Chapman:** I understand that, Dr. Johnson, but I just don't think we want to do any of this too quickly. Mr. Ash had been very consistent in his message that Geneva had no reason to be an "early adopter" of such systems. As he repeatedly said, "Let all those other health systems make the mistakes first. Then we can learn from their mistakes and make our own decision. And, in the meantime, we can keep doing well what we already do well."

**Johnson:** I appreciate that perspective, Ms. Chapman, but I have to admit, I am a bit more likely to push the envelope than Mr. Ash was. I believe introducing telemedicine would be a great boost for Geneva, helping us to better serve our patients who live far from Longwood and potentially helping us to improve patient satisfaction.

**Chapman:** But don't we already have the ability to provide excellent care for our patients? I'm just not sure what's wrong with what we do now.

**Johnson:** That's true, Ms. Chapman, but I don't think that we're looking far enough ahead. As hospitals and health systems consider new ways to interact with and care for their patient populations, we're going to be left behind. I think it would be in the best interests of Geneva to consider telemedicine on the sooner side.

**Chapman:** Well, Dr. Johnson, I disagree. I tend to believe, "If it ain't broke, don't fix it."

**Johnson:** I understand your concerns, Ms. Chapman. Thanks for sharing them with me. Would you be interested in participating in a task force charged with investigating this opportunity?

**Chapman:** I'm not sure I think this is much of an opportunity. But since you're asking, I guess I'll need to participate.

**Johnson:** Thanks so much, Ms. Chapman. I appreciate your time.

As Johnson headed back to his office, he was once more reminded that none of this was going to be easy. He was especially concerned about resistance from the physicians. Although he was a physician himself, that background did little to improve his credibility when he was making a case from the "dark side" of administration. He decided to seek out Dr. Jodi Smith, the chair of internal medicine, to gauge some of the sentiments from the physicians. He headed to her office to see if he could catch her for a moment.

## A Physician's Perspective

**Johnson:** Hi, Jodi. How's everything going?

**Smith:** Dan. Just the person I wanted to see. I heard a rumor that you were considering telemedicine for Geneva, and I wanted to make sure that it was just a rumor.

**Johnson:** Well, Jodi, the rumor is actually true. I realize I haven't been here at Geneva very long, but I've been working very hard to get a sense of this place before I propose any changes. I also realize that introducing telemedicine capabilities involves planning and careful considerations. At this point, I know there is still considerable work to be done to better understand both Geneva and the opportunities and risks associated with implementing a telemedicine service. However, I strongly believe the future of medicine will require the introduction of telemedicine capabilities to best serve our dispersed patient population.

**Smith:** That may be true, but I'm not sure the physicians really want to do this. Changing from in-person care to providing advice over a computer is an enormous change in how we practice medicine. Also, are you sure that our information technology systems are able to support high-quality telemedicine? I have heard horror stories about how physicians try to provide care remotely but problems with electronic connectivity make the "visit" a series of "can you hear me?" comments.

**Johnson:** That's something we definitely need to consider. I'd like to make consideration of this telemedicine opportunity a major goal for the coming year, and I'd appreciate it if you would consider being on a task force to make this happen. What do you think?

**Smith:** I think introducing telemedicine is a huge risk for Geneva, Dan. But I'm game to learn more. I'd be happy to join your task force.

## Considering the Resistance

Johnson recognized that, in addition to uncovering some attitudes toward telemedicine, he had learned quite a bit about Geneva's organizational culture during these exploratory conversations. The predominant culture seemed comfortable clinging to the status quo, and few individuals were open to the possibility of change. He had felt strong resistance from Chapman and Smith, and he knew that such resistance was a major hurdle that would need to be overcome for the introduction of telemedicine capabilities to proceed and succeed.

Johnson had to plan his next steps carefully. He knew that doctors valued evidence, and he had to build a good case for moving forward with the telemedicine efforts. He felt that learning more about past implementation successes and failures would be helpful, but he also suspected that other valuable information existed of which he was not aware. Johnson decided to recruit a summer resident to help him expand his search for evidence and to help inform the decision about introducing telemedicine capabilities at GHS.

## Case Questions

1. What types of information should the summer resident collect to build the overall evidence case for telemedicine at Geneva? Where should she look to find this evidence?

2. How would introduction of telemedicine capabilities affect physicians? How would it affect organizational control systems at Geneva?

3. What could be learned from speaking with other hospitals and health systems about their experiences with telemedicine? With whom would you like to speak at these organizations?

4. What would be critical success factors associated with the introduction of telemedicine capabilities at Geneva? What steps would you recommend to maximize the likelihood of success?

# ORGANIZATIONAL DESIGN

To understand how the Professional Bureaucracy
functions in its operating core, it is helpful to think of it
as a repertoire of standard programs—in effect, the set of
skills the professionals stand ready to use—which are
applied to predetermined situations, called
contingencies, [which are] also standardized.

—*Henry Mintzberg*

# COMMENTARY

Organizations are people and things combined to achieve an agreed-upon goal in a changing and resource-scarce environment. Organizations have socially defined boundaries. They have a structure, a process, and outcomes. Understanding these concepts and how they relate to one another is at the core of organization theory.

Each of these basic concepts can be subdivided. *People* include workers, professionals, managers, and trustees. *Things* include long-term assets and short-term supplies. *Combination* involves dividing people and equipment into departments and having a hierarchy aligned to the process of work and goals. *Resource scarcity* implies that achievement of goals related to improved health is constrained by the people and things available. The organization's *environment* can be described legally (laws governing behavior), economically (competition or monopoly), socially (how people define their work), and historically (our hospital is located where it is because that's where the donor gave us the land 100 years ago). *Goal achievement* can be estimated by measuring outcomes such as patient census, mortality rates, and vaccinations given. For-profit, not-for-profit, and government-run healthcare organizations (HCOs) have different legal definitions and different goals; for a for-profit organization, for example, long-run shareholder value maximization might be the goal. Organizations create different internal cultures. A faith-based organization may have a different vision and values than a for-profit organization, even though both may achieve their ends through the provision of high-quality care.

"I am a nurse working in the intensive care unit of Memorial Hospital." This simple statement describes an organization, its boundaries and goals, the work being done there, the technology in use, and a point in time. Another way to describe an organization is to explain its scarcities. Consider the statement, "We do what we can do best and let others do what they do best." It is essentially a way of understanding the "make or buy" managerial decisions that define the organization's boundary. "Our hospital needs computers and a food service, but we buy the former and contract out the latter because others can make and do these things better than we can."

Organizations must transform individual goals (e.g., my paycheck, my job satisfaction, my desire to help) into a unified, overall goal or mission. Everyone who is a member of the organization is there because it fulfills his or her personal goals. Keeping a favorable balance of all these personal incentives over time and through changing circumstances in a way that achieves organizational goals is central to the role of management.

## Understanding Organizational Design

Organizational design describes the way that elements of an organization are arranged to meet the organization's goals. These elements include and affect the people and things that are combined in the organization. Mintzberg (1979, 1983) has suggested five basic types of organizational design or structure: simple, machine bureaucracy, professional bureaucracy, divisionalized firm, and "adhocracy" (Mintzberg's term for a mutually adjusting structure). These basic types represent different ways to organize work, and some ways work better than others. However, strictly causal relationships between technology and organizational design, or between environment and design, have not yet been proven.

The basic parts of Mintzberg's organizational types are the strategic apex or top managers, middle management, the technological structure (such as planners and industrial engineers), support staff (such as personnel and security), and the operating core (workers). Each of the five types of organizational design has a different configuration of these five parts. For example, the simple organization (e.g., a doctor's office) has managers, support staff, and an operating core, but little or no technological structure or middle management.

Visually, organizational design can be depicted in an organizational chart showing relationships among these basic parts. Thus, a good organizational chart will illustrate links between and among top managers, middle management, the technological structure, support staff, and the operating core. Examples of organizational charts are provided in Case 20 and Case 26, though charts for other organizations can be considerably more complex.

The key means of organizational coordination vary according to the type of organization, and they include approaches such as direct supervision, work standardization, standardization of professional skills, standardization of outputs, and mutual adjustment (Mintzberg 1983). In a simple organization, direct supervision is the key means of coordination. In a machine bureaucracy, such as a large outpatient department, work standardization is key. In a professional bureaucracy, such as a community hospital, standardization of professional skills is a key means of coordinating the work. In a divisionalized firm, such as a multihospital system, the key means of coordination is the standardization of outputs, such as profits or market share. Finally, in an adhocracy, work is coordinated as the clinicians adjust on the spot to working with one another.

The way work is organized can be influenced by the available physical facilities or by the organization's history and the initial design of its founders.

Many doctors are not employees of hospitals because physicians traditionally have been independent professionals.

According to Mintzberg (1979, 1983), work in the operating core can be organized in one of three ways: by process or occupation (e.g., all nurses report to the director of nursing, all physicians to their department chiefs); by purpose or division, cutting across occupational specialties (e.g., all nurses and physicians report to the local clinical leadership, which may be surgery, women's health, or emergency services); or by both process and purpose, in a matrix organization. Under the matrix method of organization, all nurses report to the clinical leadership of the division for some activities and to the director of nursing for others. Matrix organization solves certain coordination problems by process and by purpose but adds another layer to management, thereby increasing coordination costs. Managers must decide when to use which form of organization and whether the benefits, if any, outweigh the costs.

## Organizational Design and Healthcare Delivery

Today, many hospitals are part of larger systems of care. Some health systems are organized to provide a "continuum of care" that includes primary care, secondary care in community hospitals, tertiary care, home care, and long-term care all in a single market area. Such integrated delivery systems bring increased managerial challenges in planning, organization, and performance measurement. Thirty years ago, a large city may have had 40 independent hospitals. Now, these hospitals have either closed or merged into a few large, competing health systems or networks. These systems are diversifying through vertical integration. Larger hospitals and health systems are looking to purchase physician practices and thereby employ rather than contract with their physician providers. At the same time, industry is going in the opposite direction. Business conglomerates with many subsidiaries and product lines are dropping those that are not performing well and sticking to "core competencies." Will healthcare follow this lead? Will these large integrated systems be dissolved back into their component parts?

Declining hospital occupancy rates, resulting from shorter lengths of stay and fewer admissions, combined with the high fixed costs of hospitals have fueled the competitive frenzy of the last few decades. This competition has led to many new organizational forms, and these changes are far from over. In addition, this competition has compelled closer attention to the wishes of the public and a growing emphasis on market understanding and patient satisfaction.

One new organizational form that has seen tremendous recent growth is the accountable care organization (ACO). The ACO delivery model involves a network of providers that forms an arrangement with a payer or payers in taking responsibility for the quality and costs of care for a particular defined patient population (Fisher and Shortell 2010; Lee et al. 2010; McClellan et al. 2010; Walker et al. 2017). Ownership and operating models for ACOs have varied: They may differ in whether they are led by physicians or by health systems, or whether they have a public sector or private sector focus. Evidence is growing that the ACO model can positively affect quality of care, increase patient-centeredness of care, and reduce costs (CMS 2014; McAlearney, Song, and Hilligoss 2017; Muhlestein 2015; Petersen and Muhlestein 2014). Still, this new model has raised issues around attribution of patients, coordination of care across institutions that are not part of the ACO, and long-term sustainability.

## Variation and Innovation in Organizational Design

Organizational variation is unending, both across the United States and around the globe. Some hospital-centered systems—such as the Hospital Corporation of America, the Voluntary Hospitals of America, or the Veterans Administration—cross healthcare markets. Health maintenance organizations (HMOs) combine the insurance function and provision of care under capitation, which is a reversal of the economic incentives of fee-for-service. Once, one could describe Kaiser Permanente and say, "That is what HMOs are or expect to be." No longer. Point-of-service (POS) plans, which give enrollees a choice of care and payment levels, have become increasingly popular. Under this model, if patients use the core physicians and hospitals, they do not make copayments; if the larger preferred provider list is used, they do. The patient can go out of the network and pay even larger copayments. However, allowing patients a greater choice of providers than they would have in an HMO makes controlling quality and costs more difficult.

Other variations in organizational design are emerging as a result of the information revolution in healthcare. With information about patients available electronically on a timely basis, providers can make some decisions about patient care alternatives without actually being present with the patient. Radiologists can read films and make recommendations remotely. Surgeons can perform surgery remotely using computer-based technologies. Telemedicine is extending the reach of providers into remote and rural areas. Patients want to communicate with their providers via e-mail or via patient portals in an electronic health record (EHR) connected to their provider's organization. Such technological innovations are encouraging HCOs to consider new approaches to healthcare service delivery that can reduce costs and improve the quality of care provided.

Process innovations are also important, as demonstrated by the spread of the Toyota Production System (TPS) or Lean production processes (Chalice

2007; Grunden 2008; Printezis and Gopalakrishnan 2007) and quality improvement methods such as Six Sigma (Trusko et al. 2007). In addition, increasing emphasis has been placed on applying best practices to HCOs, whether such practices are found within healthcare or in other fields. For instance, Fred Lee's (2004) exploration of what hospitals would do differently if they were run by Disney emphasizes the importance of culture in improving the quality of service. Berry and Seltman (2008) similarly present the findings from their extensive research into the Mayo Clinic, highlighting the fundamental roles of organizational culture and shared values in delivering high-quality care.

External organizations and foundations are promoting these efforts by helping HCOs learn improvement techniques, many of which require design changes. The Boston-based Institute for Healthcare Improvement (IHI) made important strides in addressing quality improvement issues, such as the need to reduce the number of medical errors, in its 5 Million Lives Campaign from 2006 to 2008. More recently, it has launched the 100 Million Healthier Lives Campaign as a global initiative to get 100 million people to live healthier lives by 2020. Through its website (www.ihi.org) and educational programs, IHI helps hospitals improve patient safety.

Similarly, projects funded by the Robert Wood Johnson Foundation have emphasized the need to address organizational design and quality-of-care issues. The Urgent Matters program (www.urgentmatters.org), for instance, has focused on the need to improve flow in hospital emergency departments to reduce overcrowding. The Expecting Success program (www.expectingsuccess. org) has explored ways of improving the quality of cardiovascular care provided in inpatient and community settings.

Innovations in organizational design are producing improvements in quality of care and reductions in healthcare costs. Within the United States, the Intermountain Healthcare system has successfully used TPS methods to reduce waste and improve efficiency while increasing the quality of the products it delivers (Jimmerson, Weber, and Sobek 2005). Similar results reported for Virginia Mason Medical Center of Seattle have sparked interest in both the healthcare and business communities (Spear 2005). Geisinger Health System has had success addressing issues such as clinical leadership, electronic health information systems implementation, and alignment of financial incentives to foster organizational innovation (Paulus, Davis, and Steele 2008). In addition, organizational innovations overseas have produced startling results in the area of cardiac care, as demonstrated by two hospitals in India that have been able to perform open-heart surgery for 10 percent of what such surgeries cost in the United States (Richman et al. 2008).

Despite these advancements, healthcare in the United States remains extremely expensive and of variable quality. Barriers to change include misaligned reimbursement systems, regulatory limits on innovation, and the lack of a financial incentive system for the majority of patients to seek higher value in the care they receive. Though the costs of making an international phone call, taking a transcontinental flight, and purchasing stocks are all decreasing in the United States, the healthcare system still has a need for lower-cost materials, equipment, and sites of care.

## Organizational Design and Health

Some cost-cutting measures can be initiated with little change in the way care is organized. For example, physicians can save money by using generic drugs and self-administered pregnancy tests or by substituting physician extenders, such as nurse practitioners and physician assistants, for certain tasks. The next step is to "reengineer" care—to shift emphasis toward the pursuit of disease management or population health management. Reengineering care is based on answering the question, What is the best care for a defined population, and how do we organize to achieve it? For example, how do we keep asthmatics out of the hospital? How do we reduce the amount of work productivity lost because of back pain?

The Chronic Care Model, developed by Edward Wagner of Group Health Cooperative of Puget Sound, addresses the needs associated with caring for people with chronic diseases, and it examines the roles of primary care, care coordination, and the ability of patients to care for themselves (Bodenheimer, Wagner, and Grumbach 2002; Wagner 1998; Wagner et al. 2001). Further, the ACO model may provide a new approach to population health management that engages communities (Hefner et al. 2016).

From an organizational perspective, this type of approach calls for improving the organization of care and achieving measured outcomes. In addition, self-care presents another important opportunity to improve health. Asthma, diabetes, hypertension, and stress can be largely self-managed. Community coaches meeting in church basements with groups of people who have diabetes and are trying to exercise and lose weight may be the future of healthcare focused on wellness in the community.

## The Role of Management in Organizational Design

Organizations are often described at a moment in time, like a photograph. They can also be described as changing over time, like a movie. Describing the organization as a photograph is easier, but the leader's task is to guide the organization over time—to envision a future preferred state and get the organization from its present condition to that future.

Implementing changes in organizational design can be expensive and difficult. Getting individuals and organizations to change their ways can be challenging and time consuming, and political barriers can emerge when powerful individuals or groups openly or covertly resist. One key task of today's senior health executives is to determine which organizational design will best fit tomorrow's environment and figure out how their organizations can get there ahead of others. We are indeed leading in uncertain times, with great rewards for the visionary who understands the environment well enough to predict correctly.

## Discussion Questions

1. What are the forces that lead to different decisions about organizational design? About work design?
2. What role do managers play in influencing design?
3. How does design affect the provision of care in HCOs? How does it affect the quality of care delivered? The cost of care?
4. What are the reasons for considering organizational transformation related to design?
5. How are decisions about information systems related to considerations about organizational design?
6. What are the barriers to change in healthcare organizations, and how can these be overcome?

## References

Berry, L. L., and K. D. Seltman. 2008. *Management Lessons from Mayo Clinic: Inside One of the World's Most Admired Service Organizations.* New York: McGraw-Hill.

Bodenheimer, T., E. Wagner, and K. Grumbach. 2002. "Improving Primary Care for Patients with Chronic Illness: The Chronic Care Model." *Journal of the American Medical Association* 288: 1775–79.

Centers for Medicare & Medicaid Services (CMS). 2014. "Medicare's Delivery System Reform Initiatives Achieve Significant Savings and Quality Improvements—Off to a Strong Start." *CMS Blog.* Published January 30. http://blog.cms.gov/2014/01/30/medicares-delivery-system-reform-initiatives-achieve-significant-savings-and-quality-improvements-off-to-a-strong-start/.

Chalice, R. 2007. *Improving Healthcare Using Toyota Lean Production Methods: 46 Steps for Improvement,* 2nd ed. New York: ASQ Quality Press.

Fisher, E. S., and S. M. Shortell. 2010. "Accountable Care Organizations: Accountable for What, to Whom, and How." *Journal of the American Medical Association* 304 (15): 1715–16.

Grunden, N. 2008. *The Pittsburgh Way to Efficient Healthcare: Improving Patient Care Using Toyota Based Methods.* New York: Productivity Press.

Hefner, J., B. Hilligoss, C. Siek, D. M. Walker, L. Sova, P. H. Song, and A. S. McAlearney. 2016. "Meaningful Engagement of ACOs with Communities: The New Population Health Management." *Medical Care* 54 (11): 970–76.

Jimmerson, C., D. Weber, and D. K. Sobek II. 2005. "Reducing Waste and Errors: Piloting Lean Principles at Intermountain Healthcare." *Joint Commission Journal on Quality and Patient Safety* 31 (5): 249–57.

Lee, F. 2004. *If Disney Ran Your Hospital: 9½ Things You Would Do Differently.* Bozeman, MT: Second River Healthcare Press.

Lee, T. H., L. P. Casalino, E. S. Fisher, and G. R. Wilensky. 2010. "Creating Accountable Care Organizations." *New England Journal of Medicine* 363 (15): e23.

McAlearney, A. S., P. Song, and B. Hilligoss. 2017. "Private Sector Accountable Care Organization Development: A Qualitative Study." *American Journal of Managed Care* 23 (3): 151–58.

McClellan, M., A. N. McKethan, J. L. Lewis, J. Roski, and E. S. Fisher. 2010. "A National Strategy to Put Accountable Care into Practice." *Health Affairs* 29 (5): 982–90.

Mintzberg, H. 1983. *Structure in Fives: Designing Effective Organizations.* Englewood Cliffs, NJ: Prentice Hall.

———. 1979. *The Structuring of Organizations.* Englewood Cliffs, NJ: Prentice Hall.

Muhlestein, D. 2015. "Growth and Dispersion of Accountable Care Organizations in 2015." *Health Affairs Blog.* Published March 31. http://health affairs.org/blog/2015/03/31/growth-and-dispersion-of-accountable-care-organizations-in-2015-2/.

Paulus, R. A., K. Davis, and G. D. Steele. 2008. "Continuous Innovation in Healthcare: Implications of the Geisinger Experience." *Health Affairs* 27 (5): 1235–45.

Petersen, M., and D. Muhlestein. 2014. "ACO Results: What We Know So Far." *Health Affairs Blog.* Published May 30. http://healthaffairs.org/blog/2014/05/30/aco-results-what-we-know-so-far/.

Printezis, A., and M. Gopalakrishnan. 2007. "Can a Production System Reduce Medical Errors in Healthcare?" *Quality Management in Healthcare* 16 (3): 226–38.

Richman, B. D., K. Udayakumar, W. Mitchell, and K. A. Schulman. 2008. "Lessons from India in Organizational Innovation: A Tale of Two Heart Hospitals." *Health Affairs* 27 (5): 1260–70.

Spear, S. 2005. "Fixing Healthcare from the Inside, Today." *Harvard Business Review* 83 (9): 78–91.

Trusko, B. E., C. Pexton, J. Harrington, and P. Gupta. 2007. *Improving Healthcare Quality and Cost with Six Sigma.* New York: FT Press.

Wagner, E. H. 1998. "Chronic Disease Management: What Will It Take to Improve Care for Chronic Illness?" *Efficient Clinical Practice* 1 (1): 2–4.

Wagner, E. H., B. T. Austin, C. Davis, M. Hindmarsh, J. Schaefer, and A. Bonomi. 2001. "Improving Chronic Illness Care: Translating Evidence into Action." *Health Affairs* 20 (6): 64–78.

Walker, D., J. Hefner, L. Sova, B. Hilligoss, P. Song, and A. S. McAlearney. 2017. "Implementing Accountable Care Organizations: Lessons from a Qualitative Analysis of Four Private-Sector Organizations." *Journal of Healthcare Management*. In press.

## Recommended Readings

Berenson, R. A., T. Hammons, D. N. Gans, S. Zuckerman, K. Merrell, W. S. Underwood, and A. F. Williams. 2008. "A House Is Not a Home: Keeping Patients at the Center of Practice Redesign." *Health Affairs* 27 (5): 1219–30.

Bohmer, R. M. J. 2009. *Designing Care*. Boston: Harvard Business Press.

Bush, R. W. 2007. "Reducing Waste in US Health Care Systems." *Journal of the American Medical Association* 297 (8): 871–74.

Casalino, L. P., E. A. November, R. A. Berenson, and H. H. Pham. 2008. "Hospital–Physician Relations: Two Tracks and the Decline of the Voluntary Medical Staff Model." *Health Affairs* 27 (5): 1305–14.

Christensen, C. M., Grossman, J. H., and J. Hwang. 2009. *The Innovator's Prescription*. New York: McGraw-Hill Publishers. (Chapters 4 and 5 are especially appropriate.)

Conrad, D. A., and W. L. Dowling. 1990. "Vertical Integration in Health Services: Theory and Managerial Implication." *Healthcare Management Review* 15 (4): 9–22.

Cussell, C. K., J. M. Ludden, and G. M. Moon. 2000. "Perceptions of Barriers to High-Quality Palliative Care in Hospitals." *Health Affairs* 19 (5): 166–72.

Gerteis, M., S. Edgman-Levitan, J. Daley, and T. L. Delbanco (eds.). 2002. *Through the Patient's Eyes: Understanding and Promoting Patient-Centered Care*. San Francisco: Jossey-Bass.

Glouberman, S., and H. Mintzberg. 2001a. "Managing the Care of Health and the Cure of Disease—Part I: Differentiation." *Healthcare Management Review* 26 (1): 56–69, discussion 87–89.

———. 2001b. "Managing the Care of Health and the Cure of Disease—Part II: Integration." *Healthcare Management Review* 26 (1): 70–84, discussion 87–89.

Griffith, J. R., and K. R. White. 2010. "Foundations of Excellent Care." In *Reaching Excellence in Healthcare Management*, 81–103. Chicago: Health Administration Press.

Hearld, L. R., J. A. Alexander, I. Fraser, and H. J. Jiang. 2008. "How Do Hospital Organizational Structure and Processes Affect Quality of Care?" *Medical Care Research & Review* 65 (3): 259–99.

Herzlinger, R. 2000. "Market-Driven, Focused Healthcare: The Role of Managers." *Frontiers of Health Services Management* 16 (3): 3–12.

Jha, A. K., J. B. Perlin, K. Kizer, and R. A. Dudley. 2003. "Effects of the Transformation of the Veterans Affairs Healthcare System on the Quality of Care." *New England Journal of Medicine* 310 (22): 1477–80.

Kilo, C. M. 1999. "Improving Care Through Collaboration." *Pediatrics* 103 (1): 384–92.

Kimberly, J. R., and E. Minvielle. 2003. "Quality as an Organizational Problem." In *Advances in Healthcare Organizational Theory*, edited by S. S. Mick and M. E. Wyttenbach, 205–32. San Francisco: Jossey-Bass.

Lathrop, J. P. 1993. *Restructuring Healthcare: The Patient-Focused Paradigm*. San Francisco: Jossey-Bass.

Lawrence, D. 2002. *From Chaos to Care*. Cambridge, MA: Perseus.

McAlearney, A. S. 2003. *Population Health Management: Strategies to Improve Outcomes*. Chicago: Health Administration Press.

McAlearney, A. S., K. Murray, C. Sieck, J. J. Lin, B. Bellacera, and N. A. Bickell. 2016. "The Challenge of Improving Breast Cancer Care Coordination in Safety Net Hospitals: Barriers, Facilitators and Opportunities." *Medical Care* 54 (2): 147–54.

Mehrotra, A., M. C. Wang, J. R. Lave, J. L. Adams, and E. A. McGlynn. 2008. "Retail Clinics, Primary Care Physicians, and Emergency Departments: A Comparison of Patients' Visits." *Health Affairs* 27 (5): 1272–82.

Paulus, R. A., K. Davis, and G. D. Steele. 2008. "Continuous Innovation in Healthcare: Implications of the Geisinger Experience." *Health Affairs* 27 (5): 1235–45.

Pham, H. H., J. M. Grossman, G. Cohen, and T. Bodenheimer. 2008. "Hospitalists and Care Transitions: The Divorce of Inpatient and Outpatient Care." *Health Affairs* 27 (5): 1315–27.

Richter, J., A. S. McAlearney, and M. Pennell. 2016. "The Influence of Organizational Factors on Patient Safety: Examining Successful Handoffs in Health Care." *Health Care Management Review* 41 (1): 32–41.

Robinson, J. C., and L. P. Casalino. 1996. "Vertical Integration and Organizational Networks in Healthcare." *Health Affairs* 15 (1): 7–22.

Rosenberg, C. 1987. *The Care of Strangers*. New York: Basic Books.

Rundall, T. G., S. M. Shortell, M. C. Wang, L. Casalino, T. Bodenheimer, R. R. Gillies, J. A. Schmittdiel, N. Oswald, and J. C. Robinson. 2002. "As Good As It Gets? Chronic Care Management with Nine Leading US Physician Organizations." *British Medical Journal* 325 (26): 958–61.

Scott, R. L., L. Aiken, D. Mechanic, and J. Moravcsik. 1995. "Organizational Aspects of Caring." *Milbank Quarterly* 73 (1): 77–95.

Smith, H. L. 1955. "Two Lines of Authority Are One Too Many." *Modern Hospitals* 84 (3): 59–64.

Villagra, V. G. 2004. "Integrating Disease Management into the Outpatient Delivery System During and After Managed Care." *Health Affairs* Web Exclusives W4 (May 19): 281–83.

Walker, D., J. Hefner, L. Sova, B. Hilligoss, P. Song, and A. S. McAlearney. 2017. "Implementing Accountable Care Organizations: Lessons from a Qualitative Analysis of Four Private-Sector Organizations." *Journal of Healthcare Management.* In press.

Woolf, S. H. 2004. "Patient Safety Is Not Enough: Targeting Quality Improvements to Optimize the Health of the Population." *Annals of Internal Medicine* 140: 33–36.

Woolhandler, S., T. Campbell, and D. U. Himmelstein. 2003. "Costs of Healthcare Administration in the United States and Canada Hospitals." *New England Journal of Medicine* 349 (8): 760–75.

Zhou, Y. Y., M. H. Kanter, J. J. Wang, and T. Garrido. 2010. "Improved Quality at Kaiser Permanente Through E-mail Between Physicians and Patients." *Health Affairs* 29 (7): 1370–75.

Zuckerman, H. S., D. W. Hilberman, R. M. Andersen, L. R. Burns, J. A. Alexander, and P. Torrens. 1998. "Physicians and Organizations: Strange Bedfellows or a Marriage Made in Heaven?" *Frontiers of Health Services Management* 14 (3): 3–34.

# THE CASES

In healthcare, discussion about organizational design occurs at four levels. The first is the patient care level. New questions are being asked: How do we organize the best care for asthma or hypertension or back pain? Answering this question requires a definition of "best," data on the population served, a team of staff members working to achieve the identified goals, and management support. How can the physical design of our organization improve the care and service we provide to patients? Case 25, "An Evidence-Based Design for Waterford Hospital," raises some of the issues associated with facilities design and implications for patient care, and Case 27, "We Need a Sign," presents issues related to physical design for both staff and patients in a hospital.

The second level of discussion involves issues of the design of the hospital, nursing home, and other care organizations. How do we put the component departments together? *Restructuring*, *reengineering*, *downsizing*, and *rightsizing* are the jargon terms of the moment. Case 20, "Improving Organizational Development in Health Services," presents the issues associated with centralization versus decentralization at both the health system and service line levels. Case 21, "Implementing the Office of Patient and Customer Experience at Northwell Health®," discusses the challenge of changing organizational culture to increase accountability and ensure patient-centered care. Case 22, "What Makes a Patient-Centered Medical Home?," presents the challenges associated with becoming a patient-centered medical home (PCMH).

Across the United States, hospitals, clinics, and insurers are grouping themselves together as systems of care, and this grouping strategy represents the third level of discussion about organizational design. An urban area where 30 separate hospitals once stood may now have three or four competing groups of hospitals within both regional and national health systems. The competing entities may be nonprofit, investor owned, or a mix of both. Case 23, "Quality Improvement in an Accountable Care Organization," focuses on quality improvement issues in the accountable care organization (ACO) model.

One reason behind this grouping strategy is the recognition that, with managed care and alternative financing arrangements, we will need fewer hospital beds in the future than we now have. The leaders of a single hospital left outside of a group might wonder if their hospital will be one that disappears. One way mergers occur is through the sale of a not-for-profit hospital to a for-profit group. The sale price plus the not-for-profit hospital's existing endowment are put into a nonprofit foundation. The income from this foundation's endowment is used to achieve the charitable and philanthropic goals of the original not-for-profit hospital, and the hospital, now part of the for-profit organization, is run along business lines in a competitive environment. In the rush to become one of the three or four biggest groups in an area, a health system often bases its organizational design decisions on expediency, comfort level, and speed rather than organizing to provide expeditious, excellent care. The local rush for size is of vital importance in a market oversupplied with hospitals. Any one urban hospital priced too high or of only average quality can be ignored by insurance providers negotiating contracts. For such a hospital to exist, it will have to accept whatever price the insurance providers choose to offer, which will not be high. However, if the system is large enough and includes popular, specialized, and prestigious hospitals, all insurance providers and managed care systems must deal with it. As a result, such a system will not be a "price taker" but a "price giver." It can charge full price for its services because the insurer or HMO has no choice. Case 28, "How Disruptive Should We Be?," raises the question of whether a health system should change its business model and become a focused factory to respond to market forces and patient population trends.

The fourth level of organizational design is the state or national policy level. One notable effort to change the context of healthcare delivery in the United States was the Clinton administration's unsuccessful national health plan initiative. Another was the Obama administration's passage of the Affordable Care Act. However, the current devolution of Medicaid-related decision making from the federal to the state level will also change the context of care. Some states, such as Hawaii, Oregon, and Massachusetts, have provided interesting examples of system reform, while the state of California has struggled along similar lines. Resolution of the current healthcare reform debate will undoubtedly lead to different organizational reactions, based on changes in priorities and reimbursement levels. Moving beyond the United States, Case 29, "Measuring Systematic Change Across One Health Economy in London," discusses similar issues from the perspective of the National Health Service in the United Kingdom.

The interaction of all four levels of organization and system design makes healthcare delivery a most lively arena. The field is creating unprecedented opportunities for creative leadership and the development of entirely new ways of providing better care at lower cost. New business models are being introduced, such as convenient care clinics or retail clinics in pharmacies and grocery stores, and existing organizations are being challenged to respond to competition from these new sources of care.

The coordination of many professional workers with varying skills, views of the world, and perceptions of what needs to be done, combined with the impact of licensing statutes, lies at the heart of the new designs for health services organizations. Work in large health services organizations can be organized in a variety of ways—by task or purpose, by facility, or by client group served. Case 26, "Matrix or Mess?," describes a situation in which the way work is organized creates confusion for the individual employee. Often, several different organizing principles operate in the same organization, sometimes appropriately and sometimes for historical reasons. As Clibbon and Sachs (1969) have pointed out, a laboratory is a place, obstetrics is a service focused on a health condition (i.e., pregnancy), outpatients are people, dietary is a service, intensive care is a need, day care is a category of residential status, radiology is a group of techniques, and rehabilitation is a purpose.

Many HCOs are structured in a way that is more appropriate for economic and market conditions of the time when the organizations were founded than for conditions as they are today. Organizational structure is determined in part by the nature of the organization's work, its physical facilities, its history, and the culture of the society and of like institutions. As a result, questions about what structure is truly best for a particular organization or service remain common. Case 24, "Integrating Rehabilitation Services into the Visiting Nurse Service of America," raises both structural and cultural issues associated with needed changes in organizational design.

## Reference

Clibbon, S., and M. L. Sachs. 1969. "Healthcare Facilities: An Alternative to Bailiwick Planning in Patient Fostering Spaces." *New Physician* 18: 462–71.

# CASE 20
# Improving Organizational Development in Health Services

*Ann Scheck McAlearney and Rebecca Schmale*

## Who, What, and Where?

John Shea, CEO and president of Worthington Health System (WHS), needed some time to think. He had been leading WHS for ten years and was contemplating the legacy he wanted to leave. WHS, based in the Midwest, comprised four hospitals, a home health company, and an ambulatory care service line (for basic information about the system, see exhibits 20.1 and 20.2). The system had been formed 12 years ago when two local community hospitals combined forces. The two freestanding hospitals each served distinct patient populations, with 600-bed Lincoln Hospital located downtown and 800-bed Riverview Hospital in a nearby suburb. Rather than take the name of either hospital, the organizing group elected to create a new, neutral name for the health system, and each individual hospital kept its original name. Shea was hired soon after the system's formation, so he had personally experienced most of the changes WHS had navigated.

Since the formation of WHS, the rapidly changing healthcare market and shifting patient demographics had presented a series of opportunities for WHS. Shea had successfully managed the acquisition of two other local hospitals for WHS when another local system dissolved, and he had extended the reach of WHS to the adjacent county by forming a strategic alliance with Graystone Memorial Hospital (see exhibit 20.3). Additional market changes led to the formation of Worthington Home Care and the creation of a network of ambulatory care centers that expanded WHS's reach. WHS was financially strong, and it enjoyed a positive reputation in the area, despite competition from two other health systems and several newly developed specialty hospitals.

Shea's continuing concern was the lack of "systemness" within the broad WHS system. Building community awareness of WHS as a health system had taken quite some time, and patients were still primarily loyal to the original flagship hospital, Riverview, rather than to WHS. This loyalty was also evident among employees. The Riverview staff identified with Riverview Hospital, not

| **EXHIBIT 20.1** Worthington Health System Facts at a Glance | | |
| --- | --- | --- |
| Employees | 10,400 |
| Physicians | 1,800 |
| Volunteers | 2,500 |
| Hospitals | 5 |
| Net patient revenue | $1.2 billion |
| Patient days | 370,000 |
| Community benefit | $37 million |
| Outpatient visits | 1.1 million |
| Average daily census | 960 |
| Emergency room visits | 260,000 |
| Ambulatory centers | 6 |
| Home health visits | 125,000 |

| Care Sites | Type | Beds | Employees |
|---|---|---|---|
| Riverview Hospital | Tertiary | 800 | 4,600 |
| Lincoln Hospital | Trauma | 600 | 2,980 |
| Graystone Memorial Hospital | Community | 200 | 685 |
| Mount Rising Hospital | Community | 124 | 512 |
| Fairland Memorial Hospital | Community | 95 | 450 |
| Worthington Home Care | Home health | — | 440 |
| Ambulatory care centers (6) | Health centers, urgent care, out-patient surgery | — | 690 |

**EXHIBIT 20.2**
Worthington Health System Facilities

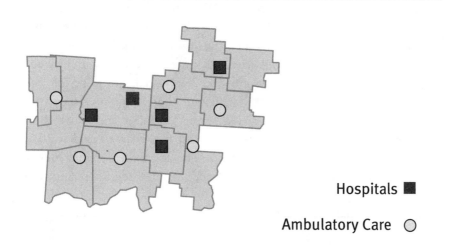

**EXHIBIT 20.3**
Worthington Health System Service Area

Hospitals ■

Ambulatory Care ○

WHS, and the Lincoln Hospital staff exhibited the same silo loyalty. When Shea had arrived at WHS, he was thrilled by the challenge of creating a true system out of the previously competing entities, but as he now reflected, he had not succeeded. He wanted his legacy to include a shift in the WHS organizational culture to one of system-focused thinking rather than entity-oriented decision making.

Several functions had been centralized in the past few years to achieve economies of scale and reduce redundancies within the system. The first functions to be centralized under the corporate umbrella were finance and supply chain. Greg Hanson, the chief financial officer, was a strong leader, and within one year, centralization saved the system more than $200 million. Some resistance to the centralization had existed, but the savings quickly made the decision difficult to dispute.

Given the current financial strength of WHS (see exhibit 20.4), Shea realized that he had an opportunity to focus on the goal of enhancing system-focused thinking. Because entity culture seemed so prevalent, Shea knew he must engage his employees to achieve systemness. He also knew that education, especially leadership development, could play a key role. One of Shea's goals was to advance WHS as a learning organization. Pursuit of this goal had led to two recent hires in the areas of organizational development and human resources (HR), and both Fiona Sinclair and Blake Snowdon seemed to sense the lack of systemness at WHS quite quickly. Shea scheduled a meeting with Sinclair and Snowdon to introduce his ideas.

## Behind the Scenes

As system vice president of organizational development, Sinclair had spent the past two months getting to know WHS and its various entities. She had come to WHS from outside the healthcare industry and had repeatedly been surprised by how "behind" she found the health system. Even basic education and training functions were still delivered at the entity level, with little sense of organizational identity at the system level. Yet Sinclair saw hope for improvement, as signaled by her own recruitment and the apparent interest of the CEO.

Snowdon, the director of HR, shared Sinclair's perspective about the fragmented nature of WHS (see the organizational chart in exhibit 20.5). He was also struck by the seeming lack of awareness about the potential for strategic human resources management to help reduce this fragmentation. Snowdon had

**EXHIBIT 20.4**
Worthington Health System Total Operating Growth

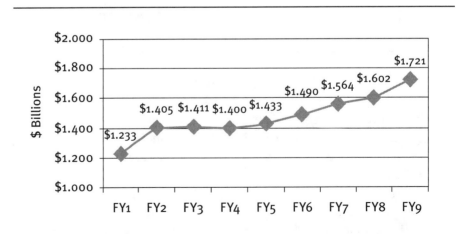

come to WHS three months ago from a smaller system based in California, and he now saw how good he had had it. Snowdon found that WHS was not a fully aligned health system that saw human resources as a strategic capability, but rather a collection of individual entities that appeared to compete among themselves for corporate-level attention. Many Riverview staff came across as arrogant because they believed they worked for the "best" hospital in the system. In contrast, Lincoln staff prized themselves on their ability to respond to the needs of the surrounding urban community, despite a largely unfavorable payer mix and staggering use of the emergency department. Snowdon had not yet characterized the cultures of the Mount Rising or Fairland hospitals, but he felt certain they were as entrenched and individualized as those of Riverview and Lincoln.

Given their similar interests and start dates, Sinclair and Snowdon were in frequent contact. Organizationally, the department of human resources reported to the chief operating officer (COO), and Snowdon was its senior

**EXHIBIT 20.5**
Worthington Health System Organizational Chart

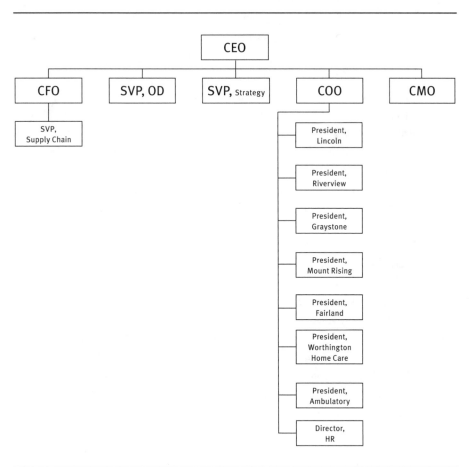

*Note:* CEO = chief executive officer; CFO = chief financial officer; CMO = chief medical officer; COO = chief operating officer; HR = human resources; OD = organizational development; SVP = senior vice president.

executive. The area of organizational development, however, was new for WHS, and Sinclair had been hired with the charge to create and build the department as she saw fit. She reported directly to CEO John Shea, but she understood the strategic importance of close ties to human resources if she was going to be able to accomplish anything with respect to organizational development.

In Sinclair's previous position, she had directed the development of a corporate university to centralize training and development for a large organization. Sinclair believed this model held promise for a health system such as WHS, but she was aware of the challenges associated with centralizing a previously decentralized and tightly controlled function. Coincidentally, Snowdon's previous role as director of human resources for a smaller health system had involved an evaluation of the corporate university model, but that system had rejected it. Instead, Snowdon's role had focused on building credibility for human resources as a strategic capability of the health system. The emphasis was on making targeted investments in strategic human resources capabilities, such as developing hiring managers' abilities to use behavioral interviewing techniques and linking individual performance evaluations to the health system's overall performance through use of a balanced scorecard.

Getting together to prepare for their meeting with Shea, Sinclair and Snowdon discussed their initial assessments of WHS. They agreed that WHS was a disjointed collection of individual entities with little loyalty to the system, but they also agreed that a fragmented culture could change. The key, they felt, would be in centralizing the education and training function for WHS at the corporate level, but they knew this idea would be met with resistance from all entities. They also knew that a move to centralize any function within WHS would fail without the commitment and support of the CEO.

## The First Meeting

Shea decided to meet with Sinclair and Snowdon in Sinclair's office, signaling his willingness to move outside the suite of executive offices to collaborate with others who were experts in their own fields. He had purposely not created an agenda for the meeting, and he instead had proposed this as a "conversation" about WHS. Shea opened the meeting with a basic question: "What can we do to make WHS feel like a system?"

Neither Sinclair nor Snowdon was timid, and they had previously agreed to be completely honest and direct with Shea. They described their early observations of WHS and the component entities, and they presented their collective assessment that, beyond the common logo and centralized payroll system, almost nothing bound WHS together as a system. Even though WHS had several corporate-level functions, such as strategic planning and marketing, the individual hospitals often seemed to replicate these functions in-house to ensure entity-level control. Particularly troublesome, Sinclair and Snowdon reported, was the training and development function; however, they also noted that this area presented a tremendous opportunity to bring WHS together.

Although Shea knew that WHS suffered from the entity-focused territoriality common to many US healthcare systems, he had been unaware of the magnitude of the problem. He was struck by the financial implications of hospital-based duplication of services. With education and training alone, duplication of training programs, evaluation processes, tracking systems, and even trainers was costing the system thousands of dollars. However, Shea was also aware that each hospital entity took training and development seriously as an entity-level capability. He knew the hospitals prided themselves on providing continuing education programs for physicians and nurses that were appropriately tailored to the hospital's perceived needs. Any move to centralize what was considered an important organizational competency would be perceived negatively and would likely be resisted. Shea knew that this issue would have to be evaluated thoroughly and, if accepted, introduced carefully.

## The Charge

Shea liked the notion of centralizing the training and development function at WHS, and he believed it could help him achieve his goal of transforming WHS into a cohesive system and learning organization. Yet he needed to be convinced that this approach could work, and that it would be worth the investment. He felt Sinclair and Snowdon were the appropriate individuals to lead the assessment process, and their newness within the system might help them uncover challenges or concerns less obvious to someone who had worked at WHS for a longer period.

Talking with Sinclair and Snowdon, Shea outlined what he would need to make his decision. First, he would need a list of the current financial and nonfinancial costs associated with decentralized training and development. Though Shea knew that Sinclair and Snowdon would not be able to cost out everything, he felt that a list and general estimate of costs could be sufficient for his purposes. Second, Shea wanted options. If, as they suspected, the centralized option was going to prove favorable, he needed to know what it could mean for WHS. Were there alternative models for centralized training and development? If so, which would be appropriate at WHS? What costs would be associated with this type of change? Further, how long would this organizational change take to implement? What would be the "value-add" of a centralized department for the entities? How could programs such as orientation, leadership development, and clinical management training reinforce a new way of thinking beyond the boundaries of each entity?

Shea asked Sinclair and Snowdon to collect the necessary data and prepare to present them to WHS senior leadership at the end of the next quarter. This timeline would give them several months to do their background research, followed by another couple of weeks to refine their assumptions and properly frame the results of their research. Shea also offered to participate in regularly scheduled meetings so that he could remain informed about their ongoing findings and any challenges they encountered. The meeting left all three feeling mutually energized, but Sinclair and Snowdon knew they had to get started right away.

## Considering the Options

After Shea left Sinclair's office, Snowdon remained to continue the discussion with Sinclair. Their first task was to plan for the work they would have to do in the coming months. In particular, they wanted to determine the scope of the project and try to get a sense of how to frame the alternatives.

Based on the preliminary conversations they had had with each other and their knowledge of the organizational development and training literature, Sinclair and Snowdon were able to outline six separate alternatives that varied by level of centralization and magnitude of organizational changes required:

1. Centralize training and development within the existing department of human resources.
2. Centralize training and development within the new department of organizational development.
3. Centralize training and development with the creation of a new structure, a corporate university, housed with the new department of organizational development.
4. Maintain decentralized delivery of training, but centralize the development function within the existing department of human resources.
5. Outsource training and development to a third-party vendor.
6. Maintain the status quo with decentralized training and development.

Given these six alternatives, Sinclair and Snowdon next had to consider what information they needed to collect to assist Shea in the decision-making process. Their biggest task was to perform an organizational assessment of WHS as a whole with respect to training and development. In particular, they needed to determine what currently was going on in education, training, and development, including where these activities occurred, who or what department provided them, and how they were delivered. With regard to education and training, they were curious about such factors as whether any programs were offered online, whether some areas of the organization collaborated with others, and how clinical training and continuing education were delivered. With regard to development, they wanted to know if any formal system was in place to track development activities, if employees in any entity or area were required to create professional development plans that could be monitored, and whether developmental programs were tied to annual performance evaluations.

Another important part of the assessment was to identify key stakeholders in the areas of training and development for each health system entity. Sinclair and Snowdon knew that organizational politics had a powerful influence on the support for or resistance to any initiative that required change. As a result, they needed to identify important decision makers within each entity and, ideally, recruit organizational champions who could help them with any change process.

Finally, to fully evaluate the different alternatives, Sinclair and Snowdon would have to develop some projections about costs associated with current operations (the sixth alternative) in comparison with the five other alternatives they had outlined. Shea had mentioned nonfinancial costs associated with training and development in addition to financial costs, so Sinclair and Snowdon needed to consider those along with the financial and nonfinancial gains that could be accrued with each alternative.

## Building the Case for Change

Shea was known for his ability to make quick decisions and then back his decisions with resource support. However, Sinclair and Snowdon knew they needed not only financial resources but also organizational commitment to ensure success for this initiative. They were excited to move forward with their ideas about centralizing the training and development function for WHS, but they knew they needed to build their case carefully.

## Case Questions

1. In addition to the items listed in the case, what other information would need to be collected to fully evaluate the centralization/ decentralization decision?
2. What should be included in developing a financial analysis of this decision?
3. What would be the nonfinancial arguments for or against centralizing training and development at Worthington Health System?
4. With whom should Sinclair and Snowdon speak when considering the impact of each alternative?

5. How might physicians and nurses be affected by the various alternatives?

6. What critical success factors would be associated with the pursuit of a centralization alternative?

7. How could a centralized organizational development department support a culture of systemness at WHS?

# CASE 21

## Implementing the Office of Patient and Customer Experience at Northwell Health®

*Sofia Agoritsas, Agnes Barden, and Sven Gierlinger*

Northwell Health® was founded in 1997 through the merger of the North Shore Health System and the Long Island Jewish (LIJ) Medical Center. Originally known as the North Shore–LIJ Health System, it took on its current name in 2016. Since its founding, the health system has grown to include 21 hospitals, more than 450 ambulatory sites, medical and graduate nursing schools, a research institute, and key clinical service lines across the New York region. As the system grew, each entity within the organization had been recognized for clinical excellence, but unique cultures existed at each site. At no point in the organization's history had a unifying, overarching culture extended across the entire health system.

Understanding the importance of defining and developing a common culture, the system's president and CEO, Michael Dowling, has led the organization to establish a unifying, overarching culture that extended across the health system. On May 2, 2015, he invited more than 4,000 organizational leaders to a leadership rally, titled "Success Is a Reflection of Leadership," at the Theatre at Madison Square Garden in New York City. There, Mr. Dowling charged the leaders to drive patient experience as a strategic priority. He challenged them to reach the 90th percentile in national patient experience rankings by the end of 2019.

At the rally, Mr. Dowling introduced Sven Gierlinger, the new chief patient experience officer (CXO), as one of the event's featured speakers. Mr. Gierlinger had a track record of distinguished performance and proven success in both the healthcare and hospitality industries. He had experience at Henry Ford Health System as well as the Ritz-Carlton Hotel Company, the luxury hotel brand recognized for its world-class service excellence.

## First Steps

As CXO, Mr. Gierlinger was the executive appointed to guide the change management process so that the organization could achieve its goal of patient satisfaction rankings in the 90th percentile. He was also responsible for leading the Office of Patient and Customer Experience (OPCE), a new structure that was being established within the organization to support the change. Mr. Gierlinger and his team were tasked with translating concepts of patient experience and patient relations into actionable behaviors. Part of this effort involved transforming the organization's focus on clinical excellence into one that demonstrated a strong culture of world-class patient- and family-centered care.

Mr. Gierlinger recruited Agnes Barden, DNP, RN, as OPCE vice president to help him lead and operationalize the cultural transformation across Northwell Health®. Prior to taking this role, Ms. Barden was the associate executive director for patient experience at LIJ Medical Center, where she had increased Hospital Consumer Assessment of Healthcare Providers and Systems (HCAHPS) scores from the 32nd percentile in 2011 to the 93rd percentile by the beginning of 2014. Thanks to her leadership in this area, LIJ Medical Center in 2014 was honored nationally by Press Ganey with the Commitment to Excellence Award, recognizing it as the academic medical center that made the greatest improvement in patient experience.

Together, Mr. Gierlinger and Ms. Barden set out to lead, influence, and inspire executive and operational teams across the highly matrixed and complex Northwell Health® organization. Their combined skill sets and expertise incorporated evidence-based knowledge specific to patient experience measurement tools, organizational change management, industry best practices, and workforce engagement and performance. They were aware that partnerships between the OPCE and other parts of the organization were more likely to be sustained if OPCE leaders provided a clear mission with realistic expectations, communicated regularly, shared responsibility for decision making, implemented rules for management, and recognized the successes of the people involved. These tasks would not be easy to achieve on their own; they became even more challenging when OPCE leaders were trying to define the culture of the organization and help guide transformational change concurrently.

## Articulating a Mission, Values, and Behavioral Expectations for the OPCE

One of the initial steps in establishing the OPCE was to identify and define its mission statement and to ensure that the statement aligned with the mission and vision of Northwell Health®.[1] The OPCE mission statement needed to sum up the direction of the unit and outline the goals that it and its leaders would aspire to accomplish. Every interaction an employee has with a patient, family member, visitor, or colleague reflects on the Northwell Health® mission. The following mission was thus established for OPCE:

Inspiring, challenging and leading Northwell Health® to design and deliver experiences our patients and customers desire

Connected to this mission, the values of the OPCE were articulated with the understanding that every role, every person, and every moment matter. Patients and customers are the center of everything the OPCE does, making *respect* and *empathy* critical, while also aligning with Northwell's core organizational values of *caring, excellence, innovation,* and *integrity.*

Next, OPCE had to articulate behavioral expectations that were aligned with its mission, values, goals, and objectives. Historically, the organization's behavioral expectations included four core behaviors for individual staff: (1) execution, (2) enabling change, (3) organizational awareness, and (4) developing self.[2] These four core behaviors, as defined in exhibit 21.1, were embedded in annual performance evaluations for all staff.

Noting a gap between the four behavioral expectations and the articulated values, Mr. Gierlinger and Ms. Barden worked with Northwell Health® human resources talent acquisition and Northwell's Center for Learning and Innovation to add two more behavioral expectations, shown in exhibit 21.2.

**EXHIBIT 21.1**
Behavioral Expectations for Northwell Health® Employees

| Behavioral Expectation | Definition |
|---|---|
| **Execution** | Displays technical and functional expertise. Takes ownership of work, structures job tasks, and maintains appropriate pace in handling multiple deadlines to achieve excellence. |
| **Enabling change** | Willingly adapts to shifting business needs and seeks opportunities to champion new processes and ideas. Anticipates and responds to change to improve work outcomes. |
| **Organizational awareness** | Understands how to overcome obstacles and ably works through the realities of a large healthcare organization. Applies best approaches to achieve business goals. |
| **Developing self** | Takes consistent action to increase knowledge and skills. Embraces challenging assignments and seeks learning opportunities to enhance performance. |

*Source:* Northwell Health® (2016).

| Behavioral Expectation | Definition |
|---|---|
| **Patient/ customer focus** | Always anticipates and exceeds the expressed and unexpressed needs of others. Builds strong relationships and delivers patient-/customer-centric solutions. |
| **Teamwork** | Inspires one another to work together to achieve organizational goals. Creates feeling of belonging and strong team morale. |

**EXHIBIT 21.2**
New Behavioral Expectations for Northwell Health® Employees

*Source:* Northwell Health® (2017a).

Starting in 2016, these new behavioral expectations were embedded into annual performance evaluations for all employees. Furthermore, competency levels for the two new expectations were thoroughly articulated, ranging from "significant improvement required" to "exceptional demonstration" (see exhibit 21.3). Clear identification of the new expectations was one of the first systemwide drivers set in place to increase accountability for each employee. As employees met these expectations, they would feel increased ownership of the improvement effort, a stronger link with the organization's culture, and a heightened awareness of the work environment.

## A Framework Is Developed: The Culture of CARE

The Culture of CARE—which stands for Connectedness, Awareness, Respect, and Empathy—is Northwell's framework for achieving the organization's mission, values, and behavioral expectations. Each component supports world-class service or the ability to exceed patient or customer expectations. The components are defined as follows:

- Connectedness—making a psychological or emotional bond between people
- Awareness—being mindful of oneself as well as the present situation and the patient's/customer's expressed or unexpressed needs
- Respect—demonstrating consideration or thoughtfulness toward patients/customers
- Empathy—the ability to understand and relate to the feelings of patients/customers from their points of view

Northwell Health® has labeled the Culture of CARE as its "tangible" culture, representing the way constituents of the organization treat colleagues, patients, families, and customers. This standardized framework aims to align the

# EXHIBIT 21.3
Competency Levels Associated with the New Behavioral Expectations

| Behavioral Expectation | Competency Level | | | |
|---|---|---|---|---|
| | **Significant Improvement Required** *The employee has demonstrated an urgent developmental need in this competency.* | **Opportunity to Develop** *The employee would benefit from development in this area.* | **Consistent Demonstration** *The employee has demonstrated proficiency in this competency.* | **Exceptional Demonstration** *The employee is a role model or coach to others.* |
| Patient/customer focus | • Does not see the value in building relationships with patients/customers.<br>• Does not make an attempt to adapt to the diverse needs of patients/customers in order to meet their expectations.<br>• Is often defensive of patient/customer feedback and is not approachable to patients/customers. | • Has started to build relationships with some patients/customers.<br>• With direction, is able to understand and meet the patient's/customer's diverse needs.<br>• Makes some effort to have a patient-/customer-centric approach but can occasionally struggle to resolve concerns and complaints. | • Builds relationships and gains trust of patients/customers.<br>• Is able to put self in patients'/customers' positions to understand their concerns.<br>• Available and willing to hear feedback from patients/customers and uses feedback to resolve concerns and complaints.<br>• Routinely meets and occasionally exceeds patient/customer expectations. | • Takes initiative to encourage peers in building relationships with their patients/customers.<br>• Always puts self in patients'/customers' positions to understand their concerns before acting.<br>• Proactively asks for patient/customer feedback and recommends solutions to make improvements.<br>• Routinely exceeds patient/customer expectations. |
| Teamwork | • Unwilling to participate in collaborative efforts.<br>• Does not share information and rarely offers support to colleagues.<br>• Shows limited consideration of the ideas and input of others. Takes credit for team accomplishments.<br>• Does not engage others in shared patient-/customer-centered problem solving. | • Collaborates on key team activities when required.<br>• Shares responsibility with and supports team members only when there is personal gain.<br>• Can occasionally let pursuit of personal goals take precedence over team agenda.<br>• Engages team members in patient-/customer-centered problem solving when there is a perceived personal benefit. | • Collaborates effectively within the team.<br>• Shares responsibility with and supports team members.<br>• Consults within the team, seeing views from all team members and listening attentively.<br>• Consistently engages others in patient-/customer-centric problem solving. | • Thrives on collaboration within the team.<br>• Shares joint responsibility with and supports team colleagues both within and outside the team environment.<br>• Consults broadly, seeking views from team members, and is willing to change own view based on feedback.<br>• Consistently places team agenda ahead of personal goals.<br>• Consistently engages others in patient-/customer-centric problem solving by sharing information and best practices. |

goals and objectives of staff and leaders across all sites and regions throughout the health system, helping Northwell Health® form one identity under one brand.

## Executive Buy-In

Executive buy-in from all across the health system was essential for building awareness of the change effort and for ensuring that improvements were supported and reinforced at all levels. To drive this commitment, executive leadership sponsored a retreat for health system executives from the major service lines and facilities across the organization. The retreat focused on the patient experience and featured video feedback from actual patients. In addition, the executives participated in a four-hour curriculum workshop developed by the OPCE, Northwell's Center for Learning and Innovation, and two outside industry leaders. Mr. Gierlinger and Ms. Barden believed that, before the curriculum was taught throughout the company, senior leaders should participate in the training so they would be able to exhibit the teachings and appropriately role-model the Culture of CARE. Evaluations and feedback about the retreat and training led to refinements of the curriculum.

Subsequent to the retreat, Mr. Gierlinger and Ms. Barden met with each of the system's executive directors and service line vice presidents to discuss the need for executive champions to lead, support, and enable the change management process at the facility and service line levels. Executives were selected for this role on the basis of their passion for patient/customer experience, interpersonal skills, organizational awareness, and role-modeling behavior. They became known as "Culture Leaders."

## Training Begins

By July 2015, 48 Culture Leaders had been selected, representing every major entity of the organization. Facilitators were then chosen to support the Culture Leaders at each site and to lead educational sessions at the site or service line. Culture Leaders and facilitators participated in a two-day training course where they learned the Culture of CARE curriculum. Culture Leaders then received additional training that focused on the roles, responsibilities, and skills involved in engaging key stakeholders. All Culture Leaders would ultimately be responsible for leading the culture change and education efforts at their designated sites and service lines. They were also expected to closely monitor patient satisfaction data.

General training throughout the system began, and in less than a year, more than 60,000 employees had been trained. The curriculum was designed to mirror the four components of CARE, and it set out to delineate evidence-based patient satisfaction standards for the system, provide frameworks for communication, teach essential skills, present video vignettes, and offer role-playing activities for each of the CARE areas. Participation in the Culture of CARE courses was a key first step to help employees understand the new expectations of the organization. Then, by pledging to CARE, employees would commit to upholding the Northwell values and mission while remaining committed to the wants and needs of patients and customers.

## Council Formation

Four councils were set up to support the structure of the OPCE and the sustainment of the cultural change: (1) the Culture Leader Council, (2) the Data Owner Council, (3) the Patient and Family Partnership Council, and (4) the Executive Steering Council.

The Culture Leader Council, consisting of the 48 Culture Leaders across the organization, would meet monthly to obtain key strategic updates from the OPCE, review performance data, and participate in peer learning and open discussion. Shared work groups were established through the council to work on implementing future steps for the OPCE.

The Data Owner Council was established to reflect the new and vital role of data owners—the people charged with ensuring data integrity and overseeing the management of patient experience data at each site. The Data Owner Council recognized the importance of quantitative data obtained through the organization's patient satisfaction surveys, as well as data obtained through comments, patient stories, letters, e-mails, and social media.

The Patient and Family Partnership Council (PFPC) was established as a collaborative forum for patients, family members, and caregivers across the system, though its efforts varied at the site level. Ms. Barden became the executive sponsor for the overall council and obtained representation from each facility. In addition, the Culture Leaders were asked to deploy extensions of the PFPC at their own sites.

The OPCE Executive Steering Council, consisting of health system senior executive leadership, ensures that system executives and their teams remain aligned in unifying the culture of the organization.

## A New Policy Is Formed

In evaluating the organization's existing policies, the OPCE realized that Northwell Health® lacked a measure that held individuals accountable and allowed for reward, recognition, or disciplinary action based on the framework provided. Therefore, the OPCE and the Northwell Health® human resources team partnered with site Culture Leaders to create such a policy.

The purpose of the new policy was to outline behavioral expectations and workplace standards related to the Culture of CARE. In addition to clearly defining the Culture of CARE, the policy delineated the six behavioral expectations for all staff, as described earlier, and four additional expectations for all Northwell leaders. Moreover, the policy included several "I" statements for each behavioral expectation to demonstrate how it could be carried out. Exhibit 21.4 provides examples of these statements.

In July 2016, the new policy was disseminated across Northwell Health®. All employees, medical staff, volunteers, students, and agency employees were now responsible and held accountable for upholding the Culture of CARE.

## Sustaining the Momentum

For a strategy to succeed, it must be supported by the proper structure. At Northwell Health®, organizational systems—including policies and procedures, formal and informal communication networks, performance management systems, job descriptions, evaluations, promotions, disciplinary processes, and data measurement—needed to align with and support the implementation of processes within the Culture of CARE.

The Culture of CARE represents a "common language" for leaders and employees, as well as a set of organizational structures, such as the stakeholder councils, for enabling, carrying out, and overseeing the change effort. As the Culture of CARE was rolled out, communication at the frontlines increased, as aspects of CARE were purposely embedded in weekly huddles with staff. A common theme and a related patient/customer story are now shared at each unit huddle—a practice followed at each site. Northwell Health® envisions additional sustainment programs for the future, including recognition programs

---

**EXHIBIT 21.4**
Examples of "I" Statements in the New Policy

**Patient/Customer Focus**
- I am welcoming, kind, courteous, and caring in all my interactions.
- I smile, greet, and make eye contact with others when appropriate.
- I take ownership in responding to and resolving concerns and complaints.

**Teamwork**
- I communicate and collaborate effectively within my team.
- I support, respect, and recognize my team members and celebrate successes.
- I speak positively and professionally about others and the organization.

linked to the achievement of behavioral expectations and leadership rounding across sites and facilities.

Within the OPCE's first year of implementation, all employees were trained in the Culture of CARE. The organization reached the 75th percentile in patient satisfaction nationally, up from the 60th percentile the year before. Looking ahead, Northwell Health® anticipates additional challenges as it attempts to refine processes, implement technology to support the changes, and further sustain the gains it has made.

## Notes

1. The mission of Northwell Health® is to improve the health of the communities it serves by providing world-class service and patient-/customer-centric care. The vision of the organization is to be a national healthcare leader that is committed to excellence, compassion, and improving the health of the community (Northwell Health® 2017b).

2. Leaders and supervisors must meet four behavioral expectations in addition to those required for all employees. These expectations are (1) managerial courage, (2) strategic agility, (3) motivating and inspiring others, and (4) developing others. Northwell leaders include employees who have one or more employees reporting to them or who are directors or above.

## Case Questions

1. What are some of the key focus areas of the OPCE strategic plan, and how might they differ in the second year of the Culture of CARE rollout?

2. What have been some of the key successes in the development of the Culture Leader role?

3. What are some of the barriers Culture Leaders face in their role?

## References

Northwell Health®. 2017a. *Employee Handbook*. Great Neck, NY: Northwell Health®.

———. 2017b. "Vision and Leadership." Accessed February 6. www.northwell.edu/about/vision-and-leadership/vision-and-leadership-mission-statement.

———. 2016. *Employee Handbook*. Great Neck, NY: Northwell Health®.

# CASE 22

## What Makes a Patient-Centered Medical Home?

*Cynthia J. Sieck, Jennifer Lynn Hefner, and Ann Scheck McAlearney*

### Introduction

Crescent Medical Practice is a midsized primary care practice in the Midwest with approximately 17,000 patients. It has 10 full-time and 5 part-time practicing physicians, and its staff includes a practice manager, 2 administrative assistants, 16 medical assistants, 5 physician assistants, 6 registered nurses, a care manager, a social worker, and a part-time nutritionist. Crescent has been in existence since 2001. The practice implemented an electronic health record (EHR) system in 2010 and a tethered patient portal (i.e., a patient portal connected to the EHR) in 2013.

Since the introduction of the EHR and patient portal, providers and staff have become more comfortable with electronic documentation and communication. In addition, patients have expressed their appreciation for the convenience of scheduling appointments and communicating with their providers through the patient portal.

This case examines Crescent's decision about whether to adopt a patient-centered medical home (PCMH) model of care. Exhibit 22.1 introduces the case's cast of characters, and exhibit 22.2 provides a timeline of key events.

---

Jill Smith, practice manager at Crescent Medical Practice

Beth Myers, a lead physician at Crescent

Rachel Piccolo, a staff nurse at Crescent

Brian Williams, a care coordinator at Crescent

Mara Thomas, an independent practice facilitator

Cici Reynolds, an administrative fellow at Crescent

Tom Kutner, a Patient and Family Experience Department employee at a local hospital

**EXHIBIT 22.1**
Cast of Characters

---

EXHIBIT 22.2
Timeline of
Key Events

**Before the Case**
- Electronic health records introduced at Crescent (2010)
- Tethered patient portal introduced (2013)

**During the Case**
- Jill Smith, practice manager at Crescent, charged with exploring transition to patient-centered medical home (PCMH)
- Jill forms Transition Management Committee
- Committee elects to hire a practice facilitator to guide the PCMH transition
- Practice facilitator delivers a report to the committee
- Administration of a patient survey about access to appointments
- Implementation of an increase in the number of same-day appointments
- Plan to enhance information technology capabilities to track patients and coordinate their care
- Development of a dashboard of metrics to compare practice performance to regional and national targets for use in tracking success of quality improvement projects
- Additional training to staff in health information technology capabilities
- Crescent considers starting a patient and family advisory group

**After the Case**
- Crescent decides to pursue PCMH certification
- Medicare starts the Comprehensive Primary Care Plus program to provide financial incentives for practices to incorporate elements similar to the PCMH standards

## The Evidence for Becoming a Patient-Centered Medical Home

The PCMH model represents a comprehensive, team-based approach to care that focuses on providing the patient with "the right care, in the right amount, at the right time" (NCQA 2014). This approach emphasizes the critical role of primary care practices in transforming the US healthcare system. Crescent is considering becoming a PCMH, and it has learned of several incentives available to PCMH practices in the area that could help offset the cost of transition to a PCMH.

Evidence suggests that the PCMH model can help engage patients and their families in the healthcare process, while also potentially improving healthcare quality and leading to cost savings (Higgins et al. 2014; Markovitz et al. 2015; NCQA 2017). In addition, the team-based structure of a PCMH may lead to greater employee satisfaction by encouraging all employees to practice at the top of their licenses and distributing care responsibilities across the team (Nielsen et al. 2012). However, for a PCMH to be effective, organizational processes must be enhanced beyond just focusing on care coordination (McWilliams 2016).

Jill Smith, practice manager at Crescent, is charged with exploring the requirements of transitioning to the PCMH model, and she begins by searching for as much information as she can find related to PCMH recognition. Jill quickly finds that the National Committee for Quality Assurance (NCQA), which recognizes PCMH practices, defines six standards that must be achieved for a practice to become a certified PCMH. These standards are listed and defined in exhibit 22.3.

Through her search, Jill learns that practices can receive NCQA recognition as a PCMH if they attain certain metrics within each of these standards. She also learns that three levels of certification exist and that the timeline for achieving each can vary depending on existing practice elements and how long it takes to implement new elements. Level 1 certification, representing the most basic PCMH, allows both paper- and electronic-based systems and stresses the importance of processes for documenting the services provided by the practice. Level 2 certification requires that the practice have some electronic means to document, plan, and coordinate care, but it does not require full electronic capabilities. Finally, Level 3 certification requires the use of an EHR for care and practice management; this level identifies the most advanced practices.

As a physician-led practice, Crescent is eligible for recognition as a PCMH, but Jill notes that the practice must first meet certain requirements in specific areas. These areas include providing patient-centered appointment access, organizing team-based care, using data for population management, providing care planning and self-care support, and implementing continuous

| Standard | Definition |
|---|---|
| Patient-centered access | Structures that meet patient needs during and after hours |
| Team-based care | Care organized to include all members and meet the cultural and linguistic needs of patients |
| Population health management | Use of data to improve the health of the population |
| Care management and support | Support for patients in management of their conditions through the use of evidence-based guidelines |
| Care coordination and care transitions | Coordination of tests, referrals, and points of transition in care |
| Performance measurement and quality improvement | Use of ongoing performance and experience data to guide quality improvement |

**EXHIBIT 22.3**
PCMH Standards Defined by NCQA

*Source:* NCQA (2014).

quality improvement. Throughout the process, Crescent will be required to provide data to NCQA to document its progress.

## Transitioning to a PCMH Model

Upon learning how comprehensive the process of becoming and maintaining status as a PCMH will be for Crescent, Jill decides to convene a PCMH Transition Management Committee. She invites a lead physician, Dr. Beth Myers; one of the staff nurses, Rachel Piccolo; and a care coordinator, Brian Williams, to join her on the committee. Collectively, the committee's role will be to provide overall direction for the process, to help staff understand the reasons for the transition and what each staff member can do in support of the effort, and to address additional practice needs identified through the transition process.

During the committee's first meeting, Jill explains to the group: "There is evidence that a new type of staff member, a practice facilitator, can assist practices with the transition to a PCMH and make the transition process more manageable."

Lead physician Dr. Myers asks, "What does that really mean? And how would that be helpful for us here at Crescent?"

Jill replies: "Apparently practice facilitators can help a practice like ours to examine current clinical, business, and organizational practices and see where there might be gaps or opportunities for improvement. Practice facilitators have been through this before, so they know what data are most helpful to guide a practice's transition to a PCMH. For us at Crescent, this means we could learn about quality improvement methods that we could apply to improve how our practice runs. Also, a skilled practice facilitator can provide feedback and coaching throughout the transition process, so we would have a resource person we could turn to when we had questions."

"That's all very well and good," notes Dr. Myers, "but how is Crescent supposed to pay for a new staff member? You know that we run on a tight budget, so it's not clear to me that bringing in a fancy consultant is going to work for us."

"Yes, that's an important point, Beth," Jill acknowledges. "But what I've learned through investigating this process is that we don't have the capability to do this on our own. If we agree that pursuing a PCMH model is the right direction for Crescent, I'm going to need help to get us there."

After more discussion, the members of the committee decide that the potential benefits of becoming a PCMH will be worth the investment in the services of a practice facilitator. Benefits include expert guidance and input from an external evaluator who can assess the status of Crescent relative to the PCMH standards and provide an action report. The hope is that these benefits will speed the process of PCMH certification and save staff time and resources, thus offsetting the cost of the facilitator.

After reaching out to her colleagues, Jill is referred to Mara Thomas, a practice facilitator based in Washington, DC. After several conversations, Jill decides that Mara's approach is a good fit for Crescent, so they finalize a contract.

Mara's first step is to learn about Crescent, so she requests that Jill send her as much background information as possible. Mara receives summaries of discussions related to the Crescent organizational structure and current clinical processes. She notes whom she would like to meet in person to learn more.

Mara's next step is to visit Crescent so she can meet with stakeholders and observe how the practice is run. In a busy first visit, Mara meets with the Transition Management Committee, speaks with several physician members of the practice, and observes practice operations. She returns for a follow-up visit two weeks later for additional meetings and further observation. Based on her findings, Mara develops a feedback report identifying areas in which Crescent would need to consider changes to become a PCMH. Mara recommends that Jill share the report with the committee, adding that she would be happy to answer any questions that come up.

## Responding to the Report

After receiving Mara's report, Jill convenes the Transition Management Committee to discuss the recommendations. Overall, the report suggested that transitioning to a PCMH would be feasible but that Crescent had quite a few steps it needed to take, as well as decisions to make.

### Defining a Direction for Crescent

First, a critical element of the PCMH model of care is the *PC* in its title: *patient-centered*. Mara notes that Crescent has to define exactly what "patient-centered care" means for the practice. In a committee discussion, Rachel, the staff nurse, notes: "I truly believe that our concept of patient-centered care must consider the whole person. We must be able to address that person's needs beyond the immediate problem-focused visit."

Care coordinator Brian echoes this sentiment: "I think it is important that our focus on patient-centered care includes supporting patients in their self-care efforts. This would mean extending support through after-visit follow-up. Also, we can leverage our patient portal to our EHR as a way to enable ongoing communication with and support by our Crescent care team."

"That sounds great," Jill says, "but I've also found that the cost of coordinating care can be considerable. It takes a lot of staff time and work to follow up with patients, provide outreach, and track patients so that they do the right thing. Actually, some early studies have shown that the costs of care coordination exceed savings for some practices, especially for practices that have already reduced overutilization and waste in their groups" (McWilliams 2016).

Jill continues: "I think we need to define what we mean by 'patient-centered care' for Crescent, but we also need to be careful about how we move forward with our PCMH transition. We need to figure out some metrics to track so that we can make sure the costs of care coordination are not swamping us."

After further discussion, the Transition Management Committee arrives at the following definition of *patient-centered care*: "Care that supports the patient as a whole person, providing access to healthcare services as well as patient records and supporting patients in making health-related decisions and engaging in self-management of their conditions."

### Identifying Staffing Needs

Mara's report noted that, given the additional care coordination requirements of the PCMH model, Crescent would need to increase staffing. According to the report, the practice would need to add the following:

- Two new care managers
- Three more physician assistants
- A second social worker
- Potentially, a pharmacist and a community services coordinator

The suggested additions represent a major expansion of both clinical and support services for Crescent, and Jill is not sure the practice can afford these increases.

### Addressing Access

Another important element of a PCMH highlighted by Mara's report was the need to ensure appropriate access to care. Access, she explained in the report, includes scheduling office hours at times that are convenient for patients and providing ways for patients to address urgent needs, such as through same-day appointments or electronic communication. Appropriate access also involves providing support to patients between office visits through such means as secure messaging through patient portals.

Reviewing current operations with the committee, Jill notes that Crescent offers appointments from 8 a.m. to 6 p.m. on Mondays through Thursdays, from 8 a.m. to 4 p.m. on Fridays, and from 9 a.m. to 2 p.m. on Saturdays. "Is this enough access?" Jill asks the group. "What evidence do we have to help us make this decision?"

"We do have openings in our schedules, but these are mostly due to patient no-shows," says Dr. Myers. "And if we offer more hours, do we have enough people who would want to work those different hours?"

"I wonder if enhancing our care coordination processes could reduce no-shows," suggests Jill.

"That's a good point," Rachel says. "But one way to gather more information about this decision is to ask our patients what they think about the schedule."

"I like that option," Jill responds. "Let's see what information we can gather."

Jill works with her administrative fellow, Cici Reynolds, to develop a short anonymous survey, and the survey is then made available for two weeks in the Crescent waiting room. The survey asks patients how long they usually have to wait to schedule an appointment and whether they have been satisfied both with the availability of same-day appointments and with the current appointment schedule.

Compiling the survey results, Cici finds that patients are generally satisfied with the current schedule but would like more same-day appointments to address urgent needs. After Cici's presentation of the findings to the committee, Jill suggests that a 10 percent increase in available same-day appointments might better meet patient access needs.

"This doesn't need to be a permanent change," notes Jill, "but we can try this for a couple of months and then reevaluate."

### Identifying a Process of Care Coordination

The next factor to address from Mara's report was care coordination. In a PCMH model, care coordination occurs at a variety of levels, one of which is coordination between primary care doctors and specialists when patients are referred for care. The committee already knew that this type of coordination was a challenge for Crescent. Across the practice, the processes for receiving outside reports have lacked consistency. Some reports have been provided in paper form, and others were scanned into the EHR; however, those scanned reports were sometimes difficult to locate during a patient encounter.

"This is actually an issue I've been considering for some time," notes Brian, the care coordinator. "And I have a suggestion. How about if we create a report for all referrals that allows the care coordinators to follow up with patients who are referred as well as monitor referral outcomes? We could also create a standardized form for all scanned reports received from outside providers."

"That sounds like a great idea!" Jill says. "Would you be willing to work with our information technology (IT) team to get this process going?"

"Of course," replies Brian. "I'd really like to get this going before we hire new care coordinators, so I'll follow up with IT right after our committee meeting."

Care coordination is also critical during times of transition for patients, particularly around discharge after a hospital stay. Mara noted that the EHR for Crescent provides a variety of features that could facilitate the identification of patients who are discharged from the hospital, but Crescent had not yet taken advantage of that capability. Reflecting on Mara's report, Jill suggests to the committee that they establish a process for care coordination after discharge.

"This might also help us address issues such as overuse of skilled nursing care, if we can monitor what is going on postdischarge," Jill adds.

"We've tried to do this in the past," Brian says, "but we need help from IT to make the process less manual. Ideally, we would like all Crescent patients to be contacted by one of our care coordinators within 48 hours of discharge to make sure they understand their discharge instructions and schedule necessary follow-up care. I'll put this on the list for my discussion with our IT experts to see if they can develop a regular report that identifies these patients. Then I'll work with the care coordinators to make it part of our work flow."

"There are other care coordination needs, too, though," notes Rachel, the staff nurse. "For instance, patients with chronic illnesses need to be seen on a regular basis to ensure adherence to their plan of care."

"Absolutely," Brian admits. "I think it would make a lot of sense to see if we could identify all patients with specific chronic illnesses. Then we could develop a schedule on which our care coordinators could reach out to identified patients who have not been seen at Crescent to assess their condition and schedule any necessary testing and office appointments."

"That's a great plan," says Jill, "but this again raises the question of cost. What if during those calls we find out the patients need help with nonmedical issues such as difficulties with transportation? The patient could be referred to the Crescent social worker, but we might then find more problems that need to be solved. Where does our role end?"

### Defining Quality Improvement Efforts

Turning to the next part of Mara's report, the committee discusses how they approach quality improvement (QI) efforts at Crescent. In the context of a PCMH, QI allows the practice to regularly assess performance, develop solutions to address areas that require improvement, and monitor progress toward its goals. Though these efforts should improve population health as well as patient and provider experiences, engaging a practice and its providers in QI can be challenging. Providers face significant time and productivity challenges and may be hesitant to change their processes or take on additional tasks. The cost of collecting and analyzing QI data can also present a barrier, and practices may not understand how to start. Obtaining buy-in from the practice, particularly from practice leadership, and beginning with a clear understanding of the resources involved are critical to the success of these efforts.

Mara is invited out for a third visit, during which she works with the committee to develop a dashboard of metrics to compare the practice's performance to regional and national targets. To facilitate buy-in across Crescent and to improve the likelihood of success for the QI efforts, the committee also develops a process for sharing the results of the QI efforts that they plan to implement across the practice. According to Mara, this process would be another important piece of the transition, because it "would allow practice members to share success, motivate each other, and promote a culture of continuous QI across Crescent."

### Identifying Health Information Technology Needs

Another important step in the transition process involves identifying new and ongoing health information technology (HIT) needs. Functionally, a PCMH practice can leverage HIT for a variety of purposes. First, practice management systems can be used to address the logistical needs of the practice, allowing for scheduling and billing. Other systems can then be used to assist with various clinical elements of the practice. For example, e-prescribing systems permit direct submission of prescriptions from the provider to the pharmacy with the goal of reducing medical errors and improving patient safety. EHRs document and store patients' health information, including visit encounters, lab and test results, prescriptions, and communications among providers. Some EHRs also include a portal through which patients can view elements of their medical record, schedule appointments, request prescription refills, and communicate with providers through secure messaging. EHRs also allow providers to examine the health outcomes of groups of patients and engage in population health management. Such technologies and systems thus help practices meet several of the PCMH goals by facilitating tracking and monitoring of segments of the patient population, improving patient access, and increasing patient safety through reduction of medical errors.

Crescent had previously implemented an EHR, so the committee's next step is to assess the features available, including the patient portal. They determine that their system meets all of the PCMH requirements but that some features are underutilized. For example, few physicians have used the registry capabilities of the EHR to engage in population health management. Thus, the committee realizes that it needs to provide additional training to all clinical staff about this system capability. This effort is in addition to Brian's current work with IT to develop systematic reports to identify discharged patients and identify individuals in need of chronic illness management.

### Obtaining Input from Patients and Families

As a final part of her report, Mara noted the importance of obtaining input from Crescent patients and families. For care to be considered "patient-centered" under the PCMH model, it has to support patients in their healthcare needs, and one way organizations can better achieve this goal is by providing a means for obtaining patient perspectives. Though Crescent regularly collects patient satisfaction data and reviews these data with staff, Jill notes that these steps are not sufficient to meet PCMH guidelines. The committee is unsure about how to do more, so Jill volunteers to speak with Tom Kutner, a colleague in the Patient and Family Experience Department of the local hospital.

Jill begins: "Hi, Tom. As I think you know, we are in the process of trying to implement a PCMH model at Crescent, and one of the areas we need to address is figuring out how to learn from our patients on a regular basis. We distribute patient satisfaction surveys, but our practice facilitator has noted that we need to do more. Do you have any thoughts about this?"

"Hi, Jill," Tom responds. "That's really great that you're working toward PCMH certification. Providing patient-centered care is so important. My recommendation for obtaining regular input from patients is to convene a patient and family advisory group. We have several of these at the hospital, and participation has been extremely rewarding to those who serve in this way."

"That sounds interesting," Jill says. "Can you tell me more about what a patient and family advisory group is?"

Tom answers: "Well, using this model, an advisory group for Crescent would be made up of patients who receive care at Crescent. The Crescent advisory group would then meet on a regular basis, and it would provide a forum where you could bring questions and ask for patient input and feedback. The group might be especially useful as part of QI, providing another perspective based on data gathered or practice changes you pilot. You could put up a flyer in the Crescent offices to recruit interested patients and families and explain how the advisory group would work."

"I think that could work well for Crescent," Jill says. "We were recently able to get some quick patient feedback by distributing a short survey in our waiting rooms, but I think the PCMH model requires creating something more formal. Thanks so much for your ideas, Tom!"

## Decision About Becoming a PCMH

At the next meeting of the Transition Management Committee, Jill addresses the group:

> Well, we've learned a lot about this process, and there is certainly a lot to consider. To summarize, though we believe that providing patient-centered care at Crescent is very important, we need to have some objectives by which we can evaluate this effort. Also, we've identified some concrete steps for moving toward becoming a

PCMH. They include increasing same-day appointment access, enhancing IT capabilities, and developing a dashboard of metrics to compare practice performance to regional and national targets, which will help track success of QI projects. We have also identified additional staffing needs. At the same time, we have uncovered a lot of unknowns about this transition. One of the biggest factors is whether we have sufficient time and resources to continue down the path toward PCMH recognition. Who is going to be accountable for these changes? I can't do this all on my own. And how will we measure our progress? On the other hand, given the direction of healthcare, can we afford not to do this? What do you all think?

## Case Questions, Part 1

1. What metrics will Crescent need to monitor to ensure success if it decides to transition to a PCMH?
2. What areas of organizational design does Crescent need to take into consideration or change if it transitions to a PCMH model? How will new staff change the design?
3. How will Jill move forward to organize the work that needs to be done for this transition? Who should be on her team?
4. How did Crescent's use of Mara, the practice facilitator, help the organization consider how to transition to a PCMH? Are there other ways practice facilitators might be used in PCMH transition efforts?
5. Crescent is considering the use of a patient and family advisory group to help it incorporate patient feedback into its transformation efforts. What other means of feedback could the practice use?

## A Year Down the Road

Crescent decides to pursue certification as a PCMH, and a year later, it learns about a new program being implemented for Medicare patients. Called the Comprehensive Primary Care Plus (CPC+) program, the initiative offers additional incentives to practices that engage in efforts to transform care delivery in five areas: (1) access and continuity of care, (2) care management, (3) comprehensiveness and coordination of care, (4) patient and caregiver engagement, and (5) planned care and population health. CPC+ provides reimbursement for care management, a performance-based incentive payment, and payment according to the Medicare Physician Fee Schedule, with an additional payment for practices that provide even more comprehensive care. Practices must apply to the program in one of two tracks that cover the five areas, with Track 2 addressing the areas more comprehensively than Track 1. If selected, practices participate for a period of five years (Centers for Medicare & Medicaid Services 2017).

## Case Questions, Part 2

6. What should Crescent consider in a decision about whether to apply to the CPC+ program?
7. In what areas are the PCMH and CPC+ programs similar?
8. What additional needs can you predict for Crescent if it is to successfully become a CPC+ program?
9. How does Donald Trump's election change the approaches you would recommend in this case?

## References

Centers for Medicare & Medicaid Services. 2017. "Comprehensive Primary Care Plus." Accessed February 8. https://innovation.cms.gov/initiatives/comprehensive-primary-care-plus.

Higgins, S., R. Chawla, C. Colombo, R. Snyder, and S. Nigam. 2014. "Medical Homes and Cost and Utilization Among High-Risk Patients." *American Journal of Managed Care* 20 (3): e61–e71.

Markovitz, A. R., J. A. Alexander, P. M. Lantz, and M. L. Paustian. 2015. "Patient-Centered Medical Home Implementation and Use of Preventive Services: The Role of Practice Socioeconomic Context." *JAMA Internal Medicine* 175 (4): 598–606.

McWilliams, J. M. 2016. "Cost Containment and the Tale of Care Coordination." *New England Journal of Medicine* 375: 2218–20.

National Committee for Quality Assurance (NCQA). 2017. "Patient-Centered Medical Home Recognition." Accessed February 8. www.ncqa.org/programs/recognition/practices/patient-centered-medical-home-pcmh.

———. 2014. *NCQA Patient-Centered Medical Home: Improving Experiences for Patients, Providers and Practice Staff.* Accessed February 8, 2017. https://www.ncqa.org/Portals/0/PCMH%20brochure-web.pdf.

Nielsen, M., B. Langner, C. Zema, T. Hacker, and P. Grundy. 2012. "Benefits of Implementing the Primary Care Patient-Centered Medical Home: A Review of Cost and Quality Results." Patient-Centered Primary Care Collaborative. Accessed February 8, 2017. www.pcpcc.org/sites/default/files/media/benefits_of_implementing_the_primary_care_pcmh.pdf.

# CASE 23

# Quality Improvement in an Accountable Care Organization

*Daniel Walker and Arthur Mora*

As Luke Billings looked out of his office window, he could see the pedestrians on the street below hurriedly walking between office buildings. He assumed they were rushing about to handle last-minute business before Thanksgiving week. Luke envied them. He too would be taking some time off to spend with family, but not before the half-day board meeting on Monday. He called out to his assistant, "Janice, have you received the final packets for the board meeting yet?" Janice walked in with a stack of papers. On the top page, Luke could see a bright logo with the words "Community ACO Performance Update" written below. Luke knew what the report contained.

## Formation and Structure of Community ACO

Founded in 2012 with Luke as the executive director, Community ACO began participating in the Medicare Shared Savings Program Track 1 one-sided risk-sharing model. With this participation, Community ACO is eligible to share in savings, if it achieves cost and quality benchmarks, without sharing the risk for any losses. Community ACO is a venture between the Glendale Health System and various primary care and specialty physicians covering the southeastern part of the state.

Glendale Health, a not-for-profit system, comprises the following:

- Four midsize acute care hospitals, with the flagship hospital located in Benton
  - Benton: 560 beds
  - Manning: 162 beds
  - Bellington: 155 beds
  - Simpson: 82 beds
- Inpatient rehabilitation and behavioral health services on the Benton campus
- Five outpatient clinics with obstetrics/gynecology, pediatrics, family medicine, and internal medicine services (employed physicians)
- One ambulatory surgery center

- One dialysis center
- Five imaging centers
- Four laboratories
- Four physical therapy and outpatient rehabilitation clinics

In addition to the facilities and services provided by Glendale Health, Community ACO allows beneficiaries access to several private-practice primary and specialty care clinics, as well as independent outpatient rehabilitation and physical therapy centers. The network size and mix seems to be well suited to care for the 19,000 attributed Medicare beneficiaries and the additional 9,000 privately insured ACO enrollees.

Potential shared savings generated by Community ACO are to be distributed as follows:

- Reinvestment in ACO: 25 percent
- Primary care physicians: 45 percent
- Specialist physicians: 15 percent
- Hospitals: 15 percent

The Community ACO governing board has 14 members, half of whom are Glendale Health representatives. The other seven board members represent primary care and various clinical specialties.

## Physician Engagement

The Community ACO board has recognized that provider buy-in to the ACO model is essential for achieving the organization's cost and quality goals. Thus, physician involvement in the development of the ACO has been prioritized. Beyond physician representation on the governing board, physician champions have been appointed at each of Glendale Health's hospitals, as well as each of the primary care and specialty clinics that are part of Community ACO. These physician champions are charged with promoting the value of the ACO model to other physicians. They advocate for care coordination and a cultural shift away from a volume focus and toward a value-based care focus.

## ACO Financial Measurement

As a participant in the Track 1 program, Community ACO is eligible to share in financial savings generated, contingent on meeting or exceeding savings and quality thresholds. First, a benchmark for total annual expenditures is developed using historical cost data for Community ACO's attributed Medicare beneficiaries. Actual annual total expenditures below the established benchmark constitute savings. To be eligible for shared savings, however, ACOs must generate financial savings in excess of a minimum savings rate that varies depending on the number of attributed beneficiaries. For 19,000 Medicare beneficiaries, Community ACO must achieve savings in excess of 2.8 percent from the benchmark expenditure figure to become eligible.

As shown in exhibit 23.1, Community ACO generated savings in excess of the 2.8 percent target in 2014. Therefore, contingent upon quality performance, it is eligible to share in savings.

## ACO Quality Measurement

Quality scoring is based on the ACO's actual level of performance on each of 33 quality measures across four domains identified by the Centers for Medicare & Medicaid Services (CMS): (1) patient/caregiver experience, (2) care coordination / patient safety, (3) preventive health, and (4) at-risk population (CMS 2015). The system used to track quality points, based on the organization's performance on each measure relative to Medicare fee-for-service (FFS) data, is shown in exhibit 23.2.

**EXHIBIT 23.1** Community ACO's 2014 Financial Performance

| 2014 Financial Performance | | | |
|---|---|---|---|
| Total Benchmark Expenditures | Total Actual Expenditures | Total Benchmark Minus Total Actual (Difference) | Difference as % of Total Benchmark |
| $218,481,692 | $211,064,488 | $7,417,204 | 3.39% |

**EXHIBIT 23.2** Sliding Scale Measure Scoring Approach

| ACO Performance Level | Quality Points |
|---|---|
| 90+ percentile FFS data or 90+ percent | 2.00 points |
| 80+ percentile FFS data or 80+ percent | 1.85 points |
| 70+ percentile FFS data or 70+ percent | 1.70 points |
| 60+ percentile FFS data or 60+ percent | 1.55 points |
| 50+ percentile FFS data or 50+ percent | 1.40 points |
| 40+ percentile FFS data or 40+ percent | 1.25 points |
| 30+ percentile FFS data or 30+ percent | 1.10 points |
| <30 percentile FFS data or <30 percent | No points |

*Source:* Reprinted from CMS (2015).

Performance below the 30th percentile for a measure results in zero points, and performance above the 90th percentile results in the maximum two points—except for the electronic health record (EHR) measure, which is double-weighted and can be worth up to four points. The total points earned for the measures in each domain are summed and divided by the total points available for that domain to produce an overall domain score of the percentage of points earned related to the points available. The percentage scores for all the domains are averaged together to generate a final overall quality score for each ACO. This score is used to determine the amount of savings the ACO shares or, if applicable, the amount of losses it owes.

Community ACO's 2014 performance, as shown in exhibit 23.3, was quite good in many areas when compared to the ACO mean and the 90th percentile of ACOs. However, it did not qualify for the maximum 50 percent of shared savings. Based on 2014 performance, Community ACO qualified for 39 percent of the shared savings generated.

## Preparing for the Board Meeting

As Luke reviewed this information prior to the board meeting, he was certain the board would be pleased with his and the ACO's performance to date. Community ACO had been rewarded for its demonstrated cost reductions and quality improvements to the tune of slightly more than $2.8 million (see exhibit 23.4). While so many other ACOs failed to generate savings or maintain quality, the Community ACO partners, according to the distribution plan, would be well compensated for the efforts they had put in since 2012. Still, Luke was uneasy as the meeting was about to begin. He knew he would be asked about the $815,892 that was left on the table by not achieving the maximum sharing rate due to quality performance. Luke knew that this was indeed the right question for them to ask.

Luke also was aware of the difficulty of the task that lay ahead. Clearly, for many metrics, such as the screening measures (ACO-19 through ACO-21), much work would be needed to approach the 90th percentile benchmark. In addition, for the measures for which Community ACO did exceed the 90th percentile, maintaining that level would likely become more difficult as ACO performance in general continues to improve.

Further, improvements would need to occur across all stakeholders, even though the stakeholders have different levels of engagement with Community ACO. For instance, each stakeholder has a different level of financial incentive in the distribution plan, and physicians, so critical to quality, may be employees or private practitioners. For some stakeholders, Medicare beneficiaries make up but a small portion of the patient population; for others, Medicare beneficiaries represent a much greater portion of their revenue.

## EXHIBIT 23.3

Community ACO 2014 Performance

| Measure | Community ACO Performance Rate | Mean Performance Rate for All ACOs | 90th Percentile |
|---|---|---|---|
| Getting timely care, appointments, and information (Measure ACO-1) | 76.32 | 80.13 | 90.00 |
| How well your doctors communicate (ACO-2) | 93.11 | 92.39 | 90.00 |
| Patients' rating of doctor (ACO-3) | 93.83 | 91.58 | 90.00 |
| Access to specialists (ACO-4) | 82.40 | 83.97 | 90.00 |
| Health promotion and education (ACO-5) | 58.13 | 58.29 | 60.71 |
| Shared decision making (ACO-6) | 77.96 | 74.60 | 76.71 |
| Risk standardized, all condition readmissions (ACO-8)* | 14.88 | 15.15 | 15.45 |
| ASC admissions: COPD or asthma in older adults (ACO-9)* | 1.44 | 1.08 | 0.27 |
| ASC admission: heart failure (ACO-10)* | 1.23 | 1.19 | 0.38 |
| Percent of primary care providers who qualified for EHR incentive payment (ACO-11) | 78.04 | 76.71 | 90.91 |
| Medication reconciliation (ACO-12) | 68.21 | 82.61 | 90.00 |
| Falls: screening for fall risk (ACO-13) | 63.44 | 45.60 | 73.38 |
| Influenza immunization (ACO-14) | 57.01 | 57.51 | 100.00 |
| Pneumococcal vaccination (ACO-15) | 49.56 | 55.03 | 100.00 |
| Adult weight screening and follow-up (ACO-16) | 65.72 | 66.75 | 100.00 |
| Tobacco use assessment and cessation intervention (ACO-17) | 90.12 | 86.79 | 90.00 |
| Depression screening (ACO-18) | 22.97 | 39.27 | 51.81 |
| Colorectal cancer screening (ACO-19) | 50.14 | 56.14 | 100.00 |
| Mammography screening (ACO-20) | 52.48 | 61.41 | 99.56 |
| Proportion of adults who had blood pressure screened in past two years (ACO-21) | 41.81 | 60.24 | 90.00 |
| Percent of beneficiaries with diabetes whose HbA1c is in poor control (> 9 percent) (ACO-27)* | 14.88 | 20.35 | 10.00 |
| Percent of beneficiaries with hypertension whose blood pressure is < 140/90 (ACO-28) | 70.88 | 68.02 | 79.65 |
| Percent of beneficiaries with IVD with complete lipid profile and LDL control < 100 mg/dl (ACO-29) | 54.62 | 57.29 | 78.81 |
| Percent of beneficiaries with IVD who use aspirin or other anti-thrombotic (ACO-30) | 83.42 | 80.79 | 97.91 |
| Beta blocker therapy for LVSD (ACO-31) | 82.72 | 82.71 | 90.00 |

* Lower rate is indicative of better performance.

*Note:* ASC = ambulatory sensitive conditions; COPD = chronic obstructive pulmonary disease; HbA1c = glycated hemoglobin; IVD = ischemic vascular disease; LDL = low-density lipoprotein; LVSD = left ventricular systolic dysfunction.

*Source:* List of measures from CMS (2015).

**EXHIBIT 23.4**

2014 Shared Savings Accounting

| Total Benchmark Expenditures | Total Actual Expenditures | Total Benchmark Minus Total Actual (Difference) | Difference as % of Total Benchmark | Quality-Determined Shared Savings Rate | Community ACO Realized Shared Savings |
|---|---|---|---|---|---|
| $218,481,692 | $211,064,488 | $7,417,204 | 3.39% | 39% | $2,892,709.56 |

Leaning back in his chair, Luke realized that he had his work cut out for him, between clarifying the various aspects of Community ACO's performance to the board and developing a quality improvement plan for the coming year. As he considered how to prioritize quality improvements and communicate the importance of quality improvement to the board and various stakeholders, Luke took comfort in knowing that the ACO incentive system is shifting the focus toward delivering and coordinating care in ways that will benefit the patient. He felt confident he was on the right track. Though ACO structure, patient attribution, physician engagement, and quality performance targets were all important, he believed these issues would all come together if he was able to motivate and encourage value-focused, high-quality coordinated care.

## Case Questions

1. Community ACO includes several hospitals and clinics within the southeastern market. What issues might emerge as a result of the Community ACO structure?

2. Community ACO is attributed a total of 28,000 patients. What does it need to do with these patients to best reduce costs and improve quality of care?

3. What barriers to physician engagement might exist in the ACO?

4. Luke's uneasiness about not meeting the maximum performance quality standards may arise out of both short-term concerns and long-term issues with the ACO model as a whole. Explain both the short-term and the long-term issues regarding meeting quality benchmarks.

5. Luke believes that the ACO model is incentivizing better approaches to care—particularly value-focused, team-based, coordinated care. How will this shift inform his management approach? What do you think is a more powerful motivator—his personal conviction or the ACO incentive structure?

## Reference

Centers for Medicare & Medicaid Services (CMS). 2015. "Medicare Shared Savings Program Quality Measure Benchmarks for the 2014 Reporting Year." Published February. www.cms.gov/Medicare/Medicare-Fee-for-Service-Payment/sharedsavingsprogram/Downloads/MSSP-QM-Benchmarks.pdf.

# ▌CASE 24

# Integrating Rehabilitation Services into the Visiting Nurse Service of America

*Jacob Victory*

O ver the last century, the Visiting Nurse Service of America (VNSA) has grown into a national home care entity. Serving 750,000 patients in 15 states annually and employing 25,000 nurses, therapists, social workers, and home health aides, VNSA earns a 5 percent profit margin on a $3 billion revenue base and has a conservative management team that monitors business and care quality targets. These divisions primarily serve the frail elderly, with thriving programs that focus on the homebound long-term care population, and target the vulnerable Medicaid and dually eligible (for Medicare and Medicaid) populations. Growing at an 8 percent rate, VNSA is proud of its current market prominence and of its origins as a nursing-based home care organization.

Indeed, nurses are considered the primary case coordinators for each patient, and from the CEO down to the nursing team leaders, nurses dominate the organization's culture and all levels of its decision-making processes, business strategy, resource allocation, and marketing. In fact, all divisions except rehabilitation services are headed by a nurse.

## Rehabilitation Services: The "Black Sheep"

VNSA's rehabilitation services, or rehab, division is the "black sheep" of the organization. It employs 3,500 physical, occupational, and speech therapists and serves about 65 percent of VNSA's patients. Rehab is considered a pseudoprogram, as it was carved out of the larger, skilled nursing–focused agency. The program reports to the vice president of operations, a clinician who is in charge of a dozen nursing-dominated programs, yet it is an ancillary service not on the senior staff's immediate radar. In fact, the program is noticed only occasionally, particularly if a therapist is late in serving an important patient or if a perceived "rehab emergency" occurs with an orthopedic patient.

VNSA patients who need rehabilitation services are primarily referred to rehab by intake nurses and nurse care coordinators. And while the organization has developed nursing teams, led by a nurse manager and supported by clinical staff, therapists are not integrated into these teams. Therapists are often informally invited to the team meetings, but the meeting agendas are strictly nursing focused, and rehab-specific issues are never addressed. Moreover, rehab has a thin management staff. Each rehab manager supervises up to 50 therapists (each with a caseload of up to 20 patients), whereas each nursing manager supervises no more than 10 nurses. VNSA's marketing and advertisements all focus on nurses providing care, even in scenarios in which a rehabilitation need is clearly depicted. This is, after all, a visiting nurse organization.

## A Change in Direction

Jeanine Bastiane, the new rehabilitation administrator, notices these issues immediately. She has a doctorate in occupational therapy and more than 25 years of experience in running hospital, nursing home, and now home-based rehab programs. She is a fun-loving but no-nonsense leader. She received the mandate to expand rehab and to bring the program to the next level to ensure innovation and market dominance of home-based rehab services. VNSA's president accepts Bastiane's plan to bring in new management talent, and a calculated effort is planned to change the culture and mind-set of the rehab division, particularly since the program has been plagued by poor management over the past decade.

Over the next year, two directors of finance and operations are hired, as is a new clinical director who is responsible for quality improvement and staff training and education. New business, financial, quality, and workforce-related metrics are developed and monitored monthly. The clinical staff is reorganized into cohesive teams, and education and retraining sessions are designed to teach clinical best practices. Scorecards are developed to monitor outcomes and service utilization. An informal rehab-specific profit and loss statement is monitored quarterly to trend revenues and expenses.

The analysis reveals that the program has annual revenues of more than $450 million and a net profit margin of 20 percent (the next most profitable program within VNSA has a margin of 4 percent). The finance and operations directors hold the rehab managers of each state accountable for meeting targets and ensuring growth, and *accountability* becomes the new catchword. Within seven months, 50 percent of rehab's management team resigns, complaining that "Big Brother" is watching. More seasoned rehab managers are immediately hired, instilling new management vigor. Though the program has been historically undernoticed, one powerful nurse executive wryly notes in a meeting, "Rehab is sure making some noise these days."

Undeniably, the noise is quite loud. The program enjoys a 22 percent increase in admissions. Bastiane persuades prominent orthopedic surgeons to refer their patients to VNSA, something the business development staff could not do. Better results than the current year are projected, and the program rates highly in employee satisfaction. Some even talk of marketing a distinct "VNSA Rehabilitation Medicine" program.

## Concerns for the Future

The noise, however, is also accompanied by what Bastiane calls "success woes," which ironically stem from the notable growth. The program is not getting the financial and human resources needed to sustain its growth rate.

First, although it brought in a $90 million profit for the organization, rehabilitation has no voice in how this profit is allocated. The money is put in an agencywide pool and used to subsidize the deficit-ridden programs and to fund investments in technology and new clinical programs.

Second, each therapist dictates where and when he or she will serve patients; any change in the service area that the therapists believe they "own" is met with raised eyebrows, veiled threats to leave the agency, and adamant resistance. Now, however, the productivity and service utilization of each therapist is the focus of a major quality improvement initiative, and each therapist is monitored to ensure that targeted weekly visit quotas are met (in order to meet demand). This additional focus has the frontline staff nervous and cautious.

Third, rehab does not have enough management and supervisory staff to monitor the clinicians. The added stress of assigning cases, monitoring utilization, reorganizing into teams, and focusing on quality of care and outcomes wears down an already thinly spread management staff.

Finally, executive administration requests that, in addition to growth, the program develop "rehabilitation packages" to sell to managed care companies, orthopedic hospitals, and specific targeted populations such as wealthy, private-paying clientele. Without additional investment in management talent or tools to monitor growth and quality, and given the historically nurse-friendly environment at VNSA, Bastiane and her team have more than a few balls to juggle.

Bastiane chews on her pencil as she leans back in her chair. Her office is quiet—her thoughts are not.

## Case Questions

1. How was the rehabilitation services division viewed before Bastiane became administrator? How was it viewed a year after her appointment?

2. What three key management challenges must Bastiane tackle first?
3. How would you advise Bastiane to better integrate rehabilitation services within VNSA?
4. How should Bastiane sell the case to obtain more financial and human resources?
5. How can she help change the current nursing culture to be more of a clinical culture?

# CASE 25

# An Evidence-Based Design for Waterford Hospital

*Ann Scheck McAlearney and Nathan Burt*

Campeon Health is a Midwestern healthcare system comprising five hospitals, ten affiliated hospitals, and an extensive ambulatory care network. Given favorable demographics and a strong bottom line, Campeon Health has recently decided to construct a new hospital in Waterford, a suburb of the larger Grouse Creek metropolitan area. In all, Grouse Creek currently contains three major hospital systems and a children's hospital, but despite steady population growth, new hospitals have been scarce. The Campeon Health facility would be the region's first newly constructed hospital in more than 22 years. Planned to be a 90-bed community hospital, Waterford Hospital could serve as a feeder hospital for the system's large flagship hospital, Lakeside Hospital, while accommodating the preferences of physicians interested in expanding their practices to include the Waterford community.

## The Charge

Prior to breaking ground for the new facility, Campeon Health has named Katherine Humphries, RN, as president of Waterford Hospital. Humphries had worked as CEO of another Campeon Health hospital for three years, and she has established a strong reputation as a transformational leader. She has been charged by the board of Campeon Health and the Campeon Health CEO to lead the initiative to design, construct, staff, and operate the new community hospital in Waterford. At the present time, the Waterford Hospital site is nothing more than a field, located across the street from an existing Campeon Health ambulatory care center.

Humphries has been given relatively free rein to design the hospital. Her years of experience as a registered nurse and as an operations leader have given her valuable insights into the delivery of care and the ways that it can be improved. She is aware that elements of evidence-based design have been shown to improve care quality for patients and workplace climate for caregivers, and she is eager to consider this approach.

## Evidence-Based Design

Evidence-based design is increasingly being used by hospitals that are trying to improve staff morale, patients' experiences, and the outcomes of care provided. Such designs are specifically used to create environments that are therapeutic, supportive of family involvement, efficient for staff performance, and restorative for workers under stress. Ultimately, evidence-based healthcare designs should result in demonstrated improvements in the organization's clinical outcomes, economic performance, productivity, customer satisfaction, and cultural measures. However, this healthcare design approach is a relatively new concept. The pool of available research and information will rarely fit a hospital's situation precisely, thus requiring critical consideration of specific design modifications and project goals.

Evidence-based design is particularly appropriate for healthcare. Physicians are accustomed to practicing, at least in part, according to evidence-based clinical guidelines and measures, while managers are increasingly using evidence-based management principles (Kovner and D'Aunno 2017). Thus, the notion of applying evidence to the task of hospital design may be well received. Further, some design principles focus on the physical characteristics that can reduce stress and contribute to the healing process, which could be especially important for patients and families dealing with the stressful and often frightening experiences common to hospital stays. Hospitals themselves have been shown to benefit—both in terms of reduced costs and increased organizational effectiveness—when applying the principles of evidence-based design (Saba and Hamilton 2006).

Evidence-based design principles incorporate a variety of elements and have in many cases been demonstrated to be effective. Design elements that have shown particular promise include exposure to sunlight, access to nature (either direct access or views), acuity-adaptable rooms, and decentralized nurse stations. Some studies have shown that climate and exposure to sunlight can influence the length of a patient's stay. One research group randomly assigned bipolar patients to sunny rooms and to rooms with less exposure to sunlight. The mean length of stay for patients exposed to greater amounts of sunlight was 3.67 days shorter than that for the control group. Similarly, patients recovering from abdominal surgery were found to have shorter hospital stays if they had a bedside window view of nature rather than windows that looked out onto a brick wall (Ulrich et al. 2004).

Well-designed rooms and buildings can bring about improved clinical outcomes in a variety of ways. An action as simple as placing an alcoholic hand-rub dispenser at the patient's bedside can yield significant improvements in practitioners' handwashing practices, thereby reducing contact infection rates. Efforts to address poor lighting, environmental distractions, and workflow interruptions can help prevent medication administration errors. Well-designed rooms can reduce the likelihood of patient falls, and good building design can reduce noise levels, thereby reducing stress for patients and caregivers (Ulrich et al. 2004).

## A Growing Evidence Base

Humphries was aware that improvements in clinical and patient satisfaction outcomes associated with the introduction of acuity-adaptable rooms were starting to become documented. In particular, she was intrigued by two examples from the recent research literature—one from Clarian Health in Indianapolis, Indiana, and one from Celebration Health in Orlando, Florida.

### Example: Clarian Health

Clarian Health switched from a traditional model of care to an acuity-adaptable model in coronary care by building an acuity-adaptable comprehensive critical coronary care floor (CCCC). The acuity-adaptable CCCC is capable of performing all necessary care in one room, from admission to discharge (Brown and Gallant 2006). Using a pre–post design to evaluate the success of the model, Clarian recorded two years of baseline data prior to CCCC adoption and then compared clinical outcomes after CCCC adoption against that baseline data.

During the baseline period, the two units that were to become the CCCC had an average of 200 intraunit transfers per month. The time spent coordinating transfers, processing paperwork, and transporting patients was considered to be non-value-added and would be better spent in direct patient care. In addition, these 200 handoffs per month elevated the risk of medical errors associated with the handoffs. After moving to an acuity-adaptable model of care, intraunit transfers were cut by 90 percent (Hendrich, Fay, and Sorrells 2004). Also noteworthy, medication errors were cut by 70 percent, likely due at least partially to the reduction in patient handoffs and transfers. Finally, patient falls decreased to a national benchmark level, and patient satisfaction increased overall (Hendrich, Fay, and Sorrells 2004).

### *Example: Celebration Health*

Celebration Health implemented an acuity-adaptable model within its new facility and saw marked improvements in clinical outcomes. In particular, patients' lengths of stay for most diagnosis-related groups (DRGs) declined significantly after the introduction of the acuity-adaptable model. Comparing data with another state, Celebration Health reported that the average length of stay for five specific DRGs in its system was 5.4 days, compared with 9.5 days reported in the state of California. Within those five DRGs, 30 percent of Celebration Health patients were discharged within four days. These length-of-stay improvements occurred with simultaneous reductions in nursing hours per patient day (Gallant and Lanning 2001).

## Financial Implications

Construction costs per square foot for an evidence-based design building are not much higher than for a traditional building, but increased costs should be anticipated. For instance, overall construction costs may be higher because of the architectural modifications necessary to introduce sunlight within 95 percent of the building or because of the greater square footage required for innovations such as acuity-adaptable rooms. From a design standpoint, introducing sunlight for internal spaces can be tricky. One solution might be to build gardens within the core spaces of a building. Though such gardens tend to be expensive, they offer visible areas for community support and can contribute to a healing environment. Acuity-adaptable rooms must be able to accommodate a large range of equipment and have space for family members; as a result, they may have to be 30 to 50 percent larger than traditional single-occupancy rooms.

At the same time, evidence-based design can reduce costs associated with utilities. The availability of sunlight throughout the building, for instance, will reduce electricity costs. Similarly, maintenance and supplies costs are typically reduced because of standardized equipment and supplies throughout the hospital.

## Capitalizing on the Opportunity

Humphries is convinced that an evidence-based design model will be appropriate for Waterford Hospital. Working with the hospital architect and contractor, she has been able to outline an evidence-based design that includes such components as acuity-adaptable patient rooms, decentralized nurse units, and liberal use of windows and open spaces to provide patients and families with access to nature. The latest architectural drawings feature all private rooms for patients, each room including a family area designed to contain a couch/bed, refrigerator, and separate television. In addition, gardens both inside and outside the hospital will have easy access points for patients, families, and hospital staff. Staff and families will also have access to respite areas, where they can go to relieve stress and deal with difficult situations and decisions. Finally, all patient areas, and 95 percent of other hospital space, are designed to have access to direct or indirect sunlight.

Overall, Humphries is pleased with the preliminary plans for Waterford Hospital. However, she knows she has a long way to go to convince hospital staff and physicians—who are generally accustomed to traditional hospital environments—that the evidence-based design model is sound and desirable. In fact, moving forward with an evidence-based design is risky if she does not get key stakeholders on board. Humphries knows her next step is to build support for the application of an evidence-based design for Waterford Hospital, but she doesn't have much time.

## Case Questions

1. Who are the key stakeholders who must support Humphries's vision for an evidence-based hospital design? How could she obtain their support?
2. What reactions might you predict from physicians regarding the use of evidence-based design at Waterford Hospital? How about from members of the Waterford community? Other local hospitals and health systems?
3. What challenges do you think Humphries and the leadership team at Waterford Hospital will face as they try to implement an acuity-adaptable model of care?

## References

Brown, K. K., and D. Gallant. 2006. "Impacting Patient Outcomes Through Design: Acuity Adaptable Care/Universal Room Design." *Critical Care Nursing Quarterly* 29 (4): 326–41.

Gallant, D., and K. Lanning. 2001. "Streamlining Patient Care Processes Through Flexible Room and Equipment Design." *Critical Care Nursing Quarterly* 24 (3): 59–76.

Hendrich, A. L., J. Fay, and A. K. Sorrells. 2004. "Effects of Acuity-Adaptable Rooms on Flow of Patients and Delivery of Care." *American Journal of Critical Care* 13 (1): 35–45.

Kovner, A. R., and T. D'Aunno (eds.). 2017. *Evidence-Based Management in Healthcare: Principles, Cases, and Perspectives*, 2nd ed. Chicago: Health Administration Press.

Saba, J., and K. Hamilton. 2006. "The Bottom Line on Evidence-Based Design." Presentation at the American College of Healthcare Executives Congress on Healthcare Leadership, Chicago.

Ulrich, R., X. Quan, C. Zimring, A. Joseph, and R. Choudhary. 2004. Unpublished paper presented at virtual seminar on healing environments, American Institute of Architects, Academy of Architecture for Health.

# CASE 26
## Matrix or Mess?

*Ann Scheck McAlearney*

Carol is excited about her newest job change. After serving as a quality improvement (QI) manager at Valley Community Hospital for the past two years, she will finally be able to put to use her expertise in both nursing and informatics by taking a new role as a clinical informaticist for the hospital. Though she felt like she had been in school forever, her experience as a nurse, her undergraduate degree in informatics, and her on-the-job training in QI have given her a broad perspective about how information technology can be usefully implemented to improve the quality of care provided at the hospital.

This new job, though, while seemingly a great fit on paper, also makes Carol a bit nervous. In her prior role in QI, she had reported to a single director. Her new position has given her a second boss, the director of information systems (IS) for the hospital. In a so-called matrix design, Carol reports to both directors and is responsible for satisfying them both.

In fact, the IS department as a whole is a matrixed department within the hospital. This organizational design for IS had been introduced because of the combination of functional and project responsibilities involved in each IS initiative. The functional areas of the department—such as budgeting, hiring, and training—are consistent regardless of project, but IS project responsibilities vary based on the nature of the project and the other hospital departments involved. For instance, a project to install a patient portal system for the hospital would have certain matters that involved the nursing department (e.g., workflow issues), as well as IS department needs dealing with technical issues, updates, training, and so forth.

As a result, each IS manager always reports to two directors—the IS director and another hospital director—based on the clinical or other operational departments served. For example, Carol was aware that the manager of ambulatory informatics reported to both the director of IS and the director of operations for the hospital. Even the IS trainers have two bosses, as they report to the IS director and the director of education for the hospital. Exhibit 26.1 shows examples of these reporting relationships, as well as where Carol's new role fits.

To Carol, this matrix arrangement for IS and QI seems to make sense given the shared goals and objectives of clinical informatics and QI within the hospital. Yet she suspects issues could arise. Carol wants to make sure she is clear about each of her boss's expectations of her and her new role, but she isn't sure how to make this transition from her original single boss to a dual reporting relationship.

**EXHIBIT 26.1**
The Information Systems Department's Matrix Design

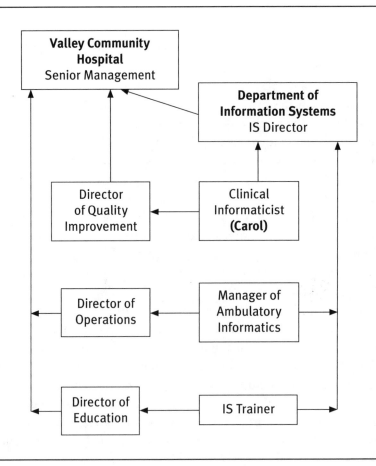

## Case Questions

1. What issues will Carol likely face in reporting to two bosses?
2. Does the matrix organizational design make sense for this hospital's IS department, or would another design be more appropriate? What would you propose?
3. What strategies can Carol use to perform well in her new role without feeling pulled in two directions?

# ▌CASE 27
# We Need a Sign

*Lindsey N. Sova and Ann Scheck McAlearney*

Gilbert Medical Center has recently opened a new, state-of-the-art cancer center, called Gilbert Cancer Center, which incorporates both a research institute and a hospital. As staff begin working in the new building, they will need time to get their bearings and understand the changes in workflow that may be required under the new arrangements. For instance, several units that used to be on one floor in the old hospital building now have been separated and accommodate patients on multiple floors or hospital wings.

Another major change is that certain hallways are now reserved for hospital staff only. These hallways have been created in addition to the regular hallways that are used by the general public. Administrators explained that the goal of introducing the staff-only hallways is to improve response times and create a space for staff to communicate "off stage." A keycard is not required for entry into all of the staff-only hallways, but the hallways tend to connect units through back entrances instead of being connected to main unit lobbies where patients and visitors would access the public elevators. The staff-only hallways also lead to staff elevators that are intended for use by hospital staff and for patient transportation.

During the planning phase for the new hospital, a stakeholder committee was convened to address facility appearance and patient satisfaction. The committee included hospital administrators and staff, providers, and patients who met regularly to discuss topics like atrium design and flow, placement of information desks, and signs to direct visitors. The conversations about signage focused on where and how often signs should be placed to direct people throughout the hospital and to other medical center buildings. Patient stakeholders raised concerns that too much signage could result in confusion for patients and visitors. Staff and providers agreed that signage should be streamlined to only those signs that are necessary to direct individuals from the main hospital entry to the places they needed to go, such as the elevators, information desk, and cafeteria. The committee members also thought the streamlined signage might reduce the likelihood of visitors wandering into staff-only hallways. By the end of the discussions, administrators felt they had a signage plan that would save money through the streamlining of signs and also result in a more satisfactory experience for people visiting the hospital.

Nonetheless, during the first few weeks of the cancer center's operations, Tyler Jones, the administrative director, receives a number of complaints about signage. Apparently, both staff and providers are getting lost trying to navigate the staff-only hallways, which results in delays with patient transports as well as late arrivals for urgent cases. A common complaint is that the staff-only hallways lack necessary signs for navigating to and from units, as well as signs to identify a unit prior to entry. Tyler was a member of the committee that discussed the number and placement of signs, so he is confused as to why these complaints are coming in, especially since the patients and visitors seem to be navigating the new hospital well.

You are an intern working for Tyler, and he has asked you to investigate these complaints and report back on the issue next week. He provides you with minutes from the stakeholder committee meetings, and he gives you contact information for the stakeholders so you can reach out to them for further details about the discussions.

## Case Questions

1. Create a plan of action for investigating the complaints. Who will you want to talk to? What questions will you ask?
2. While walking the staff hallways, you see that makeshift signs have been taped to the walls to assist in navigating the hallways. What is your next step, and how do you use this information to inform your report for Mr. Jones?

# CASE 28

## How Disruptive Should We Be?

*Anthony R. Kovner*

You are John Smith, chief operating officer of Regional Hospital, part of the Regional Health System of 15 hospitals in Eastern State. You have just read Clayton Christensen's (2009) book *The Innovator's Prescription* and have been impressed with his ideas for disrupting the business models of hospitals, physicians, and chronic care organizations. But his ideas are far different from the realities you face in managing operations at Regional Hospital.

You wonder about changing the hospital organization from a "solution shop" to a "focused factory." According to Cook and colleagues (2014, 746), "the full-service US hospital has been described organizationally as a 'solution shop,' in which medical problems are assumed to be unstructured and to require expert physicians to determine each course of care." This model leads to unwarranted variation and results in lower quality and higher costs. Mayo Clinic determined that a focused factory model—which emphasizes a uniform approach to the delivery of a limited set of high-quality services—was appropriate for 67 percent of cardiac surgery patients. Implementation of the model reduced resource use, length of stay, and cost. Variation was also markedly reduced, and outcomes were improved.

You are convinced, but how do you get other managers at Regional Hospital and Regional Health System to actively consider a focused factory model for implementation?

## Case Questions

1. What are the facts of the situation?
2. What are the reasons that an implementation structured similarly to the one at Mayo Clinic will or will not work at Regional?
3. Certainly, you will encounter stakeholder concerns about the costs of making the change, questions about how the change will affect reimbursement, and push-back from surgeons who are against the practice of "cookbook" medicine. How might you overcome other key stakeholders' opposition to the change?
4. What should you do now, and why?
5. How can you get buy-in from the system CEO while protecting your own job and not "biting off more than you can chew"?

## References

Christensen, C. M., J. H. Grossman, and J. Hwang. 2009. *The Innovator's Prescription: A Disruptive Solution for Health Care*. New York: McGraw-Hill Education.

Cook, D., J. E. Thompson, E. B. Habermann, S. L. Visscher, J. A. Dearani, V. L. Roger, and B. J. Borah. 2014. "From 'Solution Shop' Model to 'Focused Factory' in Hospital Surgery: Increasing Care Value and Predictability." *Health Affairs* 33 (5): 746–55.

## | CASE 29

# Measuring Systematic Change Across One Health Economy in London

*Sara Little*

## Background

Islington is a borough in central London where 250,000 residents live in an area just under six square miles. It is one of the most densely populated boroughs in the United Kingdom, and its population is constantly changing—about 20 percent of the population move into and out of the borough each year.

The Islington Clinical Commissioning Group commissions National Health Service activities in the borough. It was one of the first such groups to be established in England. The Islington group is led by 36 member primary care practices, and clinicians are at the forefront of everything the organization does. Like most health systems, Islington has been struggling to control the rising cost of care for people living with long-term health conditions.

## A New Program for Islington

Kathryn is an experienced public sector manager who has spent most of her career managing operations in acute care hospitals. She was recently appointed director of Islington's new integrated program. In taking this position, she has walked into a program that had formed organically over a number of months based on ideas from local primary care doctors and service managers.

Senior leaders in health and social care had been working on this program in partnership for over a year. Though the group lacked a clearly defined program, the leaders' visions about what integration—both vertical and horizontal—would look like in the end were very similar. For instance, they generally seemed to agree that it was better for patients to receive care in the community than in the hospital. Even the chief executive of the local acute care hospital agreed, despite the troubling impact such a shift would have on his own business. The senior leaders also agreed that information technology (IT) systems needed to work better together so that all clinicians, and even patients, had access to the same information. As one might expect, frontline staff were incredibly nervous about the impact such an IT strategy would have on their work.

Though improving patient outcomes was the chief goal of Kathryn's work, she had to pursue this goal while balancing long-term financial constraints. Funding was set to decrease year on year, and the chief finance officer was keen to see results quickly.

## How Can We Work Together to Move Forward?

Kathryn's biggest challenge was to get everyone to clearly describe how they would get from where they were to where they all wanted to be. The change would require years of commitment and work in a cultural environment that typically never planned more than 12 months at a time. The program, now a year in, had little to show in the way of results, despite the confidence of senior clinical leaders that the conversation had moved forward. Kathryn wondered, What else had they done in the last year other than talk?

## Case Questions

1. What kind of incentives and metrics would work in relating the hospital to primary care?
2. How can Kathryn get managers and clinicians to work together to design and implement these incentives and metrics?

# PROFESSIONAL INTEGRATION

We have altogether brought health care
from the state of having no cloth to
the state of having no quilt. The patches
are made. The stitching is the problem.

—*Donald M. Berwick*

# COMMENTARY

**P**erhaps this section of the book could be more precisely titled "Clinician Integration" rather than "Professional Integration." After all, people in so many occupations, from beauticians to ballplayers, claim to be "professionals." If we were writing about banks or airlines in a general management text, the professionals would generally represent various undifferentiated stakeholder groups of employees. Healthcare is different, however, because many of the key operatives—doctors, for instance—might not even be employed by the organization in which they work. Some physicians, nurses, social workers, dentists, and other clinicians belong to independent trade associations that represent them and look after their welfare. Sometimes, these trade associations bargain with healthcare organizations (HCOs) over the terms of employment.

This section focuses on doctors and nurses who work in large provider organizations, such as hospitals, and it examines their relationships with other professionals and with managers who claim to represent the firm's mission and goals.

## Why Is Professional Integration an Important Issue in These Organizations?

Managers and clinicians face a variety of challenges related to integrating professional and organizational goals and coordinating the work of different clinicians in taking care of patients. Doctors and nurses view their main goal as taking care of *their* patient; managers, meanwhile, view their goal as taking care of *all* patients. Some managers might include additional goals of taking care of members in a capitation plan or of people in a geographic area served. The "Triple Aim" framework, developed by the Institute for Healthcare Improvement (IHI), identifies the goals of HCOs as providing the best care (improving the patient experience) for the whole population (or for those to whom care is provided) at the lowest cost (IHI 2017). Standing in the way of these goals are various barriers to service delivery and coordination. Chief among those barriers are a fragmented care system; a wrong-sized, poorly distributed, and often underprepared workforce; and payment models that reinforce care silos and fragmentation (Knickman et al. 2016).

To simplify, we can assume that HCOs have three main parties: doctors, nurses, and managers. Further, we can also assume that these parties do not have the same interests in pursuing the Triple Aim. Doctors want to provide the highest quality of medical care to their patients, even if pursuit of this goal leads to less care for other patients under other clinicians. Nurses, meanwhile, want to provide the highest quality of nursing care to their patients and maximize what some nurses do within the scope of their licenses (which varies by state and by organization). Obviously, what nurses think they can and should do differs from what some doctors think they can and should do. In addition, payers might have specific ideas about which clinicians they want to pay—and how much they want to pay—for certain services. Managers have to approach their work in terms of providing services to all patients. Their views will likely differ from those of radiologists, for example, regarding such issues as how much radiologists should be paid for reading films. Managers generally support accreditors regarding compliance with quality metrics and payers regarding acceptable negotiated reimbursement.

Additional complications involve decisions over which services should be provided, as well as the payment for those services. Should a hospital provide chronic care services to its acute patients, and to people who are not its patients but who live in the immediate vicinity of the hospital and cannot pay for services because they lack adequate insurance? How are policies made and implemented regarding the different values and preferences of various stakeholders? Information technology complicates delivery of services even further. Which managers and clinicians have what degree of access to which electronic medical records? Who updates the records, are the records linked, and who has the access to what information?

## Fragmentation of Care

Clinicians and managers serve the patient. All too often, however, it is the patient—not the clinicians and managers—who must coordinate her own care. This arrangement results in workarounds and conflicts among providers and managers, as well as among different groups of clinicians.

One way managers and clinicians can seek to resolve conflict is by obtaining additional resources for all groups, so that the groups can bargain for what they believe to be appropriate amounts relative to peers at comparable organizations. A second way is for clinicians to become hospital employees and negotiate terms of work and pay. A unifying, integrating factor is goal agreement. The mission of the organization can be specified in measurable terms, and mechanisms can be agreed upon for measuring goal achievement, ensuring transparency, and sharing information and feedback with stakeholder groups.

Such steps, however, require a considerable amount of time to accomplish, as well as trust and goodwill. A third way to approach conflict resolution is to pursue large-scale bureaucratization of healthcare, to the point that the HCO has rules about everything and has organized ways of making rules. In such settings, HCOs must bargain over what they do, how they do it, and how they get paid by agencies of government, and then they can bargain with organizations of clinicians.

American healthcare in general has not reached agreement about how to meet these challenges. Health systems are getting larger, work is increasingly standardized, and external regulations and government payment systems are growing. Meanwhile, certain HCOs are successfully achieving their goals—and may or may not be rewarded fairly for doing so—while others are failing, going bankrupt, or being acquired. Doctors and nurses are increasingly being led by clinician managers who have developed experience and skills in representing and influencing their constituents.

Some conflict among parties is functional, and it helps to ensure that the goals of the Triple Aim are reached. Conflict is functional to the extent that claims for resources can be effectively represented and adjudicated and that trust exists among the parties. Insufficient specification of the aims may result in inadequate physician, nurse, or management advocacy on behalf of the respective constituencies. If the power of any of the three parties is too great, the result will be suboptimization—physician and nurse objectives may be achieved at the expense of managerial objectives, or vice versa. Who can be expected to pay for conflict resolution that is acceptable to all parties? Strong leverage must be exerted on behalf of those who are not directly involved in the negotiations, such as payers and patients. When health outcomes are compared across developed countries, the compensation of doctors, nurses, and managers in the United States appears to not be sustainable.

We all expect the organizations for which we work to provide a reasonable income and lifestyle, professional recognition, and participation in decision making. Of course, we do not all receive these things, as life is not always just. This casebook is written from the manager's point of view. In some instances, success in the managerial role depends on doctors or nurses *not* becoming fully unified, at least in matters of opposition to the manager. An important aspect of the manager's job—and that of physician and nurse leaders as well—is managing the expectations of constituents so that clinicians and managers get a clear and realistic view of the Triple Aim and the way it affects their expectations and performance. The goal is for the parties to envision and move toward a situation that benefits everyone—not merely doctors, nurses, or managers.

The healthcare workforce is undersized in certain specialties and oversized in others. It has shortages of primary care providers, providers in behavioral health, and providers for complex medical conditions and chronic care.

At the same time, an abundance of specialists has often resulted in unnecessary care. Care is poorly distributed based on where people live, and providers in different parts of the care system are not sufficiently incentivized to work as a coordinated team. Our training system—for doctors, nurses, and other clinicians, as well as for managers—has not prepared the workforce to work effectively in teams or collaborative settings.

Similarly, our payment system has not offered sufficient incentives to radically transform training and payment for care. In the current marketplace, as of this writing in 2017, larger organizations—whether they are health systems, insurance companies, accountable care organizations, or pharmaceutical companies and pharmacies—are capturing larger shares of the market. At the same time, the firms selling to HCOs—for instance, firms that provide information systems, run emergency departments, and manage cancer care—are growing larger as well. Larger organizations justify their market shares on the basis of their capability to produce superior outcomes—whether in quality of care, cost of care, or access to care—and government and insurance companies are increasingly rewarding provider organizations on the basis of superior performance. Evidence is needed to support these claims, but certainly HCOs are more likely to continue to grow and prosper when they do a better job of recruiting and retaining doctors, nurses (and other clinicians), and managers (and other support workers). Such organizations presumably have better governance, metrics, and ethics that contribute to higher-quality care and better service to patients.

## Summary

Professional integration is essential, because doctors, nurses, and managers cannot work together effectively when they are trained and organized as separate professions. Further, integration must be pursued in a changing environment with shifting power statuses among the three groups. Independent physicians are growing weaker, and organized physician groups are becoming more powerful. Nursing management is becoming more specialized and sophisticated, and nursing professional organizations are developing and implementing standards about the way nurses should be treated by organizations. As organizational power increases and concentrates, the scope of managers' influence grows. Managers are increasingly held accountable for organizational performance—whether doctor and nurse performance or the performance of staff in supporting doctors and nurses. Managers must be prepared to anticipate issues and respond to management and organizational challenges by making and implementing better decisions based on the best available evidence, from all sources—scientific, organizational, experiential, and stakeholder.

## Discussion Questions

1. How might you measure professional integration in large healthcare organizations?
2. What forces lead to greater or lesser integration?
3. What role do managers play in influencing professional integration?
4. What is the impact of greater or lesser professional integration on the manager?
5. What barriers exist to sufficient professional integration?
6. What might be the impact of larger healthcare organizations—and some health systems insuring patients and some insurers providing direct medical services—on professional integration?

## References

Institute for Healthcare Improvement (IHI). 2017. "IHI Triple Aim Initiative." Accessed January 20. www.ihi.org/offerings/Initiatives/TripleAim/Pages/default.aspx.

Knickman, J., K. R. R. Krishnan, H. A. Pincus, C. Blanco, D. G. Blazer, M. J. Coye, J. H. Krystal, S. L. Rauch, G. E. Simon, and B. Vitiello. 2016. "Improving Access to Effective Care for People Who Have Mental Health and Substance Use Disorders: A Vital Direction for Health and Health Care." National Academy of Medicine. Published September 19. https://nam.edu/improving-access-to-effective-care-for-people-who-have-mental-health-and-substance-use-disorders-a-vital-direction-for-health-and-health-care/.

## Recommended Readings

Berry, L. L., and K. D. Seltman. 2008. *Management Lessons from Mayo Clinic: Inside One of the World's Most Admired Service Organizations.* New York: McGraw-Hill.

Berwick, D. M. 2003. "Disseminating Innovations in Health Care." *Journal of the American Medical Association* 289 (15): 1969–75.

Blumenthal, D. 2002. "Doctors in a Wired World: Can Professionalism Survive Connectivity?" *Milbank Quarterly* 80 (3): 525–46.

Bohmer, R. M. J. 2009. *Designing Care: Aligning the Nature and Management of Health Care.* Cambridge, MA: Harvard Business Press.

Burns, L. R., and R. W. Mueller. 2008. "Hospital–Physician Collaboration: Landscape of Economic Integration and Impact on Clinical Integration." *Milbank Quarterly* 86 (3): 375–84.

Calhoun, J. C., L. Dollett, M. E. Sinioris, J. A. Wainio, P. W. Butler, J. R. Griffith, and G. L. Warden. 2008. "Development of an Interprofessional Competency Model for Healthcare Leadership." *Journal of Healthcare Management* 53 (6): 375–91.

Carlson, G., and H. Greeley. 2010. "Is the Relationship Between Your Hospital and Your Medical Staff Sustainable?" *Journal of Healthcare Management* 55 (3): 158–74.

Christensen, C. M., J. H. Grossman, and J. Hwang. 2009. *The Innovator's Prescription: A Disruptive Solution for Health Care.* New York: McGraw-Hill Education.

Cunningham, B. 2014. "The Payment Reform Paradox." *Health Affairs* 22 (5): 735–37.

Delbecq, A. L., and S. Gill. 1985. "Justice as a Prelude to Teamwork in Medical Centers." *Health Care Management Review* 10 (1): 45–51.

Djukic, M., and C. T. Kovner. 2010. "Overlap of Registered Nurse and Physician Practice: Implications for U.S. Health Care Reform." *Policy, Politics & Nursing Practice* 11 (1): 13–22.

Edmonson, A. C. 2012. *Teaming: How Organizations Learn, Innovate, and Compete in the Knowledge Economy.* San Francisco: Jossey-Bass.

Gawande, A. 2007. "The Checklist: If Something So Simple Can Transform Intensive Care, What Else Can It Do?" *The New Yorker.* Published December 10. www. newyorker.com/magazine/2007/12/10/the-checklist.

Gilmartin, M. J., and T. A. D'Aunno. 2007. "Leadership Research in Healthcare: A Review and Roadmap." *Annals of the Academy of Management* 1: 387–438.

Groopman, J. 2007. *How Doctors Think.* Boston: Houghton-Mifflin.

James, B. C., and L. A. Savitz. 2011. "How Intermountain Trimmed Health Care Costs Through Robust Quality Improvement Efforts." *Health Affairs* 30 (6): 1185–91.

Joint Commission. *Comprehensive Accreditation Manual for Hospitals.* Oak Brook Terrace, IL: Joint Commission Resources.

Lake, E. T. 2007. "The Nursing Practice Environment: Measurement and Evidence." *Medical Care Research and Review* 64 (2, Suppl.): 1045–225.

McAlearney, A. S. 2008. "Using Leadership Development Programs to Improve Quality and Efficiency in Healthcare." *Journal of Healthcare Management* 53 (5): 319–32.

McAlearney, A. S., A. N. Garman, P. H. Song, M. McHugh, J. Robbins, and M. I. Harrison. 2011. "High-Performance Work Systems in Healthcare Management, Part 2: Qualitative Evidence from Five Case Studies." *Health Care Management Review* 36 (3): 214–26.

Steele, G. D., J. A. Haynes, D. E. David, J. Tomcavage, W. F. Stewart, T. R. Graf, R. A. Paulus, K. Welkel, and J. Shikels. 2010. "How Geisinger's Advanced Medical Home Model Argues the Case for Rapid-Cycle Innovation." *Health Affairs* 29 (11): 2047–53.

# THE CASES

How do hospitals and health systems integrate the performance of managers and clinicians, and how do they facilitate sufficient alignment of performance and cooperation among teams of clinicians? In considering this question, we must address a variety of issues with organizations, clinicians, and patients, in addition to broader forces such as the concentration of healthcare systems to include insurers and providers, developments in healthcare insurance legislation and regulation at the national and state levels, and changes in the way that education in the health professions is organized and paid for.

Many of the cases in this section describe expensive and ineffective workarounds by doctors, nurses, and managers seeking to respond to fragmentation of care, misalignment of the workforce, or incentives that do not appropriately reward effective team performance. The challenge of fragmentation is clearly illustrated in Case 31, "Collaboration in Breast Cancer Care." The case raises the question of how managers can make sure women get appropriate adjuvant therapies and follow-up care given the multiple types of providers involved (e.g., primary care practitioners, radiologists, surgeons, radiation oncologists, medical oncologists), especially when not all the information systems are connected. The case covers the spectrum of diagnosis, referrals, follow-up, and the challenge of care coordination.

Case 33, "Managing the Patient Experience," describes the tensions associated with balancing quality measures and patient satisfaction, and it highlights challenges commonly faced in patient care units—specifically, the need to mediate and coordinate conflicts in which various clinicians who take care of patients do not organizationally report to the professional nominally in charge of the unit.

Case 39, "Who Is Keeping Track?," shows the effects of poor coordination between the inpatient and outpatient settings. To further complicate matters, the patient in the case faces the additional challenge of unnecessary waiting time during the transition from the emergency department to inpatient care.

A second group of cases in this section focuses on challenges related to misalignment of the workforce. This misalignment may involve a lack of integration between nursing education and nursing practice, or work issues between managers and professional nurses within hospital organizations. Case 32, "Getting from Good to Great," examines a range of issues facing the chief nursing officer (CNO) of a large, highly ranked academic medical center. The CNO reflects on how she might approach the challenge of increasing staff nurse engagement to improve nursing performance.

Another nursing case—Case 37, "When Should We Be Alarmed?"—deals with staffing ratios and considers what managers should do when ratios are not being met. How do care providers make critical decisions in allocating their scarce time? How do nurses prioritize choices, and how do hospitals train and support them to make the correct decisions?

Case 38, "Increasing the Focus on Patient Safety at First Medical Center," discusses a mechanism for professional integration, Crew Resource Management (CRM), and explores opportunities for implementation and evaluation. The CRM approach can be considered a form of matrix management, and, if used together with traditional professional organization, it may lead to better outcomes, though perhaps at higher costs.

Case 40, "Managing Relationships," focuses on the dilemma of a patient care director, and it represents a ground-level version of Case 32, "Getting from Good to Great." It considers the most important things that Betsy Cline can do to promote staff nurse engagement and morale to bring about better performance.

A third group of cases considers the lack of alignment between payment incentives and desired performance. These cases demonstrate the consequences for managers, physicians, and nurses who must attempt to achieve the Triple Aim even though often such behavior is not financially rewarded. (Consider, for instance, that reduction in inappropriate hospital admissions, a goal consistent with the Triple Aim, leads to lower hospital payments.)

Case 30, "Where the Rubber Hits the Road," deals with physician–hospital relationships and issues in coordination of care. The challenges in the case are caused in large part by inappropriate payment models (one could also say by inappropriate organizational models) in which doctors on the hospital staff compete with the hospital to provide reimbursed care, which is profitable, and to avoid providing needed care that is not adequately reimbursed. The case describes options proposed by a CEO and the reactions of key medical staff leaders.

Case 34, "The Complaining Doctor and Ambulatory Care," and Case 35, "Doctors and the Capital Budget," both highlight issues that can result from inappropriate payment incentives, as better integration among professionals and managers is impeded by their being paid by separate organizations (even if their work takes place in the same hospital). The consequences of separate structures can be seen in the behavior of attending physicians providing ambulatory care (Case 34) and medical staff doctors recommending allocation of resources in the capital budget (Case 35).

Finally, Case 36, "Doing the Right Thing When the Financials Do Not Support Palliative Care," sketches a dilemma involving issues raised in a previous case study—"The Business Case for a Hospital Palliative Care Unit," written by Kenneth R. White and J. Brian Cassel and published in the first edition of *Evidence-Based Management in Healthcare* (edited by Anthony R. Kovner, David J. Fine, and Richard D'Aquila, 2009). White and Cassel showed how faulty assumptions in the allocation of indirect costs in hospital accounting could lead to a foolish preliminary decision to close a palliative care unit. Case 36 seeks to emphasize the need for allocation of costs in hospitals to be realigned with revised payment models incenting more effective patient care performance.

# CASE 30

# Where the Rubber Hits the Road: Physician–Phelps Hospital Relationships

*Anthony R. Kovner*

In 2010, while serving as professor of healthcare management at the Robert F. Wagner School of Public Health at New York University, I was invited to visit Phelps Memorial Hospital Center in Sleepy Hollow, New York. The center's CEO, Keith Safian, wanted me to review the impact of Medicare and potential health reforms on hospital–physician collaboration.

## Competitive Position of the Hospital

Phelps is a community hospital of 235 beds that operates at 70 percent occupancy. Inpatient services include medicine, surgery, psychiatry, obstetrics, pediatrics, and physical rehabilitation. Two units of mentally ill chemical-abuse patients operate at 97 percent occupancy. Pediatrics operates at 20 to 30 percent occupancy. The emergency department had 25,000 visits in 2009.

Phelps is surrounded by other hospitals and by water. Patients do not come from the west side of the Hudson River. Phelps is part of the Stellaris alliances with Northern Westchester Hospital, Lawrence Hospital Center, and White Plains Hospital Center. The region is overbedded. Phelps collaborates *and* competes with these hospitals.

Half of Phelps's discharges are from its primary service area, and 9.5 percent are from its secondary service area. For both areas, Phelps has a 29.3 percent market share. An important nonhospital competitor is the Mt. Kisco Medical Group of 150 physicians, which is located across the street from Northern Westchester Hospital, about ten miles to the northeast.

## Phelps Medical Staff

The Phelps medical staff includes 470 individuals, 445 of whom are physicians. About 100 physicians admit 80 percent of the patients. Two small medical groups are the largest—the North Star group, which includes 14 primary care physicians, and the orthopedic group, which has 7 people. The hospital does not have enough physicians with thriving practices. The medical staff is aging—40 percent of the primary care physicians are older than age 55—and the hospital has the capacity to admit more patients. The hospital pays salaries to three obstetricians and eight internists, a family practitioner, a procedural gastroenterologist, a thoracic surgeon, and six hospitalists. Many of the directors of clinical services receive small hospital stipends; several are full-time employees.

I interviewed some key players at Phelps to learn more about the situation and to develop a case study that might benefit the physician leaders of tomorrow. Overviews of the interviews are presented in the sections that follow.

## Interview with Keith Safian, CEO

National health reform had just been passed by Congress, and Keith Safian estimates the impact on Phelps could be a negative $3.5 million each year for the next ten years. Presently, Medicare and Medicaid reimbursement to Phelps is at a rate lower than cost. Phelps operates at a 1.8 percent profit margin, while costs increased an average of 10.3 percent each year from 2007 to 2009. Phelps raises $2 to $3 million through philanthropy each year.

Safian acknowledges that the hospital has physician issues. Specialists want to be paid to be on call for the emergency department (ED). They want to be paid when they see indigent and Medicaid patients. They want to be paid for referring patients, although such payment is prohibited by law. Phelps is making some adaptations, and Safian and the chief medical officer have considered the following options:

- The hospital has recently salaried two gastroenterologists. Voluntary cardiologists have approached the CEO about partnering to perform stress tests in the hospital because reimbursement is better if these tests are done there.
- Phelps is thinking of discontinuing some outpatient mental health programs (which generate a total of 50,000 visits per year) if Medicaid cuts occur.
- The CEO does not approve of salary freezes. Phelps gave full-time employees an average 3.5 percent pay raise last year. Safian would rather cut some positions than decrease health insurance benefits.
- Phelps has started an educational program for younger physicians, the medical leaders of tomorrow. The program covers organizational and health system issues, hospital payment, and the nature of the competitive market.

- Phelps is considering building a new ambulatory surgery center on campus, although there is no pressure on operating room capacity as yet.
- Phelps has had difficulty collaborating with primary care physicians. The largest physician group has not been able to hire more primary care physicians, but it just added two specialists.

## Interview with Dr. Robert Seebacher, Medical Director of Joint Replacement Services

Phelps is the only hospital where Dr. Robert Seebacher practices. He is in a large orthopedic practice with seven partners, and they now participate only in Medicare and workers' compensation. Medicare pays $1,200 for a knee operation, whereas commercial out-of-network insurance pays $22,000. Dr. Seebacher's malpractice premiums are $110,000 per year, and office overhead is 35 percent. He performs 240 joint replacements a year; he must do 100 to pay for his malpractice insurance.

### *Views on Medicare and Hospital Adaptation*

Dr. Seebacher observes: "The United States is extremely wasteful of medical resources. For example, a 90-year-old person will find a surgeon who will do a knee or a hip replacement. So, in one year, this expends more money than that person earned in her whole life. The elderly get wonderful care now, whereas 25 years ago they didn't live long enough to receive these operations. It's hard for the hospital to stop unnecessary knee replacements or take action when every gallbladder with a stone does not need to be removed."

He adds: "Many doctors do not wish to cooperate with hospital initiatives. The current payment system divides doctors from hospitals. The hospital should form partnerships with really good physicians, as they are doing, and take care of them. If the hospital is making a lot of money on a surgeon's patients and he's getting paid below his costs, the hospital should pay him a salary.

"A current problem," Dr. Seebacher explains, "is that Phelps can't get subspecialists to take call in the ED. Phelps should subsidize these physicians—for example, hand surgeons—to take call. The chief medical officer [CMO] should have more medical directors under him, and he should look to reduce unnecessary surgery and overtreatment. Phelps should strengthen the hospitalist system, but hospitalists (and all primary care physicians) should not order 50 consults for their patients to cover themselves. There should be a more sensible focus on geriatric oversight."

### Advice to the CEO

Dr. Seebacher urges that "the CEO should listen more to the CMO. The hospital should cut away from doctors whose practice patterns are poor or wasteful. Phelps should be innovative in forming relationships with physicians. Phelps should not only look at volume but also emphasize ethical and expert care. The CEO should value the high-quality physicians he has rather than search for new people. There is too much emphasis on the patients Phelps is not getting. By definition, some of these patients won't come here anyway."

Dr. Seebacher observes: "Northern Westchester Medical Center—with its all-private rooms—appeals to patients who can pay. If Phelps shrinks, the hospital could have all private rooms. Phelps has three wards full of patients who can be frightening to other patients. Patient rooms are too small. The plant has been allowed to deteriorate. Patients see 'small, tight, dingy.' We don't have the money now to change this."

## Interview with Dr. Richard Peress, Director of Surgery

Dr. Richard Peress joined the Phelps staff in 1987 and specializes in the spine and scoliosis. He performs 50 operations a year. When he started, he brought a tertiary-level approach to Westchester County. He has recently become director of surgery.

### Views on Medicare and Hospital Adaptation

According to Dr. Peress, the sooner Medicare collapses, the better. Attempts to prop it up, he says, "won't get us where we need to go. We do what is politically expedient." Medicare has become a two-tier system, for those who can afford it and those who cannot. He believes that costs will be capped for all insurers, and charging patients more will be illegal. He observes that payments for kyphoplasty (a procedure to correct spinal fractures caused by osteoporosis) were $1,500 when he started; Medicare now pays $600. The procedure takes only 20 minutes, but the operation takes an hour of the surgeon's time; he loses money on the procedure. A plumber charges $300 an hour to unclog a toilet. For epidural injections, Dr. Peress is paid only $69 an hour, and he is putting a needle into a patient's spine.

He asks, "When does gain sharing under Medicare become fee splitting?" The hospital makes a lot of money on certain procedures, while the surgeon loses money. This raises questions about how the money can be more fairly distributed.

Dr. Peress observes that the medical staff have to change their attitudes, too. Doctors have a long history of being loners. In today's economy, the bottom line is all that counts, which is changing things for physicians. "Now all we're doing is haggling about the price." But once the hospital makes a deal with a physician, the government can't just take it away. Dr. Peress says, "I can't continue without adequate compensation."

### *Advice to the CEO*

Dr. Peress believes that decisions made by administration must be worked out so that physicians also benefit. For example, hospital online documentation that provides pay-for-performance rewards to the hospital should not be accomplished on the backs of physicians. The surge of "itinerant" physicians at Phelps pains the more loyal doctors.

Dr. Peress thinks Phelps should focus on physicians who have unique talents that are not universally available at neighboring hospitals. The hospital's advertisements could tout these physicians so that patients leap over competitor hospitals in surrounding counties. His practice, for example, draws from other hospitals in Orange and Dutchess counties. Dr. Peress wants Phelps to be a true regional spine center.

Physicians should make their case for gain sharing to a joint committee, Dr. Peress says. If a physician has the talents, she should let the committee know that. Providing high-quality care—and being personable and kind—count, too. The hospital should tell the public why physicians like Dr. Peress choose to work at Phelps. He gets better support at Phelps than he would elsewhere—for example, nursing support in the intensive care unit and care for his patients from board-certified subspecialists in cardiology, pulmonary, nephrology, and infectious disease, among other areas.

Dr. Peress feels the problem that Dr. Lawrence Faltz, the CMO, faces involves helping with the implementation and enforcement of compliance. The Stellaris computer system is a handicap because "the computer system doesn't adapt to the physicians, so we have to adapt to it."

The CEO, Safian, did what was necessary 20 years ago to get rid of the $10 million annual deficit. But Phelps cannot make money anymore just by cutting expenses; austerity is not the answer. As a new initiative, Dr. Peress is leading the implementation of a pain clinic in the old ED. He wants people to say positively about this and other services: "Phelps? Yeah, Phelps!"

## Interview with Dr. Arthur Fass, Chief of Cardiology

Dr. Arthur Fass has been chief of cardiology at Phelps since the mid-1980s. His group has three cardiologists. The hospital has two cardiology groups and a smattering of individual practitioners.

### Views on Medicare and Hospital Adaptation

Dr. Fass is very concerned that, as in his private practice, hospital reimbursement is down and costs are increasing. Physicians are now talking to Phelps and other hospitals seeking to become employees. That way, physicians can be guaranteed income, and physician employees become hospital employees, with the hospital paying their health benefits.

Dr. Fass finds that what matters to payers is not quality or thoroughness but high volume—rushing through as many patients as possible. He observes that a financial incentive exists to refer patients not to the best physicians but according to what group the physicians belong to.

Dr. Fass recommends that the CEO be sensitive to situations such as call in the ED. The CEO is asking physicians essentially to provide free service at 3:00 a.m., while the hospital itself collects a fair amount of money. Physicians should be compensated in some way for this service that they are asked to provide.

Dr. Fass observes the Phelps staff includes about 100 dedicated physicians, and 20 of those are most active in providing clinical services. The hospital should only admit new physicians to its staff if they provide service primarily from a patient care perspective rather than an economic perspective.

Physicians should be fairly compensated for what they are asked to do, Dr. Fass believes. The CEO should sit down with neurologists, for example, and set one of them up with a good salary, office space, and staff. Not having the neurologist on call affects all doctors who then are in trouble "if their patient has an acute stroke and they can't get a neurologist."

Having a relationship with a teaching hospital would also be attractive for Phelps. It might help attract primary care physicians, some of whom may be tempted to set up practice in the community.

## Interview with Dr. Lawrence Faltz, Chief Medical Officer

Dr. Lawrence Faltz joined Phelps 15 years ago after serving as chairman of medicine and residency program director at New York–Presbyterian / Queens for ten years. He specializes in rheumatology and internal medicine. Dr. Faltz is responsible for quality, credentialing, and physician discipline at Phelps, as well as for networks and academic affiliations. Dr. Faltz is active outside the hospital in the American College of Physicians, where he has held a leadership position.

### Views on Medicare and Hospital Adaptation

Dr. Faltz observes that "the docs controlled the medical system up to 1980. Since 1990, the payers have controlled the system." He notes that specialization raises costs. Before, the doctor waited to treat a hypertensive patient because of risks associated with medications. Now, the doctor can choose treatments with far fewer side effects. When the patient has blood pressure of 120/80, the doctor starts controlling for hypertension. For a pneumonia patient, the physician previously would get a chest X-ray and make seven visits. Now, the patient sees the primary care physician every day, plus the cardiology consultant, the pulmonary consultant, and the infectious disease consultant, and he gets a chest X-ray, a computed tomography (CT) scan, and an echo from the cardiologist. The patient now gets 30 services where he used to get 8. All of this adds to the cost of care.

Dr. Faltz believes that physicians need to understand their obligations as members of the hospital medical staff. Some of them see being asked to be on call as a personal attack. Doctors used to build their practice by taking call. Now there are too many specialists, so it's hard to build a practice. Physicians do not get paid sufficiently, if at all, for ED visits. Managed care companies do not give physicians a fair deal, and for many physicians, just being in practice means tremendous liability issues. Dr. Faltz believes that younger physicians do not see the profession as an all-encompassing lifestyle, as the older physicians might have.

Phelps is still run as a doctors' workshop. The hospital needs more integration of physicians and hospital by service. "We need trade-offs as to where the money is going. The hospital has to accept physician governance over some hospital issues," Dr. Faltz says. Many physician leaders at Phelps lack formal education about current health policy issues. Dr. Faltz recommends that Phelps and its physicians work together to make the newly salaried physicians productive. The present reimbursement system is not conducive to this. Phelps has to figure out how best to compete with growing medical groups, such as Mt. Kisco, that are recruiting additional physicians and taking away hospital ancillary service revenues.

Regarding call in the ED, Dr. Faltz points out that (1) subspecialists do not want call but want to keep out the competition; (2) mature practices do not need the new patient flow from the ED; and (3) primary care medical staff are unprepared to say, "If you [specialists] won't take call, we won't refer patients to you." Phelps has to move the culture. The community does not understand that, when no specialist is available after hours, patients have to be transported to another hospital. Patients view such an event as a hospital failure, not a medical staff failure. The medical staff needs to understand that the hospital and its medical staff are viewed as a single entity by the outside world. The medical staff bylaws should be changed so that physicians still have to take call even if they are 55 years old and have worked at Phelps for 20 years, which currently are grounds for exemption from call, regardless of the availability of other members of a department.

Dr. Faltz concludes: "We must see that we can't get where we want to go without each other, and we can't turn the clock back to where it was before."

## Conclusion

As I concluded my interviews, I didn't have an answer to the quandary in which the hospital and its physician leaders found themselves. On one hand, neither party seems to be netting sufficient revenue to meet revenue targets. On the other hand, neither side seems able to work out a satisfactory method of working more closely together on some kind of combined production and billing process that would meet each side's targets.

## Case Questions

1. What were the financial problems facing Phelps and its medical staff in 2010?
2. What are the options for hospital initiatives, and what do the physicians recommend?
3. How should the CEO proceed? Give a rationale for your recommendations.
4. What are the unresolved questions in the situation facing the CEO and the board? What are the risks in adopting your recommended strategy?
5. What do you recommend that the CEO and the CMO do to improve the situation?
6. How do you approach this case from the point of view of a younger physician? What do you expect from the hospital, and what do you think the hospital should expect from you?

# CASE 31

# Collaboration in Breast Cancer Care

*Ann Scheck McAlearney*

## Background

Stewart Memorial Hospital (SMH), a 900-bed safety-net hospital located in a major western city, was known for both its size and its ability to address any need a patient might have. As a result, when Molly Peterson received the news that her recent mammogram was suspicious, she decided to go to Stewart as a next step.

Not wanting to wait for an appointment, Molly decided to go to Stewart's "Breast Clinic," a weekly clinic sponsored by the hospital to help women get their questions answered and care needs met during a single visit. When she arrived on a Tuesday morning, Molly was shocked at how many women were there. Upon registering, Molly was directed to take a seat and informed that she would likely be waiting for at least an hour. Looking around the waiting room, she saw women of all ages, races, and ethnicities. Molly knew that Stewart was the place to go if you were uninsured or didn't have much insurance coverage, because they couldn't turn you away.

## Meeting New Doctors

Molly was called into the office by a medical assistant, who took her vitals and let her know that the doctor would see her soon. After another 15-minute wait, the doctor knocked gently and came through the door.

**Dr. Gayle Huerta:** Hi, Molly. My name is Dr. Gayle Huerta. I understand you are here because your last mammogram was suspicious.

**Molly:** Yes, that's right. And I'm really scared.

**Dr. Huerta:** I certainly understand that. Let's take a look and see what we should do next.

Dr. Huerta had Molly lie on the exam table and performed a thorough manual exam of both of Molly's breasts. She found a lump in Molly's right breast, and she knew that this might be the beginning of a long road for Molly. Finishing the exam, Dr. Huerta asked Molly to sit up, and she took a seat herself.

**Dr. Huerta:** In a case like this, the next step I'd recommend is for you to get a biopsy. It's a short procedure that involves taking a sample of tissue from the lump we have identified in your breast. A doctor will numb an area of your breast and insert a long needle to extract a sample of the tissue. That tissue will then be sent to the lab to see if the lump is benign, or noncancerous, or if it is malignant, meaning cancer.

**Molly:** OK, I guess that's what I have to do then. When can you do the biopsy?

**Dr. Huerta:** Actually, I don't do the biopsy myself. It is done by a radiologist who can use special tools to figure out exactly where to insert the needle. But the good news is, because you are here on our Breast Clinic day, I can refer you to a radiologist to have the procedure done today. I don't know how long you will have to wait, but would that work for you today?

**Molly:** Sure. I'm too worried to go back to work anyway.

Exiting the exam room, Dr. Huerta put in an order for a biopsy for the radiologist on duty, before moving on to see the next patient. Meanwhile, Molly got dressed and returned to the waiting room. After another hour of waiting and listening to languages she had never heard spoken before, Molly was called by a new medical assistant, who took her to a procedure room.

Looking around the procedure room, Molly was overwhelmed. She'd had X-rays during dental exams before, but this was something else. Fortunately, she didn't have to wait long, as the radiologist soon entered the room and introduced himself.

**Dr. Brian Nguyen:** Hi, I'm Dr. Brian Nguyen, and I'm here to take a sample of the lump we have identified in your right breast.

**Molly:** Hi. Yep, that's what Dr. Huerta told me would be next. Will it hurt?

**Dr. Nguyen:** You may feel a slight prick when the needle with the anesthesia is inserted to numb the area, but other than that, you should only feel pressure. Do you have any other questions?

**Molly:** Nope. I just want to get this over with.

Dr. Nguyen and his assistants performed the procedure fairly quickly, and Molly was sent home to await the results.

## Getting the Results

The following Friday, Molly received a call from Dr. Huerta's office. Picking up the phone, she was startled to hear Dr. Huerta's own voice.

**Dr. Huerta:** Hi, Molly. Is this a good time to talk?

**Molly:** Sure. What did you find?

**Dr. Huerta:** Well, unfortunately the tissue we sampled indicated that you have cancer. Are you in a place where we can talk about next steps?

The next minutes, hours, and days were a blur for Molly. All she really processed was that she had breast cancer and had to have surgery—and that she would have to wait six to eight weeks to get on the surgeon's schedule. What was she going to do for the next two months while she waited to get this cancer out of her body?

Molly went through the motions for the next seven weeks until she finally had the surgery. Two weeks later, she returned to see the surgeon, Dr. Kelsey Framer, for a follow-up appointment.

**Dr. Kelsey Framer:** Hi again, Molly. How are you doing?

**Molly:** I guess I'm OK. You got the cancer out, right?

**Dr. Framer:** Yes, the surgery was successful at removing the tumor, but there are still some steps you need to take.

**Molly:** What do you mean? I thought after surgery I would be cancer-free and able to go back to my normal life.

**Dr. Framer:** Unfortunately, it's not quite that simple. As you might recall, during the surgery where I removed the tumor, I also checked the lymph nodes under your arm for cancer cells that would indicate that the cancer had spread. And unfortunately, there were cancer cells in your lymph nodes.

**Molly:** Oh no! What does that mean now?

**Dr. Framer:** Well, in your case, more surgery is not recommended. But I will refer you to see both an oncologist, a medical doctor who specializes in treating cancer, and a radiation oncologist, another specialist who may recommend radiation therapy.

**Molly:** More doctors?!

**Dr. Framer:** Yes, I'm sorry to be the bearer of this news. As a next step, I'd like you to meet with another member of our team. Her name is Blair Haas, and she's what we call a patient navigator. She also happens to be a breast cancer survivor. Would you be open to meeting with her?

**Molly:** Do I have a choice?

**Dr. Framer:** Of course you have a choice. But I do recommend that you see her on the sooner side. She can be very helpful in this treatment and follow-up process.

**Molly:** OK, I guess that makes sense. Sure, I'll see her. How do I get an appointment?

**Dr. Framer:** Actually, she might be in the office today. Wait right here, and I'll go see if I can find Blair now. In the meantime, here is a brochure describing patient navigation.

## The Patient Navigation Process

Patient navigation, Molly learned from the brochure, aims to help patients manage the process of getting the care and treatments they need for specific health issues. In this case, the patient navigator program at SMH was funded by a grant from the American Cancer Society. The grant did not cover any healthcare services or treatments, but it did pay the salary of a part-time patient navigator to work with patients diagnosed with breast cancer. Given that a breast cancer diagnosis typically leads to an extended course of treatment that may include such elements as surgery, chemotherapy, radiation therapy, and hormone therapy, the process of "navigating" what to do next can be extremely difficult for many people. Patient navigation programs guide patients through the treatment process and ensure that they don't fall through any cracks in the system.

To Molly, this program sounded OK, but she was secretly pleased when Dr. Framer returned to the room and announced that, in fact, Blair was not currently in the clinic. Molly had had enough with this place for the day. She just wanted to go home.

Dr. Framer handed Molly a card with Blair's contact information, and she repeated her recommendation that Molly schedule an appointment with Blair. Dr. Framer also handed Molly another card with the name of a medical oncologist, and a third card with the name of a radiation oncologist.

**Dr. Framer:** So, Molly, I'm sorry we can't take care of more of this today, but these cards give you the different numbers you now need to call. With our Breast Clinic each week, it will likely be possible to get those appointments on the same day, but unfortunately we do not have a way to schedule everything at the same time.

**Molly:** Would the patient navigator also be there on that day?

**Dr. Framer:** She should be, but you'll have to call to make an appointment with her directly because she is only funded for a half-time position in our department.

Molly thanked Dr. Framer and got out of the office as quickly as she could.

Once back home, Molly took some ice cream out of the freezer and turned on the television in an attempt to distract herself from the day's news. She had started the morning expecting to be able to get on with her normal life, but now she had just learned that she had more cancer to deal with. Not only that, she was supposed to see two more new doctors and some patient navigator person. She was exhausted just thinking about it.

## The Next Day

The next morning, upon seeing the cards Dr. Framer had given her, Molly realized the previous day had not been a dream. Picking up the phone, she called the medical oncologist's office first. She was able to schedule an appointment with Dr. Amos Assad two weeks from Thursday.

Next, Molly called the number for the radiation oncologist, Dr. Julie Black, and tried to schedule an appointment for the same day as her appointment with Dr. Assad. The person who answered the call, however, explained that Dr. Black was going to be out of town that day and asked if Molly would be able to wait another week for the next available appointment. "What choice do I have?" Molly thought to herself.

Molly then picked up the third card and dialed the number for Blair, the patient navigator, but the call went to Blair's voicemail. Leaving a message, Molly didn't really know what to say other than that Dr. Framer had recommended she talk to Blair. She left a short message with her phone number and got on with her day.

## Two Weeks Later

Somehow, Molly got through the next two weeks without going crazy with concern over the cancer spreading in her body. She arrived at her appointment with Dr. Assad, and the doctor was very kind. He acknowledged that this experience was probably all very scary, and he explained that the doctors had caught the cancer relatively early, even if it had spread a bit. Dr. Assad recommended a course of chemotherapy, but he wanted Molly to meet with Dr. Black before scheduling it. Sometimes, doctors recommend that patients start with radiation and follow it with chemotherapy; other times, the opposite pathway is recommended.

**Molly:** How will I know which is the best order of treatment for me?
**Dr. Assad:** Well, after you meet with Dr. Black, she and I will consult with each other and see what we both think. We will make a recommendation for the next step, and then one or the other of our offices will reach out to schedule your next treatment.

The following week, Molly went to her appointment with Dr. Black and learned about various courses of radiation therapy. Molly found the whole experience somewhat terrifying, with lots of unfamiliar terminology and even some discussion about physics.

Once again, Molly was overwhelmed. Thinking back to her follow-up appointment with Dr. Framer, she remembered the talk about the patient navigator at SMH. At the time, she had not been all that excited to meet yet another person at the hospital, but now she thought it might be a good idea. Checking out after her appointment with Dr. Black, she asked the medical assistant, Sana Carty, about the program.

**Molly:** Hey, when I was here a few weeks ago, Dr. Framer referred me to see someone called a patient navigator. I can't remember her name, but I called her and never got a call back.

**Sana:** Oh, that would have been Blair Haas. Unfortunately, due to personal reasons, she had to take a leave of absence. I think they are trying to get a new patient navigator in to cover for her, but maybe that hasn't happened yet. Is there something I can help you with?

**Molly:** I don't know. I guess I'm just really confused about what I'm supposed to do next. I've met with all these doctors and had all these tests, but I don't know who is the right person to go to next.

**Sana:** Well, I know the process can be really overwhelming, but I think the next thing that will happen is that one of the doctor's offices will call you with a plan for your follow-up treatment.

**Molly:** OK, I guess that makes sense.

## Another Two Weeks Later

After another two weeks, Molly still had not heard anything from any of the doctors or their offices, so she decided to go back to the drawing board and call Dr. Framer's office. Dr. Framer herself called back at the end of the day.

**Dr. Framer:** Hi, Molly, how can I help you?

**Molly:** Well, Dr. Framer, I've been trying really hard to do the right thing and go to the appointments you recommended, but I'm worried because I still haven't heard about what I'm supposed to do next.

**Dr. Framer:** Were you able to meet with Blair, our patient navigator, before she went on leave?

**Molly:** No. I left her a message, but she never called back.

**Dr. Framer:** Well, that's not good. Let me look back at your chart for a minute and see if I can figure out what you should do next.

**Molly:** Thanks.

**Dr. Framer:** It looks like it has now been almost two months since your surgery. Does that sound about right?

**Molly:** Yes. Is that bad?

**Dr. Framer:** Well, it's not good, but let's see what we can do to get the process moving forward. I see you have had appointments with Dr. Assad and Dr. Black, but I don't see anything that clearly says what they recommend for your treatment plan. Let me see if I can call one or both of them now and get their ideas for next steps.

**Molly:** That would be great. Thanks so much, Dr. Framer. I'm still really worried that I have cancer in my body, and I just don't know what to do about it.

## Case Questions

1. Who should be responsible for coordinating Molly's treatments?
2. If the patient navigation program had been operating properly, what might have been different in Molly's experience?
3. If SMH had used an electronic health record, what might have been different?
4. In what ways should the organization be responsible for coordinating cancer care?
5. As a manager of the Breast Clinic at SMH, what processes would you propose to improve coordination of breast cancer care?

# CASE 32

# Getting from Good to Great: Nursing and Patient Care

*Wilhelmina Manzano and Anthony R. Kovner*

## Part 1, 2007: Nursing at University Health System
### The Question

"How do we get from 'good' to 'great'?" Andrea Rogers, chief nursing officer (CNO) of University Health System (UHS), asked Clark Kaplan, a nursing management consultant, in spring 2007.

UHS is a health system located in a large eastern city, and at the time of this conversation, it consisted of five hospitals with a budget of $4 billion. It was highly ranked nationally by *U.S. News & World Report*. "Of course, we think we're great now," Rogers continued, "but we wish to be—and be perceived as—the nation's leader in nursing."

"Whatever that means," Kaplan replied. "Do you provide the best nursing care and the best patient care, or does the nursing division feature the most focused accountability with transparency of results?"

"We've kept the focus on nursing and had to deal with competing priorities. It's easy to lose sight of the main thing and 'putting patients first' when you have to plan one, three, or five years out," Rogers noted.

### Strategic Planning at UHS

Kaplan had been hired to work with Rogers on strategic planning within nursing. His first task had been to try to evaluate the effectiveness of the existing process. He chose the following criteria for his evaluation: (1) patient and staff satisfaction, (2) nursing vacancy and turnover rates, (3) investment in and support for nursing by top management at UHS, and (4) focused accountability of the 100 patient care managers for patient care outcomes and nursing satisfaction. All of these metrics had to be taken into account across the five hospitals that made up UHS.

Rogers began by pointing to accomplishments in strategic planning during her three years as CNO. Nursing had established a hospitalwide nursing board similar to the UHS medical board that set standards of practice, governance, structure, and communication. She had also formed the Center for Nursing Excellence, which encompassed education, research, practice, professional development, credentialing, and nursing informatics. Leadership development had become a priority, and incentive performance targets had been recently implemented for staff nurses. The brand and reputation of nursing were very strong, both within and outside UHS. The president and executive vice president of UHS supported the role of nurses in taking care of patients and recognized the importance of nurses to the continued success of the organization.

Gerry Winograd, director of the Center for Nursing Excellence, explained the strategic planning process as follows: "We started in the summer of 2005, when we were evaluating whether to pursue Magnet status. The main areas we fell short in were staffing, recruitment and retention, cultural diversity, care models, and shared governance. UHS then had six initiatives for 2007, and nursing aligned itself with all of these initiatives: people development, quality and safety, serving the community, partnerships, financial and operating strengths, and advancing care." (See exhibit 32.1 for a summary of the Magnet Recognition Program.)

Top nursing leadership at UHS—a group of about 15 people, including nursing vice presidents (VPs) and the Center for Nursing Excellence staff—began meeting quarterly. With respect to shared governance, UHS developed a means by which staff nurses can participate actively in the decision-making process for patient care. Termed "patient-centered care," the model called for dialogue to be directed at the unit level concerning what staff nurses need to support their professional practice.

### Perspectives About the Strategic Planning Process

Winograd, the facilitator of the strategic planning process, coordinated stakeholders and resources. She had been in the position for seven years. Two program directors assisted her—one focusing on education and practice and

**EXHIBIT 32.1**
A Summary of
Program Review
for the Magnet
Recognition
Program

The Magnet Recognition Program was developed by the American Nurses Credentialing Center (ANCC) to recognize healthcare organizations that demonstrate nursing excellence. The program also provides a vehicle for disseminating successful nursing practices and strategies.

Focusing on high-quality patient care, nursing excellence, and innovations in professional nursing practice, the Magnet Recognition Program provides consumers with the ultimate benchmark for measuring the quality of care that they can expect to receive. When *U.S. News & World Report* assembles its annual showcase of "America's Best Hospitals," an ANCC Magnet designation is considered a key competence indicator for quality of inpatient care.

The Magnet Recognition Program is based on quality indicators and standards of nursing practice as defined in the revised third edition of the American Nurses Association *Nursing Administration: Scope & Standards of Practice* (2009). The *Scope & Standards* and other foundational documents form the base on which the Magnet environment is built. The Magnet designation process includes the appraisal of qualitative factors in nursing. These factors—the "Forces of Magnetism"—were first identified through research done in 1983. The full expression of the "Forces" is embodied in a professional environment guided by a strong visionary nursing leader who advocates and supports development and excellence in nursing practice. As a natural outcome of this effort, the Magnet program elevates the reputation and standards of the nursing profession.

The Magnet application and appraisal process is designed to bring recognition to a healthcare organization's attainment of standards of excellence in nursing. The process is long and thorough, and it demands widespread participation from the applicant organization's nurses. However, it also serves as a valuable educational experience for an organization seeking focus and direction for growth and development. Healthcare organizations find the journey to be a revealing self-assessment, creating multiple opportunities for organizational advancement, team building, and enhancement of individual professional self-esteem.

*Source*: American Nurses Credentialing Center (2008, 2017).

the other dealing with practice and with obtaining Magnet status. The nursing department leaders had mixed feelings about the costs and benefits of obtaining the Magnet designation. Some argued that Magnet status was not a reliable and valid measure of quality of patient care, whereas others believed that Magnet status was worth obtaining, even at high cost, because of perceptions in the field and for competitive reasons. According to Winograd, the most important priority for nursing in 2007 was recruitment and retention, which she said was highly dependent on nurse manager performance. Also, the division placed a high priority on increasing the time the nurse spends at the bedside, as this time leads to increased professional satisfaction and better patient care.

Ella White, VP for patient services at the North Division, suggested that the value added from centralized strategic planning for the nursing division was that "we get and give advice on best practices, collaborate, and support each other." She added, "In my job, I don't get much strategic or reflective time. Everything is a crisis, and we are always at meetings." White added that, rather than beefing up the centralized quality assurance office, the organization should place a higher priority on creating decentralized quality and safety data analyst positions. Quality and safety at UHS were centralized at the system level and across disciplines under the supervision of a physician. White needed a person dedicated to quality at North Division who worked with nurse managers at the unit level, to do the "think" work and the "look" work. The other person she needed was a safety person (for analysis of hygiene and identification and administration of medications). White argued that her administrative support was too light as a result of UHS's prioritizing heavy investments at the bedside, adding capital equipment (e.g., ultrasounds on units for insertion of lines in intensive care units, cooling blankets) and technology. Volume had increased, acuity had heightened, and patient turnover had become quicker. The state regulators, White said, want to "suck the profits out of healthcare." She concluded that strategic planning was a good, solid process in nursing at UHS but could be improved. As she noted, "We weigh, rank, and come back to the 'main thing,' but there are too many things on our list, too many priorities."

White stated, "Every nurse needs to be engaged and focused on the idea that 'It's all about the patient.' Nursing has to do better. Nursing has to raise the bar. Nursing needs to be clear about expectations. Nursing needs to understand better how we can get there. Nursing leadership will partner with staff nurses and help them achieve the UHS goal. But all nurses need to show up, participate, contribute, and be engaged in the process."

Shirley Apple, service line manager in oncology, South Division, was one of four service line directors. Her units included medical and surgical oncology (72 beds), outpatient infusion (25 chairs), radiation oncology, nurse walk-in clinics with fellows, and a few nurses who gave chemotherapy to patients not on a unit. Apple had been in her job for 12 years.

Apple participated in strategic planning in the following ways. She attended the local practice council of 10 or 12 staff. Each staff member nominated two of the nurses who served on this council, and they met 30 times a year. About 20 percent of their meeting time was spent on strategic planning. Apple also attended monthly nurse leadership meetings for the South Division, which were attended by approximately 30 nurse leaders. This group similarly spent about 20 percent of its time on strategic planning.

Apple also attended South Division nursing meetings on a division "relation-based" initiative with six other unit leaders. These nurse managers focused on raising patient satisfaction scores using a primary nursing care philosophy. After the recent implementation of the initiative on the seven units, Press Ganey patient satisfaction scores had risen significantly from the 70s to the 80s. The divisions of UHS had chosen different ways to accomplish patient care goals, and the ways were becoming more data and research driven. Children's used a family-centered model. West Division used the Planetree model. North Division used a bedside strategy. Apple observed, "This all involves a lot of hard work, and it takes a lot of time to reorganize work."

Apple was interested in ways to make nursing staff more autonomous, to increase professionalism, to encourage personal growth, and to improve management. In oncology, nurses attended education programs organized by the clinical nurse specialists and the nurse educator. Annually, 15 to 20 nurses attended the National Congress on Oncology Nursing for four days. When they returned to UHS, nurses made presentations to staff and presented seminars on what they had learned. Oncology nurses were incented to achieve oncology certification (the current certification rate is 10 percent among the 80 nurses).

Nursing leadership wanted to empower nursing managers. But Apple asked, "Does medical leadership want this goal too?" She wanted senior nursing leadership to better appreciate the amount of work that nursing and service line directors did to achieve new goals after the leadership made decisions. For example, nursing leadership initiated an anonymous, online survey on how staff nurses felt about working in the hospital; the survey took 20 to 25 minutes for each nurse to complete. During the same week that Apple had to make sure the staff nurses completed the survey, she also had to see that all nurses got their flu shots, perform evaluations for 110 people, and implement all of the special initiatives in addition to her regular work. Apple concluded, "We don't have the support we need to get the work done." But she hastened to add, "The new initiatives to put patients first do make our work so exciting!"

## Part 1 Case Questions

1. How is professional integration related to nursing division performance?
2. Why doesn't professional integration have a higher priority within the strategy planning process of the nursing division?
3. What would be a rationale for giving higher priority to professional integration in the nursing division?
4. Discuss opportunities for improving professional integration in the following areas:
   a. Among the nursing departments in the five hospitals of UHS
   b. Between doctors and nurses in the individual hospitals
   c. Between nursing and finance in the individual hospitals

## Part 2, 2011: The Nursing Division at UHS—The End of the Beginning?

### Professional Integration Progress

"What has happened in the last four years?" Andrea Rogers, CNO of UHS, asked herself, resuming her dialogue with Clark Kaplan, the nursing management consultant, in the spring of 2011.

She began to summarize: "The health system has done a lot of work responding to challenges—market share, engaging physicians in different service lines, planning a response to healthcare reform. We have more data. Our financial condition is stable, and last year was our best operating year in the past five years. In nursing, we looked at the hospital's strategic goals and asked how we can support them. We have 4,800 nurses on staff today. Our three- to five-year plan has become an eight- to ten-year plan. How do we transform care at the bedside by looking at practice? How do we care for patients safely and compassionately? How can we educate nurses at the bedside? Staff nurses must understand the context underlying what we're asking them to do."

Rogers continued: "At the same time, key issues remain:

1. Workforce issues—recruiting, retaining, and determining the right amount of staffing. The data we get are not consistent or standardized, most notably from the National Database of Nursing Quality Indicators. These data are not risk adjusted.

2. How do we partner with schools of nursing so that nurses are receiving the right educational preparation for the future? We are now affiliated with more than 20 schools of nursing. More than 1,000 nursing students were placed here last year. We seem to agree with the schools so far on what we need to do, but not on how we do it.

3. How do we respond to quality mandates from external agencies, such as The Joint Commission? How can we be 'survey ready' all of the time?

4. Financial constraints—We are asking questions about productivity and value. Can we do more in nursing for what we spend?"

### Pursuing Magnet Status

Kaplan was intrigued. "Where are you now about pursuing Magnet status?" he asked. "I've never been convinced about its scientific validity."

Rogers responded: "National best hospital rankings include Magnet status as one component now. Here we are always being asked, 'Are we going to be designated?' Only 7 percent of US hospitals have Magnet status. Our goal is to continue to get better in recruiting and retaining the best workforce, ensuring that our patient outcomes surpass all benchmarks and that patient satisfaction continues to improve. That's what is important."

## The Challenge of Accountability

"For me," Rogers continued, "a particularly important issue now is nursing manager accountability for unit performance. We're not there yet. We have top performers who buy in, and their unit outcomes show it. Yet the larger pool of nursing managers needs to understand what it means to run a service and take ownership as if this were a business. We need agreement about roles, responsibilities, partnerships, and infrastructure that support such accountabilities. And for some, their span of control is too wide for them to reasonably be accountable for all staff performance—more than 100 staff nurses report to them."

## Physician–Nurse Relationships

Kaplan interjected again. "How about the relationships between physicians and nurses? Are physicians a key barrier in empowering patient care directors to take accountability for unit performance?"

Rogers paused before replying. "We've seen tremendous improvement over the years at UHS with respect to the relationship between physicians and nurses. This starts at the top with the attitudes of the clinical chiefs. I've met with each of them to find out what they needed from nursing. We have seen great teamwork in areas where we have improved communication and handoffs. In general, I think physicians feel they need nurses, they value nurses' roles and contributions, and they are more involved and aware. The leaders don't just talk; they also do things to support nurses. I guess I would say that the culture at UHS has definitely changed."

## Looking Ahead

Rogers continued: "Our goals for the next three years focus on improving nursing practice, especially by continuing to review relevant and current practice and providing nurses with the necessary knowledge and tools to do their jobs successfully. We are also working to stabilize and right-size the workforce. In addition, we will continue to focus on nurse competencies to make sure staff keep up with the latest technology. Healthcare is so far behind other sectors, such as the financial sector. How do we get IT [information technology] to support the nurse? More specifically, how can we use IT to reduce the amount of time nurses spend walking around as opposed to at the bedside?"

## Nursing Division Performance Metrics

Rogers concluded, "The key metrics we now use in evaluating nursing division performance are (1) recruitment and retention rates and turnover rates of new graduates; (2) educational preparation of workforce and certification; (3) diversity demographics given the populations that we serve; and (4) relevant quality indicators such as rates of hospital-acquired pressure ulcers, falls with and without serious injuries, urinary tract infections, and ventilator-associated pneumonia. We also look carefully at the new HCAHPS [Hospital Consumer Assessment of Healthcare Providers and Systems] measures on patients' perceptions of care, such as nurse responsiveness, explanation of procedures, pain management, and cleanliness."

## Part 2 Case Questions

1. What changes in the environment have important implications for professional integration within the nursing division?
2. What would you recommend to Rogers about pursuing Magnet status?
3. What should Rogers do to focus on nurse manager accountability for unit performance?

## Part 3, 2016: Are We Great Yet?

UHS has grown greatly since 2007 and now comprises eight hospitals. It has remained one of the top 12 hospitals in the United States as ranked by *U.S. News & World Report*. Andrea Rogers, the chief nursing officer, has turned her attention to nurse engagement, assuming it to be associated with better patient experience and higher nursing performance. UHS does not score as highly in national rankings for nursing engagement as it does for patient safety and the quality of the patient experience.

This part of the case covers two discussions—in 2015 and 2016—between Rogers and Clark Kaplan, the nursing leadership consultant.

### The 2015 Interview and Discussion

"How can we improve conversations with nursing staff who don't meet goals, especially when it is difficult to recruit their replacements?" Rogers asked Kaplan. Rogers felt that a key challenge now was achieving consistency in benchmarked performance across all nursing units. Equally important was getting consistency among interdisciplinary teams within and across units.

#### The 2015 Nursing Strategic Plan

Nursing initiatives support the mission and vision of the health system, and nursing must be able to show that what nurses do is good for UHS. The strategic planning process for nursing is a group responsibility led by a nurse director, and it has resulted in the decision to focus on six areas:

1. Quality and patient safety
2. Advancing care and shared governance

3. Operational excellence and budget
4. Technology and innovation
5. Patient and staff experience
6. Professional development and education

As part of the annual review process, nursing managers match performance against strategic goals, but the process is difficult.

According to Rogers, "The nurse leaders and I struggle with holding people accountable. We're not very good at having critical conversations with staff. We don't replace poor performers quickly enough. When do I know it's time to tell one of them that 'This might not be the right job for you'? My question is, 'Are our nurse leaders having those crucial conversations down the line?'"

## A Meeting to Discuss Nurse Leader Engagement

In August 2015, Rogers and Kaplan met with Rogers's colleagues Nell Keller and Harry Hargle to discuss accountability and factors that might influence nurse leader engagement. Keller was the former director of nursing education and now ran special projects, and Hargle was the new UHS senior VP for human resources. A portion of their conversation follows.

**Rogers:** So what is the accountability challenge that we can respond to, as you see it?

**Keller:** UHS has made tremendous progress. Nursing is doing a terrific job. We've also made changes in senior nursing leadership, recruiting largely from the outside, and we've continued to support and develop talent from within. Nursing needs to be more proactive in making sure we are focused on and measuring the right leadership outcomes, and that we are continuously improving. The answerable questions from a strategic perspective are "How do we fairly measure nurse leader performance based on unit outcomes?" and "How do we appropriately reward nurse leaders based on achievement of those outcomes?"

**Hargle:** I see the answerable question as, "How can we recruit better nurses and nursing managers to make sure the 'retain' rate climbs from, say, 50 percent to 75 percent each year, assuming performance metrics in the strategic plan are met?" We should take the money and the time we are spending on performance appraisals and invest in better recruitment strategies, starting with an objective appraisal of what we do now and how we measure what we are looking for in new recruits. We should steal nurses who are dissatisfied working in other centers and encourage them to work here, not because we are paying them more money and benefits, but because it's a better place for nurses to work. For most of our nurses, their goals are mutually aligned with ours, they embrace our culture, they respect and admire their supervisors and colleagues, and they are passionate about improving patient care at UHS.

**Kaplan:** I think the answerable question is, "How should staff be organized to meet the goals in our strategic plan?" I would focus on accountability at the unit level for all providers, including doctors, nurses, housekeepers, social workers, and clerks. The nurse manager of the unit has developed clear objectives during the past period, based in part on input from her team, and has agreed to expected unit goals and measurable performance objectives. She gets the timely data she needs to measure outcomes and be held accountable, and she gets the support she needs from central headquarters for support services such as IT and biomedical engineering, environmental services, and food service. The nurse manager decides which problems have top priority based on present performance relative to expectations. She gets the best evidence from the scientific literature, learns from best practice at leading institutions, keeps developing leadership skills, and partners with her peers at like institutions to keep up with the scientific literature that will help her and her colleagues in leadership make better decisions in managing to achieve better outcomes.

**Rogers:** That sounds great, Clark, but the problem with this description of how things ought to be is the difficulty in focusing our priorities across boundaries. We always have too many new initiatives that have to be launched, and this creates pressure because there is too much to do and because some priorities compete with each other. We also have trouble getting reluctant nurse leaders to change when they feel threatened by the change or overconfident about the status quo.

## The 2016 Interview

One year later, Kaplan interviewed Rogers again about her reflections on accountability and how UHS was doing with nurse engagement. This follow-up interview touched on a number of topics.

### Rogers's Philosophy of Accountability

Rogers summed up her philosophy as follows: "Accountability is taking ownership of decisions. Accountability doesn't require someone checking your work. Accountability reflects your commitment and engagement, your responsibility for your actions and outcomes. You own it. It's not about excuses and looking at what someone else has done. Yes, there are many things outside of your control. But does this mean you drop the ball and walk away? What actions do you take when you are accountable?"

### Challenges Leaders Face in Being Accountable

"Performance is the bottom line," Rogers continued. "Sometimes, there is a lack of clarity about objectives. Is the team sufficiently engaged? Or are they waiting for strategic direction from above, or for human resources to make the first big move? I suggest leaders focus on what they can do locally. While they are waiting for others to initiate change, they have the ability to do some things without asking for permission, in the short term, that impact performance. That's part of being accountable."

Rogers pointed out that the issues are not only about nursing. She explained: "One challenge to nurse leaders is adequate communication across silos, especially communications with physicians. For example, one physician recently did a procedure on a patient. He didn't tell the nurse responsible for the patient about his plan, but the nurse had insight that would have influenced his decision about the procedure. The result: An unnecessary procedure was performed on the patient."

She continued: "The practice of accountability across disciplines is more challenging when physicians are not employees. Expectations are not communicated clearly, and sometimes certain messages are not acted on. We respond by going through the chain of command. In my position, I report the issue to the chief of the medical staff, who then meets with the relevant department chair, who meets with the individual physician. Sometimes remedial action—such as a suspension or a period under the supervision of an attending—is taken. The important thing is that the hospital leadership is accountable, as I am, to our patients and to the board for performance."

### It's All About Leadership

"At the end of the day," Rogers concluded, "it's all about leadership performance. Education only goes so far. In our system, we don't really have a lot of leadership turnover. Perhaps we don't have sufficient turnover and should have more. Everyone looks great on paper, but results don't always reflect that. The ultimate goal is 'great' benchmarked organizational performance."

## Part 3 Case Questions

*Note*: The first four questions pertain to the 2015 interview and discussion; the last three pertain to the 2016 interview.

1. How can Andrea Rogers shape priorities to improve nursing accountability for the patient and the care team experience?
2. What are the pros and cons of Nell Keller's suggestions? Harry Hargle's? Clark Kaplan's?

3. What evidence does Rogers need to gather over what time period to address which priority questions?

4. What process does Rogers need to follow in pursuing interventions to respond to the accountability questions raised in the case?

5. How can leadership performance continually improve? How is accountability involved?

6. How does "ownership" of accountability improve leader and organizational performance?

7. What is Rogers doing—and what can she continue to do—to improve accountability in nursing at University Health System and ultimately ensure sustained great performance?

## References

American Nurses Association (ANA). 2009. *Nursing Administration: Scope & Standards of Practice*. Silver Spring, MD: ANA.

American Nurses Credentialing Center (ANCC). 2017. "Magnet Recognition Program® Overview." Accessed February 23. www.nursecredentialing.org/Magnet/ProgramOverview.

———. 2008. *A New Model for ANCC's Magnet Recognition Program*. Accessed February 23, 2017. www.nursecredentialing.org/Documents/Magnet/New-ModelBrochure.aspx.

# CASE 33

# Managing the Patient Experience: Facing the Tension Between Quality Measures and Patient Satisfaction

*Jennifer Lynn Hefner, Susan Moffatt-Bruce, and Ann Scheck McAlearney*

**B**ryce Jackson has recently been appointed chief experience officer for Academic Medical Center (AMC), a large tertiary-care health system consisting of six hospitals with a total of 1,500 inpatient beds and an annual average of 60,000 discharges. In this role, he will oversee the Department of Patient Experience, which has responsibility for patient satisfaction data, patient family complaints/grievances, patient advocacy, volunteer services, information desks, and employee engagement. Bryce will report directly to the chief quality and patient safety officer, who is responsible for quality and performance improvement across the system.

Bryce has a decade of experience working in various middle management roles within AMC's Department of Patient Experience. During this time, he has noted a growing tension between patient satisfaction and quality measures. At AMC, although all health system leaders are tasked with improving satisfaction and quality measures, fragmentation and tension results from the involvement of different leaders tasked with improving specific metrics. Bryce recently completed a master's in healthcare administration (MHA) program through a school of public health affiliated with AMC, and he found during his studies that he is not the only one to notice the growing tension.

Prominent health administrators and researchers have noted that the current structure of the Centers for Medicare & Medicaid Services (CMS) Hospital Value-Based Purchasing (HVBP) program has contributed to, and perpetuates, this tension. One specific issue is that the CMS HVBP program now reimburses for an ever-increasing number of metrics. The pie charts in exhibits 33.1 and 33.2 illustrate the changes in the HVBP program at AMC. The proportion of the reimbursement pie that is derived from patient satisfaction scores (the Hospital Consumer Assessment of Healthcare Providers and Systems, or HCAHPS, survey) has remained relatively steady, but the other segments of this pie are continually shifting. In 2013, clinical process measures filled out the rest of the pie, but for the coming fiscal year, outcomes and efficiency will be added, incorporating a variety of metrics related to quality and patient safety.

Bryce feels that use of this reimbursement pie at AMC has resulted in fragmentation of the concept of patient experience, as well as tension among organizational leaders challenged with maximizing performance for

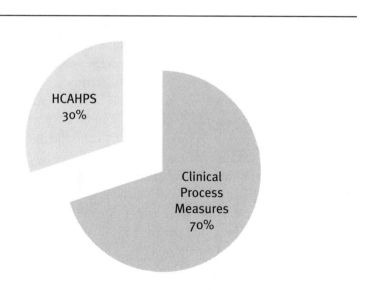

**EXHIBIT 33.1**
Breakdown of CMS Hospital Value-Based Purchasing Categories, 2013

HCAHPS
30%

Clinical Process Measures 70%

*Note:* HCAHPS = Hospital Consumer Assessment of Healthcare Providers and Systems.

**EXHIBIT 33.2**
Breakdown of
CMS Hospital
Value-Based
Purchasing
Categories,
Upcoming Fiscal
Year

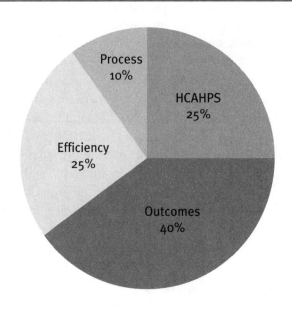

*Note:* HCAHPS = Hospital Consumer Assessment of Healthcare Providers and Systems.

the individual metrics in each leader's piece of the pie. Discussions with peers at other institutions have convinced Bryce that this problem is not isolated to AMC; in fact, these tensions are felt in health systems across the country.

The competing priorities are most evident at the point of patient care, with the patient often becoming the victim of the tension. For instance, steps taken to meet a goal in patient fall prevention—a key quality and safety metric—may be in direct conflict with a goal of improving the patient's experience as reflected in patient satisfaction scores. During his time in middle management, Bryce has been in several staff meetings where frontline nursing staff have discussed this problem. Staff are concerned that use of bed alarms will lead to hospitalized patients feeling restrained, thereby worsening their experience of care and lowering the resulting patient satisfaction scores.

Just a few months ago, a patient had been injured in a fall, triggering a patient safety event review process that highlighted this type of tension. After the fall was reported, the nurses on the care team and the physician lead reviewed the incident, and because the case was of high severity, it was discussed at the weekly significant event meeting. The administration present at the meeting called for a root cause analysis, which took 45 days and involved speaking with every party in the case. Discussions with the nurse assigned to the patient at the time of the fall noted that the patient had a bed alarm and that the alarm had gone off twice in the 24 hours preceding the fall when the patient had tried to get out of bed unassisted. Members of the staff had had a discussion about placing the patient in arm restraints, but they were concerned about infringing on the patient's rights. They knew the patient would be distraught by the use of physical restraints, but they were under great time pressure and did not know if they would be able to have a prolonged discussion with the patient about the need to have both a safe and positive experience. Staff debate about the next course of action was ongoing when the patient suffered the injury fall.

Based on this incident, and a variety of other prior experiences, Bryce has formed the opinion that much of the tension could be resolved through the development of a program to establish patient expectations. A recent large-scale survey research study, which had been included on the reading list for his capstone MHA class, indicated that patients' "met" expectations were associated with their postvisit satisfaction scores—thus supporting Bryce's idea that managing expectations may be key to solving the problem. Bryce feels that, in the ambulatory setting, patients could be provided with information about what to expect as inpatients, including the needs of the hospital and its staff, to balance safety and satisfaction. This approach would be similar to airlines' efforts to emphasize flight attendants' roles in flight safety rather than just their roles in providing passenger service on board.

Specifically, Bryce envisions appointing a multidisciplinary working group comprising all stakeholders to develop a Patient Expectation of Inpatient Care curriculum. The working group could develop an educational video to play on the hospital channel on the television in each inpatient bedroom. The video would directly present to patients the tension between satisfaction and safety and specifically highlight the recent patient fall case in which the debate over arm restraints was a factor. Each admitted patient could be directed to this video when they were assigned to a room. Bryce is confident that this approach could address the problem without involving the staff nurses directly in the education effort; nurses' direct involvement could be viewed as self-serving and would also add to their significant workload.

Bryce views his new appointment as an opportunity to address tensions, build bridges, and knock down silos. Specifically, he feels that this new role, chief experience officer, is the ideal platform from which to implement his program of patient expectation management. However, despite his enthusiasm, Bryce realizes that he must prioritize his agenda and develop a long-term plan.

## Case Questions

1. Why is patient experience a quality concern? Do you see this changing in the future?
2. How can Bryce engage his boss and his peers heading other departments to work together in support of better patient experiences?
3. How does a focus on patient education help resolve some of the tensions noted in the case?
4. What additional steps can Bryce take to better align leaders and the administrative silos mentioned in this case?

# CASE 34

## The Complaining Doctor and Ambulatory Care

*Anthony R. Kovner*

You are the assistant director for ambulatory services. An attending physician complains, "The clerks are no good in this clinic, and neither is the director of nursing." What do you say to him? Assume that the physician is an important customer.

Later during the week, he is still not satisfied. Now you are the problem. What do you do?

# CASE 35

## Doctors and the Capital Budget

*Anthony R. Kovner*

You are the hospital CEO. Doctors on the capital budget committee cannot agree on which equipment to recommend for purchase and for how much. They are way over budget. What do you say to them?

# CASE 36

## Doing the Right Thing When the Financials Do Not Support Palliative Care

*Anthony R. Kovner*

Ann Tucker, MSN, is the patient director of the palliative care unit at Community Medical Center, a large urban hospital. The palliative care unit has 20 beds and is one of 20 patient care units at the medical center. During budget time, Pat Ward, the director of nursing, tells Ann that the chief financial officer has suggested closing the palliative care unit, which is losing a small amount of money, and switching the unit to general medical care. Ann is busy with clinical work and family matters and does not have time to challenge the financial figures, but she has discussed the issue with Mary Wright, one of the oncology nurses. The following are summaries of Ann's and Mary's views:

## Ann's View

Management isn't asking the right question. The question ought to be, "What can the hospital do to provide the best care and the best experience to patients requiring palliative care?" The follow-up question is, "How can the hospital find the resources to provide that best available care?"

Ann does not find Pat Ward to be a forceful nursing leader, but rather someone "who goes along to get along." Ann has mixed feelings about taking the matter up with Dr. Paul Richards, the chief of oncology. Dr. Richards is a fiery leader and supports palliative care, but he has limited leverage with Bob Fox, the CEO, unless he is talking strictly about quality of care (relative to established evidence-based guidelines).

## Mary's View

Mary agrees with Ann's diagnosis, and she also agrees that Ann's existing responsibilities don't allow her to do anything more than writing this up. Mary suggests that Ann reach out to and meet with Sam Gold, the hospital's chief operating officer, to document the problem and ask him to investigate further. She also thinks Ann should recommend that the hospital hold up any definitive action, since there is no financial crisis, and reconsider the issue in the next budget year. Finally, Mary suggests getting the families of patients—particularly one or two members of the hospital board—involved in pressing the issue to preserve the palliative care unit. Mary says, "It's the right thing to do, you have job security, and it's the right thing for patient care."

## Case Questions

1. What is the management challenge for Community Medical Center?
2. What evidence would Sam Gold need to evaluate the alternatives he might pursue?
3. What has to happen for Ann to get a fair hearing for her justifiable concerns?

# CASE 37

# When Should We Be Alarmed?

*Susan Moffatt-Bruce and Ann Scheck McAlearney*

John, a nurse on the cardiac unit, was taking care of five patients that evening. He had started his shift at 7:00 p.m. and was getting a handoff from Lauren, the nurse who had cared for these patients for the previous 12 hours. The five patients were all stable, and all were in a medical/surgical low-acuity status. Nonetheless, the unit was far from silent.

The five patients were as follows:

- Patient 1 was receiving a continuous infusion of penicillin, and the intravenous (IV) pump kept alarming all day because the line had been placed in the elbow region.
- Patient 2 was getting an infusion of prostaglandins and was on pulse oximetry, as she had had some episodes of low oxygen the day before. Because the patient had poor circulation to her fingers, the pulse oximetry probe kept ringing "low oxygen" throughout the day, even though the patient appeared to be fine.
- Patient 3 had just had a heart attack seven days ago; he was on a heparin drip, and his blood-thinning medication was being titrated. Though this patient was up and mobile, he was considered a falls-injury risk because he was both frail and on blood thinners.
- Patient 4 was waiting to have a heart catheterization after having been admitted for undiagnosed chest pain. She was on telemetry to monitor her heart rate, which was being treated intermittently with medication, because the heart rate was on the high side.
- Patient 5 had been in the hospital for 30 days and had been having a very challenging time after vascular surgery; he was bed bound. He had a tracheostomy that was very mature and had been downsized as it was due to be removed. The patient was actively undergoing inpatient rehabilitation and was being prepared to be transferred to a rehabilitation center. Per protocol, tracheostomy patients were always on telemetry and pulse oximetry so that they could be continuously monitored.

John and Lauren did their handoffs at the doors of each of their patients' rooms. Because the patients were spread across the floor of the unit, they had to walk around the entire unit while at the same time responding to the alarms that were sounding during their sign-out. Patient 5, who was in bed and on low oxygen through his tracheostomy, had an alarm that was ringing, and when John went in to check, he noted that the probe was off the patient's finger. The patient looked stable and comfortable. John and Lauren continued their handoffs. Patient 1's IV pump alarm then began to ring when she bent her arm, and Lauren ran into the patient's room to restart the antibiotic. Patient 2 started to have alarms sound when she tried to get out of bed and her oxygen probe fell off; John quickly responded to fix the placement of the probe. Patient 3 suddenly had a disruption in his telemetry and appeared to either be flatlined or have his leads off. Both Lauren and John ran into the room and discovered that the patient had been trying to get out of bed and the leads fell off. Deciding that this patient was at a high falls-injury risk, John placed a bed alarm on Patient 3. As John and Lauren then walked out of the patient's room, the bed alarm began to sound, prompting the patient to stay in bed.

The entire handoff process took over an hour and a half, as John and Lauren relayed all the details about the patients and responded to the various alarms. By the time Lauren left, she was more than two hours over her finish time, and John had yet to do any of his individual nursing evaluations.

As John started to evaluate the patients, he heard the oxygen alarm go off in Patient 5's room. He entered the room only to find that the oxygen probe had again fallen off the patient's finger. When reminded, the patient actually put the oxygen probe back on himself. John went on to continue his nursing assessment for Patient 1. As he moved on to Patient 2, who no longer had her oxygen probe alarming, he noted that she now had her IV alarm ringing because her medication pump was running dry. Because the drug she was getting could not be interrupted, John quickly called the pharmacy so the medication would arrive as soon as possible. As John moved on to Patient 3, his phone started to ring; it was the pharmacy telling John that the important medication was ready. Because John felt he needed to quickly start the medication for Patient 2, he went back and restarted the infusion. However, when he was going into the room for Patient 2, he heard the alarm ring to signal low oxygen for Patient 5. Because he had just been in Patient 5's room and found the patient to be comfortable and able to replace the probe himself, John decided to continue to work with Patient 2; he had to get Patient 2's medication infusion restarted, because it would be life-threatening for the patient if the medication was interrupted. At the same time, the bed alarm started to ring as Patient 3 moved in his bed.

Just as John finished getting the refilled medication running for Patient 2, the heart monitor for Patient 5 started to sound. Yet because the sounds for all the types of alarms were the same, John could not tell if the sound was indicating that the leads were off or that the heart rate was actually low. He quickly finished up the infusion preparation for Patient 2 and went to help Patient 5. When he entered the room, however, he clearly saw that Patient 5 had his probe on correctly—thus the oxygen level had to be low. He found that Patient 5's heart rate and blood pressure were also very low. He immediately called a Code Blue, and the team arrived. Patient 5 was reconnected to the ventilator and had medication administered, and his vitals returned to normal. However, because the duration of his low oxygen had been prolonged, Patient 5 suffered injury to his brain.

## Case Questions

1. How do we decide on an appropriate nursing ratio for "routine" patients as they become increasingly complex? What is the role of care teams in this context?
2. How do care providers make critical decisions? How do care providers make priority choices, and how do institutions train and support providers to choose correctly?
3. What tensions exist between patient safety and patient experience in the current healthcare environment, in which we are trying to be efficient but also patient centric?
4. How do we assess the correct types of alarms that should exist for patients? How do we make the critical alarms really meaningful for the providers? What human factors must be taken into consideration in the current era of healthcare provision?
5. What strategies need to be developed to improve alarms?
6. How many alarms are really an issue, and how do we prioritize which alarms should be addressed first?

# CASE 38

# Increasing the Focus on Patient Safety at First Medical Center

*Jennifer Lynn Hefner, Susan Moffatt-Bruce, and Ann Scheck McAlearney*

At First Medical Center (FMC), the goal for the past decade has been to simultaneously improve quality and patient safety by implementing projects, initiatives, and programs either focused on an organization-wide intervention or targeted at one department, unit, or floor within the organization. This effort has resulted in a piecemeal approach to quality improvement, with one intervention layered on top of another. FMC's newly appointed chief quality and patient safety officer, Dr. Emily Frame, believes they can do better.

Emily sees a major opportunity to centralize and standardize quality initiatives through a systemwide initiative focused on both cultural change and quality improvement. Specifically, she wants to implement the Crew Resource Management (CRM) program across all units of FMC. CRM is a systematic approach to training leadership, staff, and physicians, and it incorporates customizable safety tools aimed at generating permanent culture change around patient safety. Emily is aware that adopting a unified approach to safety and quality improvement will require significant organizational change, but she believes the long-term results will justify the expected difficulty.

Given the circumstances at FMC, Emily believes that the first challenge will be to get the leaders of the institution to understand that a gap exists in patient safety and to recognize the opportunity for improvement. She is well aware that cultural transformation needs engaged leadership, and she knows that only through shared vision and purpose can such widespread programs succeed. If leaders are not engaged and supportive, the program will struggle to get off the ground, making the desired transformation virtually impossible.

Another major challenge related to executive leadership buy-in involves the financial resources necessary for implementation. Healthcare organizations have a large number of competing financial priorities, not the least of which are training and education. Training for CRM requires dedicated time away from patient care (between two and four hours), so the organization will have to backfill that nursing and physician care time. Once put into practice, however, CRM has the potential to save money by averting patient safety events. The research literature provides some evidence for these savings, particularly in critical care and surgery specialties, though systemwide implementation has never been studied. CRM has to be seen as value added and a top priority for the organization and the care of its patients.

An additional area of concern for Emily involves how she will be able to measure success. If CRM aims to improve teamwork and promote a culture of safety, how can one prove that it works? What metrics would FMC leaders, providers, and patients regard as indicators of success? As Emily well knows, cultural transformation is hard enough to define, let alone measure.

## Case Questions

1. What are the costs and potential benefits of a Crew Resource Management program?
2. What metrics could you use to measure success?
3. Does CRM make more sense in certain units than in others?

# CASE 39

# Who Is Keeping Track?

*James Ferguson and Ann Scheck McAlearney*

## Background

Hospitalists (i.e., physicians focused specifically on caring for hospitalized patients) emerged as a new medical specialty in 1996 (Wachter and Goldman 1996), and their numbers steadily increased as hospitals embraced the idea that care could be most efficiently provided by hospital-based physicians who provided only inpatient care. However, the expanding use of hospitalists nationwide has resulted in the exclusion of many local private physicians from the hospital care setting.

The integration of hospitalists into clinical practice has not been without problems, and the lack of coordination between the inpatient and outpatient settings has been particularly troublesome (McAlearney 2004). Further, within the hospital, some patients have to wait for hours to be transferred from the emergency department (ED) to the hospitalist service. When this wait is compounded with the long waits also associated with ED visits, delayed diagnosis, worsening patient health, and poor health outcomes become major concerns.

## Clint's Story

Clint was 67 years old and had been experiencing a sore throat. He went first to a local walk-in-clinic, where a physician's assistant (PA) told him his ailment was viral. The PA told him to use a mouth rinse and Tylenol as needed for discomfort. No culture was performed, and no antibiotics were prescribed.

After conditions failed to improve, Clint made an appointment with his family physician, Dr. Starr, and he brought his wife, Allison, who was an emergency medical technician (EMT). Allison explained that Clint had a rapidly progressing sore throat and that the pain had become so severe that Clint could no longer talk. She also noted that he was not even able to swallow his saliva.

Upon examination, Dr. Starr noted that Clint's mouth was red and foul smelling. Further, the uvula was pushed to the right side, and the left tonsil was obscuring most of the visible airway. Clint could hardly open his mouth and sat leaning forward to allow any secretions to drain into a soaked towel that he had brought from home.

Recognizing a potential emergency, Dr. Starr called the local ear, nose, and throat (ENT) surgeon, Dr. Hart, to arrange a meeting with the patient in the ED. Dr. Starr then typed a consult note that he faxed to the ED. He also handed a copy of the consult note to Allison with the directions that the surgeon, Dr. Hart, be paged when Clint arrived at the ED.

Upon arriving at the ED and waiting some time, Allison presented Dr. Starr's consult papers to the triage nurse. Reading the papers, the intake nurse, Margot, asked, "What is quinsy? I've never heard of that before." Allison noted that the referring doctor had felt that Clint's condition was urgent and that the surgeon, Dr. Hart, should be called now. Apparently unconvinced, Margot responded, "Well, he's breathing all right. He can wait his turn."

## Whose Patient Is This?

After waiting longer, Clint was shown to the triage area, where he was seen by a PA as part of a "fast-track" evaluation. The fast-track evaluation had been introduced as a preliminary screening step for determining whether a patient needed to be seen in the ED by a physician or could be treated by the PA as an outpatient and sent home.

The PA on duty, Mike, began the examination using his cell phone as a throat light. However, Mike complained that Clint was not cooperating and not opening his mouth wide enough to allow a good look inside. Frustrated that he was able to conduct only a minimal exam, Mike ordered a computed tomography (CT) scan. The results of the CT scan showed movement; thus no definite pathology was noted. At this point, Allison again insisted that the ENT, Dr. Hart, be contacted, and she showed Mike the consult request from Dr. Starr. Mike dismissed the request and told Allison that Clint would have to wait to be seen in the ED by a staff physician.

More time passed, and eventually an ED physician, Dr. Maple, came to examine Clint. When Dr. Maple tried to peer into the patient's mouth, however, Clint could barely open it at all. Frustrated, Dr. Maple attempted to spray an anesthetic spray into Clint's mouth to anesthetize it for better viewing, but Clint began to choke, cough, and gasp for breath. Becoming more frantic, Allison insisted that Dr. Maple read her consult note and call Dr. Hart.

After reading the note, Dr. Maple realized that the situation was truly a medical emergency, and he paged the ENT consult. Dr. Hart promptly saw Clint and rushed him to the operating room, where the abscess that was occluding his airway was drained. Clint was started on two different antibiotics and intravenous steroids. An infectious disease (ID) consult was called, and Clint was referred to the hospitalist service for admission to the hospital and subsequent inpatient care.

## Hospitalist Oversight of Hospital-Based Care

While in the hospital, Clint was seen daily by various hospitalists, but none of them seemed to be particularly well acquainted with the details of Clint's care. For instance, after Clint had been on intravenous (IV) antibiotics and pain medications for several days, Dr. Hart, the surgeon, suggested that Clint try oral medications for 24 hours prior to discharge. Dr. Hart's plan was to see if Clint could swallow oral antibiotics and not have a sudden relapse of his original symptoms.

However, because Clint's inpatient care was managed by a number of hospitalists who did not seem to communicate well with one another, Dr. Hart's treatment goal and the nuance in his changed treatment plan were not well understood across the group. In fact, once the hospitalist on duty saw that the IV medications had been discontinued, he moved to immediately discharge the patient. Further, in writing the discharge order, this hospitalist assumed that he could discharge Clint without directly checking with the surgeon or with an ID specialist about their plans of action for the patient postdischarge.

Learning about the planned discharge, Clint's family physician, Dr. Starr, came to visit him in the hospital. Both Dr. Starr and Allison were concerned that the discharge might be premature, but the discharge went through regardless. Clint was given prescriptions for both antibiotics and steroids for swelling, as well as referrals for follow-up appointments with Dr. Hart, the ENT, and an ID specialist.

## Case Questions

1. What distinct factors do you believe contributed to Clint's problems?
2. Based on your response to the first question, what strategies would you propose to reduce the likelihood of recurrences of these types of events?
3. What staff education would you recommend to streamline the patient care given in this case?
4. What communication errors can you find? How would you prevent them in the future?
5. How would you, as Margot, the intake nurse, have handled this patient?
6. How would you, as Mike, the physician assistant, have changed the outcome in this case?

## References

McAlearney, A. S. 2004. "Hospitalists and Family Physicians: Understanding Opportunities and Risks." *Journal of Family Practice* 53 (6): 473–81.

Wachter, R. M., and L. Goldman. 1996. "The Emerging Role of 'Hospitalists' in the American Health Care System." *New England Journal of Medicine* 335 (7): 514–17.

# CASE 40

# Managing Relationships: Take Care of Your Nurses

*Anthony R. Kovner*

Betsy Cline, the patient care director of the 14-bed pediatric cardiac intensive care unit (PCICU) at Children's Hospital, has held this post for two years. The unit has an $8 million budget. Cline has worked at Children's Hospital for 16 years. She spends 50 percent of her time on patient safety, 20 percent on staffing and recruitment, and 20 percent focused on nurses' satisfaction with the work and families' satisfaction with care. The remaining 10 percent of Cline's time is spent on administrative duties. She says, "What I like is working with exceptional nurses who are very smart and do what it takes with limited resources. However, we don't always feel empowered, despite the existence of shared governance, a structure I help to coordinate." Exhibit 40.1 shows the PCICU organization chart.

## Relationships with Nurses on the Unit

Nurses on the unit work three days a week, 12 hours a shift. Cline says, "My name is on the unit, not the medical director's. If anything goes wrong with the unit, they blame it on nursing. Yet I'm brushed off by people with whom I have to deal outside of the unit. For example, we have a problem with machines that analyze blood gases. I spoke with people about the technology about four weeks ago. I sent them e-mails. It's a patient safety issue, and I need the work to get done. The staff don't feel empowered if I'm not empowered. This goes for other departments as well. For example, respiratory therapy starts using a new ventilator without informing us. We have never seen this machine, nor

**EXHIBIT 40.1**
PCICU
Organization
Chart

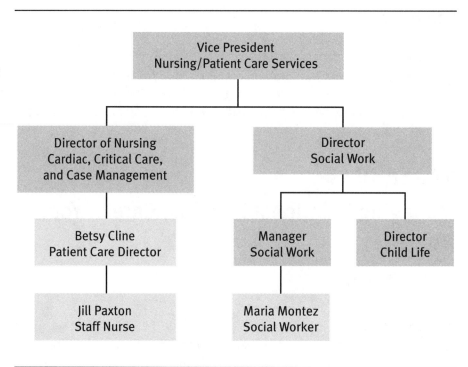

have we been in-serviced on it. They don't phone or e-mail. So I make the decision that we're not going to use the machine. With surgeons, when I tell them to wash their hands, they roll their eyes. It takes tremendous energy to deal with this."

Jill Paxton, RN, is a clinical nurse in the PCICU. She has worked in the unit for six months, having been at the hospital for nearly nine months. Paxton spends 40 percent of her time dealing with patients and families—turning, suctioning, changing dressings; 30 percent talking with physicians—negotiating plans of care and medication plans; 20 percent in medications administration and conversations with the pharmacy; and 10 percent on miscellaneous duties. She has worked on the day shift for only three weeks now, but she had also been on days for three months during orientation. Paxton says she is challenged to get the core services she needs. If she has to give a 2:00 p.m. medication and would like the medication by 1:00 p.m., she gets it by 4:00 p.m., even if she calls. She also has difficulty coordinating with the child life specialist—a specialist who breaks down medical terminology to children (e.g., "what's about to happen to you") and also deals with siblings. Paxton cannot find the cardiac transplant consultant when she needs her and doesn't have her pager number. Paxton's main satisfactions are educating the people she's working with, repairing children and seeing them go home, and helping the families.

## Relationships with Families

Cline says, "I place a clear emphasis on orienting families to the unit and showing how we do our job. We treat families with respect. Families watch me, and mentoring of nurses is important."

Paxton agrees that the unit generally does a good job supporting families. She says: "Families are kind and happy, though we do have problems with doctor and resident turnover because they typically aren't here two days in a row. The plan of care can also get lost with attendings when they change every week. Families are told different outcomes and recovery times. Families get stressed out and are often far from home. I listen to them and ask, 'Do you have any questions?' 'What do you want to see done?' 'Do you have any questions for the doctors?' I ask them if they want to participate in rounds. Sometimes we just listen. When families can't come in, they can call me every two hours because we have an in-house phone that accepts outside calls."

Cline and Paxton feel that families are an important part of what they do, that the unit has special structures and processes to involve families, and that what they are doing is generally working. But they lack concrete ways to measure unit performance in this regard.

## Relationships with Social Work

Cline says: "The hospital has a social worker who deals with heart transplant patients. This service is fragmented, and I have difficulty getting her to come to the unit. I will go to her director or to my director if I have to. I understand she has other responsibilities, but she needs to come to rounds, to deal with issues around getting nurses for home care. Of course, social workers can't wave a magic wand."

Maria Montez, the unit social worker, has worked in the PCICU for ten years. She spends 75 percent of her time on the floors with families. She works from 9:30 a.m. to 5:30 p.m., five days a week; additional social work coverage is in place at other hours. The kinds of issues Montez deals with are requests for a visiting nurse; medications and associated education; ordering of oxygen; arranging for a special intervention team at home if needed for assessment; and physical, occupational, and speech therapy. If a patient is dying, Montez discusses with nursing what they can do together when crises come up.

Montez says she has a good relationship with Cline. Montez respects the work that nurses do and helps orient new nurses to social work. She says: "We're invited to each other's rounds. The work is so intense, and there are so many patients. We've reached a level of understanding; if there's a problem, it's not personal. It's what we're all going through. We discuss each of the 37 patients in the three ICUs once a week at an interdisciplinary conference." Montez concludes, "If I could advise the hospital administrator, I would tell her to take care of your nurses."

## Case Questions

1. What are the most important things that Betsy Cline can do to "take care of her nurses" in the PCICU?
2. What are the priorities for Jill Paxton?
3. How can nurses in the PCICU judge whether the unit is doing an adequate job of supporting families?
4. What advice would you give to the hospital administrator to take care of the nurses?

# ADAPTATION

A hospital is a living organism, made up of many different parts,
having different functions, but all these must be in due proportion
and relation to each other, and to the environment, to produce
the desired general results. The stream of life which runs through
it is incessantly changing. . . . Its work is never done; its equipment
is never complete; it is always in need of new means of
diagnosis, of new instruments and medicines;
it is to try all things and hold fast
to that which is good.

*—John Shaw Billings*

# COMMENTARY

**A**dapting to external and internal pressures for and against change is a difficult challenge for the manager of any healthcare organization (HCO). The word *adaptation* suggests a view of organizational survival and growth dependent on a specific direction of change. A closer fit between environmental demands and organizational response allows the organization to attract greater or continued resources from society.

A key paradigm here comes from marketing. In quality improvement, it is called customer-mindedness. The central idea is to find out what people want and to design a product or service that meets those preferences, rather than create a product or service and try to convince people that they want it. Finding out what patients want and organizing to respond to those preferences is at the core of a customer-driven organization. In HCOs, the notion of patient-centered care is helping focus service delivery to meet those customer needs. Patient satisfaction surveys, focus groups, follow-up telephone calls after discharge, and community surveys are now widely used.

Organizations vary in their sensitivity to environmental pressures. HCOs function in complex environments, and failure to respond to pressures—such as competition, financing problems, and workforce issues—threatens their viability. In all aspects of healthcare, large organizations are getting larger and capturing market share, although many markets still have room for smaller organizations to remain viable and grow. Competitors typically cross traditional lines. For example, large health systems may contain within them a health maintenance organization (HMO), a long-term care facility, a nursing home, home health care services, and neighborhood health centers. HCOs compete with each other for patients, funding, and workforce.

Medical technologies are constantly changing. The development of new drugs continues to open up new avenues of treatment for numerous patients. Advancements in surgery have transformed the way many procedures are performed, to the point that more than 50 percent of surgery is now done in ambulatory surgery centers and doctors' offices. Hernia surgery, which once required a 20-day hospital stay, is now routinely an ambulatory procedure. Paperless electronic health records, telemetric laboratory and radiologic testing, computer-assisted laser surgery, and robotic surgery are already commonplace. Digital radiology tests taken in the United States are being read by radiologists in Australia and India. Keeping up with advances in informatics and diagnostic procedures is costly, and the benefits of those advances are difficult to forecast.

HCOs are physically located in communities, but the populations they serve may be local, regional, or even national, as consumers increasingly shop over the Internet and travel for services they believe to be higher in quality or less costly. Some patients, for instance, have surgery in India or other countries, in hopes of receiving adequate-quality care at a lower cost. But many organizations are locally controlled and require strong community relations to accomplish their purpose. For example, an HCO's relations with a church may be important in making sure that low-income mothers-to-be receive adequate prenatal services. Some HCOs are owned by a government, with the goal of meeting the healthcare needs of nearby residents. Others serve the poor to maintain their not-for-profit tax status. HCOs are often large employers. When a healthcare facility closes, the community becomes less attractive. Conversely, when a large new facility opens, it can be a boon to local union workers and firms.

HCOs receive funding from a variety of sources, each with its own rates, regulations, and conditions. The organizations often have little influence over what they get paid by large payers; in some cases, they can only respond by trying to increase volume. Payer mix is an important consideration in HCOs' decisions about what services are started, increased, decreased, or discontinued.

HCOs respond to external pressures in a variety of ways, whether by pursuing acquisitions or mergers, selling or closing services and programs, investing (or not) in highly intensive capital technology, or saturating (or not) local areas with satellite health centers. Appropriate response often requires specialized management staff engaged in planning, marketing, community relations, data generation, data analytics, and other areas. HCOs must constantly scan the environment to ensure that they can adequately respond to current developments and anticipate future trends.

## Discussion Questions

1. What are the forces that lead to various decisions about whether organizations need to change?
2. What role do managers play in organizational change and adaptation?
3. What are the barriers to change in healthcare organizations, and how can these be overcome?
4. What can HCOs do to extend the reach of their mission and to serve the surrounding communities? Are they obligated to do so?

5. Give an example of an environmental pressure affecting large group practices, and suggest alternative ways in which the group practices can adapt to these pressures.

6. How do HCOs raise the capital they need to adapt to change?

7. What are the key aspects of an HCO's commitment to realizing patient-centered care?

## Recommended Readings

Arndt, M., and B. Bigelow. 2000. "The More Things Change, the More They Stay the Same." *Health Care Management Review* 25 (1): 65–72.

Begun, J., and K. B. Heatwole. 1999. "Strategic Cycling: Shaking Complacency in Healthcare Strategic Planning." *Journal of Healthcare Management* 44 (5): 339–51.

Berkowitz, E. N. 2006. *Essentials of Healthcare Marketing*, 2nd ed. Boston: Jones & Bartlett.

Berry, L. L., and N. Bendapudi. 2003. "Clueing in Customers." *Harvard Business Review* 81 (2): 100–106.

Christensen, C. M., R. Bohmer, and J. Kenagy. 2000. "Will Disruptive Innovations Cure Health Care?" *Harvard Business Review* 78 (5): 102–12.

Collins, J. C., and J. I. Porras. 1996. "Building Your Company's Vision." *Harvard Business Review* 74 (5): 65–77.

Davenport, T. H., and J. G. Harris. 2007. *Competing on Analytics*. Boston: Harvard Business School Press.

Foreman, S. 2004. "Montefiore Medical Center in the Bronx, New York: Improving Health in an Urban Community." *Academic Medicine* 79 (12): 1154–61.

Garvin, D. A., and M. A. Roberto. 2001. "What You Don't Know About Making Decisions." *Harvard Business Review* 79 (8): 108–16.

Griffith, J. R., and K. R. White. 2016. "Internal Consulting" and "Marketing and Strategy." In *The Well-Managed Healthcare Organization*, 8th ed., 457–524. Chicago: Health Administration Press.

———. 2010. "Knowledge Management," "Human Resources Management," and "Marketing and Strategy." In *Reaching Excellence in Healthcare Management*, 201–43, 307–27. Chicago: Health Administration Press.

Griffith, J. R., and K. R. White, with P. Cahill. 2003. *Thinking Forward: Six Strategies for Highly Successful Organizations*. Chicago: Health Administration Press.

Hilligoss, B., P. H. Song, and A. S. McAlearney. 2016. "Aligning for Accountable Care: Strategic Practices for Change in Accountable Care Organizations." *Health Care Management Review* 42 (3): 192–202.

Kotter, J. P. 1995. "Leading Change: Why Transformation Efforts Fail." *Harvard Business Review* 73 (2): 59–67.

McAlearney, A. S., J. Hefner, C. Sieck, and T. R. Huerta. 2015. "The Journey Through Grief: Insights from a Qualitative Study of Electronic Health Record Implementation." *Health Services Research* 50 (2): 462–88.

Mintzberg, H. 1994. "The Fall and Rise of Strategic Planning." *Harvard Business Review* 72 (1): 107–14.

Porter, M. E., and E. O. Teisberg. 2006. *Redefining Healthcare*. Boston: Harvard Business School Press.

Reichheld, F. F. 2001. "Lead for Loyalty." *Harvard Business Review* 79 (7): 76–84.

Rindler, M. E. 2007. *Strategic Cost Reduction*. Chicago: Health Administration Press.

Robinson, J. C., and S. Dratler. 2006. "Corporate Structure and Capital Strategy at Catholic Healthcare West." *Health Affairs* 25 (1): 134–47.

Senge, P. M. 1990. *The Fifth Discipline: The Art and Practice of the Learning Organization*. New York: Doubleday Currency.

Steiger, N., and A. Balog. 2010. "Realizing Patient-Centered Care: Putting Patients in the Center, Not the Middle." *Frontiers of Health Services Management* 26 (4): 15–25.

Zuckerman, A. M. 2006. "Advancing the State of the Art in Healthcare Strategic Planning." *Frontiers of Health Services Management* 23 (2): 3–15.

# THE CASES

Adaptive capability involves organizational responses to new conditions. Healthcare organizations (HCOs) must be innovative or proactive in responding to the pressures of competitors and regulators and to the expectations of various stakeholder groups—from customers to physicians. One indicator of adaptive capability is the presence of specialized units to carry out certain functions, such as strategic planning and marketing, that are concerned specifically with adapting rather than with operations.

Strategic planning is an important managerial function. It can be conducted through a special unit, through some part of a special unit, directly by management, or by some combination of the above. Top management sees to it that information about the organization's business is gathered. Questions about the organization's mission, services, customers, competition, and strategies are addressed.

Organizations have limited problem-solving capacities. They typically avoid uncertainty, engage in biased searches for ways of adapting, act on the basis of limited knowledge, and select alternatives on the basis of past successes (Milio 1983).

Decisions to adapt can run counter to organizational goals and system maintenance. Even if the decisions can be shown, in hindsight, to have been technically appropriate, they may have been politically inappropriate. Managers may fail to consider the values of important stakeholders when they plan how to attain their mission and strategy. We are assuming, of course, that the HCO already has a carefully worked out mission and strategy, which it constantly reassesses in terms of competitive and regulatory pressures and in terms of the preferences and expectations of stakeholders, such as physicians and nurses.

The four longer case studies in this section deal with questions of adapting the organization to meet the needs of employees and patients. How these questions are answered and what strategies are selected may have consequences that are different for specific organizations and for specific managers. In Case 41, "Challenges for Mammoth Health System," a CEO, Barb Northrop, faces a series of choices about organizational priorities, given the organization's desire to become an employer of choice. In Case 42, "A Home Health Care Dilemma," two business partners consider whether their organization, C&A Home Health, should expand in response to market changes and reimbursement pressures. Next, in Case 43, "Should XYZ Healthcare Organization Make the Baldrige Journey?," Sarah Cho, an administrative fellow at XYZ, must compile information about the Baldrige program to help inform leadership's decisions about strategic direction. In Case 44, "Cultural Competency at Marion County Health Center," efforts to address problems associated with racial and ethnic health disparities and discrimination lead an administrator to carefully consider the perspectives of multiple stakeholders and the implications for the future of the health center.

The six shorter cases examine issues surrounding adaptation from multiple perspectives. In Case 45, "Shoes for the Shoemaker," a director must decide among strategic alternatives for a health management program. In Case 46, "An Investment Decision for Central Med Health System," leaders must choose between two investment options, knowing that the decision will have a major impact on product focus and delivery for the health system and have broad implications for a variety of stakeholders. In Case 47, "A New Look?," a cosmetic surgeon considers a new strategic direction for her practice in the face of increasing competition. In Case 48, "Disparities in Care at Southern Regional Health System," a CEO must take action when he is presented with evidence that his hospital has been providing disparate care across racial and ethnic categories. In Case 49, "How Can an ACO Improve the Health of Its Population?," the manager of care coordination for a new accountable care organization must consider both organizational and patient perspectives in the context of an opportunity to improve the health of the community. Finally, Case 50, "Hearing the Patient Voice," highlights the importance of considering patients' perspectives and the value of patient and family advisers in healthcare delivery.

## Reference

Milio, N. 1983. "Health Care Organizations and Innovation." In *Health Services Management: Readings and Commentary,* 2nd ed., edited by A. R. Kovner and D. Neuhauser, 448–64. Chicago: Health Administration Press.

# ▍CASE 41

# Challenges for Mammoth Health System: Becoming the Best Around

*Ann Scheck McAlearney*

## Mammoth Health System

The six hospitals that made up Mammoth Health System (MHS) enjoyed some of the best weather the United States had to offer. Nonetheless, Barb

Northrop, the chief executive officer (CEO) of MHS, had the same view as her employees—four walls of a relatively large cubicle. Her cube was one among many located on the second floor of the system's corporate office building. She had insisted on this arrangement when corporate services had moved to the new site. Senior executives, directors, managers, and staff analysts all had cubes, leaving window views for the meeting rooms and conference rooms located along the building's exterior walls.

Northrop had assumed the CEO role six months ago, and she was still trying to digest all the issues and opportunities confronting the health system. Currently, MHS was struggling to compete with the region's other major health system, and MHS had not been winning the battle. Aurora Health System, capitalizing on its reputation as an academic specialty referral center, had spent the previous five years gradually expanding its market share and luring away capable employees from MHS. Northrop's recent promotion to CEO from chief nursing officer (CNO) presented her with the new opportunity to assess reality for MHS and to make decisions that could set MHS on a better path.

## Taking Stock of MHS

When Northrop took the helm at MHS, her first step had been to assemble her executive team and get a sense of the extent of MHS's problems and opportunities. Her chief quality officer, Rebecca Robinson, was particularly helpful, especially given Robinson's access to data and expertise with data analysis.

Robinson pointed out that MHS's patient satisfaction scores were very positive, having been above 90 percent for the past three years. Northrop, however, was not convinced. She knew that patient satisfaction scores tended to be high and suspected that these scores did not tell the whole story—after all, patients were selecting Aurora hospitals over MHS hospitals. Northrop decided she needed to learn more, so she enlisted the help of her new management fellow, Kevin Pickett, to investigate patient satisfaction measurement at MHS and elsewhere.

## Patient Satisfaction Measurement

Excited about his first big project working for Northrop, Pickett began to learn everything he could about patient satisfaction. Reviewing MHS's patient satisfaction survey data, he saw that satisfaction was high and had been high for several years, just as Robinson had noted. However, he was also skeptical. What did 90 percent mean at MHS? What could this be compared to?

After doing a little digging, Pickett found that many hospitals' individually reported patient satisfaction scores were above 90 percent. In fact, high levels of patient satisfaction were touted on most hospitals' websites, but again he wondered, what did 90 percent mean?

## Examining the Evidence for Patient Satisfaction Measurement

Pickett decided to investigate the evidence further and logged into the hospital's library website, where he had access to a variety of searchable databases. Beginning a rudimentary search, he selected the PubMed database first. He then added the Academic Source Complete, Health and Consumer Information, and Business Source Complete databases, so he could search for evidence both within and outside the healthcare literature.

Knowing that the broad term "patient satisfaction" would return too many articles for him to review, Pickett used combinations of search terms— for instance, "patient satisfaction rates" and "comparison." He was still overwhelmed by the number of articles returned, so he decided to refine his search to retrieve only review articles. Pickett knew that review articles were often helpful because they reviewed and summarized a number of different articles on a given topic. Using this focused search strategy, he was able to cull through the refined search results to uncover a few key papers. He began to scan the articles so he could make sense of the evidence.

Patient satisfaction scores, Pickett learned, were less informative when surveys were conducted internally and not benchmarked against other institutions. However, national firms could conduct patient satisfaction surveys for their clients, and these firms could aggregate their data and compare individual hospitals' and health systems' scores with those of hospitals with similar characteristics. Such benchmarked comparison could provide individual hospitals with more specific information about their patient satisfaction levels. These levels would be measured in the same way that levels were measured at other hospitals, thus enabling across-hospital comparisons.

With a few more clicks, Pickett found the website for Press Ganey, a firm known for survey-based measurement of patient satisfaction in healthcare, and he began exploring the information it provided. He noted that Press Ganey did indeed provide the comparative benchmark information that MHS might find helpful, and it also offered clients an opportunity to drill down into their patient satisfaction data by providing reports by unit, by department, and so forth.

Pickett reported back to Northrop with a major recommendation: MHS should consider revising its patient satisfaction measurement program and begin to benchmark itself against other hospitals using a survey and measurement process that enables across-site comparisons as well as unit-level information on satisfaction levels.

## Getting a New Baseline

Northrop had suspected that MHS might be able to learn more from patient-based surveys, so she was not surprised by Pickett's recommendation. She then set out to obtain board-level support for the new expense of using a national firm to perform patient satisfaction surveys. She made the compelling case that the investment could provide information that would help MHS better compete against Aurora and other regional hospitals. She also highlighted the ways that benchmarked data could be used to guide efforts to improve quality of care and patient service within MHS.

The board agreed to Northrop's proposal, and the stage was set for MHS to get new patient satisfaction data. Robinson was happy to lead the process, and all was moving along nicely—until the new numbers came out.

When compared to similar hospitals and health systems across the country, MHS's patient satisfaction rates were abysmal: Only 11 percent of patients were reported to be satisfied with the care and service they received at MHS. According to the new benchmarked data, MHS was among the worst in patient satisfaction nationwide. What was going on?

## Looking Further

Northrop was surprised at the poor showing for MHS but also secretly pleased. She felt that the new information could spur MHS to implement what she considered necessary organizational changes—and she knew that organizational change was never easy. The shockingly low patient satisfaction scores could provide a "burning platform" and a sense of urgency to change things around a bit at MHS.

However, Northrop also knew that these poor numbers would not be accepted blindly by either the physicians or the board members who monitored the metrics. She enlisted Pickett's help once again to examine the unit-level patient satisfaction rates to learn more from the new surveys.

Looking further at the satisfaction data, Pickett noted that one area in particular stood out: MHS employee attitudes rated very poorly, and this issue had clearly translated to low levels of patient satisfaction. Pickett took the detailed information to Northrop and was curious about how she would react.

## Examining Employee Satisfaction Data

Northrop, who considered herself a data person, was delighted that the new data had sufficient detail to enable MHS to investigate issues that might be contributing to poor patient satisfaction. The detailed information about poor employee attitudes suggested that problems throughout MHS were contributing to the negative attitudes, and, in Northrop's eyes, these problems presented opportunities.

Because she had been an employee at MHS, Northrop knew the organization regularly collected information about employee attitudes and their satisfaction as part of its annual employee survey. She asked Pickett to investigate further and provide her with a summary of employee satisfaction survey data from the past five years.

Within the week, Pickett was able to show Northrop results of the MHS employee satisfaction survey that appeared consistent with the negative employee attitudes found in the recent patient surveys. What surprised Northrop, though, was that despite fairly low turnover rates at MHS, employees, on average, were not particularly pleased with MHS as a place to work. These findings had not changed much over the past five years.

## Employees Were Not Satisfied

The overall sense that Northrop gleaned from the survey scores was that employees considered MHS a "good" place to work because of such factors as the location, the benefits, and the fact that employees felt fairly secure about not being laid off. However, the scores indicated that MHS was far from "great." In fact, the organization showed consistently low marks in "focus on people," "caring about employee development," and "likelihood to recommend MHS as a place to work." Further, while the results showed some variation by department, they had also been relatively stable over the five years the survey had been performed.

Northrop was convinced. As she reflected to Pickett, "MHS certainly seems to have some work to do to improve employee satisfaction—and this has been the case for some time. It's time for us to start paying attention."

## Considering How to Improve

Northrop told Pickett to get Robinson and asked that both of them bring their computers and their data to the second-floor conference room. She also suggested that they bring full cups of coffee so they would be ready to tackle the problems that the data had brought to light.

When Pickett and Robinson arrived, Northrop welcomed them and immediately turned to the conference room's whiteboard to write one word: "Baldrige."

Northrop went on to explain that the Baldrige program had been established as a public–private partnership focused on quality improvement and performance excellence in US organizations. As she noted, the Baldrige Performance Excellence Program (2016b) tries to help organizations across industries improve, and it highlights three focus areas:

- Help organizations achieve best-in-class levels of performance.
- Identify and recognize role-model organizations.
- Identify and share best management practices, principles, and strategies.

Not surprisingly, Robinson was familiar with the Baldrige program, and she quickly found the program websites listing the criteria and providing information about previous winners of the Baldrige Award in the various categories (e.g., small business, education, manufacturing) (Baldrige Performance Excellence Program 2015). She discovered that, although the Baldrige Award had been presented to outstanding organizations since 1988, the first award in the healthcare sector had not been given until 2002. Since then, a handful of HCOs had been recognized with the award, but none were in MHS's local area.

Northrop was excited. Looking over Robinson's shoulder, she pointed to the information on the website about the Baldrige Criteria for Performance Excellence. The website explained that the criteria represent "a set of questions about critical aspects of managing and performing as an organization" and that the questions "work together as a unique, integrated performance management framework that any organization can use to improve overall performance" (Baldrige Performance Excellence Program 2016a). The seven criteria were listed as follows (Baldrige Performance Excellence Program 2017b):

1. Leadership
2. Strategy
3. Customers
4. Measurement, analysis, and knowledge management
5. Workforce
6. Operations
7. Results

In addition, the website offered access to the *Baldrige Excellence Framework (Health Care)*, a workbook specifically intended to guide HCOs in their Baldrige performance improvement efforts (Baldrige Performance Excellence Program 2017c).

Although Northrop knew that MHS had a long way to go, she suspected that the Baldrige Criteria could provide an evidence-based framework to guide the organization's efforts to improve in patient satisfaction and other performance areas. She was particularly concerned about the workforce focus area, given the data MHS had gathered about employee attitudes.

Reviewing the workforce materials, Northrop was particularly struck by the use of the phrase "high performance." The workforce category "addresses key workforce practices—those directed toward creating and maintaining a high-performance environment and toward engaging your workforce to enable it and your organization to adapt to change and succeed" (Baldrige Performance Excellence Program 2017a). Turning to Pickett, she asked him to investigate the notion of high-performance work practices in HCOs to see what the phrase really meant and to find additional information that could focus MHS's efforts to improve.

## Use of High-Performance Work Practices in Healthcare Organizations

Pickett's review of both peer-reviewed sources and "gray" literature (i.e., reports, articles, and information available from non-peer-reviewed sources such as trade journals, the Internet, and consultants and other organizations) showed that the topic of high-performance work practices (HPWPs) had been of interest for some time. He also found that a number of research studies had emphasized the topic within the last few years. Digging more deeply, Pickett found that a conceptual model had been proposed to examine HPWPs in HCOs (Garman et al. 2011) and that the applicability of this model had been investigated through a series of case studies of HCOs that were considered good places to work (McAlearney et al. 2011). A third article within the same series explored the issue of how HCOs might create a business case for investment in HPWPs (Song et al. 2012), although the article noted that a business case was, in practice, difficult to quantitatively establish.

As Garman and colleagues (2011, 202) state, "HPWPs can be defined as a set of practices within organizations that enhance organizational outcomes by improving the quality and effectiveness of employee performance." Their examples of such work practices include involving employees in organizational decision making, applying selective hiring practices, and using rigorous recruiting practices. Various work practices can be considered HPWP "subsystems," thus providing an organizing framework for how to think about four main areas of HPWPs: (1) staff engagement, (2) leadership alignment and development, (3) staff acquisition and development, and (4) frontline empowerment (Garman et al. 2011; McAlearney et al. 2011). McAlearney and colleagues (2011) elaborate on the subsystems as follows:

### HPWP Subsystem 1: Staff Engagement

Communicating mission and vision

Information sharing

Employee involvement in decision making

Performance-driven rewards/recognition

### HPWP Subsystem 2: Leadership Alignment/Development

Leadership training linked to organizational goals

Succession planning

Performance-contingent rewards

### HPWP Subsystem 3: Staff Acquisition/Development

Rigorous recruiting

Selective hiring

Career development

Extensive training

### HPWP Subsystem 4: Frontline Empowerment

Employment security

Employment safety

Reduced status distinctions

Teams/decentralized decision making

Pickett himself had been introduced to MHS through the highly selective fellowship application process, but he did not know how other employees were recruited and selected across the various MHS entities. Further, he knew from his review of the most recent MHS employee survey that the vast majority of employees did not feel included in MHS decisions—whether at the individual job level, at the unit level, or at the broader organization level. As Pickett reflected on the practices and subsystems in the proposed model for HPWPs in HCOs, he sensed that MHS had a long way to go.

## Moving Ahead

Northrop knew that focusing on people was the right thing to do, but she also knew that she could not change the organization on her own. Given MHS's poor marks in both patient and employee satisfaction, she suspected that the HPWP model might provide a framework for examining MHS's "people practices" and for uncovering specific areas for improvement. Baseline data in both areas had clearly shown that MHS was far from perfect; thus the case could be made that the status quo was no longer acceptable. Still, as the literature was starting to show (e.g., Song et al. 2012), investment in HPWPs was generally considered a "leap of faith"—not a decision known to demonstrate a proven return on investment.

Northrop was also aware that the Baldrige process was costly. The application process itself was expensive, to say nothing of the organizational changes the system would have to make to present a convincing case for performance excellence.

As Northrop reviewed the evidence that Robinson and Pickett had presented, she wondered what she should do next. She knew that she needed the support of her executive leadership team and solid commitment from the health system's board if she was going to make progress and transform MHS. However, she also knew that she had to proceed carefully if she was going to propose substantial changes for the organization—especially considering that she had only been leading MHS for a short time.

## Case Questions

1. What are Northrop's current options for MHS? What are the pros and cons of the different options she might recommend?
2. What option do you recommend that Northrop propose for MHS? Why?
3. Given the option you select, outline a proposal that Northrop could use to make her case to the board. What do you need to include in your proposal to make this case as strong as possible? What additional information would you need to support this proposal?
4. Describe a communications plan that Northrop can use to present the outline of this proposal to MHS employees. Again, what should be included in this plan? Is there anything that should be left out?

## References

Baldrige Performance Excellence Program. 2017a. "Baldrige Criteria Commentary (Health Care)." National Institute of Standards and Technology. Updated January 12. www.nist.gov/baldrige/baldrige-criteria-commentary-health-care.
———. 2017b. *2017–2018 Baldrige Excellence Framework: A Systems Approach to Improving Your Organization's Performance.* Gaithersburg, MD: US Department of Commerce, National Institute of Standards and Technology.
———. 2017c. "2017–2018 Baldrige Excellence Framework (Health Care)." National Institute of Standards and Technology. Updated January 12. www.nist.gov/baldrige/publications/baldrige-excellence-framework/health-care.

———. 2016a. "Baldrige FAQs: The Baldrige Excellence Framework and Criteria." National Institute of Standards and Technology. Updated September 21. www.nist.gov/baldrige/baldrige-faqs-baldrige-excellence-framework-and-criteria.

———. 2016b. "What We Do." National Institute of Standards and Technology. Updated September 21. www.nist.gov/baldrige/about/what_we_do.cfm.

———. 2015. "Baldrige Award Recipient Information." National Institute of Standards and Technology. Updated December. http://patapsco.nist.gov/Award_Recipients/index.cfm.

Garman, A., A. S. McAlearney, M. Harrison, P. Song, and M. McHugh. 2011. "High-Performance Work Systems in Health Care Management, Part 1: Development of an Evidence-Informed Model." *Health Care Management Review* 36 (3): 201–13.

McAlearney, A. S., A. Garman, P. Song, M. McHugh, J. Robbins, and M. Harrison. 2011. "High-Performance Work Systems in Health Care Management, Part 2: Qualitative Evidence from Five Case Studies." *Health Care Management Review* 36 (3): 214–26.

Song, P., J. Robbins, A. Garman, and A. S. McAlearney. 2012. "High-Performance Work Systems in Health Care, Part 3: The Role of the Business Case." *Health Care Management Review* 37 (2): 110–21.

# CASE 42

# A Home Health Care Dilemma: Considering Expansion

*Terri Menser, Barbara Barash, and Ann Scheck McAlearney*

Ashley had started as a licensed practical nurse (LPN) and shift lead at True Care, a home health care agency; her focus was providing care to patients with severe spinal cord injuries. After three years of additional part-time training, Ashley recently completed a bridge program to become a registered nurse (RN). The patient population that she serves requires care from both a certified nursing assistant (CNA) for patients' daily living needs and from an LPN or RN for medical care and medication management. Typical care usually includes medication, documentation of vital signs, and a complete examination of the patient. Many patients with spinal cord injury need around-the-clock care, requiring rotating twelve-hour shifts.

During her time at True Care, Ashley has seen a constant turnover of LPNs and supervisors, and supervisors have had great difficulty balancing the combination of clinical and administrative demands. As a result of the management turnover, procedures seemed to be constantly changing, challenging any semblance of consistency. Employees were left confused, frustrated, and ultimately demotivated. Consequently, patients suffered, as staff failed to show up for assigned appointments. Ashley was concerned that the staff were starting to miss simple diagnoses during patient assessment; she knew that these misses could lead to increased healthcare utilization (e.g., unnecessary emergency department visits). In addition, with each change in supervisors came a change in the manner and duration of employee training. Ashley suspected that this variability in training might have affected the quality of training received by new hires. It may also have affected employees' adherence to proper safety and infection control protocols.

## Considering a New Approach

In discussions with Craig, True Care's office manager, Ashley had often talked about the issues True Care faced and the improvements she would make if she were in the position to do so. Craig had started his healthcare career in medical billing prior to switching to home health care. Like Ashley, he had just finished his own advanced degree, a master of health administration (MHA). Craig's passion for home health stemmed from personal experience: His older brother was partially paralyzed and required home care. Growing up, Craig had learned of home health care's complexity, and he understood the field from the client's perspective. He thought Ashley's ideas were sound. He became convinced that together they could establish a better home health care agency, and he was eager to explore the option of forming a new business with her. Craig had tremendous confidence in Ashley's abilities and had come to trust her implicitly; thus she was an ideal business partner. Craig was confident that his background in healthcare management, finance, and information technology; his unique perspective on patient care; and Ashley's experience and knowledge of the home health industry would enable them to succeed.

Ashley and Craig sat together and discussed the type of business they would create. Craig stressed the importance of hiring nurses who genuinely listened to patients' needs and took care to make patients and their families feel at ease in their own homes. Ashley and Craig also discussed how to attract and retain high-quality nurses for their agency. Craig recalled his family's experience "breaking in" new nurses. This process involved having the nurse learn the patient's routine, understand the home environment and physical surroundings, and meet family and friends with whom the nurse would interact. Ashley and Craig knew that developing trust and comfort between caregiver and patient took time, so minimizing staff turnover was crucial. Ashley also noted the importance of ensuring work–life balance for their staff. Coming to agreement about their goals for a new agency, Ashley and Craig decided the time was right to start planning the launch of their new business, C&A Home Health.

## The Planning Process

Ashley and Craig knew that proper planning was of paramount importance for realizing success. Much time was devoted to getting up to speed on (1) the relevant rules and regulations for the home health care industry, (2) the details specific to worker's compensation, and (3) the requirements for documentation. Ashley and Craig learned that in 2009 there were 33,000 Medicare-certified home health agencies and that the annual expenditures for the home health care industry were projected to have exceeded 70 billion dollars that year (National Association for Home Care and Hospice 2010). They had discussed at length whether C&A should undergo the Medicare/Medicaid certification processes, and they decided against doing so, at least initially.

In her current position, Ashley cared solely for patients with spinal cord injuries, and Craig thought they should continue that focus with C&A—both because they had experience with such a business and because the specific focus provided a competitive advantage that stemmed from genuine concern and understanding. The market they were preparing to enter had other established home health agencies, but none of those agencies focused their services on a defined population as Craig and Ashley planned to do.

As they sorted out the details of running their own home health agency, Craig's prior experience in healthcare—particularly his hiring experience and his payroll responsibilities at True Care—proved invaluable. He was charged with the responsibility for initially drafting C&A's business plan, creating the budget documents, and compiling content for the company website—all skills he learned in his MHA program. Ashley focused her energies on creating the policies and procedures manual and crafting training materials for new employees. They consulted with a lawyer who would review all documents and provide feedback to make sure their business foundation was sound.

## The Early Years for C&A Home Health

As C&A Home Health got off the ground, Ashley and Craig had to work almost nonstop. Operating a new business in the healthcare environment has a steep learning curve because of the highly regulated nature of the field. Ashley and Craig initially hired three experienced LPNs and one CNA whom they knew. Doing so allowed Ashley to dedicate most of her time to overseeing the clinical side of the business as the director of clinical services. They were fortunate that many of Ashley's clients—and some of the clients of the newly hired staff—chose to switch to C&A, providing immediate income. They were able to start their company with a client base of 19. C&A gradually added staff over time as its client list grew; eventually, the client list reached its current level of 42 patients.

Ashley and Craig were well aware that, even though working in the home health sector often paid more than working in long-term care facilities or inpatient settings, not all aspects of working in the field were ideal. For instance, home health typically requires travel, and nurses work alone in clients' homes. Thus, the nurse becomes, in practice, a care team of one that bears almost complete responsibility for a patient's welfare. Ashley recalled that True Care had shown little regard for work–life balance and had frequently scheduled shifts for employees that did not allow adequate rest time between shifts. She and Craig understood the importance of minimizing employee turnover, so they wanted to make sure their staff felt understood and appreciated. By offering wages above the market average and promoting their supportive organizational culture, C&A was able to maintain an adequate staffing level, in spite of the fact that the home health industry had a deficit of available and trained nurses.

Ashley and Craig knew that employees could easily feel isolated in delivering home care, so one of their areas of focus was trying to create a team environment in the face of the solitary work required. They understood that nurses needed to be able to ask questions and have professional discussions on a regular basis. To promote this team environment, Ashley and Craig decided to convene bimonthly meetings so that, as the team continued to grow, employees could get to know one another and build professional relationships. In addition, to facilitate ongoing communication among coworkers, C&A provided all employees with cell phones and laptops, which were used to securely document patient information (e.g., vitals) and to communicate with the C&A team through secure messaging. Further, Ashley and Craig scheduled monthly in-service sessions to enable face-to-face interactions among staff and to ensure attention to ongoing training and staff development needs. The in-service trainings also covered shifts in healthcare policy—which helped the staff stay abreast of developments affecting home care and clinical areas—and ensured that the staff would be regularly updated about C&A procedures and any clinical changes they needed to consider.

## Capitalizing on Success

Buoyed by their success, Craig has been pushing to expand the population that C&A serves. He wants to include older adults and children with special needs. Ashley, however, is concerned that this level of expansion would increase demand beyond their current capacity. She is hesitant to hire new employees too quickly, because an influx of new nurses would undoubtedly affect the existing employees and potentially disrupt the work environment. Ashley also knows that finding high-quality nurses is difficult, and she wonders if they would need to find another RN to be a second clinical supervisor for the agency if they added more LPNs. One option Craig suggested is hiring another RN who has experience serving the proposed new patient populations; this RN could fill a new role as assistant director of clinical care.

Ashley is most concerned about the complexity related to accepting new payer types, specifically Medicare. Documentation required by the Centers for Medicare & Medicaid Services (CMS) seems daunting, and Ashley knows that accepting Medicare subjects C&A to random audit reviews. Ashley has heard horror stories associated with Medicare audits. She knows that if CMS finds inconsistencies in the documentation justifying patients' homebound status and the need for skilled services, additional files will be audited. Every document in a patient's chart must have dates and times for visits that are billed, and any errors in documentation will result in CMS requesting a refund from the organization. Very recently, Ashley had heard of a postreview CMS refund request of over $100,000.

These concerns do not preclude the possibility of accepting Medicare, but they do warrant caution and careful consideration. As C&A's clinical director, Ashley has worked hard to educate the nursing staff about proper documentation protocols, and she is afraid that adding new documentation protocols specific to Medicare might create confusion. Also, given the importance of fully complying with set documentation protocols, she dreads the new mountain of requisite forms, as well as the need to learn all about relevant CMS policies and procedures. For example, Ashley knows that CMS can only be billed during a limited time period (i.e., organizations only have a month from the date of the service to bill CMS), and this requirement may necessitate organizational and process changes for C&A.

Ashley knows that if C&A decides to accept new payer types, additional trainings for current staff will be required. She wonders if it might make more sense to expand in a more minor way—but how? At some point, the company's current office space—a comfortable two-room space in a local medical office building—may become insufficient. Ashley knows that the building has no available adjoining office space, so increasing space for additional staff members would be complicated. With all these thoughts rushing around her head, Ashley begins to feel overwhelmed.

The prospect of expanding their business seems daunting, but it is also exciting. Ashley enjoys the administrative side of healthcare because it allows her to learn new skills and overcome barriers while still having the patient interactions and connections that first attracted her to the field.

## Expanding the Home Health Business

Ashley and Craig decide to do some research so they can better understand the opportunities and threats that exist in the home health market. Their three main options for expansion are (1) accepting additional payer sources, (2) adding new services, and (3) covering new markets. Selling the business might also have been an option, but because Ashley and Craig are both motivated to continue in the field, they took it off the table.

Craig knows that, to expand the business, C&A needs to focus on increasing revenue through one or more of the following means: increasing the number of clients, increasing the revenue per visit, or increasing the number of visits. Craig is confident that, with some additional resources, they could begin managing 60 patients; the goal would be to continue to expand to accommodate up to 100 patients next year. Craig notes that increasing the number of patients would be preferable to increasing the number of patient visits, because the latter is dependent on the medical necessity of each patient.

Regarding new payers, Ashley and Craig both know that accepting patients with Medicare and Medicaid coverage will require additional certifications and significant energies to ensure the appropriate documentation and approval processes for each. Further, Medicaid and Medicare patients represent two new patient populations—children with special needs and older adults—that C&A does not currently serve. Including additional services might require hiring new staff. Moreover, increasing the number of overall visits would likely require them to expand into new areas and potentially move their office. Given the current state of C&A's finances, Craig believes he could create a well-managed plan to execute some of these changes, but first he needs to determine what direction C&A should pursue.

Ashley questions whether expanding the patient population C&A serves is the wisest choice. She is concerned about the prospect of having to understand and comply with so many new rules and regulations specific to children with special needs and elderly populations. She is also concerned that an expansion of care to 100 patients would require both additional staff and the shifting of current workloads. Ashley recognizes that many of the nursing skills used to care for C&A's current patient population are readily transferable to patients with special needs and older adults, but she wants to consider alternatives. One idea she has is to launch a modest marketing campaign that might help to promote further growth of C&A without requiring drastic changes to the current business model. Another option that seems less risky would be to focus on expanding geographically.

Ashley decides to organize her thoughts on paper so that she is prepared to discuss the options with Craig and make an informed decision about C&A's next steps. She starts by noting the organization's strengths:

- A true commitment to patient care, stemming from both her experience as a care provider and Craig's perspective on patient care
- Consistently low employee turnover rates
- Efficient use of information technology to track patients
- Craig's degree and background, as well as their combined knowledge of the home health care industry

Continuing her analysis, Ashley begins to consider the organization's weaknesses. She believes the organization's main weakness is its limited experience providing care to a broad range of patients, but she knows C&A has other weaknesses as well. She and Craig need to make a decision about how to expand, but she wants to make sure they choose the most appropriate alternative for C&A.

## Case Questions

1. Choose a city to be C&A's location, and complete a brief SWOT analysis (i.e., an analysis of strengths, weaknesses, opportunities, and threats) for the agency. Use the information presented in the case and any relevant outside sources.
2. Of the questions that came to mind while you were completing the SWOT analysis, which were you unable to answer based on the information presented in the case? Make a list of those questions.
3. What expansion alternative do you recommend for C&A Home Health?
4. What are the dangers associated with business size? Can a home health agency be too small or too large?

## Reference

National Association for Home Care and Hospice. 2010. "Basic Statistics About Home Care." Accessed March 10, 2017. www.nahc.org/assets/1/7/10hc_stats.pdf.

# CASE 43

## Should XYZ Healthcare Organization Make the Baldrige Journey?

*John R. Griffith*

*Note*: Much of this case has been abstracted from a longer document. Though the case remains long, the editors felt that the level of detail was necessary to accurately present a good portion of the Baldrige process to students.

Sarah Cho is an administrative fellow at XYZ—a large healthcare organization (HCO) that operates three inpatient sites and extensive outpatient, rehabilitation, and home care services—and the organization's chief operating officer (COO) has just asked her to investigate what would be involved if XYZ were to consider the "Baldrige journey." Sarah gathers whatever information she can find on the Internet and in the literature, and she outlines the basics:

- The Baldrige program is run by a federal agency and a voluntary consortium, with programs in most states.
- Healthcare winners generally perform at top-quartile levels or better on a "balanced scorecard" of quality, patient satisfaction, worker satisfaction, and financial performance.
- Winners pursue multiple rounds of annual applications—collectively known as the "journey"—which seems to take several years. Clearly, an HCO can go part of the way and then quit, but nothing is published about anybody but winners.
- The winners' documentation is available on the program's website (at http://patapsco.nist.gov/Award_Recipients/index.cfm). The 2015 winner, Charleston Area Medical Center (CAMC), provided a clear but challenging roadmap. It is 55 pages long and hard to read.
- The Baldrige Framework provides a set of questions to prompt in-depth study of work processes. Applications must follow the Framework. The Baldrige website provides descriptive advice and encouragement.
- The Baldrige Framework specifies 11 core values and concepts (Baldrige Performance Excellence Program 2017):
    - Systems perspective
    - Visionary leadership
    - Customer-focused excellence
    - Valuing people
    - Organizational learning and agility
    - Focus on success
    - Managing for innovation
    - Management by fact
    - Societal responsibility
    - Ethics and transparency
    - Delivering value and results
- These core values drive the Framework's six process categories—leadership; strategy; customers; measurement, analysis, and knowledge management; workforce; and operations—which in turn drive a results category (Baldrige Performance Excellence Program 2017).
- Healthcare winners have similarities in their model for high-performance HCOs. The model has about eight components, divided between continuous improvement activities and a "servant leadership" culture. The model is not traditional, and it is not simple.

- One article (Griffith 2015) suggests that, although the model adds to some costs, it is cost effective overall and tends to pay for itself in early years. Much of the return on investment is in reduced cost of care. Individual patients are treated better, faster, and more cheaply.

Reflecting on what she has learned, Sarah notes to herself that Baldrige seems like a good idea but that it involves a lot of hard work. XYZ's COO obviously thinks the idea merits further study. Sarah notes that XYZ has similarities to CAMC, the 2015 winner. She feels that if she and the rest of XYZ's team studied the model and the way CAMC implemented it, they would have enough information to decide whether to apply and whether to make the journey. Sarah begins outlining a shorter version of CAMC's Baldrige documentation to help the team better understand both the model and the journey.

## Condensed Description of Charleston Area Medical Center (CAMC), Based on Its 2015 Baldrige Application Summary

This section includes excerpts from CAMC's (2015) Baldrige application summary. The application includes an organizational profile and a description of achievements and improvements across seven categories: (1) leadership; (2) strategy; (3) customers; (4) measurement, analysis, and knowledge management; (5) workforce; (6) operations; and (7) results.

### Organizational Profile

CAMC is a $900-million teaching healthcare organization in West Virginia. Its 4 inpatient and 34 outpatient sites provide more than half the care in its county and a substantial fraction of all the care in the state. It employs 2,000 nurses and 5,000 other employees. It has 800 affiliated physicians, including 160 medical residents. It has not-for-profit governance with a 17-member board. It identifies West Virginia University–Charleston and several critical suppliers as key partners.

CAMC's (2015, ii) mission is "Striving to provide the best health care to every patient, every day." Its vision is to be recognized as the following:

- BEST place to receive patient-centered care
- BEST place to work
- BEST place to practice medicine
- BEST place to learn
- BEST place to refer patients

CAMC's values are quality, service with compassion, respect, integrity, stewardship, and safety, and its core competency is "Improving the health and economics of our community." CAMC (2015) has an explicit strategy to "Grow Our Own" professional and nonprofessional workforce.

CAMC operates in a rural, economically challenged state with a declining population, and less than half of the residents are employed. The CAMC (2015, i–ii) application states:

> [CAMC seeks] to not only deliver the BEST care to our patients but also to increase our competitive advantage as a low cost provider in the region. . . . [W]e expect to achieve an annual $10 million reduction in our costs, resulting in cost reduction of $155 million since 2002. We are also . . . using a holistic sustainability model that helps us to ensure we can deliver on our mission and create success now and in the future.

As a regional referral center, CAMC has expanded its services to West Virginia critical access hospitals, health departments, and other rural care sites, providing telemedicine, creating a Partners in Health Network, and leading a Coalition for Community Health in its home county.

In 2014, CAMC (2015, iii) changed its accrediting body to Det Norske Veritas and Germanischer Lloyd Healthcare (DNV) "because the DNV accreditation is: 1) process driven, 2) uses the ISO 9001 methodology, and 3) is better aligned with our Baldrige performance improvement journey." It also deliberately enhanced its benchmarking and best-practice intelligence. The application states (CAMC 2015, v):

> CAMC is a founding member of QUEST, a Premier and IHI [Institute for Healthcare Improvement] national hospital collaborative, comprised of a subset of 350 high performing hospitals that submit detailed comparative information. . . . QUEST provides national benchmarks based on the top decile and top quartile performance of organizations shown to outperform most U.S. hospitals.

### Category 7: Results

Results are the focus of the seventh category in the Baldrige application, but for the purposes of this discussion, we will address them first. CAMC reports extensively on results, in response to the emphasis on results in the Baldrige scoring system. Within the results category, the scoring system puts 120 points on clinical outcomes and 330 points on other areas; thus, results account for a total of 450 of the system's 1,000 points. Of the other six categories, the only one weighted over 100 is Category 1, leadership, with 120.

## Clinical Care
### Outcomes
CAMC (2015) uses benchmarks and competitor data from several national companies. According to its application, CAMC ranks in the top decile in aggregate inpatient patient safety, complications, and mortality, and it ranks as "better than expected" on 13 relatively common inpatient diagnoses. The overall rankings are supported by details in the areas of heart failure mortality, orthopedic and neurological trauma, and obstetrics/gynecology mortality. CAMC claims to be West Virginia's leader in preventing avoidable readmissions. CAMC has reduced urinary tract infections in pediatric patients in the intensive care unit to 0 over the course of 2.5 years. It has approached 90 percent on breastfeeding in maternity care settings, substantially above local and national averages. It has reduced central line infections in trauma cases to 0 since January 2014. On the potentially avoidable admissions rate, a commercially prepared analysis, CAMC reports that it is substantially better than its competitors and national medians. CAMC's overall readmission rate is in the top quartile as reported by Premier.

### Processes
CAMC (2015) is top decile in most Centers for Medicare & Medicaid Services measures. It claims 100 percent compliance on children's asthma treatment and "outperforms local competitors" on mammogram follow-up (CAMC 2015, 35). It exceeds guidelines for stroke anticlotting response and American College of Surgeons standards for trauma response. CAMC has "sustained high performance" in starting treatment for Priority 1 Trauma. It has pushed inpatient medication accuracy checking to over 98 percent, which it claims is benchmark. It has reduced blood transfusion by one third. Oxygenation of premature infants has dropped from 40 percent to 20 percent in eight years, surpassing national averages. CAMC has reduced positive tests for bacteria after cleaning to less than a third of its 2012 values, better than recommended standards. Outpatient medication records are 100 percent reconciled and 100 percent provided to patients. CAMC is top decile in meeting standards for disseminating critical lab results. It has achieved 100 percent full documentation of chemotherapy plans. The emergency department lab and X-ray reporting times exceed standards. CAMC has increased postdischarge primary care appointments to near 90 percent.

### Structural Quality Measures
CAMC (2015) exceeds standards on all types of emergency drills. It surpasses network suppliers' standards on system availability and on help desk and problem resolution. Inventory turnover exceeds benchmarks; supply failures are near zero. CAMC's facilities management costs were reduced 8 percent in 2013 and 11 percent in 2014.

## Patient Satisfaction

CAMC's (2015) overall inpatient satisfaction is less than top quartile, although it is better than that of the organization's competitors. (Many Baldrige winners are top decile.) CAMC identified physician and nurse attitudes as an opportunity for improvement (OFI). Some of CAMC's Hospital Consumer Assessment of Healthcare Providers and Systems (HCAHPS) measures were near top decile. Nurse–patient communication remains less than top quartile, but the organization has reached top decile in discharge information communication.

Outpatient satisfaction is near top decile, although OFIs are reported in communication, courtesy, and physician contact time. Emergency satisfaction has risen to levels equal to those of other Baldrige recipients. Emergency "loyalty" is top decile. CAMC has a strong following on social media, and it has successfully marketed several specialty services. CAMC claims that it is the community leader in name recognition and perception of quality.

## Workforce Management

CAMC (2015) has about 11 percent overall turnover and 9 percent nursing turnover per year. It is top decile in time to fill, with only 20 days for nursing vacancies. It operates substantially better than Occupational Safety and Health Administration (OSHA) standards on injuries and return to work.

CAMC (2015) maintains 100 percent continuing education compliance for both physicians and nurses. Employee survey questions on patient focus, respect for management, loyalty, and overall satisfaction show CAMC near top decile in nursing and within top decile for physicians and other workers. CAMC claims near 100 percent satisfaction with training, and internal training is effective in retaining new nursing employees. Physicians and trustees report satisfaction with leadership and governance. CAMC promoted internally for 86 percent of openings. It spent 6 percent of payroll on education.

## Leadership and Governance

CAMC (2015) is a "disproportionate share hospital" with 11 percent uncompensated care. It contributes 15 percent of net revenues to community benefit, approaching twice the national average. CAMC won 87 percent of appeals on Medicare denials, substantially above average. All research review, Medicare, OSHA, and accreditation requirements are met. CAMC has won voluntary accreditation for pulmonary rehabilitation, stroke, breast, and children's care. CAMC lists eight national and two state awards for excellence. Several represent "top decile" or better achievements.

CAMC documents reduced energy consumption and contributes to smoking reduction among high school students. It documents a strong audit and compliance program.

### Finance and Market

CAMC (2015) estimates its total economic impact (i.e., money spent in West Virginia) at $775 million per year, one of the largest impacts in the state. It works with the Ford Foundation to promote "wealth creation" in the region. CAMC claims "intelligent risks" in expanding community benefits, acquiring a small HCO outside of Charleston, and taking on an improvement project with a contractor.

CAMC's (2015) operating margin at least equals the teaching hospital median. Expense per adjusted discharge is near the best quartile as identified by the Council of Teaching Hospitals. The bond rating has improved to A3+ (Moody's). Medicare costs per patient are below average. Labor costs per patient day have been reduced and are best quartile. CAMC has about 200 days' cash on hand and about 40 days in receivables. It has sustained a 40 percent debt-to-equity ratio. CAMC has reduced costs every year since 2005. It raises some funds from community contributions. Net assets have increased annually since 2010.

CAMC has sustained market share in most specialties and increased share in some specialties.

### *Category 1: Leadership*

Senior leaders at CAMC (2015) guide the organization via the Leadership System (LS), shown in exhibit 43.1.

CAMC (2015, 1) developed the LS six years into its journey, and its purpose is "to guide the organization and provide a systematic approach to deploy the mission, vision, values and the expectations for how we lead." The application continues:

> The foundation of the system is our mission and vision pillars. At the center are our patients and families. Every leader is expected to role model our values and demonstrate strong communication and listening skills. The numbers [in the outer circle of the diagram] represent what a leader must accomplish. Leaders must understand the key requirements of their stakeholders in order to provide the *best health care to every patient, every day* (our mission) by setting direction, aligning and cascading goals to the workforce, implementing action plans, achieving plans, mentoring and developing people, and changing systems and structures to support performance improvement (PI). This is augmented by actions every leader must role model and cannot delegate (arrows). . . . [The system] is fully deployed . . . to build leadership skills, commitment, and PI. We measure the effectiveness of the LS through the achievement of our goals and the employee engagement survey.

CAMC promotes the system extensively and repeatedly, and it expects its key partners to support the system. The application describes the evaluation of senior leaders (SL) according to the system (CAMC 2015, 1):

**EXHIBIT 43.1**
CAMC
Leadership
System

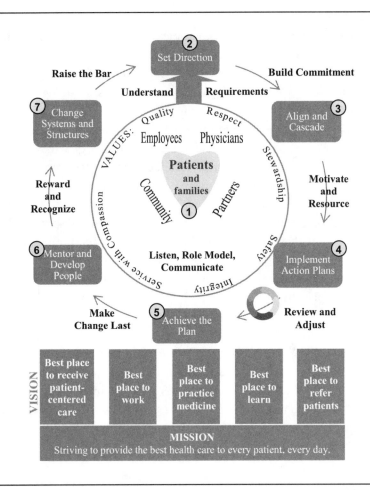

*Source:* Reprinted from CAMC (2015, 1).

SL are evaluated annually on their effectiveness in role modeling the values and how their actions reflect a commitment to these values. As examples, *Quality* is demonstrated by SL serving as champions for PI teams and *Stewardship* is reflected through service on community boards, volunteer activities and wise use of resources.

CAMC (2015) implements its vision using the Enterprise Systems Model shown in exhibit 43.2. The model identifies the expected contributions of all CAMC and partner activities, dividing them into three categories: those that "guide," those that "do work," and those that "support." The model diagram includes five multicolored circles that represent the Define, Measure, Analyze, Improve, and Control (DMAIC) approach to continuous improvement. These "cycles of learning," which are analogous to annual budget cycles, begin with a focus on customers' requirements and are expected of all people and processes related to patient and customer support.

**EXHIBIT 43.2**

Enterprise Systems Model

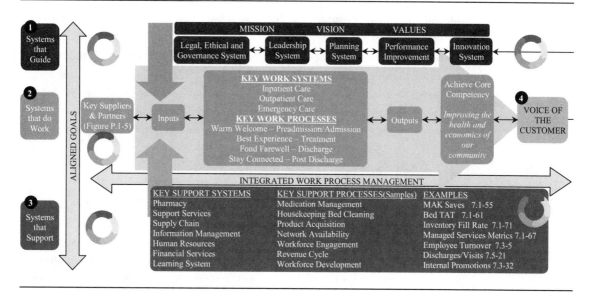

*Source:* Reprinted from CAMC (2015, 27).

The CAMC (2015, 2) states:

> Achievement of the strategic objectives and organizational agility is accomplished through SL reviews . . . , down to the performance results of every leader. . . . SL participate in succession planning and the development of organizational leaders by identifying: 1) succession planning positions; 2) who could fill each position short-term; 3) the status of each succession plan candidate; and 4) by leading, guiding and mentoring selected candidates. A culture of patient safety is created and promoted though our values, the LS, and by including safety in the *operational* sustainability factors review process.

The application explains further, describing the role of the board of trustees (BOT) in CEO performance evaluation (CAMC 2015, 4):

> The BOT Compensation Committee evaluates the performance of the CEO based on 1) achieving BOT approved annual goal and BIG DOT [strategic scorecard] targets as defined by the CEO's Individual Scorecard, and 2) role modeling the organization's values. Executive compensation is determined based on the performance evaluation of these areas and development opportunities are identified annually. . . . The CEO evaluates direct reports using the same process with recommendations reviewed and approved by the BOT Compensation Committee. . . . [A]ll SL participat[ed] in a

multi-rater survey process aligned with our CAMC LS competencies. Each SL used the feedback to create a development plan to improve their personal effectiveness as leaders. . . . An annual Board self-assessment identifies areas for improvement and educational needs for the Board. As a cycle of learning, each committee is now evaluated and committee chairs are responsible for reviewing the results and developing an improvement plan, if needed. Individual board member competencies are evaluated annually by the BOT Nominating Committee and any individual performance improvement issues are addressed with the board member by the CEO and BOT Chair. Additionally, board members identify gaps in their personal learning and these are addressed through overall BOT, Board committee, or individual learning.

In 2015, CAMC expanded the role of the BOT Nominating Committee and made it a Governance Committee, to enhance accountability for systematic centralized review of governance processes. The CAMC (2015, 3) organizational governance system establishes accountability for senior leaders' actions through legal and ethical requirements and audit processes. It sets annual performance goals for the CEO and approves "performance planners" for each senior leader that follow from the strategic plan. Strategic plan results are reviewed by the board's seven committees and reported quarterly at full board meetings. The board's Compensation Committee reviews the achievements of the CEO and senior leaders relative to their performance goals each year. A standardized format for senior leader scorecards links the leaders' performance and creates line-of-sight accountability.

CAMC's system to promote legal and ethical behavior is illustrated in exhibit 43.3. The application further describes the organization's efforts in this area (CAMC 2015, 4–5):

We systematically validate that we have the appropriate requirements, they are deployed through training, and use is validated through audit. Our BOT, BOT Audit Committee, Compliance Committee, Ethics Committee and SL enable and monitor ethical behavior throughout the governance structure and organization and with interactions with WF [workforce], patients, partners and others through a seven step Ethical Compliance Guidance and Validation process.

The application explains the role of the chief compliance officer (CAMC 2015, 1):

The Chief Compliance Officer, a SL, has responsibility for oversight and reports directly to the BOT's Audit Committee on findings. Corrective action results and Compliance Hotline outcomes are used for organizational learning. Recent cycles of learning have resulted in revisions to required annual in-services for all employees and improvements to audit [procedures].

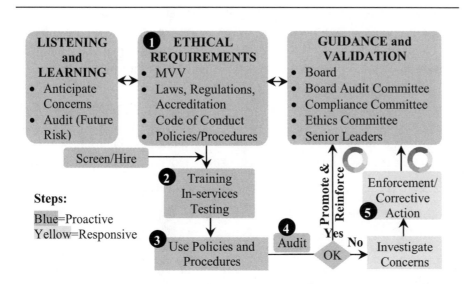

**EXHIBIT 43.3**
Legal and
Ethical Behavior

*Note:* MVV = mission, vision, and values.

*Source:* Reprinted from CAMC (2015, 5).

CAMC also uses external audits and Safety Committee environment-of-care assessments to identify adverse risks.

CAMC leadership also focuses on the organization's societal responsibilities. The application states (CAMC 2015, 5):

> Social considerations include the Community Needs Assessment and Civic Affairs requests and contributions. . . . We also provide GME programs, a Nurse Anesthesia school, nursing and allied health education financial support, visiting residencies and student rotations. . . . Our community benefit for health professionals' education is over $40 million annually.

## Category 2: Strategy

Strategy development at CAMC (2015, 6) is "a closed-loop cycle that ensures our: *strategies* are developed; *goals* and *action plans* have *performance measures* with comparisons; *goals* and *action plans* are deployed; and *performance* is analyzed, improved and innovated." It follows a four-phase, 16-step strategic planning process (SPP), shown in exhibit 43.4. The Planning Department manages the process and supplies data. As the 16 steps are executed, a specific leader monitors each of the CAMC mission and vision pillars (shown in exhibit 43.1).

CAMC begins its strategy development process by reviewing the prior year's planning activity and making improvements to the process itself. Senior leadership coordinates the cycle through a formally appointed "senior planning team" (SPT in exhibit 43.4.), which includes all senior leaders, all clinical directors, and West Virginia University–Charleston and the information management company (key partners). Board committees, medical staff officers, the Physician Advisory Council, the CAMC physician group, nursing councils, the workforce, and medical residents provide formal input to the planning.

The eight-month commitment to phases I through III is designed both to select the right goals and to gain universal understanding and support. Plan development is guided by a formal strategic analysis, shown in exhibit 43.5. The phrase "Blind Spots," which appears repeatedly in both exhibit 43.4 and exhibit 43.5, indicates a systematic double-check for errors, particularly omissions.

**EXHIBIT 43.4**
Strategic Planning and Deployment Process

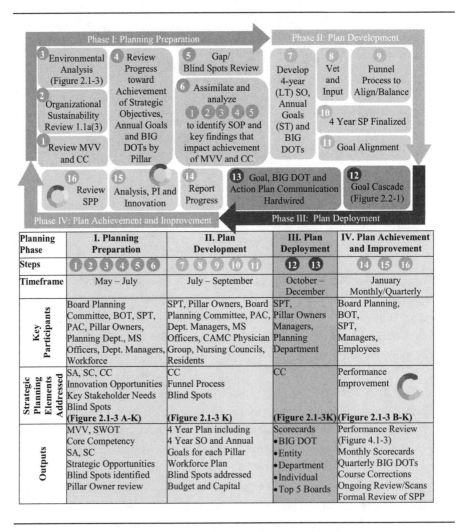

| Planning Phase | I. Planning Preparation | II. Plan Development | III. Plan Deployment | IV. Plan Achievement and Improvement |
|---|---|---|---|---|
| Steps | 1 2 3 4 5 6 | 7 8 9 10 11 | 12 13 | 14 15 16 |
| Timeframe | May – July | July – September | October – December | January Monthly/Quarterly |
| Key Participants | Board Planning Committee, BOT, SPT, PAC, Pillar Owners, Planning Dept., MS Officers, Dept. Managers, Workforce | SPT, Pillar Owners, Board Planning Committee, PAC, Dept. Managers, MS Officers, CAMC Physician Group, Nursing Councils, Residents | SPT, Pillar Owners Managers, Planning Department | Board Planning, BOT, SPT, Managers, Employees |
| Strategic Planning Elements Addressed | SA, SC, CC Innovation Opportunities Key Stakeholder Needs Blind Spots **(Figure 2.1-3 A-K)** | CC Funnel Process Blind Spots **(Figure 2.1-3 K)** | CC **(Figure 2.1-3K)** | Performance Improvement **(Figure 2.1-3 B-K)** |
| Outputs | MVV, SWOT Core Competency SA, SC Strategic Opportunities Blind Spots identified Pillar Owner review | 4 Year Plan including 4 Year SO and Annual Goals for each Pillar Workforce Plan Blind Spots addressed Budget and Capital | Scorecards • BIG DOT • Entity • Department • Individual • Top 5 Boards | Performance Review (Figure 4.1-3) Monthly Scorecards Quarterly BIG DOTs Course Corrections Ongoing Review/Scans Formal Review of SPP |

*Note*: BOT = board of trustees; CC = core competency; MS = medical staff; MVV = mission, vision, and values; PAC = Physician Advisory Council; SA = strategic advantage; SC = strategic challenge; SO = strategic objective; SPP = strategic planning process; SPT = senior planning team. Figure numbers in the exhibit refer to elements from the longer application document from which content for this case was abstracted.

*Source*: Reprinted from CAMC (2015, 6).

**EXHIBIT 43.5**
Environmental Analysis Inputs into the Strategic Planning Process

| | Collect | Processes to Analyze and Develop Information | Who Involved |
|---|---|---|---|
| | | **STRATEGIC CHALLENGES, STRATEGIC ADVANTAGES, STRATEGIC OPPORTUNITIES** | |
| **A SWOT** | MVV, CC; Organizational Sustainability Review; Environmental Analysis; Ability to Execute; Gap and Blind Spot review | Steps 1–5 of the SPP, SWOT from each Department and SWOT Development Process, Identify Risks to Future Success, SC, SA, Identify Strategic Opportunities | CSO, SPT, PAC, All Depts. |
| | | **RISKS TO CAMCHS FUTURE SUCCESS** | |
| **B Technology** | Technology Scans; Supplier, Partner and Workforce Input; Figure 4.2-3 Data and Information Availability, Safety; Competitor Technology; Disruptive Technology | Cost/Benefit Analysis; Assess technology needed to achieve SO, Annual Goals and work processes; Explore systems to allow use of Big Data for insight and action; Blind Spots | SPT, Suppliers, Partners, Vendors, PAC, MS |
| **C Markets** | Market and Competitor Data; Figure P.2-1 Market Share & Key Competitors; Figure 3.1-2 Patient/Other Customer VOC Listening and Learning Posts | Marketplace Blind Spots; Market Share and Market Analysis Report; Mergers and Acquisitions; Scenario Planning | Planning Dept., Board Planning, SPT, PAC, Mgrs. |
| **D Health Care Services** | National, State and Local Data; Community Needs Assessment; Figure P.1-1 Health Care Service Offerings; Figure 1.2-2 Community Support; Figure 4.1-2 Comparative Data Selection Process; Changes in Health Care Delivery Role of Local Businesses | Identification of Program Gaps; Comparable Organizations' Future Performance; Listening Posts, Risk Assessment; Societal Well Being; 10 year forecast for demand for inpatient and outpatient services; Blind Spots | Board Quality and Planning, Planning Dept, SPT, MS, PAC, Community |
| **E Patient/ Stakeholder Preferences** | Satisfaction Surveys; Complaints; Figure 3.2-4 Complaint Management Process; Safety; Shifts in Patient Care Delivery Locations; Figure 3.1-2 Listening Posts; Figure 3.1-1 Customer Communication System | HCAHPS and Satisfaction Survey Reviews, Patient Experience Aggregated VOC Reports; A3 Problem Solving; Blind Spots | Patient Experience Council, BPTL Pillar Owner, SET, SPT |
| **F Competition** | Market Assessment; Figure 3.1-2 Listening Posts; Figure 3.2-3 Customer Relationship Model; Competitor Strengths and Weaknesses; Non-Traditional Competitors | Trend Analysis; Future Performance; Referral Pattern Shifts; Competitive Blind Spots, Potential New Entrants into the Market Blind Spots | Planning Dept., Board Planning Committee, SPT |
| **G Economy** | National, State and Local Issues; Business/Industry Closures; Financial Market Reviews; Unemployment | Review Trends and Industry Intelligence; Blind Spots | Board Finance Committee, SPT |
| **H Innovation** | Innovation Inventory; Gaps Identified in Figure 2.1-5 | Learnings from systems that outperform others; Figure 2.1-5 Innovation Process; Figure 6.1-3 Innovation Management | SPT |
| | | **CHANGES TO THE REGULATORY ENVIRONMENT** | |
| **I Regulatory Environment** | National, State and Local Regulatory, Legal and Ethical Requirements; Legislative Briefs; Figure 1.1-1 Incinerator Report, Recycling, Energy Study, Safety, ISO and NIAHO | Review Survey Results; Gap Analysis; Audits; Mock Surveys; Concurrent Review; Gaps for ISO and NIAHO standards; Gaps in Key Support Processes; Blind Spots | Safety Dept, SPT, Compliance, Legal, Suppliers, Partners |
| | | **ABILITY TO EXECUTE THE STRATEGIC PLAN** | |
| **J Sustainability** | 1.1a(3); Organizational Sustainability Reports | Organizational Sustainability Factors Review; Blind Spots | SPT |
| **K Ability to Execute** | Governance System; CC; BIG DOTs; Scorecards; Figure 6.1-1 Enterprise Systems Model; Workforce Capability and Capacity; Listening Posts; Figure 1.1-1 Leadership System; Figure 4.1-3 Organizational Performance and Capabilities Review; Organizational Sustainability Reports | Annual review of process performance for these systems and processes; CC review; Funnel Process; BIG DOT Approach and Review; Annual review of Health Care Service Work Process Requirements; Review of Support Process Performance; Review Key Support Process Performance and Gaps; Blind Spots | Executive Council, SPT, CEO, COO, CFO, CSO |
| | | **BLIND SPOTS – See the Blue Notations in the Analysis Column** | |

*Note:* Numbers in the exhibit refer to elements from the longer application document from which content for this case was abstracted.

*Source:* Reprinted from CAMC (2015, 7).

Exhibit 43.5 presents a rigorous environmental analysis that includes both an assessment of strengths, weaknesses, opportunities, and threats—that is, a SWOT analysis—and a systematic review of forces for change. The chart specifies multiple analyses shared across the planning team, and it indicates which groups hold responsibility over the final plan. Perhaps most importantly, the planning process concludes with "Sustainability" and "Ability to Execute" (lines J and K in the exhibit); at this part of the process, all managers understand (1) what their annual goals are, (2) how these goals contribute to CAMC's mission, (3) how they expect to achieve their goals, (4) how they and their team will be rewarded, and (5) what help to expect if a goal is in danger.

CAMC's process produces a rolling, four-year, long-range plan; a short-term annual plan; and a continuous review component that allows rapid response to unexpected changes. Any failure or difficulty in completing the plan is unexpected and thus subject to rapid response.

The CAMC goal-setting process deliberately emphasizes mission and vision, deemphasizing traditional goals focused on margin and financial performance. Note that the words *margin* and *profit* do not appear in exhibit 43.4 or exhibit 43.5. Cost reduction, however, is a recognized benefit, referenced twice in exhibit 43.5.

CAMC (2015) maintains a budget planning cycle that coincides with the strategic planning process and incorporates the annual budget, capital, workforce, information system, and medical staff development plans. Thus, resources to support the various action plans are built into the budget, and long-term budget needs are incorporated into the operating and capital budget allocation processes.

Workforce plans are integrated with the budgeting process to address specific staffing and training needs. They identify changes to workforce capability and capacity.

Once a plan is adopted, progress toward goals is carefully monitored. Each department maintains a "Top 5" board that identifies its priority areas of improvement. The boards serve as a means for deploying action plans and as a working visual communication tool. The tracking of progress toward goals is further described as follows (CAMC 2015, 10):

> SL and department managers enter progress on their action plans quarterly and monthly into the on-line goal system. SL review progress monthly with their direct reports. The EC [Executive Council] and BOT conduct quarterly progress reviews towards goals and targets relative to the system BIG DOTs [strategic scorecard measures] and hospital measures. Improvement teams/innovation processes are implemented if the need for course correction is identified.

For the 2015 strategic planning process, CAMC (2015, 9) used its strategic challenges and strategic advantages to develop a list of its top 20 goals:

1. Improve processes that support our customer service vision and timeliness of responding to key customer needs.
2. Deploy standardized processes for communication with patients/families.
3. Improve use of Soarian and workflows. *NEW GOAL: Replace Siemens/Soarian with Cerner IT system.*
4. Accelerate coding and clinical documentation improvements.
5. Improve appropriate use.
6. Improve evidence-based care reliability.
7. Improve effectiveness of transitions of care to reduce readmissions.
8. Deploy TCT [Transforming Care Together] to all nursing and selected ancillary departments. Value Stream Map key processes in ED [emergency department], OR [operating room], CDL [Circulatory Dynamics Laboratory] and Ambulatory areas.
9. Improve safety systems to reduce harm.
10. Identify at least one opportunity in each department from the 2014 Employee Survey and develop an action plan for improvement.
11. Fill gaps in identified critical medical staff recruitment needs.
12. Implement a Medical Staff leadership program.
13. Define our Physician Enterprise Model.
14. Improve integration of research and academic programs and learners to Quality and Patient Safety structure, processes, QIPS [Quality Improvement and Patient Safety] and research.
15. Incorporate Individual Leadership Learning Plans in all Leadership Performance Planners (front line leaders up).
16. Grow identified service lines.
17. Achieve budgeted bottom-line.
18. Improve cost, efficiency and productivity.
19. Implement plan to improve the health of our communities.
20. Identify affiliation opportunities.

These goals all have specific benchmarks and are linked to unit goals, if applicable.

CAMC (2015, i) developed an innovative team approach to care, known as Transforming Care Together (TCT), which is "aimed at redesigning patient work processes to reduce waste, increase direct time at the patient's bedside and improve the overall quality of care." The deployment of TCT to all clinical areas has resulted in meaningful change and improved satisfaction for both patients and staff.

### *Category 3: Customers*

CAMC (2015) has a dominant market share (about 40 percent) that has been increasing slowly. CAMC customer relations results (described in Section 7.2 of the application) are generally improving, approaching top quartile, and leading those of CAMC's competitors by small margins. The organization has segmented its markets carefully, by clinical need, care site, and communications approach. It has recognized its physicians as both workforce and referral source. It has established 15 key listening and support mechanisms, and it has identified a leader or team in control of each. CAMC integrates these efforts through a Service Excellence Team that meets monthly. The team has created five "action teams": (1) Standards, (2) Measurement, (3) Recognition, (4) Communication, and (5) Innovation. CAMC addresses identified problems through the "Top 5" boards.

CAMC's patient contact systems are summarized in exhibit 43.6. The organization has invested in extensive outreach, including telemedicine support, community education, a health improvement coalition, health fairs, and social media. To understand its markets, CAMC uses surveys (principally HCAHPS), with the assistance of a national information company that provides comparative data. It also uses complaints, worker observations, and rounding to identify patient needs. Complaint management software supports both analysis and rapid response. CAMC (2015, 11) explains:

> Our marketing team monitors and receives alerts via email and Smartphone apps when CAMC keywords are used in online venues. Compliments or complaints posted are reviewed at least hourly. When a posting requires follow-up, our marketing team responds by email or phone call.

Responses requiring multiple inputs are routed to a 24/7 on-call administrator or to the appropriate individual. Follow-up includes rounding and patient call-backs. CAMC (2015, 12) continues:

> The effectiveness of social media campaigns is evaluated monthly. . . . Data from rounding and social media are populated in [a] dashboard and are part of the aggregated monthly VOC [Voice of the Customer] report.

CAMC uses customer data in its branding activities, targeting specific populations. It has extended its planning process to identify unmet health needs—an effort that has led to the development of a weight-loss center and a program to combat child obesity. CAMC reinforces its brand through the use of social media, and it maintains an extensive website that includes clinical information for patients.

**EXHIBIT 43.6**
Patient and
Other Customer
Support

| Key Communication and Support Mechanisms | Patients/ Families | Community | Physicians | Payors |
|---|---|---|---|---|
| **Seek Information and Assistance** | | | | |
| Direct Contact | X | X | X | X |
| CAMC Website/Public Reporting Websites/Social Media (YouTube, Twitter, Facebook) | X | X | X | X |
| Publications — Vital Signs, CAMC Today | X | X | X | X |
| Health Fairs and Community Education | X | X | | |
| **Obtain Services** | | | | |
| Physician Match | X | X | | |
| Web-based Registration | X | X | | |
| Community Liaisons | X | X | X | X |
| Transfer Center | X | | X | |
| Telemedicine | X | X | | |
| Partners in Health | X | X | X | X |
| **VOC / Complaints** | | | | |
| Rounding for Outcomes | X | | | |
| Administrator On-Call | X | | X | X |
| Letter/Fax/Email/Phone | X | X | X | X |
| Cipher Health/Discharge Follow-up Calls | X | | | |

*Source:* Reprinted from CAMC (2015, 14).

CAMC's demand analysis and forecasting are integrated into its knowledge management (discussed further in the next section). Actual usage trends, environmental and market assessment, and input from national experts are incorporated into the strategic planning process "to determine if patient and other customer requirements are being met or exceeded and if new requirements are needed" (CAMC 2015, 13). The Voice of the Customer report and environmental assessment data help CAMC's leadership identify new markets, attract new patients/customers, and create opportunities to expand relationships with current patients/customers.

CAMC has invested in a multipart program to deploy customer-focused thinking throughout its sites. The program is supervised by the Service Excellence Team and includes the following features (CAMC 2015):

- An employee handbook that defines key actions and describes their integration into annual performance reviews
- A monthly e-communication highlighting key service points
- A monthly "Service Excellence Café" featuring "fun activities that promote our standards of behavior"
- A training program for new hires that uses the AIDET (Acknowledge, Introduce, Duration, Explanation, and Thank You) model, reinforced at the work sites
- A playbook of best practices for critical customer concerns, in which a "key play" is selected quarterly and promoted systemwide with specific deliverables
- A checklist that incorporates customer expectations into key work processes, beginning with a standardized "warm welcome"

CAMC has a fully automated complaint system, with aggressive analysis and follow-up. Workers are trained in a "HEART" response—which stands for *hear* them, *empathize*, *apologize*, *resolve* promptly, and *thank* them—and authorized to do service recovery. Complaints are analyzed and summarized monthly for the departments and annually for the board. Departments are expected to review reports and initiate process corrections if needed.

### Category 4: Measurement, Analysis, and Knowledge Management

Exhibit 43.7 shows that CAMC (2015) measures virtually every aspect of its operations, processing thousands of values each month, reporting dozens to every manager, and focusing on quantified improvement goals. Every CAMC measure must be valid, reliable, and collectible. It must also be related to strategic objectives, subject to operator control, and have outside comparisons or benchmarks. CAMC ranks benchmarks from nine sources, beginning with rigorously standardized national measures, but also including competitor or "recognized leader" data. The system of measures and benchmarks is reviewed and improved as part of the strategic planning process and continuous improvement programs. Progress is monitored by the assigned pillar owners.

CAMC (2015) pursues performance improvement in a three-phase system.

- *Phase 1: Identification.* This phase involves identifying high-performing units and operations through performance review findings, rounding, audits, quality initiatives, and benchmarking.

**EXHIBIT 43.7**

Organizational Performance and Capabilities Review (Sample Only)

| When | CA | N/MS | SS | SL | P | BOT |
|------|----|----|----|----|----|----|
| **DAILY** | | | | | | |
| Safety (patient/WF) | x | x | x | | x | |
| Census/volume/staffing | x | x | x | x | x | |
| Admissions/referrals | x | x | x | | x | |
| Productivity | x | x | x | | x | |
| Social media | x | x | x | x | x | |
| Satisfaction/quality | x | x | | | | |
| Top 5 board | x | x | x | | x | |
| **WEEKLY** | | | | | | |
| Rounding | x | x | | | x | |
| Productivity/financials | x | x | x | x | x | |
| Patient satisfaction | x | x | x | x | x | |
| PI projects (single point lessons, A3) | x | x | x | x | x | |
| **MONTHLY** | | | | | | |
| Clinical outcomes | x | x | | x | x | |
| Rounding | x | x | x | x | x | |
| Scorecards | x | x | x | x | x | |
| Financial performance | x | x | x | x | x | |
| TCT project status | | | | x | | |

**Analysis to Ensure Valid Conclusions**

DAILY:
- Variance (daily vs. budget)
- Trending
- Review of Quantros
- Social media monitored by Marketing and issues communicated
- Patient compliments and complaints
- Work process in process measures
- Support process requirements

WEEKLY:
- Trending/variances
- Patient complaint themes reviewed
- Process change
- Root cause analysis

MONTHLY:
- Social media campaigns
- Budget target vs. actual
- Statistical comparison
- Action plan evaluation
- All Top 5 boards and scorecards

**Decisions Made**

DAILY:
- Daily operational changes
- Service recovery
- Safety/regulatory
- Resource pool/call-offs
- Physician notification
- Patient flow
- Performance improvement

WEEKLY:
- Safety/regulatory
- Staffing/recruitment
- Recognition
- Reinforce action plans
- Service recovery
- Operational changes

MONTHLY:
- Modify social media campaigns
- Modify action plans for Top 5 boards
- Resource allocation/new teams
- Budget changes
- Business development

**Information Flow** → → → FOCUS ON ACTION BASED ON SIZE OF VARIANCE, TREND, RISK ← See exhibit 43.4.

*(continued)*

**EXHIBIT 43.7**
Organizational Performance and Capabilities Review (Sample Only) *(continued)*

| When | | CA | N/MS | SS | SL | P | BOT | Analysis to Ensure Valid Conclusions | Decisions Made |
|------|------|----|------|----|----|----|-----|--------------------------------------|----------------|
| **QUARTERLY** | | | | | | | | • Budget target vs. actual<br>• Statistical comparison<br>• Work/support process in-process & outcomes<br>• Action plan evaluation<br>• Aggregation of patient experience data<br>• Identification of current performance gaps and gaps for projected year-end performance | Address performance gaps:<br>• Safety/regulatory<br>• Resource allocation/changes<br>• Operational changes<br>• Modify action plans<br>• Opportunities for PI/Innovation |
| Patient satisfaction | | x | x | x | x | x | x | | |
| BIG DOTs / goals / action plans / cascaded measures / financials | | x | x | x | x | x | x | | |
| Social media trending | | | x | | x | | | | |
| Work process | | x | x | x | x | x | | | |
| **ANNUAL/BIANNUAL** | | | | | | | | • Social media campaigns<br>• Budget target vs. actual<br>• Gaps in performance<br>• Action plan evaluation and scorecard review<br>• Year-end results compared to annual projected performance compared to benchmarks<br>• Impact of year-end results on strategic planning process accomplishment<br>• Gap analysis: current performance versus year-end actual; differences between projections of our future performance and BIG DOT performance targets | • Messaging approaches for social media tailored to key customer requirements<br>• Safety/regulatory<br>• Recognition<br>• Action plan modification/new plans<br>• Opportunities for PI/innovation<br>• Organizational success and success compared to competitor performance<br>• Strategic opportunity and Innovation<br>• Changes in structure, key work systems, key work processes, support processes<br>• Strategic planning process and organizational review processes |
| Workforce performance reviews | | x | x | x | x | x | x | | |
| Employee satisfaction | | x | x | x | x | x | x | | |
| Physician satisfaction | | x | x | x | x | x | x | | |
| Patient safety culture | | x | x | x | x | x | x | | |
| Strategic plan achievement of:<br>• BIG DOTs<br>• annual goals<br>• action plans<br>• cascaded measures | | x | x | x | x | x | x | | |
| **CONTINUOUS** | | | | | | | | • Shifts in technology, market, services, competition, economy, regulatory environment | • Change in strategic objectives, annual goals, action plans to adapt to shifts in market conditions; shift in priority |
| Environmental analysis | | | | x | | x | x | | |

*Information Flow*

FOCUS ON ACTION BASED ON SIZE OF VARIANCE, TREND, RISK
See exhibit 43.4.

*Note:* CA = clinical areas; N/MS = clinical nursing and medical staff; SS = support services; SL = senior leaders; P = partners; BOT = board of trustees.

*Source:* Adapted from CAMC (2015, 18).

- *Phase 2: Spread.* The second phase promotes the spread of best practices through the use of department huddles, Six Sigma report-outs, Top 5 boards, nursing councils, PI plans, single point lessons (one-page process descriptions for teaching and reference), and standardized training.
- *Phase 3: Sustain.* The third phase uses 30 intra- and cross-functional committees to oversee operating units, and it builds on CAMC's performance improvement culture and learning environment to promote evidence-based care and thought leadership. Improvement and innovation success are recognized with Quality Awards.

As CAMC (2015, 18) gained experience and knowledge over the course of several cycles, it established a team dedicated to spreading improvements, a change acceleration model, and a prioritization matrix to integrate best practices. The Transforming Care Together approach—an "innovative management and care delivery model" to build team-based care—arose from the organizational performance and capability review process. Similarly, cycles of improvement led to the deployment of the Top 5 boards to all CAMC departments.

CAMC (2015) uses 15 projection methods to understand trends in its data. The organization's focus is on moving all BIG DOTs—that is, strategic scorecard measures—to top decile performance, if such a benchmark is available; otherwise, the focus is on continuous improvement. If gaps exist, they are addressed either through continuous improvement or deliberate innovation strategies. The decision about whether to pursue innovation strategies is based on specific criteria, including whether "30 percent or greater improvement" or "a new level of performance" is required (CAMC 2015, 19).

The application explains (CAMC 2015, 19):

> We deploy PI priorities and opportunities to work groups and functional-level operations throughout the organization through the goal cascade process. . . . [P]riorities and opportunities are also deployed to our key suppliers/partners through the same cascade process to ensure organizational alignment. The BOT Quality Committee provides oversight for prioritization of PI and innovation opportunities.

Further describing its organizational learning, CAMC (2015, 20) states:

> [We] embed learning in the way our organization operates through our innovation forcing functions, culture drivers and established processes and measures at the organizational, SL, middle management, and WF levels. . . . This promotes learning as part of daily work, problem solving and best practice sharing. When a process is improved and innovated, it becomes part of our work systems and work processes which are managed through our DMAIC process.

Quantitative data must be carefully collected, protected, and monitored. CAMC (2015, 20) continues:

> At the *base level*, we utilize equipment and infrastructure systems that incorporate device-level, file-level, and database level integrity checks, as well as hardware integrity checks. At the *application program level*, we utilize database integrity checks, edits of input and interfaced data, and end-user data validation procedures. At the *application system level*, we conduct component and integrated testing, and employ acceptance criteria which must be met before systems are placed into production. We also produce "balancing reports" to allow our end-users to help detect errors in data entry or interfaces.

CAMC protects its data through routine practices ranging from Health Insurance Portability and Accountability Act (HIPAA) training to audits and specific risk assessments. The application states (CAMC 2015, 20):

> This systematic [data security] process includes: 1) investigation and remediation of any anomalies on a daily basis; 2) upgrading systems with supported versions of the operation system; 3) removing administrative privileges on common desktop accounts; and 4) hardening devices with [an] enhanced mitigation toolkit. Best practices are identified and guide selection and implementation of defense tactics such as layered security and security policy.

CAMC (2015) maintains redundant power and computing backups to ensure 99.95 percent reliability, a disaster recovery system, and explicit downtime procedures.

### Category 5: Workforce

CAMC (2015, 24) deliberately and carefully fosters "an organizational culture that is characterized by open communication, high performance work and engagement through our LS." This culture permeates all aspects of CAMC's work.

As part of the annual review process, CAMC's human resource planning team reviews workforce staffing levels, capabilities, and needs to develop short- and long-term plans for each site and job category. The criterion is goal achievement rather than cost minimization—that is, it focuses on ability to improve outcomes rather than on an input standard such as hours per unit of output. In 2012, CAMC increased clinical full-time equivalents (FTEs) to meet productivity and safety targets. It developed a clinical resource float pool and temporary staff to fill resource needs. The plans support recruitment strategy and provide early warning and reassignment opportunities to potentially redundant workers.

CAMC seeks internal candidates for all positions before it recruits new workers. New workers, including physicians and volunteers, are subject to structured interviews, evaluation, credentialing, and background checks. New hires must agree to CAMC's mission, vision, and values. Extensive training and close mentoring ensure that new workers become both capable and comfortable on the job. CAMC (2015, 22) states: "Key requirements of patients and other customers are integrated into our behavioral standard expectations and performance matrix for every employee and are embedded through orientation and training processes."

CAMC's (2015) "Grow Our Own" strategy encourages workers to expand their skills (see the examples in exhibit 43.8). The organization has developed a number of career ladders through cross-training and increasing job competencies. CAMC has 171 medical fellows, supports several other professional training programs, and holds West Virginia University–Charleston as a key partner. It systematically promotes health employment among K–12 students and provides assistance for collegiate study.

The application describes CAMC's (2015, 26) Workforce Learning and Development System (WLDS):

> We evaluate the effectiveness of our WLDS using Kirkpatrick's four levels of learning. For example, [instruction and training activities] validate specific required job competencies of a WF member. WLDS efficiency is evaluated by key factors such as cost against level of participation and effectiveness, frequency of course offerings, rapid spread of new knowledge, and convenient access.

CAMC actively participates in local and regional recruitment events and strives to recruit a diverse workforce. It provides diversity awareness training to new employees and includes patient diversity considerations in other education.

CAMC's (2015, 24) performance management system supports engagement and high performance by "evaluating, compensating, rewarding, and recognizing" the workforce. The application explains:

> WF engagement is assessed through a systematic approach that includes both formal and informal approaches. Our annual Employee Satisfaction and Engagement survey is our formal approach to obtain feedback from the WF segments. . . . We solicit additional feedback through specific surveys tailored to our nurses, physicians (employed and private) and our volunteers.

CAMC analyzes annual employee survey data for the following purposes:

- To identify the questions that have the greatest correlation to engagement
- To determine elements for different work groups and segments
- To identify themes and trends for all segments, entities, hospitals, and departments

**EXHIBIT 43.8**

Examples of Education/Training Addressing Learning and Development

| Educational Offerings | Learning and Development System Requirements | How Offerings Support Organizational and Personal Development—Distinctions |
|---|---|---|
| Clinical conferences | Core competency; focus on patients | Largest provider in the state |
| Service Excellence Team service plus training | Core competency; action plans; focus on patients and customers | "Service excellence" behaviors (10,257 trained to date) |
| Transforming Care Together | Performance improvement and innovation/ action plans | More time at the bedside; workforce efficiencies |
| Research day | Innovation | Translates research to practice |
| Simulation program | Innovation; translate learning to application | State-of-the-art technology; reinforces new knowledge/skills on the job |
| Ethics in the Round | Ethical healthcare | Promotes values and ethical practice |
| Information technology (ISO 9001, ICD-10, Soarian) | Ethical business practice; focus on patients; strategic challenge | Embraces cutting-edge technology for patient care delivery |
| Continuing medical education | New knowledge and skill | National accreditation with commendation |
| Universal curriculum for residents | New knowledge and skill; focus on patients | Meets or exceeds benchmarks on Accreditation Council for Graduate Medical Education survey |
| CAMC University Leadership Development Program | Transfer of knowledge; workforce development; new knowledge and skill | Grow Our Own; highly qualified leaders (> 85% of leaders promoted from within); leadership capability and capacity |
| Nursing Leadership Development Program | Transfer of knowledge; action plans; strategic challenge; workforce development; new knowledge and skill | Grow Our Own; highly qualified nursing leaders (greater than 90% promoted from within) |
| Crucial Conversations / Team Training / Just Culture | Focus on patients; performance improvement; new knowledge and skill | Learning environment; enhancing patient safety culture; 3,007 workforce members trained |
| EduTrack | New knowledge and skill; focus on patients | Employee in-service/training portal; live and computer-based offerings |
| Medical Explorers | Strategic challenge; innovation; workforce development | 20–30 high school students participate each school year; focus on future workforce |
| Imagine U Virtual Surgery Experience | Strategic challenge; innovation; workforce development | 10,347 students from 30 high schools (2007–2014); focus on future workforce |
| Junior Volunteers | Strategic advantage; workforce development | 50+ Junior Volunteers per year |

*Source:* Adapted from CAMC (2015, 25).

The CAMC application (2015, 24) explains: "We identify departments with lower leadership scores, and pair them with managers who are most successful to assist with developing improvement plans through sharing best practices."

CAMC also measures and strives to improve workplace health, security, and accessibility. The application states (CAMC 2015, 23):

[CAMC] provides WF training emphasizing personal security, [managing] workplace violence, crisis intervention and identification of workplace hazards. . . . Cycles of learning led to the redesign of units to increase efficiency and to decrease potential WF injuries.

Exhibit 43.9 highlights CAMC's work environment strategies related to health, security, and accessibility.

CAMC has a carefully developed compensation structure and uses a broad spectrum of rewards (see exhibit 43.10). The application states, "We conduct an annual systematic analysis of the compensation and benefit structure to determine if changes are needed to support our WF via services, benefits and policies" (CAMC 2015, 23).

## EXHIBIT 43.9
Health, Security, and Accessibility Performance

| | Strategies Tailored to Work Environment | Key Measure/Goal | Results |
|---|---|---|---|
| Health | • WF compliance with influenza vaccine<br>• Pre-employment physicals<br>• Fitness for duty testing | 100% eligible WF | Figure 7.3-9 |
| | • Transitional Return to Work program with temporary job restriction | 100% of eligible WF placed | Figure 7.3-10 |
| | • Wellness — screening, weight loss, nutrition, and fitness | Program participants | (AOS) |
| Safety | • Required annual safety training<br>• Environmental rounding/Safety audits<br>• Infection prevention procedures<br>• Hazardous materials procedures<br>• Ergonomic assessments<br>• Chemical inventory process<br>• Blood borne pathogen review | Reduction in overall accident/injury rate | Figure 7.3-11 |
| Security | • 24-hour campus security<br>• Associate/vendor identification badges<br>• Escorts and car assistance<br>• Code Gray: combative help | Reduction in personal thefts | (AOS) |
| Access | • Card readers for access<br>• Security desk (ED/Mother/Baby)<br>• 24/7 surveillance<br>• Security rounds/Security station 24/7 ED | Number of safety incidents | (AOS) |

*Note*: AOS = available on site. CAMC has additional assessment data not included in the application. Figure numbers in the exhibit refer to elements from the longer application document from which content for this case was abstracted.

*Source*: Reprinted from CAMC (2015, 23).

EXHIBIT 43.10
Reward and
Recognition
Methods

| Reward & Recognition | High Performance | Innovation and Intelligent Risk Taking | Patient Focused Care | Workforce | Physicians |
|---|:---:|:---:|:---:|:---:|:---:|
| Heart & Soul | x | x | x | x | x |
| Volunteer Celebration | | | x | x | |
| Thank You Notes | x | x | x | x | x |
| Rounding | x | | x | x | x |
| Service Award Program & Dinner | x | | | x | |
| Service Award Recognition Boards | x | | | x | |
| Quality Awards | x | x | x | x | x |
| HCAHPS | x | x | x | x | x |
| On the Spot | x | | x | x | |
| KEEP/ASP Program | x | | x | x | x |
| Medical Staff Recognition Dinner | | | x | x | x |
| Nurse Excellence Award | x | x | x | x | |
| DAISY Award | x | x | x | x | |
| Medical Staff Employee Recognition | x | x | x | x | x |

*Source:* Reprinted from CAMC (2015, 24).

The application states (CAMC 2015, 25):

Monetary compensation and non-monetary recognition are essential to create and sustain high performance and contribute to daily engagement and strategic performance ownership. All regular status employees are eligible for an annual merit-based increase and an incentive award when annual goals and BIG DOTs are achieved. Quality performance incentives may be added at the hospital or service level to reward achieving quality or regulatory targets. Skill-based compensation plans provide incentives and rewards for individuals who attain career ladder achievement, specified certifications or other competencies in targeted professional or technical positions.

## *Category 6: Operations*

CAMC (2015, 27) claims that its Enterprise System (shown previously in exhibit 43.2) supports a systematic process for achieving best practice:

> We begin with the MVV . . . and customer requirement inputs. Guidance is provided by legal and ethical standards and governance system, the LS [see exhibit 43.1], the SPP [see exhibit 43.4], PI System, and Innovation Systems.

The design of healthcare services and work processes at CAMC (2015) is based on patients' and other customers' key requirements. They incorporate

1. all customer requirements and existing key work processes;
2. best practices;
3. organizational knowledge, including evidence-based medicine;
4. patient and other customer value; and
5. value stream mapping or design to identify key performance indicators.

An Impact Leadership Committee monitors process design teams and supplies necessary resources.

Implementation at CAMC (2015) is also carefully managed, incorporating

1. standardization of the process;
2. deployment via policies and procedures;
3. dissemination of learning through one-page task descriptions and job instruction/training; and
4. oversight through in-process and performance measures.

The application further describes the implementation process (CAMC 2015, 27):

> Oversight for this process is the responsibility of the SL process owner who monitors key performance measures and in-process measures. . . . If there is a gap in performance, a cycle of learning using DMAIC is initiated and action plans are modified.

CAMC (2015, v) believes that "Improvement is everywhere," and the breadth and depth of the organization's improvement efforts are highlighted in exhibit 43.11. It claims over 15 years' experience with Six Sigma, with 8 full-time Six Sigma Black Belts and 92 Green Belts. It expanded the Shewhart cycle for continuous improvement—which traditionally involves cycles of Plan, Do, Check, and Act—to its DMAIC approach of Define, Measure, Analyze, Improve, and Control (see exhibit 43.12). CAMC (2015, 28) tracks "in-process

EXHIBIT 43.11
Performance
Improvement
Breadth and
Depth

## IMPROVEMENT IS EVERYWHERE

Improvement is CAMC Health System wide from the Board to every employee:
- **Organizational Level:** Baldrige
- **System and Process Level:** Enterprise Systems Model
- **Department Level:** Improvement Projects
- **Individual Level:** PI training starting at orientation

## IMPROVEMENT IS SYSTEMATIC

Process Improvement uses:
- **Process Improvement Methodology:** DMAIC
- **Tools:** 5S, Lean, Visual Management, A3 Problem Solving, Waste Walk, Standardized Work, Root Cause Analysis, ISO 9001 and others

## IMPROVEMENT IS FACT BASED

Improvement is evaluated:
- **Improvement Tracking:** Top 5 Boards, Scorecards
- **Performance Verification and Accountability:** Organization Performance and Capabilities Review, Performance Management System

## IMPROVEMENT IS MATURE (Started in 1989)

Improvement is shared:
- More than 67 Committees

**Performance is integrated:**
- Organizational Knowledge Management

*Source:* Reprinted from CAMC (2015, v).

and outcome measures for every work process and for every customer segment," and its Top 5 boards focus departments and partners on improvement priorities.

CAMC (2015, 28) analyzes patient care "at multiple touchpoints before, during, and after each visit," and it maps patient experience to (1) "understand key requirements" and (2) "enable us to explain healthcare service delivery processes and likely outcomes to set realistic patient expectations." The application further describes CAMC's efforts in "defining a *Patient Experience Pathway*" and standardizing key actions that need to occur at the various phases of customer interaction.

During the admission process, the patient's decision-making preferences, consent, and Advance Medical Directive forms are entered into the nursing database in the electronic record. The patient takes part in a systematic orientation process that uses both two-way communication and written information. After admission, patients' daily goals are written on the white boards in their rooms, and an Interdisciplinary Plan of Care (IPOC) process helps ensure that

| Define | • Determine strategic opportunity for improvement (data driven)<br>• Identify customer requirements<br>• Define the problem |
|---|---|
| Measure | • Develop process measures based on criteria<br>• Collect process data<br>• Check the data quality and identify benchmarks<br>• Understand process behavior<br>• Baseline process capability and potential |
| Analyze | • Analyze the process<br>• Develop theories and ideas (potential root causes)<br>• Analyze the data (trends and benchmarks)<br>• Verify root causes and understand cause and effect |
| Improve | • Plan improvement strategies<br>• Pilot strategies<br>• Measure effectiveness<br>• Implement improvements and re-measure as needed |
| Control | • Standardize new process<br>• Sustain<br>• Spread improvements |

**EXHIBIT 43.12**
The DMAIC
Process for
Improvement

*Note:* This symbol signifies use of DMAIC process for improvement throughout this application.
*Source:* Reprinted from CAMC (2015, v).

patient and family goals are met. Rounding helps coordinate care. Rounding and other listening post data are trended and analyzed for OFIs.

Exhibits 43.13a and 43.13b show how customer requirements are factored into key work and support processes for inpatient, outpatient, and emergency department care.

CAMC's (2015) sepsis procedures provide a clinical example of its Enterprise System in action. The Institute for Healthcare Improvement's QUEST collaborative had helped CAMC identify sepsis as the highest cause of preventable mortality, so it became a key goal and BIG DOT. In repeated improvement cycles, teams with physician leaders developed best practices to reduce mortality:

- Preadmission efforts focused on staff training in nursing homes to promote early identification and intervention, to allow prompt treatment, and to avoid unnecessary hospitalization.
- Improvements at the admission stage included an ED nurse's protocol that identifies high-risk patients and triggers a sepsis evaluation, the sepsis treatment bundle, and notification to an intensivist physician.

**EXHIBIT 43.13A**

Key Work Processes

| Key Work Processes | | Key Requirements 7.1(a) | Measures 7.1b(1) | Results |
|---|---|---|---|---|
| Preadmission Admission | Warm Welcome | High quality, safe care Respectful attitude Knowledge and skills Timeliness/Ease through the system | IP - Uninsured Patient Conversion OP - Third Next Available Appointment ED - ED Turnaround Times by Hospital | 7.1-54 7.1-52–7.1-53 7.2-19 |
| Treatment | Best Experience | High quality, safe care Knowledge and skills Timeliness/Responsiveness Communication | IP - Medication Administration Saves OP - Documented Plan for Chemotherapy ED - ED Priority 1 Trauma | 7.1-55 7.1-58 7.1-41 |
| Discharge | Fond Farewell | High quality, safe care Communication Coordination of care Timeliness | IP - Average Length of Stay OP - Medication Reconciliation on OP Chart ED - Lab ED Turnaround Time | (AOS) 7.1-44 7.1-59 |
| Post Discharge | Stay Connected | High quality, safe care Communication Coordination of care with next provider | IP - Primary Care Practitioner Appointments Scheduled OP - Follow-Up Mammogram after Screening Copy of Medications Provided | 7.1-63 7.1-48 7.1-43 |

*Note*: AOS = available on site. CAMC has additional assessment data not included in the application. Numbers in the exhibit refer to sections of the longer application document from which content for this case was abstracted.

*Source*: Reprinted from CAMC (2015, 28).

- Improvements during treatment included a system that triggers an early intervention alert in response to changes in the vital signs of a hospitalized patient, as well as medication protocols that decrease ventilator and intensive care unit days.
- Discharge improvements focused on follow-up with the patient's physician and education for the patient and family about risk factors.
- Postdischarge practices emphasized communication to increase medical staff awareness of prevention and early identification.

As a result of these work process improvements, CAMC saved 1,613 lives from 2011 to 2014. As of June 2016, the total was 1,798.

CAMC's approach to supply chain management is similarly systematic. It evaluates new supply requests in an eight-step process that includes analysis of clinically oriented value, environmental issues, source and distribution, and training materials. The application explains (CAMC 2015, 30):

> Supplier performance is measured and evaluated monthly for fill rates, invoice discrepancies, service issues and returns. Bi-annual or annual scheduled business reviews are conducted with suppliers for learning and alignment of service

**EXHIBIT 43.13B**

Key Support Systems and Processes (Partial List)

| Key Support Processes | Organizational Support Requirements | Measures 7.1b(1) | Results |
|---|---|---|---|
| *Work System Key Requirements are addressed by each Key Support System* | | | |
| Medication Management | **Inpatient** High quality, safe care Communication/respect Responsiveness/ timeliness | Missing First Dose Review MAK Saves | (AOS) 7.1-55 |
| Housekeeping Bed Cleaning | | Bed Turnaround Times | 7.1-61 |
| Product Acquisition | | Inventory Fill Rates | 7.1-71 |
| Network Availability | **Outpatient** High quality, safe care Communication Timeliness | Network and Server Availability, IT Help Desk, Help Desk Customer Survey Managed Services Metrics | 7.1-67 |
| Workforce Engagement | | Overall Employee/Nursing Turnover Time to Fill New Positions Employees Living the Values | 7.3-5; 6, 7, 29 |
| Revenue Cycle | **ED** Timeliness High quality, safe care | Inpatient Discharges Outpatient Visits Emergency Room Visits | 7.5-21, 25, 26 |
| Workforce Development | | Internal Promotions | 7.3-32 |

*Note*: AOS = available on site. CAMC has additional assessment data not included in the application. Numbers in the exhibit refer to sections of the longer application document from which content for this case was abstracted.

*Source*: Reprinted from CAMC (2015, 28).

expectations. Key Distribution Supplier scorecards are used to provide feedback on service issues, reported product failures and business related issues.

The application describes the request for proposal (RFP) process in use at CAMC (2015, 30):

We use an extensive RFP process with specific criteria for selecting our group purchasing organization (GPO) and other suppliers. . . . All vendors must meet CAMC's defined credentialing criteria before being granted access to the hospital or performing any sales or educational visits. We also use our GPO and other suppliers to help us achieve efficiency in supply cost management, support innovation through researching new technology and products, and provide a forum for networking to share best practices.

Examples of improved operations cited by CAMC (2015) include cycles of improvement that raised drug delivery effectiveness from 90 to 99 percent in three years and the development of a "5S" tool that all nursing units used to standardize the organization of medications, clean/dirty supplies, forms, equipment, and linen supplies.

Concerning safety, the application states (CAMC 2015, 30):

Our safety system addresses proactive accident prevention by: 1) defining job requirements, 2) assessing the individual's ability to perform required functions, 3) defining policies and processes to safely perform tasks, 4) providing PPE [personal protective equipment], and 5) training at orientation annually/or more frequently when changes in duties occur. 6) Inspection strategies are deployed across the system through leadership rounding and safety, facility and security rounds. 7) Auditing processes are systematically used for targeted issues and include hand hygiene, semi-annual departmental inspections, and use of outside consultants.

When system failures occur, they are reviewed using the DMAIC process. Changes are deployed via single-page memos and safety alerts.

CAMC (2015) is prepared for disasters and emergencies and conducts routine training, simulations, and drills. Its systems have met two challenging tests—first in 2012, when 70 percent of West Virginia was without power, and then in 2014, when a major flood contaminated the water supply. The sites functioned under emergency conditions for several days.

## Next Steps

Sarah Cho has now spent a considerable amount of time reviewing CAMC's Baldrige documentation and summarizing her findings as they might relate to XYZ. In completing her summary, Sarah decided not to draw too many comparisons between CAMC and XYZ, because other members of the team know XYZ so much better than she does. However, as she worked, she recognized that a key issue will be getting everybody to understand the differences—not just the senior team, but all managers.

When finished, Sarah is surprised to find that her "summary" is more than 8,000 words long. "Nobody will read all of this," she thinks. "Do I now have to develop a summary of the summary?"

## Case Questions

1. What should Sarah include in a two-page executive summary of the summary she has created?
2. Sarah also thinks she needs an "elevator speech." It starts with something like, "XYZ is great, but we can make it greater. It's a win–win for everybody—patients, caregivers, other XYZ associates." Help her finish the speech by adding 250 words about why the Baldrige journey is a good idea for XYZ.

3. What should the chief operating officer be thinking? Before she tells Sarah to present the summary to the senior leadership, what actions should she take as COO?

## References

Baldrige Performance Excellence Program. 2017. *2017–2018 Baldrige Excellence Framework: A Systems Approach to Improving Your Organization's Performance.* Gaithersburg, MD: US Department of Commerce, National Institute of Standards and Technology.

Charleston Area Medical Center (CAMC). 2015. "2015 Malcolm Baldrige National Quality Award Application." Accessed March 7, 2017. http://patapsco.nist.gov/Award_Recipients/PDF_Files/CAMC%20Health%20System%20Application%20Summary.pdf.

Griffith, J. R. 2015. "Understanding High-Reliability Organizations: Are Baldrige Recipients Models?" *Journal of Healthcare Management* 60 (1): 44–61.

# ▌CASE 44

# Cultural Competency at Marion County Health Center

*Maria Jorina and Ann Scheck McAlearney*

**M**arion County Health Center (MCHC), a not-for-profit community health center, is located in the West. Within its women's clinic, MCHC runs a breast cancer screening program intended to provide preventive services and educational programs to women residing in the county. The clinic offers screening mammograms, clinical breast exams, sexually transmitted disease (STD) testing, pregnancy counseling, and a variety of instructive materials on cancer and health promotion for women. The clinic's patient population reflects the racial makeup of the county: 60 percent of its patients are white, 30 percent are African American, and the remaining 10 percent represent a mix of Native American, Asian, and other racial groups. About 65 percent of the clinic's patients are age 40 or older, and many are poor and unemployed.

When Patricia Cole, the new administrator of MCHC, reviewed the most recent health center statistics reporting breast cancer screening rates, she was concerned to see not only that MCHC rates were below the state and national averages but also, most disconcertingly, that white women had consistently higher rates of initial and repeated screening visits than their African American counterparts. Annual mammogram screenings are currently recommended for women older than age 40, when self and clinical breast exams are considered less effective at detecting cancer. Because many of the center's patients are older than 40, low rates of breast cancer screening were troubling, to say the least. In addition, Cole was well aware of the continual emphasis from the Colorado Office of Minority Health on reducing healthcare disparities among racial and ethnic minorities. Given that MCHC's mission pledged to "provide access to care regardless of race, ethnicity, or country of origin," Cole wondered what factors might be contributing to this disparity and what she as the health center's administrator could do about it. She decided to ask Emily Parsons, the director of all MCHC screening programs, to investigate.

## A Review of Breast Cancer Screening Services at MCHC

After receiving her assignment from Cole, Parsons went directly to the MCHC women's clinic so that she could see, firsthand, how care was being provided. Upon entering the clinic, she first noticed that most of the women in the waiting room were white. She also saw a number of brochures placed on the counters and coffee tables situated in the waiting room. The brochures covered subjects ranging from STD prevention and pregnancy to cervical and breast cancer screening.

Parsons wanted to speak with some of the physicians working at the clinic to learn about how the physicians interacted with their patients. She was particularly interested in learning under what circumstances and how often the topic of breast cancer screening was brought up during patient visits. Fortunately, all four clinic physicians agreed to brief meetings, so Parsons cleared her schedule.

## The Physicians' Perspectives

Parsons's meetings with the four clinic physicians were strikingly similar. MCHC physicians appeared to believe that the benefits of breast cancer screening were already well known. Further, several physicians noted that, because MCHC's breast cancer screening program had been extensively advertised in the local media, they did not feel obligated to emphasize the benefits of screening to the patients they saw in the clinic. As all four physicians noted, MCHC provided educational materials at the clinic that were widely available for patients to read while they waited for their appointments; thus, the physicians did not feel the need to specifically discuss screening during the short periods of time they had with their patients. The physicians' collective sentiment appeared to be that, if a patient had questions, she could raise those questions during the visit. Parsons was surprised by such conviction, especially given that three of the four physicians were women.

Parsons also got the impression that the physicians did not believe that early breast cancer screening was equally beneficial for all patients. Several of the physicians made comments to the effect that "most African American women did not see their providers regularly anyway," so telling them about the screening program was considered a waste of the physicians' time. Another physician believed that, because African American women were statistically less likely to get breast cancer, they did not need the same amount of health education on the topic. When Parsons brought up MCHC's mission, all four physicians expressed a sincere belief that they were providing care equally.

A final impression from her meetings was that the physicians did not seem to feel comfortable discussing the importance of breast cancer screening with patients because they had not received specific training about how to introduce and discuss the subject. Several physicians noted that they found communicating with nonwhite patients to be especially difficult, in part because they felt some of the patients lacked sufficient knowledge of medical terminology to fully understand what the physicians were saying. All four physicians expressed a sentiment that relating to nonwhite patients was generally impaired by racial and cultural differences.

## Some Patients' Perspectives

Parsons was quite startled by the physicians' comments and felt that she needed to learn even more about what was going on in the clinic. She wanted to ask patients what they thought about the benefits of screening, see if they had any questions, and see if they would share their thoughts about the need to perform breast self-exams. She obtained permission from MCHC's institutional review board to speak with patients about their experiences and perspectives. Parsons then interviewed a number of women—both white and African American—at the end of their clinic visits to better understand their views about breast cancer screening.

Among the women who agreed to be interviewed, the majority of white patients expressed general satisfaction with MCHC's breast cancer screening program and noted that it had indeed been well publicized in the local media. With few exceptions, this group believed that breast cancer screening was beneficial to all women and that screening should be a part of health promotion programs throughout the county. A majority of women in this group also commented that they did not feel the clinic's physicians brought up cancer screening first and that patients often had to ask about it themselves.

The African American women's responses painted quite a different picture for Parsons. A great majority of these women believed breast cancer screening was only necessary when recommended by the physician, and many reported that they did not feel comfortable asking about screening if the doctor did not bring it up. When asked whether they had seen advertisements for MCHC's screening program on television or in local newspapers, the majority of African American women said they had not. Many of these women did not have cable television, and most did not regularly read a newspaper. Further, most of the African American women Parsons interviewed were not aware of the benefits of breast self-examinations and reported not knowing how to do them.

Many of the African American women reported that they had difficulty seeing a physician on a regular basis. Some women noted that doctor visits were inconvenient, with several expressing frustration that a visit the clinic required asking for time off work. A couple of women also commented that the clinic's location was an issue, because they had to take two buses to get there. Several other women complained that a visit to the clinic required them to pay for daycare for their children, which was an expense they could not always afford.

## Additional Issues Surface

After hearing from both the physicians and a number of patients, Parsons presented her findings to Cole. Parsons's view was that the MCHC physicians were not culturally competent and seemed unable to relate to their nonwhite patients. Cole could not disagree.

To make matters worse, Cole then told Parsons about a letter of complaint she had recently received from one of the MCHC employees in the clinical quality department. In the letter, the employee expressed dissatisfaction with the MCHC work environment and provided several examples of insensitivity on the part of MCHC staff members, who were reportedly ignorant about cultural differences and intolerant of this employee's religious practices.

## Cultural Differences Among Employees

An ongoing shortage of domestically trained medical staff has been a common problem for healthcare organizations throughout the United States, and MCHC was no exception. To meet its staffing needs, MCHC had begun hiring foreign-trained candidates to fill vacant patient coordinator positions. Most recently, the department of clinical quality had hired a new patient coordinator, a Pakistani female, whose duties included greeting and assisting patients and visitors, helping patients with scheduling tests and procedures, obtaining test results, maintaining the accuracy of patient information in the health center database, and resolving issues related to insurance claims and referrals.

This newly hired patient coordinator, Ms. Neely, had come to the United States ten years previously and had worked in healthcare for that entire time. Neely had received nursing training in Pakistan, and she had worked there as a registered nurse for five years. Since coming to the United States, Neely had taken and passed the National Council Licensure Examination for Registered Nurses (NCLEX-RN) and obtained a license from the state of Illinois, where she initially resided. Neely had recently moved to Colorado, where MCHC was located. Though she applied initially for an RN position posted on the MCHC website, she was instead offered a patient coordinator job. Even though Neely felt she was overqualified for the patient coordinator position and deserved the RN position instead, she felt obligated to accept the position to support herself and her teenage daughter. In addition, the human resources manager had assured Neely during the job interview that her position could been seen as a stepping stone and that, with more experience and a Colorado state license, she would be given additional challenges and responsibilities.

## A Complaint About Cultural Competency

In her letter to the MCHC administrator, Neely complained that, after having worked at MCHC for nine months and having obtained a Colorado RN license, she still had not been given an opportunity to take on more challenging tasks. She believed the nurse supervisor micromanaged her work, and she perceived that she was given too many "boring" tasks, such as resolving patient insurance claims and scheduling tests. Further, she noted that there had been no discussion about a promotion any time soon. Neely also felt that her colleagues and supervisors looked down on her because of her nationality and accent. She stated that colleagues spoke noticeably louder when addressing her and made it obvious that her accent was difficult for them to understand. She further commented that colleagues always appeared uninterested when she talked about her culture and traditions. Finally, Neely stated that, on several occasions, her supervisor had expressed discontent when she requested time off for her religious holidays.

## Incorporating Additional Evidence

Upon receiving this letter, Cole recalled having overheard one of Neely's colleagues, Ms. Gilbert, complaining to another staff member about issues in the clinical quality department. Cole suggested that Parsons talk to Gilbert and continue her investigation.

Parsons found Gilbert in her office, and Gilbert was more than willing to talk about what was going on in the department. One of Gilbert's college friends, who had been a Marion County resident all her life, had applied for the patient coordinator position at the same time as Neely, and Gilbert was surprised and disappointed that her friend did not get the job. Gilbert told Parsons that she believed all jobs should be offered first to domestically trained professionals who have the skills and competencies to provide adequate services to the MCHC population.

Next, Gilbert explained that she and her colleagues felt Neely was being culturally insensitive by bringing her traditional Pakistani dishes—which contained spices that most people at MCHC were not used to—to office potlucks and holiday parties. Gilbert and her colleagues felt that Neely, having lived in the United States for at least ten years, should be able to make traditional American dishes by now.

Third, Gilbert noted that she and her colleagues felt Neely was being unprofessional by leaving her workplace several times a day to perform her prayers. Neely's absences, Gilbert explained, could cause important calls to be missed and the continuity of patient care to be disrupted.

Finally, Gilbert complained that Neely—because her faith required her to always wear *shalwar kameez*, a traditional Pakistani garment of pants and a tunic—was able to bend office rules by wearing "relaxed" clothing every day of the week instead of only on Fridays, as allowed for the other staff. Even though Neely wore a white medical coat on top of her shalwar kameez, everyone felt she was not following the rules. In summary, Gilbert's account indicated that the department felt a general distrust toward Neely, regardless of her performance as a patient coordinator.

## Now What?

Parsons scheduled an appointment with Cole to discuss the additional information she had learned from her meeting with Gilbert. Both Parsons and Cole realized that Gilbert's comments could be interpreted as just one person's opinion, but they also sensed that the comments represented a wider problem, given the letter Neely had sent to Cole.

Cole was both unhappy and perplexed with the situation she now faced at MCHC. While in college and graduate school, she had learned about racial and ethnic health disparities, discrimination, biases, and the importance of cultural diversity, but she had never personally dealt with the issues before. Nor had she ever expected to find them in her workplace. Cole recognized that MCHC clearly had some issues to resolve around both discrimination and cultural competency, and she had to take the lead to develop an appropriate strategy.

## Case Questions

1. What are the cultural competency problems that MCHC faces? What makes these problems similar to one another, and what makes them different?
2. What organizational and cultural barriers can be identified in this case?
3. What strategies should be developed to overcome these barriers?
4. What kind of priority should these problems have for Cole, the MCHC administrator? Does Cole have to act as the sole decision maker in this situation? Who else could be involved in developing strategies to address these problems?
5. Whose interests should be considered in this situation and at what cost?

# CASE 45
## Shoes for the Shoemaker

*Anthony R. Kovner*

Tim Collins is the new director of the health management program at the Urban School of public and nonprofit management. The school has about 1,000 students and 40 full-time and 60 part-time faculty. The health management program represents 20 percent of the school's enrollment. The small school is breaking even financially. Collins teaches strategic management, and the dean, Sam Ivins, has asked him to develop a strategic plan for the health management program.

## Estimate of the Situation

Collins is heavily scheduled and has many other duties, including carrying out his own research. He gets no additional compensation for being program director. He talks to a variety of stakeholders in the program—faculty, admissions, students, alumni, and colleagues running programs at other schools—and gathers the following evidence:

- Applications to the health management program are down, but admissions are steady.
- The faculty has suffered the retirements of two senior faculty members, one of whom Collins was hired to replace.
- The faculty's research productivity is low.
- No online courses are offered.
- Placements for students remain good; students get jobs at competitive salaries.
- The school has a weak relationship with alumni, whose support is minimal.

On the plus side, both the school and the health management program have a rich tradition. Several of the school's faculty, including Collins, are notable scholars. Further, the program is fully accredited.

## Alternative Plans of Action

Collins has come up with three possible responses to the management challenge he faces in strategically planning for the program. He plans to discuss them with faculty.

These three options are as follows:

- Option 1: Do nothing. The program has essentially been following this option since the last program director resigned. The only positive move since the resignation was the hiring of Collins.
- Option 2: Shut down the program or merge it into another school. Along these lines, the health management program could be merged with the management department of the school, the program could partner with the large medical center owned by the university, or the program could merge with the business school.
- Option 3: Invest in the health management program, and make it distinctive. This option requires funds currently not available through the regular budgeting processes, as well as entrepreneurial talent. To pursue this option, one tactic would be to appoint a full-time clinical director of the program. Other tactics would be to aggressively recruit adjunct professors and to partner with managers at large medical centers. Consideration should also be given to expanding the executive

degree program, initiating online courses, and focusing the traditional program around evidence-based management.

## Case Questions

1. For each of the three options, what are the keys to ensure that implementation is successful?
2. Which option do you recommend that Collins choose, and how should he proceed?

# CASE 46

# An Investment Decision for Central Med Health System

*Emily Allinder, Jason Dopoulos, Breanne Taylor, David Reisman, Erick Vidmar, Jason Waibel, and Ann Scheck McAlearney*

## Background

Central Med Health System (CMHS) was created on January 1, 1996, with the mission of "providing expert healthcare to the people of North Central Iowa." The nonprofit organization comprises two general, acute care hospitals, Central Med Hospital and Shelty Hospital, with a combined total of 395 beds. The service area covers six counties in North Central Iowa: Rich, Crawford, Ashville, Morris, Huron, and Knowell counties. Central Med is the largest provider of healthcare services between the cities of Cletan and Flagship. The health system provides a complete range of primary care and specialty practices. Central Med Hospital offers a Level II trauma center and a Level II perinatal department. Other featured services include cardiac care, comprehensive neurological services, cancer care, behavioral health, maternity services, sports medicine, surgical services, pediatric therapy services, speech therapy services, industrial health and safety services, home care, and hospice care.

All services and business units are driven by the mission, vision, and values of CMHS. Central Med's vision is to provide "expert care close to home." The organization seeks to be the provider of choice for residents of North Central Iowa, and it strives to dissuade residents from traveling to Cletan or Flagship for care. The core values as stated by Central Med include the following:

- *Quality*: We will be known for excellence in all that we do.
- *Customer service*: We will work to fulfill the individual needs of every patient, family member, and visitor.
- *Innovation*: We will continually strive to develop and work with the latest processes and technologies available in every department.
- *Teamwork*: Our staff will work together to provide our patients with the best care possible.

## Financial Status

CMHS is a financially stable organization. Operating margins have been consistent with similar "BBB" bond-rated organizations over the past three years and currently stand at 3 percent. A $12 million endowment provides consistent investment returns, which contributed to a total margin of 8 percent last fiscal year. CMHS maintains a prudent balance sheet with a debt-to-capitalization ratio of 25 percent. Days cash on hand has averaged 225 over the last three years, and the current ratio was 2.5 last year, demonstrating the system's ability to cover its operating expenses. CMHS has historically used debt to finance capital projects, but due to evaporation of liquidity in the municipal bond markets, the system has decided to fund certain projects with cash from operations.

## The Problem

Like other nonprofit healthcare providers, CMHS struggles to enhance patient care with limited financial and capital resources. Investments in new clinical programs are evaluated carefully to ensure that patients have access to the appropriate new programs and services. CMHS strives to balance the need to invest in the clinical programs that are most important to its patient population with the need to remain financially viable.

CMHS leadership is currently faced with a difficult decision. The system has $13 million to invest in a clinical expansion project, and stakeholders throughout the organization differ in their ideas about which program is most deserving of the new capital investment. Whereas certain members of the leadership team want to invest in an expanded radiation oncology program, others are interested in bolstering heart services by enhancing the interventional cardiology program.

### Option 1: Radiation Oncology
The American Cancer Society, the *Journal of Oncology Management*, the Health Care Advisory Board, and other expert sources project a 20 to 25 percent

increase in the number of newly diagnosed cancer cases in the next ten years. In addition to this increase in newly diagnosed cases, the five-year relative survival rate has increased significantly as a result of newer technologies and treatments. As people live longer, the demand for cancer services will grow.

Dr. Moh, the only radiation oncologist at CMHS, sees up to 70 patients a day, which is 40 percent more patients than the average radiation oncologist sees. The facilities are cramped and the schedule is tight, but somehow he is able to complete the day's work. Perhaps the friendly culture of CMHS keeps the staff content with current operations, but Dr. Moh believes something needs to be done differently to continue to provide high-quality care.

Every radiation oncology department in the country needs two components: a board-certified radiation oncologist and the essential equipment to create a treatment plan. CMHS has both of these components, but many people have become concerned that the department will need additional equipment to accommodate treatment plans. Linear accelerators are traditionally used to program a patient's treatment plan and can be accessed for each appointment. CMHS currently has two machines and averages between 40 and 50 patients per day. The literature recommends that one machine treat 30 to 35 patients per day; thus, to meet demand, CMHS must have two machines running. Technical difficulties are a problem because CMHS's linear accelerators are unmatched. If one machine goes down, the patient plan for that machine cannot be transferred to the other machine. This issue results in wasted time and resources.

In addition, Dr. Moh is concerned that CMHS is vulnerable to competitors who might want to enter the radiation oncology market in CMHS's primary service areas. Such competition would be difficult for CMHS to withstand given its current facilities. Dr. Moh knows he needs to act quickly to secure the future success of the program.

## Option 2: Interventional Cardiology

Although the cardiology program has been quite successful for CMHS, further investment in the interventional cardiology segment of the department is desperately needed. Current industry trends favor interventional cardiology procedures over traditional open-heart operations, and expert industry organizations predict that these trends will continue. CMHS needs to make a significant investment in its interventional cardiology program if it wants to retain and expand market share in this specialty.

Cholesterol-lowering and antihypertensive medications introduced over the past ten years have resulted in significantly extended life spans for cardiology patients. However, Americans leading more sedentary lifestyles and eating high-fat diets have contributed to a larger number of patients requiring specialized cardiac care. As the number of patients requiring specialized cardiology care continues to increase throughout the service area, CMHS has been struggling to expand its service offerings to this patient population. At the same time, a large competing health system in the area has recently invested in a significant expansion of its cardiovascular service line. Dr. Peak, an interventional cardiologist and CMHS's director of cardiology, knows that to ensure the future success of the cardiology division, he needs to secure additional financial support from hospital leadership.

The cardiology program at CMHS has overcome significant challenges in the past. Several years ago, the division faced a need for more cardiac surgeons and operating rooms to handle the increased number of coronary artery bypass graft procedures. The solution to the problem was to remodel the cardiac operating rooms and recruit several highly qualified physicians. The program has since become one of the more profitable units at CMHS and a model that other divisions within the hospital hope to emulate.

Advances in treatment options for cardiology patients have focused on minimally invasive interventional procedures that are more comfortable for patients and have significantly reduced recovery times. In fact, the number of minimally invasive interventional cardiology procedures performed at CMHS has nearly doubled in the past few years. These procedures are completed in specially designed treatment areas where sophisticated imaging equipment is used to guide small catheters and instruments through patients' cardiovascular systems. The single interventional cardiology suite at CMHS is no longer adequate to serve this expanding clinical need. Dr. Peak knows that CMHS needs to invest significant capital in the creation of additional interventional cardiology treatment areas if it hopes to retain market share in this competitive environment.

### Implications of the Investment Decision

Given CMHS's location, the health system is continually concerned about its ability to retain market share and avoid losing patients to hospitals in Cletan or Flagship. Although the financial stability and reputation of CMHS are enviable, the hospital has been unwilling to expand beyond the North Central Iowa region. Further, CMHS's clear mission and strong organizational culture have made affiliation options, such as alliances or other cooperative arrangements with competitors, virtually impossible to consider. As a result, any CMHS investment will be pursued on its own.

In previous discussions about investment options, hospital leadership had proposed other possible uses for the $13 million. However, the board has rejected the other alternatives and has narrowed the options to the two currently on the table. In addition, the board is unwilling to further explore avenues that might make the two options jointly possible. Even though an exclusive investment in radiation oncology will threaten the success of the interventional cardiology program, and vice versa, the board wants to force a decision between the two, and it wants the decision made now.

## Case Questions

1. What are the pros and cons of each alternative investment? Does the radiation oncology project or the enhanced interventional cardiology program better align with CMHS's mission and vision? Why?
2. Whom does CMHS serve? At what cost?
3. Which stakeholders at CMHS will be affected by this decision? Which stakeholders should be included in discussions about which alternative investment to pursue?
4. What additional information would you need to make a solid business decision? Are there nonfinancial data you should consider?
5. What implications would exist for the alternative service that is not selected for investment? What might happen to volume and market share for that service?
6. If the two alternatives were not mutually exclusive, what types of financing strategies would you propose to permit investment in both options?

# CASE 47
## A New Look?

*Ann Scheck McAlearney and Sarah M. Roesch*

D r. Elinor Cooke is a renowned cosmetic surgeon, highly dedicated to healing and restoring well-being for those affected by aesthetic issues. She believes that her line of work builds the confidence and self-esteem of those who seek her services. Dr. Cooke received her medical degree from Case Western Reserve University and then completed four years of residency and two additional years of residency in plastic surgery at the Ohio State University Hospitals. Dr. Cooke's current practice, North City Aesthetic and Plastic Surgery, Inc., affiliated with Northside Community Hospital, is in a suburb of Cleveland on a beautiful wooded lot next to Lake Erie. In addition to Dr. Cooke, one other doctor—Dr. Ryan Thomas, who specializes in men's reconstructive surgery—is affiliated with North City. The practice also employs two nurses and an office manager. It has an excellent reputation and is known for its compassionate approach to care.

Although North City Aesthetic and Plastic Surgery is considered one of the premier practices in the Midwest market area, Dr. Cooke is concerned about some of the changes she has observed in the field of plastic surgery. When she started her practice in the early 1980s, cosmetic surgery was a relatively new field. Plastic surgery was available for people affected by disfigurement but not readily available for those who wanted to fix something just because they did not like their appearance. Over the years, Hollywood, new techniques, and new trends sparked tremendous growth in the cosmetic surgery industry, and with this growth, the profile of a typical cosmetic surgery practice changed. Whereas patients used to be amazed that a tummy tuck, breast augmentation, facelift, or rhinoplasty was possible, now the average patient tends to want more than surgery alone.

Another trend Dr. Cooke has observed is the increasing level of competition for aesthetic surgery services. She has been aware of the expanding availability of surgical procedures through ambulatory surgery centers, but a recent invitation to a "Botox party" event provided evidence of a new competitive threat—even if the quality of care provided at such events might be suspect. Dr. Cooke's North City practice has managed to grow based on patients' word-of-mouth recommendations and other physicians' referrals rather than through advertising. Yet given local and regional competition for well-paying patients, Dr. Cooke knows that she must develop her own strategy to ensure that the practice can survive and thrive into the future.

Dr. Cooke has a bachelor's degree in business and is a problem solver by nature, and she is continually looking for ways to grow her practice's business. In considering the new trends in the aesthetic surgery area, Dr. Cooke senses that she has a choice to make. Abdominoplasty (tummy tuck) is the most popular form of surgery that she performs. After surgery, the patient often has trouble with activities such as moving from a sitting to a standing position, walking, and caring for the postoperative drains. Dr. Cooke has often thought that the practice could consider offering a 24-hour care alternative for postoperative patients.

One particularly intriguing option is to develop a "hideaway" where aesthetic surgery clients could relax and recover after their procedures. She knows that her patients desire complete confidentiality at all times and that they want a high degree of professional and personal attention before, during, and after the procedures. A hideaway would allow Dr. Cooke to provide top-notch medical care in a spalike atmosphere, and it would enable her staff to offer professional and personal attention to healing patients during the days following surgery. Given her knowledge of the important connections between individuals' minds and their bodies, Dr. Cooke is certain that a relaxing atmosphere would enhance the healing process while offering a safe place for recovery. Moreover, no other facility in the Cleveland area offers such a service, so Dr. Cooke feels the hideaway would definitely give her practice an edge over competitors.

Dr. Cooke suspects that this hideaway concept would have considerable appeal to her well-heeled patients; however, she knows that potential patients are not the only people she would need to consider in developing a new approach for the North City practice. When she shared her idea with Dr. Thomas, he was less than enthusiastic. Dr. Thomas reminded her that they were surgeons, not innkeepers. He noted that the overhead costs associated with such a practice change would be high, and he was particularly worried about management of the facility. Dr. Thomas also brought up the issue of insurance liability. Then he mentioned that he had heard that St. Clare's, another community hospital, was also looking into opening a similar type of facility not too far away.

Understanding Dr. Thomas's concerns, Dr. Cooke is discouraged but not defeated. The lease on the practice's current building will soon be up, so she knows she must make a decision quickly. The possibility of a similar facility opening at St. Clare's motivates Dr. Cooke to further investigate her idea. She feels her building's scenic locale—on a beautiful wooded lot with lake views— would be perfect for a postoperative hideaway, and she thinks Dr. Thomas's male patients would also benefit from a discreet setting in which to recover.

## Case Questions

1. What are the pros and cons of changing the focus of Dr. Cooke's practice?
2. How would you expect the various stakeholders (e.g., patients, referring physicians, Northside Community Hospital, her professional colleagues) to react to Dr. Cooke's new business concept?
3. What would you recommend for Dr. Cooke?

# CASE 48
# Disparities in Care at Southern Regional Health System

*Ann Scheck McAlearney*

Theo Hank leaned back in his chair and closed his eyes. He had been afraid that the reports would contain bad news, and he now had to figure out what to do with this new information. Flipping through the first binder on his desk—reporting results of the recent Robert Wood Johnson Foundation–sponsored assessment of the cardiovascular care provided by his organization—he was increasingly concerned.

Southern Regional Health System was based in Jackson, Mississippi, an area known for its diverse population and high poverty rates. Poverty and unemployment in the area affected whites and nonwhites differently: Black and Hispanic residents were about three times more likely than white residents to live in poverty, black residents were two and a half times more likely than whites to be unemployed, and Hispanic residents were more than twice as likely as whites to be unemployed. Beyond poverty and unemployment concerns, however, was the issue of disparities in healthcare—that is, different care being given to different patients. Although such disparities had received increasing attention nationwide, Hank thought that the care provided at Southern Regional was "color-blind." Under the health system's mission of providing "excellent quality of care for all," he assumed that the care was equitably delivered across patients and patient populations.

Apparently, this was not the case. The first report presented heart care data that had been collected over the past year, and it showed significant disparities in the care provided by Southern Regional. For instance, using the four core measures for heart failure that the Centers for Medicare & Medicaid Services currently collects and reports, the data indicated that only 41 percent of Southern Regional's patients were receiving all recommended heart failure care and that the number was lower for nonwhite patients than it was for whites. Whereas 68 percent of whites received all recommended care, the comparable number among nonwhites was just 27 percent. Disparities were also apparent in the percentage of heart failure patients who received discharge instructions: Only 65 percent of Hispanic patients received the information, compared to 85 percent of non-Hispanic patients. Also troubling Hank was the fact that none of the measures was close to 100 percent. The data clearly indicated that the care provided at Southern Regional was not the type of care Hank would want offered to his own family. He truly did not understand how his hospital could be providing such disparate care.

The second binder on his desk offered little information to ease his concerns. This report, the "Assessment of Organizational Readiness to Change" for Southern Regional, showed that few individuals in the hospital were aware of the nationwide problem of disparities in care and that even fewer were aware that such an issue might be problematic within their own hospital. The evaluation also showed a strong tendency among hospital employees and physicians to resist proposed changes and instead "go with the flow."

Hank now possessed data showing significant gaps in the care provided to African American and Hispanic patients relative to white patients, and he knew that he had to bring this issue to the forefront of hospital concerns. A meaningful reduction in these disparities would be a legacy he would love to leave. Yet he still was not sure how best to address this issue at Southern Regional.

## Case Questions

1. What should Hank do with the information contained in these reports?
2. What reactions would you predict Hank might receive from various hospital stakeholders, such as other executives, physicians, board members, or the community?
3. What can Hank do to raise the level of urgency at Southern Regional Health System to address the issue of disparities in care?
4. What are the constraints he will face?

# | CASE 49

# How Can an ACO Improve the Health of Its Population?

*Ann Scheck McAlearney*

Vandalia Care, an accountable care organization (ACO), had been successfully developed as part of Vandalia Medical Center (VMC), but the new ACO's leadership had become concerned. Specifically, they worried that their mission to reduce care costs while improving the health of the population was at risk. In the six months since Vandalia Care had been established, the number of patients served had increased, but VMC was having difficulty determining whether and how the ACO model was having an impact on the health of its population.

VMC had an electronic health record (EHR) that was operational in both inpatient and outpatient settings, but not all providers could access all elements of the EHR. Now that Vandalia Care had been implemented, a new problem arose with respect to data. Vandalia Care had associated hospitals and providers, but because of the way ACO contracts were written, patients attributed to the ACO were not required to use those facilities and clinicians. As a result, when patients attributed to Vandalia Care visited providers external to the ACO, data about those visits were virtually impossible to collect. Considering that Vandalia Care's goal is to improve the health of the entire ACO population, lack of access to the comprehensive health records of all attributed patients was problematic.

Lindsey Dillow, the new manager of care coordination for Vandalia Care, wanted to help solve this problem. Drawing from recent research on ACO development (McAlearney, Song, and Hilligoss 2017), Dillow believed that Vandalia Care patients, like other ACO patients, did not know they were actually part of the ACO. Patients might be loyal to their primary care physicians, but when they needed specialty care or hospitalization, they went wherever they wanted to go, regardless of whether the setting was part of Vandalia Care. As a result, Dillow did not know these patients had sought services outside the ACO until she received claims data several months after the admission or visit, thus significantly compromising her ability to coordinate care. Further, costs that could have been controlled via ACO contracts with specialists, hospitals, and even skilled nursing facilities were left unchecked.

Vandalia Care's launch had included a mass mailing to members of the community, but Dillow believed more needed to be done to engage patients and community members in improving their health. She knew that the ACO's leadership was open to supporting a major initiative to connect with the community, so she needed to carefully consider her strategy. Dillow recognized that a true focus on population health management had to be less about branding the ACO and more about engaging consumers and encouraging them to care about their health. In particular, she believed that an important element of this outreach had to focus on connecting physicians with community members. She wondered whether focusing on a particular segment of the population first—children, for instance—made sense, or whether staging her outreach plan by geographic area or community was a better alternative. Dillow had access to the Vandalia EHR to inform her plan, but she needed to figure out what to do first.

## Case Questions

1. How could the EHR be used to improve population health management?
2. What kinds of community outreach might be effective for Vandalia Care? What kinds of outreach might be perceived less favorably?
3. Is there a population group or area that should be targeted first? Why and how?

## Reference

McAlearney, A. S., P. Song, and B. Hilligoss. 2017. "Private Sector Accountable Care Organization Development: A Qualitative Study." *American Journal of Managed Care* 23 (3): 151–58.

# CASE 50

# Hearing the Patient Voice: Working with Patient and Family Advisers to Improve the Patient Experience

*Cynthia J. Sieck*

## Background

Healthcare systems are increasingly seeking opportunities to solicit and incorporate patient perspectives in an effort to provide more patient-centered care. Patient satisfaction surveys provide some insight into patient perceptions, particularly about how well the organization is achieving its goals related to communication and the care experience. In addition, many organizations use patient and family advisory councils to better understand how patients experience care, as well as to improve the way care is delivered.

## The Case: A Patient Adviser's Perspective

Karen Williams is a 56-year-old breast cancer survivor who is also living with diabetes and cardiovascular disease. For the last ten years, Karen has been receiving most of her medical care from the University Health Network (UHN), which includes primary care clinics, general hospital services, a cancer center, and a heart hospital. For the last two years, Karen has served as a patient adviser for UHN's Patient and Family Advisory Council. The council consists of 12 patients from a variety of backgrounds who have received care at one or more of UHN's hospitals or clinics. They meet monthly to provide feedback about various projects presented to them by UHN staff members.

Karen's current project with the council involves the development of a new information brochure/packet to be provided to all patients throughout UHN. She and five other advisers sit on a brochure committee with six staff members from the patient experience and marketing departments. The initial meeting begins with an introduction of committee members and a summary of the work the committee wishes to accomplish. The committee is charged with assessing the usefulness of current brochures and information sheets, identifying hospital services that are particularly in need of additional explanation, and selecting pictures from various options and templates provided.

Throughout the six months of the project, the committee tours each hospital and takes notes about how the delivery of information to patients might be improved through the use of a patient- and family-focused brochure/packet. At monthly meetings, committee members receive updates on plans for marketing communications to patients, and they provide feedback. When patient advisers and staff members disagree on a decision, Sue, the director of the patient experience department, facilitates a discussion followed by a vote. Sue also checks in with the advisers to learn about any challenges they face while participating on the committee. After the committee reaches a decision, Karen and two other patient advisers are invited to submit their brochure suggestions to UHN administrators.

At the end of the project, Sue asks each adviser what they liked about serving on the committee, what was challenging, and what they would change in future efforts. Karen reports that she appreciated receiving meeting agendas in advance so that she could prepare. She also feels that the project leader established an open and welcoming tone throughout the project, so that advisers felt comfortable providing their comments. However, she says she sometimes had difficulty attending meetings that were scheduled during UHN staff's workday, as it conflicted with her own workday. She suggests that future efforts provide remote access and focus on greater document-sharing capabilities.

## Case Questions

1. What in Karen's background made her input on UHN projects particularly relevant?
2. How did the brochure committee facilitate patient adviser input?
3. What are some other ways the committee could have sought input from patients?

# ACCOUNTABILITY

Let's not be too hasty: speed is a dangerous thing.
Untimely measures bring repentance.
Certainly, and unhappily, many things are wrong in the Colony.
But is there anything human without some fault?
And after all, you see, we do move forward.

—*C. P. Cavafy*

# COMMENTARY

**A**ddressing the increasingly important concept of accountability, Rachel (2012) succinctly states, "Where a culture of accountability exists, people do what they say they'll do." She further specifies several common concepts that are at the core of accountability:

- Obligation—a duty that usually comes with consequences
- Willingness—acceptance by choice or without reluctance
- Intent—the purpose behind the plan
- Ownership—having power or control
- Commitment—feeling emotionally compelled

Brinkley (2013) assumes that values form the basis of culture and that culture drives performance. Furthermore, she suggests that culture cannot be left unattended because, in the absence of purposeful culture shaping, cultures develop by default. Donnellan (2013, 25) writes that purposeful ethical behavior is good for business in any organization and that, in healthcare, it "will result in enhanced patient care, a committed and satisfied staff, efficient care delivery, and increased market share."

To our knowledge, none of the above assertions has been proved scientifically, but they represent our assumptions in presenting this section of the book. We know that we would prefer to work in—and receive care in—an ethical and accountable organization.

Accountability involves a wide range of subtopics, various loci in the organization, and questions that are variably answerable. We focus here on organizational and managerial accountability. How is the organization accountable to whom and for what, and how is the manager accountable for what to the organization and to herself? Accountability is closely related to ethics, and the word *ethics*, like *accountability*, covers a wide waterfront of interpretations. In our understanding, the difference in practice is that ethics focuses more on the espousing of values, whereas accountability speaks to the organization doing what it says it will do.

Accountability is said to be a good thing, although it costs managers scarce time. Managers must specify who will be accountable for what, obtain agreement on this specification, make such agreement transparent, influence expectations, and oversee the reporting of performance. All of these tasks must occur while the manager presumably has more important things to do—taking care of patient care issues and supporting his family, for instance. The relationship between higher accountability and better performance has never been tested, nor proven, to our knowledge.

In some ways, accountability can be seen as a marketing approach. The organization will be accountable for its performance, and therefore customers should trust the organization and go to it for care. We assume that, if a competitor is accountable and our organization is not, other things being equal, patients and customers will go to the competitor. Of course, a focus on accountability is not a widely used marketing slogan, nor a necessarily effective one. Telling customers that they are "in good hands" may provide assurance in general, but providing that assurance on the ground when the waits are long is a different task. So what are we to make of accountability in the real world?

Two factors are vital in implementing accountability: (1) a specification of organizational performance that is mutually agreed upon in advance by stakeholders and (2) the capability of managers to control the resources and behavior necessary to achieve such specified performance objectives.

## Expectations of Organizational Performance

Stakeholders assess organizational performance in a variety of ways. Some organizations use "balanced scorecards" as strategic management tools. In promoting the balanced scorecard approach, Kaplan and Norton (1996) have identified four perspectives: (1) financial (e.g., return on investment, market share); (2) customer service; (3) internal business processes (e.g., hospital readmission rate for the same illness); and (4) learning and growth, keyed to employee morale and suggestions.

Management accountability ranges accordingly across the four perspectives on the scorecard. For example, with regard to customer service, managers can undertake marketing studies to learn about patients' preferences and the services they would like delivered. Managers can also aid in the reorganization of work so that fewer clinicians provide more services for each patient. Managers can similarly reevaluate organizational routines regularly in terms of impact on patient and physician convenience.

To further focus on service, managers can tour the facility regularly. Managers can let patients know what service levels they should expect and let clinicians know what behavior is expected from them. Managers can report regularly to stakeholders about performance, plans, and issues, and stakeholders, including patients and employees, can serve on policymaking and advisory committees. Management information systems can focus on obtaining data to improve services. Useful data may include information about the population served; use of various services; quantity, cost, and quality of service; and patient and provider satisfaction. Summaries of reports by regulators and accreditors can be shared with stakeholder groups. Managers can analyze organizational goals and performance; trends in turnover, overtime, and absenteeism; and developments in fundraising, profitability, and new capital equipment. Other areas of organizational performance—for instance, organizational decision-making processes—should also be examined and addressed.

By making itself more formally accountable, organizational leadership incurs substantial costs in terms of management time spent on the process, dollars spent on information system upgrades, and conflicts raised by discussions about present and future direction. But the leadership may also reap substantial benefits, including plans and initiatives that are more acceptable to stakeholders and therefore more feasible to implement; greater commitment from key clinicians to organizational goals; and a sharper focus on the organization's mission, which justifies goals to employees and customers and makes goals easier to attain.

Society gives resources to high-performing organizations that add value to inputs and provide goods and services. The owners of such organizations have five functions, according to Pointer and Orlikoff (2002): (1) formulating a vision and key goals and ensuring that strategy is aligned with the vision and goals; (2) ensuring high levels of management performance; (3) ensuring high-quality care; (4) ensuring financial health; and (5) ensuring the board's effectiveness and efficiency. The chief executive officer (CEO) is the board's agent on site.

## Stakeholder Claims on the Organization

Organizational performance can be improved—or negatively affected—by such forces as legislation, regulation, and the media. Consider Medicare, for example: As payments are reduced, costs may shift to other payers, and beneficiaries' access and well-being may decrease (certainly as some physicians choose to no longer participate in the Medicare program). Managers generally have less control over external stakeholders than they do over stakeholders within their organization.

Healthcare is a particularly challenging field because of the difficulties in specifying measurable outcomes and in gaining agreement among stakeholders with different ideas about goals, strategies, and the appropriate roles for nonprofit governing boards. Some healthcare organizations, however, have made great advances in the area of accountability.

According to Berry and Bendapudi (2003, 100), the Mayo Clinic manages "a set of visual and experiential clues" to make clear to patients that care is organized around their needs rather than around doctors' schedules or hospital processes. Mayo employees are hired because they embrace the organization's values; these values are then emphasized through training and reinforced by the culture of the workplace. Further, to encourage collaboration among professionals, physicians at Mayo are paid salaries—meaning that they do not lose income if they refer a patient to another doctor. Sophisticated internal paging systems, telephones, and videoconferences facilitate communication, and electronic medical records have been fully implemented. The facilities are "designed explicitly to relieve stress, offer a place of refuge, create positive distractions, convey caring and respect, symbolize competence, minimize the impression of crowding, facilitate wayfinding, and accommodate families" (Berry and Bendapudi 2003, 105).

To promote accountability across the organization, managers can ensure that key stakeholders are identified and that their expectations and satisfaction levels are regularly measured. For greater objectivity in this regard, measurement can be done by external organizations explicitly organized for this purpose.

## Discussion Questions

1. How would you know if a health system or accountable care organization is sufficiently accountable to its stakeholders?
2. How, if at all, does being an "ethical" organization differ from being an "accountable" organization?
3. How would you structure an organization to ensure that its culture of accountability is actually enacted?
4. For which (if any) stakeholders is "accountability of healthcare organizations" a high priority? Is it a high priority for patients and consumers?
5. How would you propose to evaluate a CEO for making her healthcare organization sufficiently accountable over a period of time?

## References

Berry, L. L., and N. Bendapudi. 2003. "Clueing in Customers." *Harvard Business Review* 81 (2): 100–106.

Brinkley, R. W. 2013. "The Case for Values as a Basis for Organizational Culture." *Frontiers of Health Services Management* 30 (1): 3–13.

Donnellan, J. J. 2013. "A Moral Compass for Management Decision Making: A Healthcare CEO's Reflections." *Frontiers of Health Services Management* 30 (1): 14–26.

Kaplan, R. S., and D. P. Norton. 1996. "Using the Balanced Scorecard as a Strategic Management System." *Harvard Business Review* 74 (1): 75–85.

Pointer, D. D., and J. E. Orlikoff. 2002. *Getting to Great: Principles of Health Care Organization Governance*. San Francisco: Jossey-Bass.

Rachel, M. R. 2012. "Accountability: A Concept Worth Revisiting." *American Nurse Today*. Published March. www.americannursetoday.com/accountability-a-concept-worth-revisiting.

## Recommended Readings

Berwick, D. M., T. W. Nolan, and J. Whittington. 2008. "The Triple Aim: Care, Health, and Cost." *Health Affairs* 27 (3): 759–69.

Blustein, J., and B. E. Weinstein. 2016. "Opening the Market for Lower Cost Hearing Aids: Regulatory Change Can Improve the Health of Older Americans." *American Journal of Public Health* 106 (6): 1032–35.

Bush, J. 2014. *Where Does It Hurt?: An Entrepreneur's Guide to Fixing Health Care*. New York: Portfolio/Penguin.

Casolino, L. P., N. Erb, M. S. Joshi, and S. M. Shortell. 2015. "Accountable Care Organizations and Population Health Organizations." *Journal of Health Politics, Policy and Law* 40 (4): 821–37.

Citizens Budget Committee. 2016. *What Ails Medicaid in New York? And Does the Medicare Redesign Team Have a Cure?* Published May. http://nyachnyc.org/wp-content/uploads/2016/05/Citizens-Budget-Commission-What-Ails-Medicaid-in-New-York.pdf.

Fisher, E. S., S. M. Shortell, S. A. Kreindler, A. D. Van Citters, and B. K. Larson. 2012. "A Framework for Evaluating the Formation, Implementation, and Performance of Accountable Care Organizations." *Health Affairs* 31 (11): 2368–78.

Fox, D. M. 2015. "Commentary: Patients' Rights Matter in Regulating ACOs." *Journal of Health Politics, Policy and Law* 40 (4): 903–08.

Friedlaender, J. 2016. "Beating a Cancer Death Sentence." *Health Affairs* 35 (7): 1333–37.

Hefner, J. L., B. Hilligoss, C. Sieck, D. M. Walker, L. Sova, P. H. Song, and A. S. McAlearney. 2016. "Meaningful Engagement of ACOs with Communities: The New Population Health Management." *Medical Care* 54 (11): 970–76.

King, C. J., and J. L. Roach. 2016. "Community Health Needs Assessments: A Framework for America's Hospitals." *Population Health Management* 19 (2): 78–80.

Knickman, J. R., and A. R. Kovner. 2015. "The Future of Health Care Delivery and Health Policy." In *Jonas & Kovner's Health Care Delivery in the United States*, 11th ed., edited by J. R. Knickman and A. R. Kovner, 333–42. New York: Springer.

Kovner, A. R. 1994. "The Hospital Community Benefit Standards Program and Health Reform." *Hospital and Health Services Administration* 39 (2): 143–57.

Lutz, S. 2007. "Transparency—'Deal or No Deal'?" *Frontiers of Health Services Management* 23 (3): 13–23.

McAlearney, A. S., D. Terris, J. Hardacre, P. Spurgeon, C. Brown, A. Baumgart, and M. E. Nyström. 2014. "Organizational Coherence in Health Care Organizations: Conceptual Guidance to Facilitate Quality Improvement and Organizational Change." *Quality Management in Health Care* 23 (4): 254–67.

McWilliams, J. M., L. A. Hatfield, M. E. Chernew, B. E. Landon, and A. L. Schwartz. 2016. "Early Performance of Accountable Care Organizations." *New England Journal of Medicine* 374 (24): 2357–66.

Noble, D. J., and L. P. Casolino. 2013. "Can Accountable Care Organizations Improve Population Health? Should They Try?" *Journal of the American Medical Association* 309 (11): 1119–20.

Paulus, R. A., K. Davis, and G. D. Steele. 2008. "Continuous Innovation in Health Care: Implications of the Geisinger Experience." *Health Affairs* 27 (5): 1235–45.

Porter, M. E., and R. S. Kaplan. 2016. "How to Pay for Health Care." *Harvard Business Review* 94 (7–8): 88–98, 100, 134.

Reid, T. R. 2009. *The Healing of America: A Global Quest for Better, Cheaper, and Fairer Health Care.* New York: Penguin.

Robbins, J., and A. S. McAlearney. 2016. "Encouraging Employees to Speak Up to Prevent Infections: Opportunities to Leverage Quality Improvement and Care Management Processes." *American Journal of Infection Control* 44 (1): 1224–30.

Schroeder, S. A. 2006. "What to Do with a Patient Who Smokes." *Journal of the American Medical Association* 294 (4): 482–87.

Topol, E. 2015. *The Patient Will See You Now: The Future of Medicine Is in Your Hands.* New York: Basic Books.

White, K. R., and J. R. Griffith. 2016. "Population Health." In *The Well-Managed Healthcare Organization*, 8th ed., 281–316. Chicago: Health Administration Press.

# THE CASES

This section of the book has four longer cases and eight shorter cases dealing with the topic of accountability. The cases aim to generate thoughtful discussion, often going beyond the roles of managers in healthcare organizations (HCOs) and exploring ethical questions that managers face as individuals, as part of their communities, and as citizens.

Imagine that a patient gets bad care, complains about it, and gets no satisfaction. Who is responsible for the bad care, and what can the person listening to the complaint do about the situation? The listener has to hear what the complainant is saying and document it. Then she has to share the complaint with someone who can do something about it. A standard response to any complaint is the following:

> We're sorry for what happened. I will see that it does not happen again. If you like, you can enter a hearing process and receive a more formal response to your complaint. Through that process, we can better understand all sides of the issue and determine what can be done. If, for example, you had to wait because we were short-staffed, we can explain what we are doing to prevent similar shortages in the future. If you suffered injuries or financial loss, we can compensate you or take your claim to an arbitrator or a mediator who will help us decide what to do.

Responding to a complaint takes time, and the time of both the complainant and the listener are scarce. The best approach, of course, is to minimize the number of complaints by ensuring that services are organized properly in the first place, as discussed in other parts of this book.

In Case 51, "Letter to the CEO," a hospital CEO receives a letter from a patient and spouse detailing an experience of inadequate and inefficient care. The complainants are not looking for payment or to sue anyone or to get anyone in trouble; they just want to improve care at the hospital. How should the CEO respond? Of course, the CEO should acknowledge the letter, offer to meet with the patient and spouse, and ask the involved department heads to respond. But the detailed list of problems seems to suggest that major change is needed at the hospital. In initiating such change, how should the CEO set standards for accountability, establish transparency, and open channels of communication between the patients and families and the institution's leadership?

Case 52, "Whose Hospital?," recounts the firing of hospital CEO Don Wherry. A class could be devoted to whether Wherry should have been fired, or whether he should have resigned. Perhaps more interesting, however, would be a discussion of how Wherry's problems could have been prevented. After all, several months earlier, he had received a favorable evaluation. A larger question could focus on how well the board of the hospital represents the community served, as well as how the community served should be defined. What role did the medical staff play in Wherry's firing, and what role should it have played?

In Case 53, "Managed Care Cautionary Tale," a distinction can be made between legal and moral accountability. What responsibility does the ownership of an HCO have in the first place of siting the organization in an area serving paying patients rather than in an area of medical need? And then, once sited, how does the HCO establish policies to limit the losses on nonpaying patients and the referral of such patients to other centers that already are overloaded but get public funding to meet this need? Precisely, what is the accountability of the HCO to regularly inform AIDS-diagnosed patients that they would get better care management services if they left the health plan? By law, "dumping patients" is unethical and illegal. Does this "referring" amount to "dumping" or not?

A different accountability question arises in Case 54, "Dr. Fisher's Patient," when a doctor finds that a patient's attempts to specify treatment goals for himself and track his own progress are measurably improving care, increasing patient satisfaction, and controlling costs. What can the doctor do with this information? Not all patients will be willing to exert such self-discipline, and educating patients to take measurements, maintain records, and change behavior will be a challenge. Further, the time required to educate patients on these matters represents an opportunity cost that would prevent the organization from providing other services. What should management do? The costs and benefits of such an intervention for other members of the plan are unknown.

The shorter cases at the end of this section are similarly varied. In Case 55, "Coordination of Cancer Care," a wealthy patient describes challenges he faces as he seeks to coordinate his own pancreatic cancer care. In a more perfect world, he would have received more help in coordinating this care. But what happens to patients who lack his means? And does the patient have a responsibility to report and improve the poor care coordination he experiences in his own care?

Case 56, "What Benefits the Community," deals with a hospital's efforts to comply with guidelines regarding level of charity care. A simple solution for the hospital might be to raise the level of charity care above the minimum level, either by liberally interpreting what counts as "charity care" or by extending the reach of monies devoted to providing services for patients who cannot afford to pay. Discussion of this situation can prompt other questions as well, including whether large hospitals should be granted tax exemption in the first place, given that the great majority of their revenue is provided by paying patients. Alternatively, when hospitals do have to provide charity care, consideration should be given to measuring the outcomes of that care rather than merely the expenditures.

Case 57, "CEO Compensation," does not question the usual way CEO compensation is decided, which is by hiring a consultant, comparing salaries at comparable institutions, and recommending the level at which the CEO be paid. Our guess is that most CEOs of large institutions, at least in healthcare, are paid too much but that a small percentage are paid too little. Many hospitals could pay much less than they do and still attract excellent managers or leaders to be CEOs; at the same time, those leaders who are extremely effective in spurring higher organizational performance are worth much more than the other CEOs included in salary comparisons. In reading this case, students should also consider: At this level of pay, how important is compensation in Kyle's decision about whether to take the new job?

Case 58, "What's in a Name?," raises a variety of questions related to donations, donor reputations, and what donors expect in return—for instance, naming rights. Does the reputation of the donor—or the way the donor made its money—matter? For example, what if a physician accused of fraud wants to name a hospital conference room after himself? Should he be allowed to do so? An additional question involves timing: Should the room be named when the pledge is made or not until the money is received?

Case 59, "Patient Satisfaction in an Inner-City Hospital," raises several issues related to heavy demand in inner-city hospitals. Assuming that opening more inpatient beds is not a viable solution, how can hospital leadership tackle the problem of long waiting times? Differential waiting times, based on the different levels of urgency of patients' conditions, are appropriate, but what can the hospital do to ensure that the triage process is handled effectively? Another question involves patient expectations for the wait. If the wait is long but the patient has no health risk, what factors affect patient satisfaction with the wait?

Case 60, "Medically Assisted Living," raises a number of difficult questions about the appropriate use of a patient's resources when the patient is 92 years old, physically well but mentally frail, and prefers living at home. The woman in the case would be safer in a medically assisted facility but insists on remaining in her apartment, even as it increasingly eats up her savings. When should the woman's daughter insist that her mother be moved, if ever? What is society's responsibility for the care of old people who can no longer take care of themselves?

Case 61, "Patients and Data Privacy," presents a situation in which a doctor suspects that a patient—a former football player whose symptoms hint at Alzheimer's disease—is withholding information about his mental health, possibly because of privacy concerns related to the use of electronic health records. What should the doctor do to change the patient's behavior? How might one's answer change if the patient were actively considering suicide because "life is no longer worth living"?

In Case 62, "Saving Primary Care in Vancouver," Dr. Zachary faces a serious management challenge. She has three options as to what she should do next: (1) continue solo practice for as long as she can; (2) close her practice and work at a walk-in clinic or with a group practice; or (3) fight to save family practice through political and grass roots advocacy.

# CASE 51
# Letter to the CEO

*Anonymous*

Reprinted with permission from *Quality Management in Health Care* 14 (4): 219–33. 2005. Copyright Lippincott Williams & Wilkins, Inc.

## Dear Chief Executive Officer: The Perceptions of a Recently Discharged Patient

Editor's Note: *The following material represents a report based on the actual hospital experience of a health professional and his wife, who also is a health professional. They are well qualified to make the assessments set forth in this report.* Quality Management in Health Care *is treating this as a quality management case study, and, to preserve the authors' confidentiality, is omitting their names and that of the hospital.*

### Foreword
Dear CEO,

Attached is a description of my recent experience at your hospital. I and my wife share this with you because we are committed to improving the delivery of health care services in hospitals. We believe that our perceptions reflect problems in the system of care and are in no way meant to reflect upon individuals. We hope you will find the perceptions useful.

We have many professional colleagues and many friends who work at your hospital. We plan to continue to get our health care there. In fact, I expect to have another operation there 3 months from now.

We shall be happy to discuss any aspect of care with you or your staff, and do whatever we can to improve care. We plan to share this document with my physicians and with your Director of Nursing.

Sincerely,
Patient and Spouse

## *Perceptions of a Hospital Experience*

Operation: Cardiac Arterial Bypass Graft (CABG) October 2004

Operative Report:

I. Semi-urgent coronary bypass grafting employing aortosaphenous bypass grafts to the first and second circumflex marginal coronary artery.

II. Anastomosis of the right internal mammary artery (skeletonized) to the right coronary artery.

III. Anastomosis of the left internal mammary artery (as a pedicule) to the left anterior descending coronary artery (2 venous and 2 arterial grafts).

The heart was returned to the pericardial cavity. The heart spontaneously defibrillated in a few minutes. The procedure was tolerated well and the patient was discharged from the operating room in good general condition.

This is our story of a common surgical procedure that saves lives every day, but is painful and stressful for patients and their families. The heart has spiritual meaning—our "heartfelt" thanks; "I love you with all my heart." We also know that we cannot live without our hearts. Knowing that my heart would stop beating for a large part of the surgery brought with it the special fear of truly being on the brink of death or of coming back (or not coming back from the dead). My wife and I were both terrified.

I underwent cardiac catheterization at an urban medical center in the Fall. The surgical plan at that time included insertion of a stent. However, the physician found a 70% blockage of the main anterior artery and similar damage to the posterior vessel. He said, "In 2004, in this city, a stent is not an option." The bypass graft had to wait until Plavix, the drug I took in anticipation of the stent, had passed out of my system. This circumstance was similar to that experienced by former President Clinton earlier in the year. The cardiologist required that I be given heparin, and kept under continuous hospital monitoring until a quadruple bypass could be performed 6 days later.

The quadruple bypass graft was performed by an outstanding surgeon, who typically performs more than 300 each year. Four days later I was sent home with plans for rehabilitation therapy to begin in 3 weeks. As I write this account 5 weeks after surgery, I am up and about and feeling much healthier, with more energy than before the surgery. So we could conclude that nothing went wrong.

But, can we be so sure? True enough, the attending physicians provided excellent technical care and were also admirably comforting. The nurses were extremely pleasant and, for the most part, efficient. Nevertheless, we observed numerous errors or potential errors (near misses) in the way that ancillary staff, nurses, and even some physicians failed in or neglected their responsibilities, both medical and humane. There were system failures, largely in the provision of nonclinical, so-called hotel services. Opportunities were lost for staff to teach and provide emotional support, and that seriously marred the entire hospital experience. We have organized this narrative on the following themes.

### Errors and Potential Errors

1. *Potential infections:* I never observed any physician, nurse, or staff member wash hands before approaching us, nor were we told that they had washed elsewhere.
2. *Fire hazards:* At least 8 gurneys, in addition to wheelchairs and linen carts, clogged the hallway outside my room, in violation of state regulations and JCAHO standards.
3. *Medication error:* Late one afternoon, a physician prescribed Cipro to be administered twice daily. A nurse gave me the first dose that evening. The next day she brought only 1 dose.

    Only on the third day she did follow orders and deliver morning and evening doses.
4. *Potential medication error:* The evening nurse came to say goodnight on one of the presurgery nights because she said she had nothing else to do for me. Only after my spouse asked about prescribed bedtime medications did the nurse leave to check, and returned to say, "Oh, I see he does have medications and I didn't see that in the computer." My spouse asked why these medications were not found in the computer.

    The nurse replied, "Oh, I guess they *are* listed for 10:00 PM. I'll get them for you." That same night, Proscar, one of my drugs, was missing from the medication drawer. The same nurse finally had to get Proscar from the pharmacy and brought it to me at 11:30 PM.
5. *Potential unnoticed cardiac event:* Another nurse left my heart monitor disconnected for 40 minutes prior to my transfer to another unit, explaining that he needed to have me ready for the transport crew. (Disconnecting a monitor takes about 3 seconds.)
6. *Potential blood clot:* At one point, the registered nurse failed to notice that the heparin intravenous bag was empty. My wife had to call him, and it took him more than 15 minutes to replace the fluid.

7. *Allergic reaction to tape:* I broke out in a skin rash from tape used during the cardiac catheterization. My wife told a physician resident, who ordered silver nitrate. On the evening before surgery, my wife told the surgical resident about the tape allergy, recommending that he not use the same tape during surgery. The resident said that the allergy was not recorded in the chart and asked us to find out from the catheterization laboratory what kind of tape they had used.

   But that was an impossible assignment for a patient or spouse. My wife asked that at least a yellow self-stick be put on the chart to note the tape problem. The resident told us to remember to tell the surgeons about it in the morning.

   As our anxiety about the surgery mounted, my wife called a nurse acquaintance on the hospital staff. She finally was able to learn the name of the offending tape (Dermaclear) and placed a large warning on the chart.

8. *Informed consent:* The same surgical resident asked me to sign a consent form that did not specify any surgical procedure. He said that he would fill it in afterwards.

9. *Potential delayed recovery.* Three days after surgery, I was too tired to speak to the physical therapist (PT) who visited with instructions. The PT called my wife at home and asked her to be available the next day to help persuade me to participate in therapy. They set a time for the meeting; my wife arrived on time, but the PT failed to appear at all that day.

10. *Potential dental problems:* I occupied 2 private rooms in sequence during my stay. Neither had a toothbrush, floss, or toothpaste. There was a mouthwash of some sort—but not the kind that studies have shown works as well as dental floss in preventing gum problems.

### System Failures
Absence of follow-up

1. A cardiology fellow, who worked me up in preadmission testing, promised to attend the cardiac catheterization but never showed up.

2. The evening before surgery, the anesthesia resident was unable to confirm that the attending anesthesiologist would be present throughout the cardiac surgery and would be handling only 1 patient. The resident's reaction to my inquiries suggested that she considered them bizarre. She said she would find out, but never returned with an answer. Once again, my wife called someone she knew, who verified that the anesthesiologist would be handling only my case.

## Poor Communication

1. Immediately after the catheterization and prior to surgery, the cardiologist called my wife to report that I would have to be monitored and remain in the hospital until surgery. He had already told me the same thing. But when I arrived in the postcatheterization unit, a nurse congratulated me on going home that day. Similarly, a patient facilitator for the catheterization service left a message for my wife that she could take me home in a few hours.

2. I and the entire unit had no phone service for several hours one day. On another day, my extension number, untypically, did not match the room number. So my callers ended up disturbing another patient.

3. No one explained how to get a newspaper. My wife or a physician friend brought one each morning by 8:00 AM. Only days later did we learn that a newspaper deliverer came to the floor each morning.

4. We could not get TV service for several hours in one of the rooms. The TV service's phone was continually busy.

5. No one told us what personal clothing and supplies to bring to the hospital either for the catheterization or for the surgery.

6. No one informed us how we could make use of helpful volunteers, social services, or pastoral counseling. We never saw a nutritionist, who could have explained the presurgery diet, which seemed low on salt, or the desirable posthospital diet.

7. No one explained how to work the electric bed. It may surprise readers, but my wife, a nurse, did not know either (but being a public health nurse she soon figured it out).

8. When my wife was asked to leave the recovery room following her brief visit with me, the nurse offered a phone number for checking on my condition during the night. Confident that she had a contact with a registered nurse (RN), my wife left the hospital. But when she called the number a few hours later she got the main switchboard operator who reported on my condition, secondhand.

## Insensitivity to Patients

1. At 10:30 PM, the night before the surgery, several nurses were laughing and talking outside of my room for one half hour, until I requested quiet.

2. On at least 2 occasions, nurses spoke loudly over the speaker in my room, in search of a nurse who was not there.

3. The waiting area of the cardiac catheterization laboratory was in the corner of a crowded, cold hallway, with only 1 chair for me. My wife had to stand. There was no privacy for me in a patient gown. Hospital staff passed regularly through this hallway, threading between us and the laboratory equipment that cluttered the hall.

## Environment and Housekeeping

1. My private room featured a broken chair, dirty windows, and inadequate light for reading. The nurse sent for a reading lamp, which arrived the next day, broken. The lamp was never fixed or replaced. On several occasions, full waste baskets were not emptied. The bathroom towels were thin and worn.

2. Environment: The room temperature in one of my rooms was consistently either too hot or too cold.

3. Unnecessary moves: The postangiogram unit was closed from Saturday noon to Monday morning, forcing my transfer to another floor—up one crowded elevator, down another.

4. When I arrived in the new unit, there was no holder for my cardiac monitor, and I had to carry it in my hand for several hours.

5. Missing belongings: When transferred from one unit to another, my belongings were not transferred with me. It took several requests and phone calls to retrieve them.

## Food Service

The food was consistently tasteless, sometimes delivered late (after 10:00 AM one morning) and, one evening, to the wrong room. We were never told that we could bring in take-out food (at least prior to surgery, we did anyway). On one occasion, my wife saw a dietary manager in the visitor cafeteria and told him that my food had been found in another unit and that it was cold. He advised her to call the dietary department and ask the nutritionist to provide a new meal. When my wife called, the woman who answered the phone said rudely, "We don't have a nutritionist here. He should never have told you that." She finally agreed to send up a new meal.

## Lost Opportunities (to Provide Comfort, Improve Health, and/or Improve Safety)

1. No one gave us information or any educational materials about cardiac disease, risks affecting the course of disease after discharge, or behavior that might keep me healthy. By flipping the TV channels, we saw that

the hospital has some educational videos on various topics, including meditation.

2. The cardiac surgery house staff (which sometimes included a nurse practitioner) usually visited in groups of 5 or more, but never introduced themselves by name or professional title. They spoke in murmurs, mainly to each other. They actually stood away from me, as if I had a communicable disease. They never provided emotional support or taught us anything about my illness or approaches to preventing future cardiac problems.

3. Only nurse friends, who visited me, offered emotional support or asked about our feelings and fears. Only 1 hospital aide offered hope, a hug, and kind words before surgery. My wife asked for a visiting nurse following discharge. The hospital nurse declined. She then asked for physical therapy at home and one of the nurses said that a PT would be arranged, but it never was.

## Discussion

According to a physician friend, I am incredibly lucky that I was diagnosed and treated as quickly as I was. Another physician told us "of people with my problem 10% die each year." For probably saving my life we are grateful to talented and caring physicians and nurses. Our internist is the real hero for following up on my vague and not very serious symptoms. We are grateful that we have adequate insurance and live in the United States, where I had to wait only 1 week to get the echocardiogram that began my course of care. We were fully paid by our employer during my recovery and my wife's care for me in the hospital.

Fortunately for us, we had the financial resources to go back and forth to the hospital, fly in our children, and buy whatever I wanted, from takeout food to TV and phone. We worry about people who do not have our resources, notably health insurance, or who do not speak English, have no primary care physicians who care about them, and whose spouses cannot manage to arrange good patient care.

There were many wonderful RNs and aides who cared for me. One of the RNs got me up to the chair, got me to use the nebulizer, and arranged for me to have a bed bath. That is ordinary nursing care in some hospitals, but we saw it as especially kind.

Nothing we encountered resulted in poor outcomes, but there were too many near misses, and we suspect similar mishaps occur at almost all hospitals.

The near misses usually are not reported and therefore do not inspire changes in hospital routines. Hospital managers and others can claim that our negative experiences were minor (some would say petty—like the non-functioning TV) and blame a lack of adequate funding. The managers might make a similar claim about the "lost" opportunities we noted, saying "There is a nursing shortage." This is not the place to discuss revenues and expenses, except to note that the hospital charged more than $68,000 for this 11-day stay, not including physician fees.

We believe that many of the problems we have identified result not from inadequate resources, but rather from insufficient focus on patients and a lack of accountability for performance at the patient level of care. If our experience is typical, it has important implications for hospital administrators and for the training of patient care managers.

## Case Questions

1. How do you feel about the level of patient care given in this medical center? How do you think other patients feel? The doctors? The managers?
2. What are some of the problems with patient care in this hospital? What are the most important problems that the manager can do something about?
3. What are the causes of these problems?
4. As the hospital CEO, what would you do if you had received this memorandum?
5. How would you have solved the problems to which the memorandum refers?
6. What organizational factors would constrain implementation of your recommended solutions?
7. How would you, as the CEO, overcome these constraints?

# CASE 52
# Whose Hospital?

*Anthony R. Kovner*

The year was 1979, and Tony DeFalco, a 42-year-old electrical engineer and president of the board of trustees of Brendan Hospital in Lockhart, East State, wondered what he had done wrong. Why had this happened to him again? What should he do now?

The trustees had voted, at first 10 to 6 and then unanimously, to fire Don Wherry, the CEO. The hospital had hired Wherry, who had been DeFalco's personal choice from more than 200 candidates, just 18 months earlier. Around the time of Wherry's hiring, DeFalco had told the trustees that he shared the burdens of managing Brendan Hospital with Wherry and that there was no way of dissociating Wherry's decisions from his own. So in a way, DeFalco pondered, the board should have fired him, too.

DeFalco had lived in Lockhart all his life, and he commuted one-and-a-half hours each day to his office at National Electric. DeFalco loved the town, even though it was one of the poorest towns in the poorest county in central East State. Lockhart had a population of about 50,000, of which 30 percent were Italian, 25 percent Puerto Rican, and 10 percent Jewish. The leading industries in the town were lumber, auto parts manufacturing, and agriculture.

## The Situation at Brendan Hospital

On June 7, 1979, DeFalco had received a call from Joe Black, president of the Brendan Hospital medical staff. Black told him that some doctors and nurses had met over the weekend to discuss charges against Wherry and that they would be holding a mass meeting about the charges at the hospital the following night. Upon receiving the news, DeFalco called Wherry, who had been giving a lecture to healthcare administration faculty in Montreal, Canada, about the relationship between a CEO and the board of trustees. Wherry was as shocked as DeFalco had been, and he returned immediately to Lockhart.

That night, DeFalco and Wherry went to a hospital foundation meeting near the hospital cafeteria where the mass meeting was being held. DeFalco and Wherry had been planning the foundation meeting for several months; it had been scheduled and rescheduled to ensure that all eight of the prominent townspeople could attend. The key reasons for forming the foundation were to enlist the energies of community leaders in hospital fund-raising, thereby freeing the hospital board for more effective policymaking, and to shield hospital donations from the state rate-setting authority. Brendan Hospital had held its first annual horse show the previous fall, and the event was a success, largely through the efforts of DeFalco and two dedicated physicians who owned the stable. The event netted $10,000 and created goodwill in the community; the show and all proceeds were dedicated to the hospital.

Because the foundation meeting was important—and because they had not been invited to attend the mass meeting—DeFalco and Wherry attended the foundation meeting as scheduled. There, they elicited a great deal of verbal support for the foundation, and for DeFalco's leadership. The community leaders were familiar with problems of employee discontent in their own businesses and with the political maneuverings of former Brendan medical staff. The issues surrounding Wherry would all calm down, no doubt. The wife of the town's leading industrialist said she appreciated DeFalco's frankness in sharing the hospital's problems with them.

Of course, everything was not yet calm. Attendees at the mass meeting had produced a petition to get rid of Wherry, and it was signed by half the medical staff and half the employees as well. A leadership committee of four doctors and nurses demanded Wherry's immediate resignation. Further, rumors circulated that, if the board didn't vote Wherry out, the committee wanted the board's resignation as well. (See exhibit 52.1 for an organizational chart of Brendan Hospital.)

Brendan Hospital had a site visit for Joint Commission accreditation scheduled for that Thursday and Friday, and a board meeting was held on Wednesday afternoon, before the site visit. After much discussion, the board decided to meet with the staff and employee representatives on the following Monday. The accreditation site visit somehow went smoothly.

That Monday afternoon, the four doctor and nurse representatives met with the board, noting that they could not speak for the others. They delivered the petition to DeFalco, who read it to the trustees. The petition stated that the undersigned demanded Wherry's resignation because he was "incompetent, devious, lacked leadership, had shown unprofessional conduct, and had committed negligent acts." The representatives would not discuss the matter further at that time, as they had been delegated only to deliver the petition. DeFalco then scheduled another board meeting for the following Wednesday afternoon, June 22. At that meeting, the board would hear all the charges against Wherry, and Wherry would be able to confront his accusers.

The June 22 meeting was attended by 8 physicians, 18 registered nurses, 5 department heads, a laboratory supervisor, a dietary aide, and the medical staff secretary. All but one of the 18 hospital trustees were in attendance, including Wherry, who was a member of the board. The meeting was held in the tasteful new boardroom of Brendan Hospital, complete with oak tables and plush burgundy carpeting.

## The Accusers' Charges

A summary of the committee's presentation against Wherry, with statements from numerous committee members, follows:

**Perrocchio:** The most important thing we have to discuss today is patient care. That's why all of us are here. Many of us are here not because we have a personal gripe, but because we want to do what's best for the patient.

**Tully (department head):** Mr. Wherry humiliated and intimidated three department heads: Mr. O'Brien, Mrs. Williamson, and Mr. Queen.

**EXHIBIT 52.1**
Brendan
Hospital
Organization
Chart, Board of
Trustees

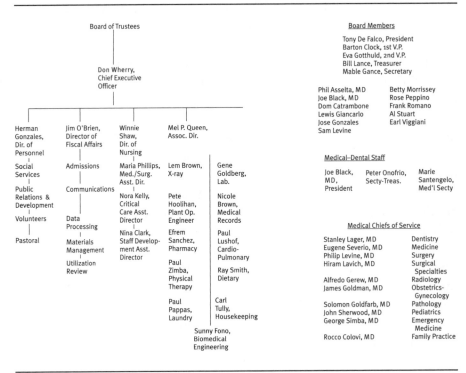

**Board of Trustees**

Don Wherry,
Chief Executive
Officer

| | | | |
|---|---|---|---|
| Herman Gonzales, Dir. of Personnel | Jim O'Brien, Director of Fiscal Affairs | Winnie Shaw, Dir. of Nursing | Mel P. Queen, Assoc. Dir. |
| Social Services | Admissions | Maria Phillips, Med./Surg. Asst. Dir. | Lem Brown, X-ray | Gene Goldberg, Lab. |
| Public Relations & Development | Communications | Nora Kelly, Critical Care Asst. Director | Pete Hoolihan, Plant Op. Engineer | Nicole Brown, Medical Records |
| Volunteers | Data Processing | Nina Clark, Staff Development Asst. Director | Efrem Sanchez, Pharmacy | Paul Lushof, Cardio-Pulmonary |
| Pastoral | Materials Management | | Paul Zimba, Physical Therapy | Ray Smith, Dietary |
| | Utilization Review | | Paul Pappas, Laundry | Carl Tully, Housekeeping |
| | | | Sunny Fono, Biomedical Engineering | |

**Board Members**

Tony De Falco, President
Barton Clock, 1st V.P.
Eva Gotthuld, 2nd V.P.
Bill Lance, Treasurer
Mable Gance, Secretary

Phil Asselta, MD          Betty Morrissey
Joe Black, MD             Rose Peppino
Dom Catrambone           Frank Romano
Lewis Giancarlo          Al Stuart
Jose Gonzales            Earl Viggiani
Sam Levine

**Medical–Dental Staff**

Joe Black, MD, President    Peter Onofrio, Secty.-Treas.    Marie Santengelo, Med'l Secty

**Medical Chiefs of Service**

Stanley Lager, MD          Dentistry
Eugene Severio, MD         Medicine
Philip Levine, MD          Surgery
Hiram Lavich, MD           Surgical Specialties
Alfredo Gerew, MD          Radiology
James Goldman, MD          Obstetrics-Gynecology
Solomon Goldfarb, MD       Pathology
John Sherwood, MD          Pediatrics
George Simba, MD           Emergency Medicine
Rocco Colovi, MD           Family Practice

**Pappas (department head):** There is a bad morale problem in the laundry.

**Patrocelli (supervisor):** Laboratory morale is low. There are too many people in other departments and not enough personnel in our department. Companies who deliver to us have put us on COD.

**Fong (department head):** Mr. Wherry humiliated Mr. Queen.

**Frew:** There has been a problem in staffing new areas of the hospital. We were told that these would be adequately staffed. I realize they haven't opened yet.

**Tontellino:** Several months ago, a nursing survey was sent around by Mr. Wherry, and we all sent in our responses. We have received no response from Mr. Wherry about the survey.

**Carter (RN):** We need more help on the floors.

**Greenberg:** Insensitivity is the problem. The administrator, as you can see from all the comments made so far, is insensitive to the people who work in the hospital.

**Santengelo (medical staff secretary):** The director of volunteers' salary should have been explained to the rest of us. Employees should continue to get Christmas bonuses. It means a lot to many of them. Mr. Wherry has created a whole lot of unnecessary paperwork. I don't feel he heard what we were telling him.

**Lafrance (RN):** There has been a lack of communication between administration and employees. Mr. Wherry has actually asked people to give him the solution to a problem they presented to him.

**Shaw (RN and former director of nursing):** Mr. Wherry used four-letter words in his office with me. He called one of our attending physicians a . . . .

**Levari (RN):** When there was a bomb scare, Mr. Wherry came to the hospital and stayed for 20 minutes. Then he left before the police came, which I definitely think was wrong.

**Leon (RN):** It took Mr. Wherry ten months to call a meeting with the head nurses. Problems in nursing have to be solved around here by the nursing department.

**Kelly (RN and assistant director):** The problem has been lack of communication. I was humiliated when I presented a memo to Mr. Wherry about increases in operating room expenses. He said he couldn't understand what was in the memo, although it was right in front of him. His whole manner was rude.

**Phillips (RN and assistant director):** When the state inspector came on one of her inspections, she said that Mr. Wherry should be dumped.

**Santengelo:** He told Dr. Burns one thing and me another when we needed extra help in my office.

**Bernstein (RN):** Mr. Wherry was evasive and showed a lack of concern. He asked me for my suggestions. I told him to put an ad in the paper to get more help, and it was in the next day. Nurses were not present at administrative meetings.

**Brown (department head):** Mr. Wherry said Dr. Black would also have to sign an X-ray equipment request for $100,000. That is poor leadership.

**Ferrari (RN):** I didn't like the tone of his response when I called him at home to ask about treating a Jehovah's Witness in the emergency room. When we call Mr. Queen, the associate administrator, we nurses never experience that kind of problem.

**Lashof (department head):** I felt intimidated by Mr. Wherry. The hospital has a morale problem that interferes with patient care.

**Brown:** He said to me, "If you can't handle the problem [we were having in X-ray], I'll find someone who can."

**Charlotte (RN):** I've had a problem with my insurance, and the personnel department still hasn't gotten back to me for three weeks now. I am divorced and have a little girl, and it's really creating a hardship for me. I don't understand why Mr. Gonzales, the personnel director, hasn't gotten back to me. I've called him about it many times.

**Lafrance:** Mr. Wherry sounded upset and annoyed when I called him at home about the electrical fire in maternity.

**Gerew:** The problem is communication. Mr. Wherry promised something and didn't deliver. I have been working here for three years trying to develop a first-class radiology department. How can we cut costs and improve service in the outpatient department? I asked for help from fiscal affairs and I didn't get any.

**Lavich:** The family no longer has any confidence in its father. There was a unanimous vote of no confidence for Mr. Wherry in my department.

**Greenberg:** Mr. Wherry has a repressive style. There has been a tremendous turnover of personnel in the nursing department since he became the administrator.

**Mendez:** There is poor morale at the hospital. The nurses are upset. Mr. Wherry used derogatory language concerning foreign medical graduates. This was in the student administrative resident's report on what to do about the emergency room. Let's remove what is causing the problem.

**Black (president of the medical staff):** Department heads should be on board committees. No one came around and told department heads that they were appreciated. People at Shop-N-Bag make more money than nurses. Our medical people want to be appreciated, too.

**Frew:** Tony DeFalco, the board president, is seen as being in Mr. Wherry's pocket. There must be accountability for the situation that arose. I have no personal grievance. Accountability starts at the top.

**Black:** Dr. Fanchini was behind a good deal of what I was doing. A lot of critical things have happened, making for a crisis situation. Dr. Simba was hired to head up the emergency room, without adequate participation of the medical staff. Dr. Fanchini resigned as a board member. Dr. Burns resigned as president of the medical staff because of his personal problems. Mr. Wherry said that Dr. Severio was not really a cardiologist. The radiologists at Clarksville Hospital asked for emergency privileges. What made the medical staff unhappy was when Mr. Wherry said we weren't going to get a CT [computed tomography] scanner and when he said that there were no problems in nursing morale. At the meeting of the medical executive committee held this Monday night, June 20, the committee reaffirmed our lack of support for Mr. Wherry, giving him a vote of no confidence by a vote of 10 for the motion, 1 against, and 1 abstaining.

Listening to the doctors and nurses, DeFalco felt as though he were a spectator watching a Greek tragedy. As the committee representatives left the boardroom, DeFalco remembered a similar meeting just two years earlier, when the board met in the old private dining room. At that meeting, the board was voting to dismiss the previous administrator of 22 years, Phil Drew. Drew allegedly had not kept up with the times, and some doctors said he had sexually harassed several nurses. The hospital at that time also was not doing well financially. DeFalco considered

Drew a good man and regretted what had happened. He had promised himself that he would do everything in his power to prevent such a situation from repeating.

## Wherry's Defense

"First, I'd like to go through the state of the hospital as it was when I got here," Wherry began his defense. For background, see the list of Brendan Hospital's goals and accomplishments from 1978, shown in exhibit 52.2; see exhibit 52.3 for a list of the 1979 goals.

| 1978 Goals | 1978 Accomplishments |
|---|---|
| 1. Stabilize hospital finances | • $75,000 surplus<br>• Improved Medicaid and Blue Cross reimbursement<br>• Expenditures reduced in line with lower than expected occupancy |
| 2. Increase fund-raising | • Modernization fund pledges on target<br>• Successful first annual horse show |
| 3. Improve hospital morale | • Regular employee–administration meetings<br>• Regular publication of *Brendan News* |
| 4. Improve quality of nursing care | • High patient evaluations in survey<br>• New director of nursing recruited |
| 5. Organize department of emergency medicine | • Department organized and Dr. George Simba recruited as chief |
| 6. Establish effective management information and control system | • Implemented auditors' recommendation<br>• Evaluating new data processing alternatives |
| 7. Increase communication with Spanish-speaking community | • Several meetings held with Hispanic leaders<br>• Increased Hispanic staff in patient areas, including social services |
| 8. Increase accountability of medical departments for quality assurance | • Board resolution requiring annual reports<br>• Joint conference committee and trustee seminar for better communication between medical staff and trustees |
| 9. Increase community participation in long-range planning | • Four community members added to long-range planning committee<br>• Wide distribution of annual report with attendance encouraged at annual meeting |
| 10. On-schedule, on-budget, fully accredited new wing | • New wing scheduled to open in April 1979<br>• Building roughly within budget and on schedule |

**EXHIBIT 52.2**
Brendan Hospital's 1978 Goals and Accomplishments (from the 1978 Annual Report)

EXHIBIT 52.3
Brendan
Hospital's 1979
Goals (from the
1978 Annual
Report)

1. Stabilize hospital finances and improve cash flow
2. Improve board, administration, and medical staff communication
3. Increase hospital involvement of Spanish-speaking community
4. Fill administrative vacancies and recruit needed medical staff
5. Increase pediatric and obstetrical inpatient occupancy
6. Accomplish complete availability of new wing by April and obtain full hospital accreditation
7. Establish quality assurance programs for all professional departments
8. Establish productivity and efficiency goals for all hospital departments
9. Develop an operational long-range plan, including time and dollar estimates for new programs
10. Continue to contain increases in hospital costs

Wherry was nervous as he spoke, but DeFalco thought he seemed perfectly assured of himself, confident in the rightness of his cause. That confidence was probably one of the things the doctors held against him. Wherry had attended Princeton University and Harvard Business School, and he had worked for a government regulatory agency in hospital cost containment before taking the Brendan job.

Wherry continued his statement, describing conditions at the time he was hired.

**Wherry:** There was bad leadership in the nursing department and in several other departments, a lack of medical staff leadership, and few competent department heads. Nursing is a difficult occupation. Morale is always a problem in this department. These are young people with children; they are working evenings, nights, and weekends; and the work is physically, emotionally, and administratively demanding. The doctors at this hospital are like doctors in other hospitals similar to Brendan, fearful of anything that threatens to affect their livelihood or freedom. I can understand that. But there is a small, embittered group with axes to grind against me.

I have been busy with the finances of the hospital and in improving external relationships with Latinos, state officials, and other groups. Mel Queen, the associate administrator, has been busy with the new construction and the move into our new $5 million wing.

We've had a new director of nursing on board for five weeks now, and I wish that everyone would have just given her a chance. Dr. Burns's resignation as president of the medical staff didn't help me any, and I have had a director of personnel, Gonzales, with acute personal problems, which has been a problem for me, too. Next, it's quite unusual for someone to have to defend himself on the spot to a list of specific charges that I have been waiting for these past 13 days and just now have been made aware of. I think the way this whole thing has been handled by the doctor and nurse ringleaders is disgraceful. The charges they have made are largely not true and could not be proved even if they were true. Even if the charges are true to a substantial extent, there is still not sufficient reason for your discharging me, certainly not suddenly, as they are demanding you to.

The doctors are out to get me because I'm doing the job that you've been paying me to do, that I'm evaluated on, and for which I received a very good evaluation and a big raise at the end of last year, presumably because I was doing a good job. [For Wherry's evaluation, see appendix A; for DeFalco's raise letter, see appendix B.]

Certainly, none of you have told me to stop doing what I have been doing to ensure quality, contain costs, and improve service. During the past year, I gathered information for the medical staff on a new reappointment worksheet so that reappointments aren't made on a rubber stamp process every two years. I pointed out the problems that the low inpatient census in pediatrics would create in retaining the beds in the years to come. I obtained model rules and regulations for the medical staff and shared these with the president, Dr. Black. I questioned the effectiveness of the tissue committee, which hasn't been meeting consistently and has produced only perfunctory minutes when it has met. I investigated the performance of the audit committee after our delegated status under the Professional Standards Review Organization was placed in question by a visiting physician, Dr. Lordi. I suggested we explore mandated physician donations to the hospital, as was passed and implemented two years ago by another East State hospital. When we received patient complaints about doctors, I took them up with the respective chiefs of departments. I investigated the assertion by a lab technician that tests were being reported and not done by the laboratory. I questioned and had to renegotiate remuneration of pathologists and radiologists, all with knowledge of the president of the board, Mr. DeFalco, and I have done nothing without involving the medical executive committee.

I have been involved in the lengthy and frustrating process of getting support from other hospitals for a CT scanner and in justifying financial feasibility of the CT scanner at this hospital. I have suggested ways to recruit needed physicians into Lockhart and have shared with the staff other approaches used by East State hospitals, such as a guaranteed income for the first year. I followed up a trustee's question about the appropriateness of fetal monitoring with the chief of obstetrics and gynecology, and I worked out a satisfactory response to poor ophthalmology coverage in the emergency room with the chief of ophthalmology. I became involved in trying to convince one of our three pathologists not to resign because of a run-in with the chief of pathology. I have to get after physicians who do not indicate final diagnosis or complete their charts on time, because this delays needed cash flow for the hospital. I suggested that the hospital develop a model program for providing day hospital and other care to the elderly and chronically ill, and sought the cooperation of State University in designing a research protocol to measure the need for such services. This action was resented by several members of the staff—although we have not gone ahead with the state research program pending staff approval, and, if they disapprove, I said we would not go ahead with it.

I initiated a study of how we can prevent malpractice at the hospital and conveyed board disapproval of radiology equipment, which we had scheduled to buy but couldn't afford because other radiology equipment broke down in an unforeseen way. There are several very difficult physicians on the medical executive committee who have never gotten along with any administrator or with other physicians. I am the one who has to discuss with the surgeons and the radiologists ways to decrease costs in their units when these costs are way above the state medians, and we have to reduce them or face financial penalties.

As far as nursing goes, here is a list of what I have done: I have met with all shifts, with head nurses, with supervisors, and regularly with the director and assistant directors. I hired a new director and fired an old assistant director whom the nurses had said showed favoritism, lied to them, and overpromised. This was opposed, by the way, by Dr. Fanchini, former director of obstetrics and gynecology. I hired an expert nursing consultant to help us develop appropriate goals and ways of meeting these goals. I was in the process of obtaining the services of an operations research consultant, at no cost to the hospital, to help us with our scheduling problems. We implemented a study done by an administrative resident on improved staffing and scheduling. I pointed out all the problems of authoritarian leadership, lack of adequate quality assurance programs, and lack of appropriate scheduling and budgeting to the previous nursing director, which is why she had to be demoted. Mrs. Shaw always tried to do her best, but she lacked the proper education and skills. I obtained 15 additional approved nursing positions, including one additional full-time RN in in-service and an additional $80,000 for in-service, from the state rate setters, something that no one has been able to do at this hospital for the past eight years. Our expenditures in nursing are already above the state median. I obtained a staffing plan from another hospital for the director of nursing and influenced her to distribute a questionnaire to all nurses to better find out their feelings and ideas.

I could go through each of the charges made by the people assembled here, but it won't really prove anything. Yes, I did call a doctor a [four-letter word] in my office. Yes, I did leave the hospital after the bomb scare before the police came, but only after I was convinced that it was just a scare. I had a meeting to go to in Urban City, and I called one hour later to see that everything was all right. I think it is significant that none of the department heads supposedly humiliated by me showed up at this meeting. You have asked me to resign, but I'm not going to resign. That would not solve the hospital's problems. Firing me will not solve the bad nursing morale here or the doctor distrust. It will show the doctors and nurses and the community who runs this hospital. Is it the board of trustees or some doctors and nurses (the nurses are mainly being used by the doctors)? Whose head will these doctors be asking for the next time they want to get rid of somebody? The bond issue set for next month that could refinance our debt on the new wing will not go through if you fire me. And we shall have a $355,000 payment to make in August, which will be difficult to meet.

"Does anybody have any questions?" DeFalco asked the other trustees. There were a few questions, but nothing significant—no major contradictions of anything Wherry had said. The trustees then asked Wherry to leave the room and told him that they would make a decision.

That evening, after dinner with his wife and teenagers, DeFalco watched a baseball game on television. He couldn't get his mind off the board meeting, the vote 10 to 6 against Wherry, and the ultimate unanimous vote to dismiss him with two months' severance.

## Board Comments

During the week leading up to the board meeting, DeFalco had made a point to discuss the Wherry situation with the other 16 trustees. The following, to the best of his recollection, represents the essence of their comments to him.

**Clock (age 55, life insurance salesman, first vice president of the board, former mayor, DeFalco's longtime confidant):** I have been one of Don Wherry's strongest supporters since he got here and before he got here. I was a member of the search committee that selected Don, as you remember. I still like Don personally, really I do, but it has become obvious to me, at least, that Don can no longer manage the hospital. Whether Don is right or wrong, the docs don't like him. [Wherry had told DeFalco that Clock sold life insurance to a lot of doctors.] Don's biggest mistakes have been in not firing Mel Queen, the associate administrator, who never has supported him properly, and Winnie Shaw, the ex-director of nursing, whom he should never have kept around and I told him so.

**Gotthuld (age 50, second vice president of the hospital board, president of the board of Preston College, wife of a beer distributor):** You know, I have been spending one or two weeks out of every month in Vermont, where we bought a distributorship, and last year Sam and I spent six months on a luxury liner trip around the world. So I really don't know what's going on that well. As chairman of the executive committee, I know we gave Don a good evaluation and so, if he isn't acting properly as chief executive officer, then at least part of the fault is ours. I see no reason to fire Don abruptly because of these alleged charges.

**Lance (age 45, president of a local lumber company, treasurer of the hospital, chairman of the buildings and grounds committee):** I have always been one of Don Wherry's closest friends, although he may not admit it now. I think Don could do an excellent job managing a university hospital, but he definitely cannot do the job here at Brendan and we should get rid of him now. Don might care more than anyone else, certainly more than I do, about the welfare of the hospital employees, but he just hasn't communicated that to them.

**Gonce (age 65, RN, secretary of the hospital, recently returned from University Hospital in Urban City where she was recovering from a heart attack):** Tony, you know I fought bitterly against Don Wherry's coming to Brendan in the first place. I voted then for Mel Queen, the associate administrator, to do the job, and I vote for him now to do a better job than Don Wherry. Don should be working for the government somewhere, not in a small town. Mel Queen will make an excellent administrator of Brendan Hospital. We should have given it to him in the first place.

**Giancarlo (age 60, president of a local canning firm, newly elected to the board in January):** I don't know much about the facts of the situation, Tony. I like Don Wherry personally, but obviously the doctors and many of the employees are unhappy with him. They must be listened to. It doesn't seem that anything they are complaining about is new or isolated.

**Gonzales (age 40, secondary school teacher, one of Don Wherry's strongest supporters):** I see what Don has done to meet with all the Latino leaders without any crisis, to hear out our problems and respond to us. Don has reorganized and improved services in the emergency room, hired a Spanish-speaking social work assistant, and increased the number of minority supervisors. I am not that impressed, really, by these charges. There's no meat to them. I think this is just a bunch of doctors trying to get rid of Don as they got rid of Mr. Drew, the last CEO, and I do not think the board should bow down to them this time.

**Peppino (age 34, senior bank vice president):** Knowing Don Wherry as I do, I can understand a lot of the charges and sympathize with those making the complaints. Don Wherry is cold and authoritative, and if he knows so much, maybe that isn't what the job needs anyway. Mel Queen can run the hospital perfectly well, I'm convinced of that. And if the doctors are going to stop admitting patients as they threaten to do, they must feel very strongly about Don Wherry. It's important to calm the doctors down and get on with business as usual, and the sooner the better. Don Wherry will have no problem finding a job somewhere else. Maybe he was going to leave Lockhart anyway after a few more years.

**Black (age 45, president of the medical staff):** We have to get rid of this guy. He's nothing but trouble. I tried to work with him, but the guys don't like him. Maybe it's because he went to Princeton or something. He gives the guys this feeling that he feels superior to us. He's the big-time administrator, and we're the lowly doctors. We'd much prefer Mel Queen running the hospital. We don't have to put up with this Wherry guy, and now's the time to get rid of him.

**Romano (age 50, president of a lumber company, newly elected to the board in January):** I feel the way Lew Giancarlo does. I never thought being elected to this board would involve all these problems, and I'm certainly spending more time on this darn hospital than I would like to be spending. It's a tough thing for this Wherry guy. I like Don personally, but I really think we're going to have more problems with him than without him.

**Levine (age 45, attorney, newly elected to the board in January):** I think this is disgraceful what we're doing to Don. I don't like the way the whole thing was done, even if Don has made mistakes. You don't treat an employee this way, certainly not the chief executive officer. But I don't think that Don has handled it right, either. He should have gone to the mass meeting and defended himself. He should have organized people to speak on his behalf. That's the advice I would have given Don as a lawyer. And I think it's a darn shame this has to happen. It doesn't have to happen, really, if someone would only stand up and fight for Don and his cause. I'm doing the best that I can, but I've only been on the board a short time, and therefore I feel I'm limited in what I can do.

**Morrissey (age 47, housewife):** Don and his wife Sue are personal friends of mine, but I can't let that get in the way of making the right decision for the hospital. Don is certainly a brilliant guy who cares about people and doesn't want to see the patient or the consumer taken advantage of. He wants to do all the right things, and he has done a lot of the right things. The hospital is a safer, warmer, financially sounder place than it was when Don took over. I'm certainly going to vote for Don. I'm sorry, but I don't feel I know enough to be really energetic about this.

**Viggiani (age 60, owner of a large real estate firm, chairman of the county Democratic Party):** I think it's a terrible thing what they're doing to Don. It's just like with the other guy, Phil Drew. This guy has always been there when we needed him. He works night and day. If anything's the matter, then it must be our fault because this guy has been doing what we've been telling him to do. He hasn't done anything without telling the doctors and us first. I think it's a disgrace.

**Asselta (age 70, general practitioner):** The staff just doesn't like him. I like Don Wherry. I know he's been trying to do the right thing. I've tried to help Don, after I made sure of him, every way I can. You know my wife has been very sick, and I haven't been able to attend to hospital affairs lately as I would like. I guess I'll go along with the majority, either way.

**Goldman (age 61, chief of obstetrics and gynecology, newly elected to the board in January):** I don't think the man knows how to manage the hospital, asking the employees to come up with the solutions to their own problems. That's bad management. Our group is against him.

**Catrambone (age 50, director of a large funeral home):** Tony, I'm only sorry I won't be at the meeting to speak for Don. There's a right and a wrong, and I can tell the difference. Ask yourself who is right and who is wrong, and you've got to vote for Don Wherry. I happen to think he's a pretty fair manager to boot. I wish you would count my vote. Since my open-heart surgery, I've got to be in Rochester, Minnesota, for my annual heart examination.

**Stuart (age 41, senior vice president of the same bank of which Mrs. Peppino is assistant vice president):** I don't like Don Wherry. [Wherry had told DeFalco that Stuart and Peppino were against him because he gave all the bank business, per finance committee recommendation, to a competing bank.] I never have. I served with him on the personnel committee, and we were usually in disagreement. Don always made me feel somehow that I was ignorant, that he felt himself superior to me. This is not how he should have acted. And I'm sure a lot of the employees feel the same way about Don that I do.

| **APPENDIX A** Summary of Don Wherry's CEO Evaluation (November 25, 1978) | Rating 1–5 (1 is high, 5 is low) | |
|---|---|---|
| | **Self** | **Avg. Trustee** |
| **I. Goal Achievement** | | |
| 1. Stabilize hospital finances | 1 | 2.7 |
| 2. Increase fund-raising | 3 | 3.6 |
| 3. Improve hospital morale | 3 | 4.9 |
| 4. Improve quality of nursing care | 1 | 3.7 |

| | | | |
|---|---|---|---|
| 5. Organize emergency room department | 1 | 2.9 | |
| 6. Establish an effective management information and control system | 2 | 2.1 | |
| 7. Maintain on-schedule, on-budget west wing building program | 3 | 2.3 | |
| 8. Establish plan for utilization of west wing and integration with total hospital operations | 3 | 2.1 | |
| 9. Increase communications with the growing Spanish-speaking community | 1 | 3.1 | |
| 10. Increase accountability of medical departments for quality assurance | 1 | 3.1 | |
| 11. Prepare to obtain three-year hospital accreditation upon completion of west wing | 3 | 1.9 | |
| 12. Increase community participation in hospital long-range planning | 1 | 2.2 | |

**APPENDIX A**

Summary of Don Wherry's CEO Evaluation (November 25, 1978)

*(continued)*

**CEO Remarks:**
1. The CEO is goal-oriented.
2. He needs to spend yet more time developing consensus and persuading key stakeholders and earning their respect.

**Trustee Remarks:**
1. Many of these "specifics" are difficult for an outside director to judge.
2. I think the CEO's contributions are acceptable except in items 3 and 4, where they should have been significantly greater.
3. Morale is a question.
4. The CEO is doing a fine job for Brendan.
5. The CEO's capability is great for achieving all goals. Sometimes his motives are not understood, and some obstacles are not of his doing.
6. The answers to some of these questions are based more on perceptions than actual knowledge.

**President's Remarks:**
I agree that the CEO is goal-oriented. He has attained goals we have given him about as well as anyone could reasonably expect.

| **II. System Maintenance** | 2 | 3.5 |
|---|---|---|

**CEO Remarks:**
1. Given what the CEO was hired to do, a certain amount of distrust is inevitable.
2. The CEO tries diligently to establish regular and continuing dialogue with all key hospital groups and individuals.

**Trustee Remarks:**
1. The greatest weaknesses in this category are in maintaining adequate commitment of employees to organizational goals and developing adequate trust between management and medical staff.
2. The board is not made aware of exactly the number of employees needed and the department that has this need. There seems to be a feeling of unrest among the administrative staff (department heads). Trust between management and medical staff is currently very poor.

*(continued)*

**APPENDIX A**
Summary of
Don Wherry's
CEO Evaluation
(November 25,
1978)
*(continued)*

3. The CEO's capabilities are limitless, but I feel he has developed a schism between himself and the medical staff.
4. Small areas of difference need to be cleared by better communication and understanding of mutual problems. The main problem area is with doctor contracts.
5. I suspect that the only positive factor in the above list would be "maintaining adequate administrative and control systems."

**President's Remarks:**
1. Our "hospital system" has undoubtedly provided sufficient patient care of adequate quality at reasonable cost. I therefore believe the trustee evaluation to be too low in this area.
2. A mistrust of the administration by the medical staff does exist. I am also apprehensive about the "team play" of the administrative staff. We must address these problems in 1979.

**III. Relationships with Important External Publics**   1        2.1

**CEO Remarks:**
The hospital has done well with licensing, regulatory, and reimbursement agencies, and with other provider agencies during 1978. The CEO speaks frequently to consumer organizations and volunteer groups as well and has been well received.

**Trustee Remarks:**
1. The CEO has done an especially good job with third-party payers.
2. This is definitely the CEO's strongest area.
3. Excellent record.

**President's Remarks:**
I am pleased with the CEO's accomplishments in this area.

**IV. Management Roles**

| | | |
|---|---|---|
| 1. Interpersonal | 3 | 3.6 |
| 2. Informational | 1 | 2.4 |
| 3. Decisional | 1 | 2.8 |

**CEO Remarks:**
The CEO is intelligent and quick. He works long hours and is subject to constant pressures. He cannot possibly talk at length continuously with 18 trustees, 40 key doctors, 20 department heads, and other key personnel outside the hospital. He must try harder to be cheerful, quiet, friendly, and low-key.

**Trustee Remarks:**
1. I think the CEO has done a good job in 1978, especially in view of what he walked into.
2. The CEO has weakness in providing motivation, also in recognizing disturbances of uneasiness within the hospital personnel and in dealing with incompetent or unproductive personnel.

**APPENDIX A**
Summary of
Don Wherry's
CEO Evaluation
(November 25,
1978)
*(continued)*

3. The CEO seems to be seeking many changes. His method for achieving them isn't always productive. The CEO has great potential but doesn't seem to implement it well.
4. I'm not too sure if the CEO is handling personnel adequately. Morale has not improved within the hospital.
5. The CEO has done and is doing an outstanding job. I am proud to work with him and would give him even higher marks if possible.
6. The CEO is excellent on a one-to-one basis. He handles groups well. He is anxious to please and to get cooperation.

**President's Remarks:**

1. Changes in staff personnel in 1978 have hampered the efficiency and effectiveness of this group. When stability of this group occurs, provided the right group has been chosen, improvement in hospital management will be most evident.
2. The dissemination of information is exceptional.
3. I have confidence in the decisions that are being made. I am not sure about their method of implementation.

**V. President's Summary**

1. Areas of Evaluation:
   The CEO has exceeded my expectations. In sum total, I am extremely pleased with his accomplishments.
2. Strengths:
   Planning, establishing priorities, dealing with regulatory agencies, understanding and articulating hospital organization, financial management, intelligence, creativity, ability to negotiate, potential, sincerity, and directness
3. Weaknesses:
   Impatience and aloofness (coldness)
4. Uncertainties:
   Evaluation of personnel, evaluation of situations, employee motivation, and nonpeer and subordinate relationships
5. Recommendations:
   Attempt to gain trust and respect of medical staff.
   Improve trust and respect of employees in presence of others.
   Refrain from reprimanding employees in the presence of others.
   Work toward having assistant responsible for day-to-day operation of hospital.
   Continue to attempt to improve morale.
   Improve patience; realize that few people can match his intelligence quotient.
   Continue to develop administrative staff.
6. Conclusion:
   The CEO has performed well in 1978. He has acceptably attained his goals. As a new manager, he has been severely tested by the board of trustees, medical staff, and employees, and he has withstood their challenge. I believe his inherent intelligence will allow him to correct any and all identifiable deficiencies.

*(continued)*

**APPENDIX A**
Summary of
Don Wherry's
CEO Evaluation
(November 25,
1978)
(continued)

The CEO's self-evaluation was extremely accurate. It is comforting to know that he has the ability to correctly assess his strengths and weaknesses. The following elements will be necessary for his continued success:

a. Constructive advice and support by board of trustees
b. Trust of medical staff
c. Melding of administrative staff into a stable, competent, and qualified team with common objectives

**APPENDIX B**
Letter from
Tony DeFalco to
Don Wherry on
January 10, 1979

**Personal and Confidential**

January 10, 1979
Mr. Don Wherry
Brendan Hospital
Lockhart, East State

Dear Don,

The Board of Trustees of Brendan Hospital, on January 8, 1979, unanimously approved a 10 percent increase in your annual salary along with a $500 increase in automobile allowance for 1979. The above increases will result in a per annum salary of $57,750 and an automobile allowance of $2,300. Your receipt of this letter provides you with the authority to make the stipulated adjustments effective January 1, 1979.

Our board believes that you have done an outstanding job as our chief executive officer and hopes that the above increases have fairly rewarded your effort.

Very truly yours,
Tony DeFalco, President
Brendan Hospital Board of Trustees

## Case Questions

1. How do you feel about what happened to Don Wherry?
2. Do you feel the board was justified in acting as it did?
3. What could Wherry have done differently to avoid being fired? What could the board have done to prevent this? Should the medical board have acted any differently?
4. Should Wherry have resigned as the board wished him to?
5. Whose hospital is Brendan Hospital? What are the consequences of this being the case—for consumers, patients, managers, physicians, and trustees?

# CASE 53

# Managed Care Cautionary Tale: A Case Study in Risk Adjustment and Patient Dumping

*Zachary Pruitt and Barbara Langland-Orban*

Reprinted with permission from the *Journal of Health Administration Education* 33 (3): 475–86. 2016. Exhibit numbers have been revised for the purpose of this publication.

## Introduction

This case is modeled after true events that occurred at WellCare Health Plans, Inc. (Gentry & Wells, 2010). In addition to patient dumping, a whistleblower complaint alleged significant false claims violations in the State of Florida (FBI, 2012). It should be noted that one of the authors of this case study was present when federal agents raided the headquarters of the managed care organization. However, the case uses fictitious names for the characters and events have been constructed for purpose of teaching students the complexities of patient dumping, risk adjustment, and financial incentives.

## Case
### Guns, badges, and bulletproof vests

Josh Thompson once worked in the managed care sector, proudly believing that HMOs could advance population health and align payment incentives with quality care. That was before hundreds of state and federal agents occupied his company's offices. A whistleblower at the publicly traded health plan collaborated with the FBI by wearing a wire like a television character. For 18 months, the whistleblower bravely and secretly recorded hundreds of hours of conversation with health plan employees. This included executives and even with Josh, who was a compliance analyst. The whistleblower alleged serious fraud.

"Step away from your computers!" federal agents yelled. They were wearing guns, badges, and bulletproof vests.

One agent pulled Josh aside. "Sir, come with me. Are you carrying a weapon?"

Josh stammered, "No, just a BlackBerry."

The agent confiscated Josh's phone and computer, and escorted him to an empty office. "Nice offices you've got here," the agent said looking out the window at the manicured grounds three floors below.

"Yes. And we have a gym." Josh talked too much when he was nervous.

With the door closed, two federal officers stared coldly at Josh. "Kind of suspicious that a Medicaid health plan could afford offices like these. Makes you wonder . . ."

Josh flushed. "Um, well, you see, we're paid through capitation, so . . ."

"What's capitation?" one agent interrupted.

"Capitation, as in *per capita?* No? Okay. Put simply, our health plan is paid an average per-member-per-month fee by the state Medicaid program to cover all health care expenses for our members. When a patient's costs exceed the capitation payment to the health plan, the plan loses money. Too many money-losing patients enrolled in a health plan is called adverse selection, which negatively impacts our profits. We have hundreds of thousands of members in our health plans, so if we do our job right, we're profitable," Josh explained.

The suspicious agent asked, "What do you mean, 'do your job right'?"

Josh further explained, "Well, there are two ways to make a profit: keep patients healthy to avoid expensive health care costs or avoid the sick patients."

"I see. And which way does *your company* make a profit?" asked the agent.

Josh knew his characterization of the managed care business model was overly simplistic. In reality, the story was more complicated, but he understood the basic value proposition of managed care. Josh continued to explain the company's perspective. "The population health approach targets individuals with some common characteristic, such as a diagnosis. Then, we design care management interventions for that sub-population. We are responsible for patient education, care coordination, or anything that makes them healthier."

The agents gave Josh blank stares.

Josh continued, "For example, if diabetics are not adherent to their medications, then their health care costs can become really high. So, managed care has the incentive to implement medication adherence improvement programs that can save thousands of dollars a year." According to Roebuck et al. (2011), over $4,000 a year is saved when compared to diabetics that are non-adherent to their medications.

The agents looked at each other and then back at Josh. "Does it work that way with all patients? Or does your company 'avoid the sick patients,' as you say?" The agent pulled out his note pad. "Tell me about the patient dumping, Josh."

A rush of memories went through Josh's mind. Actually, he *had* witnessed the problem at his company. Little did he know that the issue would so dramatically resurface. Long before Josh's sequestration and interrogation on that terrible day, Josh had uncovered a patient dumping scheme.

## *Population health dilemma*

Nancy McGregor, as a nurse case manager, was usually weary of non-clinical "bean counters," but Josh had built a solid relationship with her, working long hours together on a compliance project. Case managers are nurses responsible for working with high-risk patients to identify patient needs with the aims of improving health and reducing costs. The health plan case managers coordinate care for patients in collaboration with medical providers in the health plan's network.

Nancy revealed that, throughout the prior year, case managers regularly had informed AIDS-diagnosed patients that they would get better care management services if they left the health plan. Sadly, this may have been true due to a Medicaid program that was designed to provide quality care to such patients. Nancy McGregor and her case management team had a dilemma. They could provide basic case management for AIDS-diagnosed members *and risk losing money.* Or they could encourage the patient to leave their health plan to obtain enhanced case management services, which would save the company money while also improving the care provided to the patient. Her boss was aware of the issue. Nancy told Josh that case managers had been rewarded with a dinner at an expensive restaurant for getting patients to leave the health plan.

Her boss Steve Sorensen was the director of population health. His job entailed creating analytical reports to identify high-risk members and working with the case management team to reduce health service utilization and costs. He also worked with the quality improvement team to improve quality of care measures. Steve reported to the vice president of revenue optimization, but he also had a "dotted-line" reporting relationship to the medical director at the health plan.

Josh questioned Steve Sorensen about his concerns. Sorensen bragged that there had once been a very effective program to remove health plan members diagnosed with AIDS, but that it had been recently discontinued. "Our membership initiative effectively channeled these patients to other sources of health care financing," the director wrote in an email. "These patients received enhanced services through a different Medicaid program. This created a win-win scenario for our health plan and the patients."

Familiar with the rules, Josh knew that encouraging any member to leave the health plan was strictly prohibited. Dumping patients is unethical and illegal. Josh explained to Steve Sorensen and his team of case managers that the patient dumping program should not be revived. However, the director of population health endured his admonishment with indifference. Their strategy had already changed.

### The internal audit

Josh's role as a compliance analyst was to monitor health plan operations for compliance with federal and state regulations in order to promote health of the members and to assure that the services are delivered according to contracts with the government. This meant that he regularly engaged in audits of internal processes, policies, and procedures. He hoped to eventually become the company's Chief Compliance officer.

After auditing their existing HIV/AIDS case management activities, Josh discovered two causes for ending the patient dumping "initiative." First, he learned that a competing Medicaid HMO was marketing to patients diagnosed with HIV or AIDS. This meant the highest risk patients tended to prefer the competitor over Josh's health plan. The phenomenon of having a sicker than average membership mix is called adverse selection. Josh was unsure why the competitor chose to market to an unfavorable patient population. Nevertheless, many patients were leaving their plan, so patient dumping was unnecessary.

Secondly, Josh learned that the case managers were selective about which members received case management services. The case managers skimped on the lauded population health management efforts for HIV-positive patients—no coordination of care, no patient education, no medication adherence interventions for HIV patients not yet diagnosed with AIDS. By ignoring HIV-positive members, they increased the chances that the HIV-positive patients would choose to leave for another plan. It appeared to be a passive-aggressive effort to achieve favorable risk selection.

However, for AIDS-diagnosed patients, a fairly aggressive medication adherence protocol was followed. Josh was confused. Why the medication adherence program only for the higher risk AIDS-diagnosed members?

### The financial analysis

For this question, Josh needed to dig a little deeper. Josh asked the health plan's finance analyst, Cara Morgan, to pull some data on the issue. Her data analysis made the reason clear—the incentives just were not aligned to encourage care interventions for HIV-positive patients, not yet diagnosed with AIDS.

Josh knew that by this time the state Medicaid program had already begun to address the patient dumping problem. Risk adjustment policies are responses to the fundamental challenges with capitation—nefarious behaviors, such as patient dumping, or anti-competitive practices, such as favorable risk selection (Eggleston, Ellis, & Lu, 2012). The Medicaid program instituted a risk-adjusted capitation method that prospectively paid monthly capitation fees to health plans based on the severity of disease of their members. The risk-adjusted capitation fees were intended to help reduce the incentive for health plans to avoid really sick and *costly* members.

Under risk-adjusted payments, sicker patients result in higher per-member-per-month (PMPM) capitation fees. For example, Josh's HMO was paid a different capitation rate for the HIV and AIDS disease categories. The monthly capitation payment for an HIV-positive enrollee was approximately $1,600 per month and approximately $2,400 per month for an enrollee diagnosed with AIDS. The difference in the risk-adjusted capitation rate accounted for the additional health care services and pharmacy costs associated with the progression of HIV infection to AIDS-defining illnesses (Pruitt, Robst, Langland-Orban, & Brooks, 2015).

Josh figured that Steve Sorenson's population health management plan was to focus on the higher revenue population. Perversely, the risk-adjusted capitation actually incentivized disease progression. The payment to the health plan increased if the disease worsens from HIV-positive to AIDS. If a health plan skimped on case management for the HIV-positive group and waited until the patient progressed to an AIDS diagnosis, then the risk-adjusted capitated premium would increase substantially, from $1,600 to $2,400, as shown in exhibit 53.1.

Yet, this did not explain why the case managers were assisting the sicker AIDS-diagnosed members, but not the less costly HIV-positive group. As exhibit 53.1 shows, while the revenue was higher, the profits were actually less with the AIDS-diagnosed group.

Josh then realized that much of the costs of HIV/AIDS care was in pharmaceuticals. These costly drugs were important to keeping patients' immune system strong (U.S. DHHS, 2011). Yet, among this Medicaid-insured population, the adherence to these drugs was very low—less than a quarter of all members stayed with the regimen as prescribed (Pruitt, Robst, Langland-Orban, & Brooks, 2015). Cara suggested some further analysis.

When Cara divided the population of HIV/AIDS members into two groups based on their medication adherence behavior, it made sense. Josh understood why HIV-positive members did not get any attention from the case managers. For HIV-positive members prescribed drugs, the non-adherent group were $320 PMPM in *profit* on average, as shown in exhibit 53.2. However, for the adherent HIV-positive group, the *loss* was $338 PMPM, as shown in exhibit 53.3. The health plan would have no short-term financial incentive to create adherence interventions for the HIV-positive patients. For AIDS-diagnosed members, however, adherence interventions make financial sense—$96 PMPM in profit for the non-adherent group, but $383 PMPM in profit for the adherent group, on average.

|  | HIV-positive | AIDS-diagnosed |
|---|---|---|
| Capitation | $1,600 | $2,400 |
| Expenditures | $1,439 | $2,250 |
| Profit (Loss) | $  161 | $  150 |

**EXHIBIT 53.1**
Overall HIV/
AIDS Capitation
and Mean
Expenditures

EXHIBIT 53.2
Non-adherent
HIV/AIDS Group
Capitation
and Mean
Expenditures

|  | HIV-positive | AIDS-diagnosed |
|---|---|---|
| Capitation | $1,600 | $2,400 |
| Expenditures | $1,280 | $2,304 |
| Profit (Loss) | $ 320 | $  96 |

EXHIBIT 53.3
Adherent HIV/
AIDS Group
Capitation
and Mean
Expenditures

|  | HIV-positive | AIDS-diagnosed |
|---|---|---|
| Capitation | $1,600 | $2,400 |
| Expenditures | $1,938 | $ 2,017 |
| Profit (Loss) | ($338) | $  383 |

### The transplant investigation

"Mr. Thompson?" the agent asked as Josh gazed silently out the office window. "Mr. Thompson, did you hear what we asked you about patient dumping?"

"Yes, sorry," Josh said. "A while back, I was made aware of a program to encourage members with AIDS to leave our plan for another state Medicaid program. At the time I learned of it, though, it was no longer active."

"What about transplant patients?" the suspicious FBI agent asked.

Josh told them everything he knew about the HIV/AIDS patient issue, but he was not aware of transplant patient dumping. The whistleblower's official complaint reported the health plan's case managers systematically persuaded unprofitable *organ transplant* patients to leave the health plan. He was not under investigation, per se. Still, Josh regretted that he failed to report what he knew at the time to the authorities.

### A Tiffany & Co. piggy bank

For Josh and many of his colleagues, this event was marked with a professional depression, recognizing participation in a fog of complicity. The raid, indictments, trial, and eventual prison sentences for some executives were life-altering events for them. The health plan executives made terrible mistakes, actions driven by hubris. Josh knew them to some extent. One gave Josh's family a lovely gift for the birth of his first child. The beautiful hand-painted porcelain piggy bank from Tiffany & Co. still sits in his son's room. When Josh sees it, he often reflects on the shame and sadness these former executives must feel at the loss of their careers, reputations, and freedom. It was a long, sad fall from Tiffany & Co. to prison.

Even for Josh and his colleagues, the vast majority of whom were not involved in fraud, the scandal was a defining moment. His confidence in managed care waned somewhat; however, he knows that many health plan employees make the right ethical choices. Josh's experience provides a heightened sense of awareness of how health policy influences professional behaviors, good and bad, providing a cautionary tale for health services executives and policymakers.

## Post Script

While risk-adjusted payments are necessary to discourage patient dumping in risk-based payment systems, it may encourage nefarious behaviors described in this case; namely, it may discourage prevention of disease (Eggleston, Ellis, & Lu, 2012). To combat this weakness, efforts are underway to complement risk-adjusted payment schemes with quality of care performance measurement and incentives. For example, Medicare's Shared Savings Program offers risk-adjusted capitations, but only rewards Accountable Care Organizations for controlling costs while meeting stringent quality standards (Salmon, Sanderson, Walters, Kennedy & Muney, 2012). Medicare has also reduced risk selection in the Medicare Advantage managed care program (McWilliams, Hsu, & Newhouse, 2012), and beginning with the Affordable Care Act, has complemented this risk adjustment effort with Star Rating System performance measurement (Reid, Deb, Howell, & Shrank, 2013). Other organizational reforms, such as patient-centered medical homes, combine risk-adjustment with bonuses to incentivize performance (Newhouse, Garber, Graham, McCoy, Mancher, & Kibria, 2013).

The case is based on an actual whistleblower complaint that alleged patient dumping (Hellein v. WellCare, et al., 2010). However, the resulting federal case was ultimately overshadowed by the false claims reporting to the State of Florida by WellCare employees. According to the FBI, the case was eventually settled for over $200 million, and the whistleblower received over $20 million in compensation (U.S. Attorney's Office Middle District of Florida, 2012). Five executives were convicted of fraud and sentenced to prison (Tillman, 2014).

## References

Abrahamson, K., & Durham, M. (2010). Integrating sociological theory into the case study experience. *The Journal of Health Administration Education*, 27(3).

American College of Healthcare Executives. (2011). ACHE code of ethics.

Eggleston, K., Ellis, R.P., & Lu, M. (2012). Risk adjustment and prevention. *Canadian Journal of Economics/Revue canadienne d'économique*, 45(4), 1586–1607.

Gentry, C. and Wells, M. (2010, June 28). "Unsealed complaint slams WellCare" Health News Florida. Retrieved from: http://hnfarchives.org/hnf_stories/read/unsealed_complaint_slams_wellcare

McAlearney, A.S. & Kovner, A.R., Neuhauser, D. (2013). Health services management: readings, cases, and commentary. *Health Administration Press*.

McWilliams, J. M., Hsu, J., & Newhouse, J. P. (2012). New risk-adjustment system was associated with reduced favorable selection in Medicare Advantage. *Health Affairs*, 31(12), 2630–2640

National Center for Healthcare Leadership. (2006). Healthcare Leadership Competency Model, v2.1. Retrieved from: http://www.nchl.org/Documents/NavLink/ NCHL_Competency_Model-full_uid892012226572.pdf

Newhouse, J. P., Garber, A. M., Graham, R. P., McCoy, M. A., Mancher, M., & Kibria, A. (Eds.). (2013). Variation in Health Care Spending: Target Decision Making, Not Geography. National Academies Press.

Pruitt, Z., Robst, J., Langland Orban, B., & Brooks, R.G. (2015). Healthcare Costs Associated with Antiretroviral Adherence Among Medicaid Patients. *Applied health economics and health policy.* 13(1), 69–80.

Reid, R. O., Deb, P., Howell, B. L., & Shrank, W. H. (2013). Association between Medicare Advantage plan star ratings and enrollment. JAMA, 309(3), 267–274.

Roebuck, M. C., Liberman, J.N., Gemmill-Toyama, M., & Brennan, T.A. (2011). Medication adherence leads to lower health care use and costs despite increased drug spending. *Health Affairs*, 30(1), 91–99.

Salmon, R.B., Sanderson, M.I., Walters, B.A., Kennedy, K., Flores, R.C., & Muney, A.M. (2012). A collaborative accountable care model in three practices showed promising early results on costs and quality of care. *Health Affairs*, 31(11), 2379–2387.

Tillman, J. (May 19, 2014). "Judge sentences former WellCare execs to prison in Medicaid fraud." *Tampa Bay Times*. Retrieved from: http://www. tampabay.com/news/courts/criminal/judge-sentences-former-wellcare- execs-to-prison-in-medicaid-fraud/2180459

U.S. Attorney's Office Middle District of Florida. (2012). *Florida-Based WellCare Health Plans Agrees to Pay $137.5 Million to Resolve False Claims Act Allegations.* Washington, D.C.: U.S. Federal Bureau of Investigations. Retrieved from: https://www.fbi.gov/tampa/press-releases/2012/florida-based-wellcare- health-plans-agrees-to-pay-137.5-million-to-resolve-false-claims-act-allegations

U.S. Department of Health and Human Services. (2011). Guidelines for the Use of Antiretroviral Agents in HIV-1-Infected Adults and Adolescents. Washington, D.C.: Office of AIDS Research Advisory Council. Retrieved from: http://www. aidsinfo.nih.gov/ContentFiles/AdultandAdolescentGL.pdf

U.S. ex. rel. Sean J. Hellein v. WellCare Health Plans, Inc. et al., Case No. 8.06-CV-01079-T-30TGW. (M.D. Fla. 21 June 2010).

## Case Questions

1. Which competencies from the National Center for Healthcare Leadership Competency Model are relevant to the behaviors of individuals in this case?

2. What are the benefits and caveats of risk-adjusted capitation? How could the caveats of capitation be reconciled or improved in the HIV/AIDS example provided in this case (see exhibits 53.2 and 53.3)?

3. Using the American College of Healthcare Executives Code of Ethics, how should the case managers address the dilemma between advancing the best interest of their patients versus the best interest of the organization? How should the director of population health address the dilemma?

4. What challenges exist in targeting population health management interventions for high-risk patients? To what extent is this a priority for organizations focused on population health (e.g., ACOs)?

5. What alternative actions could Josh have taken when he discovered the patient-dumping program existed, and what are the anticipated consequences of each proposed action?

6. Who in the organization should be held accountable for the issues described in the case? What should be the consequences?

# CASE 54

# Dr. Fisher's Patient

*Duncan Neuhauser*

## The Improvement Committee at Hillside Village Hospital

The 30-bed Hillside Village Hospital is one of five hospitals that make up a rural, regional accountable care system (RACS). The Hillside Village improvement committee has the assignment of guiding the improvement of measured outcomes, patient satisfaction, and lowered costs for the system in general and for Hillside Village Hospital in particular. The four other hospitals in the RACS have similar committees and will share results.

The Hillside Village committee is having one of its regular meetings. The committee includes Sally Marsden, the management representative for the system who has executive responsibility for the improvement committees; Dr. Frederica Fisher, a physician representative; and Robert Smith, the vice president of nursing and patient care. Their preliminary discussion follows:

**Sally Marsden:** As you all know, we are working on ways to measurably improve care and patient satisfaction, as well as control costs. If we can do this and measure our improvements, we will qualify for supplementary third-party payments. We are almost in reach of our goals.

Dr. Fisher has sent us a report from one of her patients. The question before us is this: Is this patient's example relevant to our goals? Can we learn from it and apply our learning to other patients?

**Dr. Frederica Fisher:** In the past, it was easier for the doctor to give orders to be followed by the patient. The patient would listen to what was recommended and take the doctor's advice. Now, though, more patients want to and insist on participating in their own care. This report I am sharing involves an extremely unusual patient. I will call him "John" so he will remain anonymous. John is a retired quality engineer for a big defense contractor, and he has carried out his own experiment about the effects of his drug treatment. Perhaps there are more patients who would do this if we encouraged them. If so, it might help us with our system goals.

**Robert Smith:** This is an interesting idea. As we know, new drugs are approved for use after large randomized controlled trials [RCTs] show that their use results in better outcomes than alternative treatments. For instance, a possible result of an RCT is that, in the control group, 30 out of 100 patients get better, whereas, in the treatment group, 60 out of 100 patients get better. This difference is significant and unlikely to be due to chance. Yet these results also indicate that the remaining 40 out of 100 treatment patients could be taking the drug without benefiting. If we could find out who those patients are and stop their use of the drug, we would save 40 percent of these treatment costs. Dr. Fisher's patient's experience may provide a picture of how we could do this more broadly.

**Marsden:** Do you really think we could get more of our patients to do this kind of self-assessment? And do you think it will work? We need to figure out whether we should encourage this, and if so how.

**Smith:** Right now, we have a couple of advanced practice nurses who might be interested in leading a patient support group to help patients do such self-evaluations. It would involve changing what they do on a daily basis, but they might be open to the challenge.

**Marsden:** For our next meeting, can we have a plan to present to the RACS leadership group?

## Randomized Controlled Trials vs. Person-Specific Evidence

Randomized controlled clinical trials can answer the question, On average for a defined population, and other things held equal, does this treatment make a significant difference? If the RCT produces clear, positive evidence, the treatment is considered appropriate and will likely be approved for use. Physicians with knowledge and experience can then match the treatment to conditions, and pharmacists and package inserts can give generalized information on the treatment's benefits and side effects. However, a critical next step might be to pursue person-specific evidence—that is, to find out if such a treatment benefits an individual person.

Can individual patients carry out their own quantified experiments to understand how they benefit—or do not benefit—from a drug or treatment? Dr. Fisher's patient tried to conduct such an experiment about his own treatment, and other patients might be similarly interested. The experience of Dr. Fisher's patient highlights the opportunity for individual patients to play a role in data collection and analysis, and it has provided the impetus for the RACS leadership to further consider this option. The ultimate goal would be to make this type of individual assessment as accurate, cheap, and simple as possible.

The example provided by Dr. Fisher's patient illustrates the methodologic issues that arise and the results that can be achieved with this person-specific approach.

## The Prescription for Dr. Fisher's Patient

John was a 75-year-old man with an enlargement of the prostate—benign prostatic hyperplasia—that resulted in a frequent need to get up at night to urinate. Nocturia, as this need is known, is common among elderly men, and getting up as many as five times a night is an inconvenient but not life-threatening condition. John's primary care physician, Dr. Fisher, prescribed the drug tamsulosin hydrochloride (brand name Flomax) to be taken one pill (0.4 mg capsule) per day. John was taking no other medications.

When John went to fill his prescription, the RiteAid pharmacist gave out a standardized fact sheet for patients. According to the fact sheet, two expected benefits of the medication were (1) a reduction in the need to urinate often and (2) a stronger urine stream. Two side effects, however, were (1) dizziness and (2) runny nose. The usual cost of this drug was $119.99 (US dollars) for a 30-day supply; with insurance coverage, it cost $12 for John out of pocket. In addition, upon John's request, the pharmacist included the technical package insert from Sandoz, the drug maker. Information about the drug is available via DailyMed (2015).

Upon reading the package insert, John found the clinical evidence in support of the drug to be of high quality. In the two studies described, the statistical analysis was commendable, and, controlling for the placebo effect, the evidence for efficacy was strong. That said, the insert was missing some information that could help John answer the question of whether the treatment would work for him.

The reported trials used two outcome measures: urine flow and the American Urological Association (AUA) symptom score. However, a literature reference to the AUA score was not provided; in fact, the insert had no literature references at all. Given his background in quality control, John would have particularly liked to have seen a distribution of the outcome scores. The insert stated that more people benefit from the drug than from any placebo effect, but John wondered how many patients experienced no or minimal benefit. These people, if they could be identified, could avoid costs and risks by not taking a pill that did not benefit them.

## John's Question: "Does This Treatment Work for Me?"

For John, the medication had four outcomes of potential concern—two benefits and two side effects—and he wanted to examine the trade-off between the positive and negative effects. To help evaluate the trade-off, John applied a utility score to each outcome to reflect how important it was to his quality of life. The utility scores were either 1 or 0; a score of 1 indicated that the outcome was predicted to affect his quality of life, and a score of 0 indicated that it was not. Of the four outcomes John considered, he assigned scores of 1 to two of them: the benefit of reducing the number of times he needed to get up during the night and the side effect of dizziness. He assigned scores of 0 to the two outcomes about which he was not concerned: urine stream and runny nose.

Determining how to appropriately measure the dependent variables—particularly the number of times "up"—was a challenge, and it took John several months to work this out. Ultimately, he decided to measure the times "up" by tracking each night of sleep as follows: *sleep/up/sleep/up/sleep/up* (with the final "up" being the moment he woke up to start his day). For an "up" to count for the purpose of the study, it had to be bracketed by "sleep" before and after. The example of *sleep/up/sleep/up/sleep/up*, therefore, would yield a score of two "up" counts.

Once John started taking the medication, the symptoms of dizziness became apparent. With Dr. Fisher's permission, John started to take the pill every other day, and he tracked the number of times he had to get up each night. His collection of data included the date, whether he took a pill that day, the number of times he was up at night, the level of exercise he had gotten the previous day, and notes about any special cause variation.

Between July 15 and September 11, 2014, John conducted a 55-day individual trial. For 28 of those days, he had taken a pill the night before; for the other 27 days, he had not. For the 28 days after taking the pill, John got up an average of 2.22 times per night. In contrast, for the 27 days without the pill, John got up an average of 2.39 times. John thus found that the medicine made an improvement in his health as measured by fewer "ups" during the night when he took the medication. He was now ready to conduct a full experiment.

# Factors to Consider in John's Experiment
## The Placebo Effect

Studies often use blinding to control for a placebo effect, to ensure that the observed outcome is a result of the treatment itself and not just the person's belief in that treatment. In this experiment, however, John considered the placebo effect part of the benefit of treatment and purposely did not control for it.

## Control Variables

John chose exercise as a control variable because exercise seemed to lead to better sleep. John's level of exercise each day was largely dependent on weather factors, such as subzero temperatures and rain. It was also influenced by the need to complete such tasks as snow shoveling, yard work, log splitting, and walking, all of which could be considered exercise.

For John's experiment, measurement of exercise evolved into a four-point scale. Routine walking and the climbing of 10 to 20 flights of stairs amounted to the baseline measure of daily exercise, which was recorded as $E(0)$. Days in which John completed additional exercise received higher scores. Days with an additional 15 minutes of heavy exercise received a score of $E(1)$; 30 minutes of exercise to the point of perspiring and being out of breath produced a score of $E(2)$; and more than an hour of such exercise warranted a score of $E(3)$. (Notably, although these standards of exercise worked for John, they might not be suitable for people of different ages and fitness levels.)

## Side Effects

Of the two possible side effects, the runny nose was deemed unimportant and therefore not included in the study. John was concerned, however, with the other side effect, dizziness. In fact, his desire to reduce dizzy spells was one reason he started taking the drug only on alternate days.

Through close examination of his activities, John found that the dizziness side effect was almost entirely associated with one specific behavior pattern: It occurred when John would stand up and climb a flight of stairs after having been seated at his computer for half an hour or more. After John became aware of this link, the side effect became both predictable and controllable.

## Special Cause Variation

The concept of special cause variation comes from quality improvement thinking, and it suggests that an extreme outlying result can potentially be dropped from the analysis if that result has a clearly known plausible explanation outside of the factors being studied. This approach can narrow the distribution for a series of outcomes and provide clues to help with understanding variance.

During one night of the study, John's neighbor's house caught fire. Seven fire trucks rushed to extinguish the fire, but the house ultimately burned down. Obviously, the event disrupted both John's sleep and his data collection the following day. As a result, that time frame was counted as a special cause and excluded from the analysis. Other, less dramatic factors also affected John's measurement of times "up"—for instance, the large family cat jumping on the bed at 4:00 a.m. (John noted, "There is no snooze button on a cat that wants its breakfast.")

## The Findings from John's Experiment

Traditional RCT design compares two groups of patients—one group that receives the treatment and another that serves as the control group. Factorial design involves the use of multiple variables at once, and it can show both first-order effects and interaction effects between the individual variables (Montgomery 2013; Olsson et al. 2005; Neuhauser 2005).

John's experiment used a factorial approach to analyze three variables—taking the pill, level of exercise, and number of times up at night—and their interactions. He also considered the interaction effect of exercise combined with taking the pill. Using this approach, John gained much more information than he would have gotten from an RCT using a single variable. The results of John's experiment are displayed in exhibit 54.1.

Reviewing these results, John found that there was an interaction effect between exercise and taking the pill. Without exercise, taking the pill reduced

**EXHIBIT 54.1**
Results of John's Factorial Experiment

| Exercise | Pill Taken | Number of Days Observed | Average Number of Times Up at Night |
|----------|-----------|-------------------------|-------------------------------------|
| Minimal E(0) | Yes | 20 | 2.65 |
|  | No | 15 | 3.00 |
| Low — E(1) | Yes | 12 | 2.00 |
|  | No | 16 | 1.88 |
| Medium — E(2) | Yes | 10 | 2.90 |
|  | No | 11 | 2.09 |
| High — E(3) | Yes | 30 | 2.20 |
|  | No | 24 | 2.13 |

*Note:* E(0) to E(3) refers to the levels of exercise described in the text. The pill is one tamsulosin 0.4 mg capsule taken. A total of 138 days were tracked between Nov. 1, 2014, and March 31, 2015.

the frequency of getting up at night from an average of 3.00 times to an average of 2.65 times. However, when combined with any level of exercise, taking the pill actually made the number of "ups" increase. This interaction effect surprised John and led to a new treatment strategy: He decided to take the pill only when he had not exercised beyond the $E(0)$ level, and he tried to increase the number of days with higher levels of exercise.

John tried this approach for 12 days, from April 24 to May 5, 2015. During this period, all but two days had exercise scores of $E(1)$ or higher; therefore, only two pills were taken. During this time, the average number of "ups" was 1.67; however, if the two pill days were excluded, the average number dropped to 1.3. Furthermore, John's use of pills during this period dropped to just one pill every six days. When compared to the originally prescribed dosage of one pill per day, the reduced use of pills could be translated into an 83 percent reduction in medication costs.

John's health status, as measured by the number of "ups," went from 2.31 in 2014 to 1.67 in 2015—an improvement of 28 percent, or .64 "ups" per night. John decided that this result represented a clinically significant difference. Further, his data suggested that additional improvement might be possible if he could increase the number of high-exercise days. (John also was intrigued by studies he had heard about indicating that mice that exercised more were less likely to get cancer.)

A couple of months later, John found another variable that was associated with his number of "ups": the number of hours he spent in bed. Other things being equal, the longer he stayed in bed, the greater the likelihood he would need to get up.

## Considering the Results

John's experiment is presented here as an example of how measurement and factorial design can be used to gain a better understanding of a person's health condition, lower costs, and improve measured quality. John's quality and side effect measures are unique to him, and the specific results of his study should not be generalized to anyone else. Instead, John and Dr. Fisher have proposed that this approach to "the quantified self" serve as a companion to other sources of clinical evidence, such as clinical trials, clinician knowledge, and the pharmacist's expertise (Topol 2015). However, a number of additional factors should be considered when putting an individualized experimental approach into practice.

### *Statistical Versus Clinical Significance*

Because this approach does not involve comparing the individual's results to those of another population, statistical significance is not an issue; what matters is clinical significance. Is the reduction of one "up" in five days worth the effort? If not, how big does the difference have to be to justify the costs and side effects? In John's experiment, he considered the difference between 2.31 and 1.67 "ups" to be clinically significant.

Many experiments and comparisons of this type might benefit from the collection of baseline data before a medication is started; however, delaying treatment for a month or more to allow for this data collection might not always be feasible.

### Human Subjects Review

Human subjects review is an important consideration in research and experimentation, but it is not designed to deal with personal improvement efforts such as John's experiment. A person should be able to carefully examine his or her own health as a matter of individual liberty and freedom, and the person does not need anyone's permission to do so. In this example, permission was not sought from any organization, and the data collected were not entered into a site that would then own the data.

### More Sophisticated Statistics and Analytics

A great variety of fancy statistical methods can be applied to this experimental approach, including control charts, regression models, utility scores, and decision analysis (Olsson et al. 2005). John's experiment, for instance, could have been enhanced, for statistical purposes, by levels of exercise that were randomly or purposely assigned. However, to do so would miss the key point of this example—to show that an average person can do this type of analysis at minimal cost and provide valuable new data about their health.

### Measurement Errors

Errors in measurement and recording—and failures of short-term memory—are certainly possible in this type of experiment. Regular daily recording of the measured variables reduces but does not eliminate this problem.

### Applying This Method in Practice

This method is not appropriate for patients who require constant monitoring, and it is less useful when variables are measured less frequently than once a week (Topol 2015). But between those extremes lie opportunities for study across a wide range of medical domains. Such areas may involve exercise, hypertension, stress, blood sugar (Solodky et al. 1998), smoking, substance abuse, asthma (Alemi and Neuhauser 2004), diet, study habits, and other behaviors (Neuhauser, Provost, and Bergman 2011; Agency for Healthcare Research and Quality 2014) that may help in the management of chronic conditions.

### Key Distinctions

How does this individualized experimental approach compare with RCTs that use many patients and a standardized outcome measure? The following are some important distinctions between the two approaches:

1. *The unit of analysis.* By changing the unit of analysis from one patient to one patient-day, the individualized approach allows for the collection of more information quickly and cheaply.

2. *Generalizability.* The individualized approach does not aim to produce results that can be generalized beyond the individual. Therefore, it does not require a lot of the statistical analysis that an RCT might need to examine differences between groups due to chance. In the case of a single patient, the patient is not a sample but rather the statistical universe.

3. *The dependent variable.* RCTs require the use of the same dependent variable for all participants, and the variable must be measured the same way for everyone. The individualized approach, on the other hand, can account for the fact that patient outcome preferences differ, and it acknowledges that measurement of results and side effects may have to be handled differently to obtain optimal outcome measures for a specific person.

   In John's experiment, he assigned utility scores to the four outcomes of potential concern. Two of them (times "up" and dizziness) received utility scores of 1, and the other two (urine stream and runny nose) received scores of 0, based on John's preferences. Other patients might have different utility scores for those outcomes and, even with similar trial results, recommend a different optimal treatment. Furthermore, an individual's utility scores may change over time. When one outcome is managed, another outcome might start gaining relevance to the individual, thus driving the score higher. The package insert for John's medication described trials that used the AUA score as a metric for all the patients. Yet an individual considering these scores would want to know the distribution of these scores in order to design his own optimal treatment. A patient might also wish to know how the symptoms were actually measured in the trials.

4. *Randomized versus alternative assignment.* Randomized assignment of patients in a clinical trial is generally to be expected. John's factorial design, however, used an alternate-day approach. Alternating treatment and nontreatment days for an individual seems unlikely to introduce bias from unknown variables. It also made sense based on the pharmacokinetics of the drug related to the rate of absorption.

5. *Costs of the study.* The standard RCT can cost millions of dollars and take years to complete. In contrast, an individualized factorial approach costs little or nothing, depending on one's perspective. In John's study, it required a pen and paper to record at least four data points each day and a simple pocket calculator for addition and division.

## How Can the Lessons from John's Experiment Be Applied?

John's experiment used a factorial design to show the impact of several variables and their interaction on his health status. By doing so, he was able to understand and reduce unwanted side effects, lower the costs of medication by 83 percent, and improve his measured health status by 28 percent. The experiment clearly demonstrated that a patient can benefit from developing a quantified multifactor model of his own treatment and health status.

If this practice costs next to nothing to do, saves money, and improves measured health status, why is it not used ubiquitously? What are the barriers? To start, physicians lack the time, and they do not receive reimbursement for such studies. In addition, reducing pill use, in the short term, is not in the drug company's economic interest (although, in the long run, having drugs that truly benefit the patient is). Some online services may be able to do this kind of analysis, but such applications and programs often make ownership of the data a condition of use, so the data can be resold for a profit. Finally, a lot of people simply do not like numbers.

Despite these obstacles, John's experience shows great potential for improving health management in creative ways. For instance, what if people who had prescription costs exceeding $50 dollars a day were only reimbursed if they joined a support group and routinely collected their own data? Patients who reduced their costs and improved their health status might then get some of the savings.

In practice, many aspects of health can be measured daily, including blood pressure, blood sugar, exercise, smoking, stress, mental health, pulse, medication compliance, asthma, and diet. The individualized approach used in John's experiment was extremely low cost and could be easily applied to such conditions. Further, a key indicator of successful chronic disease management is when the patient has an accurate multivariate model of her condition even if only a few variables can easily be measured.

Dr. Fisher's patient had certainly given the Hillside Village improvement committee a lot to think about. In addition to helping John successfully manage his own condition, John's experiment represented promise for better self-management of chronic conditions for numerous future patients. Sally Marsden and her colleagues agreed to further explore how the organization could build on John's experience to help advance the system's goals.


## Case Questions

1. Is this approach to participatory care worth pursuing? Is there another strategy you might propose that could help lower costs and improve quality?
2. For what kind of patient is this approach appropriate?

3. How do we find interested practitioners and patients who might like to try this approach?

4. What incentives can be created to get patients, providers, and health plans to support this approach?

5. How would you measure the program's success (or failure)?

6. How would you create a cultural climate in a healthcare organization that would be receptive to patient participation?

## References

Agency for Healthcare Research and Quality. 2014. *Design and Implementation of N-of-1 Trials: A User's Guide*. Rockville, MD: Agency for Healthcare Research and Quality.

Alemi, F., and D. Neuhauser. 2004. "Control Charts for Time Between Asthma Attacks." *Joint Commission Journal on Quality and Safety* 30 (2): 95–102.

DailyMed. 2015. "Tamsulosin Hydrochloride Capsule." Updated December 24. https://dailymed.nlm.nih.gov/dailymed/drugInfo.cfm?setid=fb120098-b007-4a33-80b8-b7279c7668ee.

Montgomery, D. C. 2013. *Design and Analysis of Experiments*, 8th ed. New York: John Wiley & Sons.

Neuhauser, D. 2005. "Why the Design of Experiments Just May Transform Health Care." *Quality Management in Health Care* 14 (4): 217–18.

Neuhauser, D., L. Provost, and B. Bergman. 2011. "The Meaning of Variation to Healthcare Managers, Clinical and Health-Services Researchers, and Individual Patients." *BMJ Quality and Safety* 20 (Supplement 1): i36–i40.

Olsson, J., D. Terris, M. Elg, J. Lundberg, and S. Lindblad. 2005. "The One-Person Randomized Controlled Trial." *Quality Management in Health Care* 14 (4): 206–16.

Solodky, C., H. Chen, P. Jones, and D. Neuhauser. 1998. "Patients as Partners in Clinical Research." *Medical Care* 36 (8, Supplement): AS13–AS20.

Topol, E. 2015. *The Patient Will See You Now: The Future of Medicine Is in Your Hands*. New York: Basic Books.

# CASE 55

# Coordination of Cancer Care: Notes from a Pancreatic Cancer Patient

*Anthony R. Kovner*

The following are comments from a pancreatic cancer patient:

I have received care from MD Anderson, the University of Pennsylvania, and cancer physicians in Milwaukee, Chicago (where I live), and Johns Hopkins. I've linked with PanCan Advocacy at both the national and local levels. Recently I've been trying to find out where clinical studies are being done on the use of immunotherapy for pancreatic cancer. No physician has been able to tell me anything about this. I learned from a University of Pennsylvania newsletter, forwarded to me by a friend, that a "dream team" was working on treating pancreatic cancer.

I've learned of three trials going on, and they take two forms: One type focuses on modifying white corpuscles so cancer cells don't recognize and defend against them, and the second type involves vaccines. I can't get into this first trial because my disease isn't metastatic (it hasn't spread beyond my pancreas). At the same time, I've been unable to learn about the other two trials except by hit and miss. I have been told to find benefactors of the trials, but I don't want to pursue this option unless it is a last resort. I've learned that a trial at Sloan Kettering in New York is not open for new patients. I'll call again just in case. In the meantime, I have no idea where else reputable hospitals may be carrying on these trials.

Right now, I don't know what I don't know. And no one seems to know. No one medical professional has told me that this is the direction I should take. My oncologist can help me evaluate my options, but this is complex. He does immunotherapy on other organs, so I don't know what he knows about the pancreas. From what I've seen and heard, everyone seems to have tunnel vision. People don't think about issues or patients or options beyond their own circle of interest. They may be terrific during treatment, but that is not enough to help. Also, it's not that they want to protect their own turf. I find no one in the medical profession is currently capable of helping me. And I really don't know the solution. I'm grateful for the treatment I am receiving and that I have enough money to search for other interventions that might help me. While I'm in Philadelphia, I'm staying overnight because these appointment visits around clinical trials have a way of being cancelled. I want to make sure I can see the doctor and find out any information that can help me learn about what I can do next.

## Case Questions

1. Who should be in charge of coordinating cancer care for a patient like this?
2. How can the patient find out who can help him?
3. How should the patient react if his oncologist says, "This is how we take care of patients with your problem in our system"?

# CASE 56

# What Benefits the Community?

*Paula H. Song and Ann Scheck McAlearney*

**B**arney Wiseman looked at his hospital's most recent community benefit report. His hospital has been reporting its community benefit activities for years, well before the state required all not-for-profit hospitals to report their activities annually to the state attorney general's office. Year after year, Wiseman's department submitted the report, but there had never been any feedback from the state about his hospital's level of community benefit or activities.

Today, though, the community benefit report took on new significance. The big news of the week was from the neighboring state of Illinois, which had moved to revoke the property tax exemption status of three hospitals. If Illinois succeeded, these three hospitals would be responsible for property taxes, which could translate into a new financial burden involving millions of dollars. Illinois had identified these three hospitals when it reviewed the levels of charity care provided by hospitals in the state. The three hospitals had been singled out because they were deemed to be providing only "low" levels of charity care, ranging from 0.96 percent to 1.85 percent of patient care revenue, according to the Illinois Department of Revenue (Japsen 2011).

However, as Wiseman knew, the "appropriate" level of charity care that a not-for-profit hospital should provide had not yet been defined. Hospitals typically provide a range of services that could be considered community benefits, from hosting community health fairs to providing health services that are often unprofitable, such as emergency department services, burn units, and counseling services. In addition, many hospitals are reimbursed by Medicare and Medicaid at levels below the cost of the services they deliver; thus, these unreimbursed costs could be seen as part of a benefit to the community. Other activities, such as providing graduate medical education and performing unfunded research, are also typically understood to benefit the broader community hospitals serve. Whether and how to count these activities when evaluating a hospital's community benefits are still unclear.

Wiseman had always thought that his hospital provided care and services well above the "acceptable" level for community benefits, but the situation in Illinois made him question if it really did. Moreover, Wiseman began to wonder if his current community benefit report adequately accounted for all of the community benefits the hospital provided, well beyond charity care.

## Case Questions

1. Who should benefit from a hospital's community benefits? (Who are the hospital's stakeholders, and how do they benefit?)
2. How much community benefit should not-for-profit hospitals provide?
3. What activities, other than charity care, should be counted as community benefits?
4. What are the implications if a not-for-profit hospital's tax-exempt status is revoked?

## Reference

Japsen, B. 2011. "State Challenging Hospitals' Tax Exemptions." *New York Times*. Published September 10. www.nytimes.com/2011/09/11/us/11cnchospitals.html.

# CASE 57

# CEO Compensation: How Much Is Too Much?

*Terri Menser*

Kyle Martin has worked in healthcare since he graduated with a master's degree in healthcare administration in 2002. He has dedicated himself to his job, often exceeding 60 hours a week, with the goal of becoming a CEO before his fortieth birthday. Kyle started out as the director of a small group practice and then transitioned to working as a senior practice manager for Green Valley Hospital. There, he has worked his way up, serving as administrator for surgical specialties throughout the state and then as chief innovation officer for the last four years.

Now, at the age of 38, Kyle is close to realizing his goal. He is in the final stages of negotiation for the CEO position at Maple Park Hospital, Green Valley's main competitor. Maple Park recently forced out its CEO, Scott Villa, because of poor performance, marked by diminishing quality of care and decreased patient and employee satisfaction scores. Mr. Villa's base salary had totaled $700,000 annually, which is not surprising given that the industry average in 2009 was approximately $600,000 (Joynt et al. 2014).

The hiring committee at Maple Park has decided that Kyle is the clear choice for the job, largely because of his extensive knowledge of the local market and his familiarity with hospital operations from a variety of perspectives. However, taking over Maple Park would be a challenge for any executive, and especially for Kyle, who will be new to CEO-level leadership and is younger than much of the staff. In the immediate future, Maple Park will face challenges in increasing its operational efficiency and addressing its rising turnover rates.

Andrew Henderson is the newest member of Maple Park's board of directors, and he has been asked to take the first pass at devising better metrics to determine the new CEO's compensation package. In preparing for this task, Andrew has read everything he can find related to hospital CEO compensation. One sentence from a study published in *JAMA Internal Medicine* keeps coming to mind (Joynt et al. 2014, 66):

> Whether linking CEO compensation to quality metrics would lead to better care is unknown; an alternative possibility is that linking CEO compensation explicitly to quality metrics could have unintended consequences, such as reducing hospitals' incentive to provide care to medically or socially complex populations.

Andrew takes seriously his responsibility for drafting the initial compensation guidelines. He wants to be fair, and he wants to attract the best possible candidate for the CEO position. Although he was uncomfortable with Mr. Villa's seemingly singular focus on profits, Andrew understands the importance of financial incentives to motivate and retain the CEO. He strives to find a balance between providing those incentives and setting performance metrics that will benefit the organization.

Meanwhile, the decision to leave Green Valley is not one that Kyle is taking lightly. Though he looks forward to taking on a new challenge, he knows he must weigh the pros and cons of the move and consider his work–life balance. Kyle knows that the easiest way to advance his career is to change jobs, but going to work directly for the competition almost feels disloyal. He has spent the last 12 years at Green Valley, enjoys his work, and gets along well with his coworkers. His current base salary is $350,000, which affords him a comfortable life. The details of the new compensation package are still being finalized. The new salary information will certainly influence his decision, but he is being careful to weigh all other relevant factors as well. Kyle has been married for ten years and has a four-year-old girl. He wants to be the best husband and father he can be, and he knows this new position will require long hours.

As he prepares to decide between these two career trajectories, Kyle writes a list of questions to discuss with the hiring committee. He hopes the answers will help him sort out his remaining concerns.

## Case Questions

1. In your own words, explain the meaning of the quotation from Joynt and colleagues (2014).
2. Do you believe quality measures (e.g., readmission rates) are a fair measure of a CEO's performance? Provide support for your answer.
3. From Kyle's perspective, briefly discuss the main pros and cons of accepting the new position.
4. What questions would you ask the hiring committee if you were Kyle?
5. What factors might help you determine the salary level that you would consider a fair offer?

## Reference

Joynt, K. E., S. T. Le, E. J. Orav, and A. K. Jha. 2014. "Compensation of Chief Executive Officers at Nonprofit US Hospitals." *JAMA Internal Medicine* 174 (1): 61–67.

# CASE 58
# What's in a Name?

*Ann Scheck McAlearney and Sarah M. Roesch*

Donna Taylor was on her way to the mall to pick up an item that was being donated for a carnival silent auction benefiting her daughter's school. In her head, she was going over the last-minute list of things she had to do to get ready for that night's carnival. Taylor really didn't have anything to worry about, because she was a master planner of fund-raisers and community service events. Ten years ago, she had worked in the insurance industry, but after her third child she left her job to stay home with her kids. Taylor enjoyed staying home with her children but had found herself seeking additional outside responsibilities to help her feel useful. Taylor became active in the community through volunteerism and participated in many service projects offered by the Junior League, YWCA Women's Board, and Children's Hospital Auxiliary. She also participated in various capital campaigns and was a natural fund-raiser. Taylor was an organized, creative, and capable worker who quickly climbed the volunteer hierarchy and became a leader within these organizations. As her three daughters each entered school, she also became active in their school's parent–teacher association; this involvement had led to her current run to the mall to pick up the donated auction item.

While sprinting into the mall to gather her item, Taylor let out a deep sigh as she passed the Ashley and Mitch store. Taylor's oldest daughter, Stella, was in the sixth grade and just getting interested in fashion, and a pair of Ashley and Mitch jeans was at the top of Stella's birthday list. Taylor shook her head at the large poster—a photo of three scantily clothed teenage models—in Ashley and Mitch's window. Ashley and Mitch was infamous for its use of risqué promotional material and sexual imagery to entice preteens and teens to buy its clothing. Taylor was no prude, but she found this type of marketing sleazy and demeaning to young people. The strategy certainly seemed to work, however, as most preteens she knew were very interested in Ashley and Mitch's clothing. Taylor was able to shrug her shoulders at the poster with a mental note that "it's only clothes," but she knew her daughter would not be getting those jeans for her birthday.

Taylor hurried to pick up her donation. Back in the car, she again went over her mental list for the fund-raiser. Having decided that she had everything covered, she was just beginning to relax when the news came on the radio. The reporter was explaining that the local Children's Hospital would soon be renaming its emergency room "The Ashley and Mitch Emergency Department and Trauma Center" in exchange for a $10 million donation. With this new information, Taylor was struck by the realization that maybe it wasn't "only clothes." Taylor thought back to several of her family's past middle-of-the-night trips to Children's Hospital and remembered how thankful she was that her children had such a good place to go in emergency situations. She also thought about the hours she spent volunteering at Children's Hospital, pushing a book cart and delivering books to patients. Taylor knew that $10 million could do a lot for a children's hospital. Yet to name an emergency room after a company known for its use of sexual image marketing to target preteens and teens? She wasn't convinced. As the mother of three preteen girls, Taylor knew how insecurities about image could damage self-esteem. Furthermore, she was struck by the apparent inconsistency between Ashley and Mitch's message and Children's Hospital's mission of "protection and caring for children." As she approached the school for the carnival fund-raiser, Taylor's confusion had changed to anger at Children's Hospital for deciding to associate with a company notorious for egregious advertising.

Upon arriving at the school, the first person Taylor ran into was her fund-raising cochair, Meg Flynn. After telling Flynn about the partnership between Ashley and Mitch and Children's Hospital, she was amazed that Flynn seemed ambivalent. Flynn's first response was to ask, "Why would Children's turn down such a large donation? They would be crazy to turn down that kind of money for all it could do to improve healthcare for children." Flynn further pointed out that, despite the advertising, the consumer is the one with the true power. "No one is forced to buy Ashley and Mitch clothing. People can choose to look away." Flynn also suggested that maybe Ashley and Mitch owes something to the consumer—considering it makes millions of dollars each year selling its inappropriate clothing—and *should* give back to children. Taylor understood Flynn's points and realized that $10 million is a sizable donation, but she didn't think she could just look the other way. Taylor thought Ashley and Mitch should donate the money but not get naming rights, which seemed inappropriate for a field focused on health and well-being.

## Case Questions

1. What are the pros and cons for Children's Hospital in accepting the donation from Ashley and Mitch in exchange for naming rights?
2. Are there alternatives, such as a donation without naming rights, that you might propose?
3. Given the sentiments among community members, should the hospital work with the community to establish donation guidelines? Or are such decisions only relevant to the hospital itself?
4. Should guidelines be established about which companies or industries are allowed to donate money?

# CASE 59

# Patient Satisfaction in an Inner-City Hospital

*Claudia Caine and Anthony R. Kovner*

Lutheran Medical Center is a 400-bed, inner-city, community teaching hospital in Southwest Brooklyn. It is also one of only two Level I trauma centers in the borough of Brooklyn. Three major competing hospitals are within five miles of the hospital, and this competition continually challenges the hospital's efforts to grow and gain market share. Lutheran's community is made up mainly of immigrants and blue-collar wage earners. The payer mix is 75 percent Medicare and Medicaid. Recent efforts, therefore, have focused on reaching out to the neighboring community of Bay Ridge, where the population is dense, better insured, and facing the closure of its only hospital (one of the aforementioned three hospitals).

Given New York's low reimbursement rates and the high costs of providing healthcare there (e.g., wages, malpractice, benefits), the hospital must keep 90 percent of its beds filled to break even. Lutheran is already known as a low-cost provider, so its ability to further cut costs is limited; hence, growth is its only real option. However, most administrators know that hospitals that are routinely filled at more than 85 percent present many challenges. Safety, quality of care, and patient satisfaction must be given greater attention at those hospitals than at hospitals with lower, more comfortable occupancy rates. Thus, Lutheran's primary objective is to achieve growth and maintenance of high census while still improving quality of care, safety, and patient satisfaction levels.

To pursue this objective, the hospital years ago embarked upon an effort to dramatically improve its emergency department (ED). Generally known to be the hospital's "front door" to the community, the ED accounts for more than 70 percent of Lutheran's admissions. Lutheran believes that, if the ED works smoothly, patient satisfaction will go up, first impressions will be positive, quality of care and patient safety will be improved, and more and more residents of the community, and beyond, will choose the hospital for care.

Starting in 2002, the hospital set out to do three main things in an effort to become the ED of choice in Brooklyn:

1. Replace the leadership of the ED
2. Expand the ED's space by 60 percent and modernize it
3. Redesign all ED systems and processes

The project had several specific, measurable goals:

1. To increase the percentage of patients who report being "satisfied" or "very satisfied" from 52 to 70 percent
2. To increase the number of visits from 147 to 175 per day
3. To have a provider see every patient within 30 minutes of the patient's arrival in the ED
4. To have fewer than 2 percent of patients return to the ED for a second visit within 48 hours of their first visit
5. To hire 100 percent ED-trained physicians in the ED

The project began in 2002 and was completed in 2006. The first step was to replace the leadership. The leaders, at the start, were reluctant to change and were not familiar with national best-practice models in ED care. Also, 80 percent of the physicians were not ED-trained. Replacing the chairman and the vice president of nursing for the ED took one year. Turning over the staff to have 100 percent ED-trained physicians required three and a half years.

Next, in 2005, the hospital formed an ED Process Redesign Task Force. Previous leadership had attempted a process redesign in 2002 but failed. A major lesson learned at that time was that redesign and overhaul are impossible without the right leadership in place. The new redesign effort was led by the hospital chief operating officer and the new chairman of the ED. The other members of the team included the chief nursing officer, the vice president of nursing for the ED, the nurse manager for the ED, the ED educator, and the vice president of operations responsible for the ED.

The process redesign had seven main results:

1. A care team model was created for the ED, allowing small groupings of patients to be treated by a team that included a medical doctor (MD), nurse, and aide.
2. A position called the "ED patient navigator" was created. This person was available to communicate with referring physicians about their patients and serve as a case manager for ED patients.
3. The role of the ED nursing care coordinator / charge nurse was redefined so that the person became the daily "director" of movement, operations, and oversight of the entire ED.
4. The traditional nursing triage model was replaced with a combined triage/fast-track model. Physician assistants (PAs) replaced nurses at triage, and the PAs triaged, treated, and released patients or triaged and moved patients to the main ED as appropriate.
5. All ED staff were given portable internal zone phones to improve communications and reduce the noise level.
6. Paper charts were replaced with a fully automated medical record and tracking system.
7. Bedside registration was implemented, so patients went directly from triage to an ED bed without stopping to be registered.

Within 18 months of the creation of the process redesign team, the following occurred:

1. Patient visits went from 147 to 172 per day.
2. The average door-to-provider (MD or PA) time went from 90 minutes to 30 minutes.
3. All MDs were ED-trained.
4. Only 2 percent of patients needed to return to the ED within 48 hours of their initial visit.
5. ED patient satisfaction went from 52 to 66 percent (still four percentage points short of the goal).

Clearly, the team members were disappointed by the lack of progress in patient satisfaction, but they were not confused by it. The reason was that, as patient volume increased, the number of available hospital beds remained fixed, so patients waited longer as more time was needed to move patients from the ED to a hospital bed. Because the hospital must remain at over 90 percent occupancy to break even, adding beds would have created operating losses for the institution—an option the team did not have available.

The next challenge then involved improving patient satisfaction given the increasing wait times for hospital beds. The team took the following actions:

1. It added a team of physicians to the ED to provide care to admitted patients who were awaiting beds.
2. It created a labor–management joint team to improve patient flow on the inpatient units (with a goal of discharging patients within four hours of a discharge clearance note being written by a physician).
3. It created the ED Diplomat program, which is a daily rotation of senior hospital leaders from 2:00 p.m. to 8:00 p.m. The leaders meet with each ED patient who has a long wait, explain the wait, manage expectations, and give free hospital television services and free parking when appropriate.
4. It increased nurse and nurse aide staffing in the ED.
5. It arranged for patients to wait on more comfortable beds, instead of on stretchers.
6. It began a program to provide food and telephones for patients in the ED.
7. It opened a discharge lounge for patients awaiting discharge, so that beds can open up sooner.
8. It created housekeeping and transport "SWAT" teams to facilitate room turnovers on inpatient floors.

The most recent measurements indicate that patient satisfaction in the ED has increased to 75 percent. However, calling this improvement an upward trend is premature.

## Case Question

1. What more can this hospital do to address its challenges? Keep in mind that opening more inpatient beds would cost upward of $1.5 million and put the already ailing institution into a negative financial position.

# CASE 60
## Medically Assisted Living

*Anthony R. Kovner*

S am started up the car and prepared to drive with his wife, Alice, home to the city. They had just eaten dinner in Rosedale, a suburb, with Alice's 92-year-old mother, Tania, and they left Tania on the steps of her apartment building, near the restaurant. Tania had asked Alice to walk her up the steps to the building and then go with her in the elevator up to her apartment, but Alice said no. Tania asked again, adding "please," but Alice explained: "If you're not well enough to take the elevator up to the third floor, you're not well enough to live here anymore. It would be much easier for you to move into assisted living."

This exchange was the latest chapter in a conversation that had been going on for months. Sam recalled the resistance they had encountered getting Tania to give up her car keys and get rid of her car. Alice had subsequently persuaded Tania to get a home care aide to help out three afternoons a week, and that arrangement seemed to worked well. Tania has plenty of money, but Alice is concerned about Tania living alone. Tania has recently had several health misadventures necessitating trips to urgent care or the hospital emergency room. Those incidents required help from neighbors, as Alice and her sister-in-law both live more than half an hour away.

Sam kept his thoughts to himself during the argument, but he wondered, "Where's the problem?" Alice is clearly anxious about what might happen should her mother have an accident or a stroke. Alice also feels her mother would do better in a medically assisted living facility with regularly scheduled meals, opportunities for social engagement, and nursing support. But as Sam kept thinking, he came to a new realization: "This is what Alice is going to do to me, and I wouldn't want to be put in a medically assisted living facility either." Alice is 12 years younger than Sam and still working.

## Case Questions

1. Where's the "problem" in this case? For Tania? For Alice? For Sam?
2. What are Alice's alternatives in this case? What are the pros and cons of each alternative?
3. How could you organize a search of options that represents an evidence-based review of the literature?

4. How are the challenges that Tania faces met in other developed countries?

# CASE 61
## Patients and Data Privacy

*Daniel Walker*

**D**r. Mylene Figuero entered one of her examination rooms to see her next patient, a man in his mid-fifties, sitting waiting for her. As she sat down in front of the computer showing his electronic health record (EHR), she recognized the patient as a famous former football player. She asked what brought him in today, and in response, the patient immediately launched into a description of his issues. He had recently been experiencing confusion and having difficulty focusing.

As Dr. Figuero began to type the information into the EHR, however, the patient became more reluctant to talk freely about his situation. She prompted him to continue, but the man clammed up, telling her that he had just not been sleeping well and that he had to leave. Dr. Figuero was worried that the patient was withholding information about his mental health, and she thought that his symptoms, combined with his history as a football player, hinted at Alzheimer's disease.

Dr. Figuero had seen this type of behavior before, and she thought it had become more common among her patients since she switched from paper charts to the electronic record. She worried that patients might be concerned about the privacy of their health information once it was available in the digital world. Indeed, she had just read an article about an EHR system that had been hacked at a nearby hospital. She felt confident that her own EHR system was safe, because she had purposefully chosen a platform with two-factor authentication and added security features. Still, she suspected that patients might not trust that the system was secure, and she wondered how their concerns over the privacy of sensitive health information might change their interactions with their doctors.

## Case Questions

1. Why might the patient's withholding of information concern Dr. Figuero? Why might the patient withhold information?

2. Assuming Dr. Figuero is correct that the withholding is a result of the patient's privacy concerns, what could she do to change that behavior?

# CASE 62
## Saving Primary Care in Vancouver

*Caroline Wang*

D r. Shannon Zachary, a family doctor of 30 years practicing in Vancouver, British Columbia, Canada, faces some hard choices. She is devoted to her patients and sees the practice of medicine as a calling, but she must now confront the harsh reality that traditional family practice is on the brink of extinction in British Columbia.

Independent family practitioners who work in solo or small group practices are rapidly disappearing, as they are not being replaced after they retire or leave practice. In fact, for the past two decades, many practicing family physicians who provide "full-service" comprehensive, longitudinal care have been unable to find associates or new doctors willing to take over their practices when the older physicians retire. Instead, Dr. Zachary has noted, today's younger family medicine graduates overwhelmingly prefer to work in "walk-in clinics" that are proliferating throughout the province, or as hospitalists specializing in hospital medicine (i.e., inpatient care). Both of those options tend to provide higher incomes and better lifestyles than family practice does.

At the same time, an estimated 200,000 British Columbians do not have a family doctor. In fact, Victoria, the provincial capital, has a large senior population but no family physicians who are accepting new patients. An experienced family doctor who knows her patients can provide valuable continuity of care, and Dr. Zachary is concerned that the loss of this continuity will be especially problematic for the elderly, as well as for patients who have chronic, complex diseases. People without a regular family doctor may have no choice but to wait in line at a walk-in clinic or go to a hospital emergency department (ED) to address more urgent problems. Walk-in clinics that provide short visits for episodic care are not well suited for many patients' needs: Some visitors to such clinics have noted that they see a different doctor each time for only a few minutes, with the doctors, frequently without eye contact, addressing "only one problem per visit."

Dr. Zachary believes that the impending demise of traditional family practice in British Columbia is the result of decades of system neglect and devaluation of the general practitioner's professional services. Treating a patient in primary care requires spending time with the person to deal with multiple problems and chronic conditions, in addition to providing preventive care and counseling. However, under the publicly funded Medicare program that provides universal first-dollar coverage for physicians' services, all family doctors in British Columbia are paid the same flat fee for an office visit (expected to last five to seven minutes), regardless of the actual duration of the visit and the complexity of services provided.

From her years of practice, Dr. Zachary understands the importance of experienced family physicians in caring for older patients with multiple chronic diseases. As the gatekeepers in primary care, traditional family physicians skillfully manage the vast majority of acute and chronic conditions for their patients, many of whom are on multiple medications; coordinate and evaluate myriad diagnostic tests and ongoing treatments; and arrange referrals for specialist consults, with some waiting lists ranging from several months to a year. Such dedicated family doctors work long hours "running on the treadmill" to keep patients alive and to keep the system from collapse, yet, as they age, they have come to be regarded dismissively as "dinosaurs." What will happen when they are gone?

Dr. Zachary knows that a longitudinal doctor–patient relationship based on trust is crucial for high-quality, patient-centered primary care. Timely access to appropriate treatment can prevent complications, avoid duplication of tests and services, and reduce the risks of misdiagnosis and medical errors. A strong primary care foundation improves outcomes at a lower cost, which results in better health for the population.

Dr. Zachary reflects on her earlier years of practice, when all family physicians provided comprehensive longitudinal care, offered 24/7 on-call services, and visited their patients in hospitals and nursing homes. At that time, everybody had a family doctor, and the Canadian healthcare system was considered the best in the world. Today, many family physicians who provide longitudinal care for patients with chronic, complex diseases and who routinely manage multiple problems per visit complain that they work twice the number of hours per day but earn only half the income of doctors practicing at walk-in clinics.

Newer annual incentive payments for the management of a few single chronic diseases, such as diabetes, and the introduction of a complex care fee have not been successful in attracting new graduates to "full-service" family practice. Important system issues remain unaddressed: Notably, family physicians are required to provide 24/7 on-call availability to their patients without compensation, and they receive no remuneration for administrative duties, such as arrangement of referrals and coordination of care. Further, the inability of family physicians to find locum physicians to cover their practice when they are away for vacation, sickness, maternity leave, or continuing medical education are burdens that increase the risk of physician burnout.

In this system of private delivery of publicly funded services, family practitioners are responsible for their overhead costs but have no control over their fees. The vast majority of physicians work under fee-for-service arrangements and bill the British Columbia Medical Services Plan for services rendered. Billing is done in accordance with a physician fee schedule that is determined by contract negotiations between the provincial medical association and the provincial government. Laws forbid the "extra-billing" of patients for medically necessary services above the Medicare rates; however, these rates have not kept up with inflation, the rising cost of living, or growing office overhead costs.

With the apparent lack of political will and leadership to spur reform in this area, the future of family medicine as the cornerstone of the Canadian healthcare system looks bleaker with each passing year. When the system essentially punishes family doctors for practicing good medicine, today's new graduates—who tend to have large student debt loads and who place a high value on work–life balance—are naturally going to pursue other areas. And with this new generation of doctors voting with their feet, the culture of medicine is changing from a profession to a business.

The disintegration of primary care increases the fragmentation of patient care and heightens the risk of duplication and medical errors. Patients often must wait many hours to be seen in hospital EDs, and they may have to wait several months to a year for consultations with specialists, elective surgery, or advanced diagnostic tests such as magnetic resonance imaging scans. With shortages of doctors and nurses, a lack of hospital beds and long-term care facilities, and even ambulances operating over capacity, the universal public healthcare system in Canada is stretched to its limit. It is also in constant gridlock, despite a desperate need for reform to serve the needs of an aging population.

Dr. Zachary believes that physicians should play a vital role, both as patient advocates and as leaders, in driving health system innovations that support high-quality, evidence-based practice. Her passion is to use her experience and knowledge to develop patient-centered models of integrated primary care and thereby improve population health. She considers three potential options, each with risks and benefits, for what she should do:

1. *Continue working in her current solo practice and look after her patients with chronic, complex diseases for as long as possible or until she retires.* She knows that her patients need and appreciate her care. Although this option would provide her with great professional satisfaction and autonomy, she would have to work longer hours to see more patients if she wishes to maintain a viable practice. Doing so could possibly result in burnout and is likely not sustainable.

2. *Close her medical practice and work in a walk-in clinic (providing simple, episodic care) or join a group practice.* This option would enable her

to earn a higher income and work part-time without losing money. However, it would reduce her autonomy and professional satisfaction, both of which she values highly.

3. *Fight to save family practice in the province through political and grassroots advocacy efforts to change the healthcare delivery and payment systems.* This option represents an opportunity to shape the future of integrated primary care and to support independent practitioners who provide comprehensive services and continuity of care. Dr. Zachary would seek to build such a movement with a coalition of like-minded doctors and citizens who wish to transform the healthcare system. This effort, of course, would require significant time and energy, and it would demand maximum flexibility and autonomy in her own practice.

Dr. Zachary believes she can use her medical practice as a laboratory of reform to build a new practice model that supports solo and small-group independent practitioners who wish to deliver high-quality, evidence-based, culturally sensitive care. The model she envisions is based on the four pillars of primary care—first contact, comprehensive care, longitudinal care, and coordinated care—with a whole-person orientation and a longitudinal doctor–patient relationship as the result. The practice model is integrated with other family practitioners, specialists, and allied health professionals in acute care and community care who will work as a "virtual team" with the patient in the center.

The goal for such a model is to provide services that are timely, efficient, effective, and compassionate across the care continuum for every patient. Serving the community's needs also involves identifying the gaps and challenges of vulnerable groups, such as new immigrants and the large numbers of ethnic Chinese patients in Vancouver who face language barriers. Dr. Zachary must convince other like-minded physicians and health professionals to form a collaborative network and enlist community leaders to support such an initiative. She would also need funding to plan and implement an evidence-based model as a pilot project with evaluation and practice-based research.

Dr. Zachary believes that strengthening the future of family practice is essential for the development of an integrated patient-centered system that serves the community and meets the "triple aim" goals of improved care, reduced costs, and better health. Well-designed payment reforms are needed to align incentives with quality and value. Key challenges will be to develop new quality measures that are meaningful for patients, to minimize bureaucratic intrusions that interfere with patient care, and to objectively evaluate the outcomes and performances of practitioners and of models being proposed for system redesign. Evidence-based approaches are vital for determining what interventions do and do not work, supporting continuous learning, informing policy decisions for accountable care, and restoring excellence to the Canadian healthcare system.

## Case Questions

1. How should Dr. Zachary evaluate the alternatives she outlines for her future? What are the pros and cons of each option?

2. If Dr. Zachary decides to pursue health reform using her practice as a laboratory, what stakeholders will she need to recruit to help her in the effort?

3. What additional evidence can Dr. Zachary gather to build her case for reform?

# INDEX

Note: Italicized page locators refer to figures or tables in exhibits.

# ABOUT THE EDITORS

**Ann Scheck McAlearney, ScD, MS**, is professor of family medicine and vice chair for research in the Department of Family Medicine at the Ohio State University (OSU) College of Medicine. She also holds courtesy appointments at OSU as professor in the Division of Health Services Management and Policy at the College of Public Health and as professor of pediatrics. In 19 years at OSU, Dr. McAlearney has taught a variety of courses in organizational management, leadership, and strategic management for master's and doctoral-level students, as well as a course on healthcare organization and financing for medical students. She has 25 years of health services research experience and has authored more than 200 peer-reviewed publications, 10 books (mostly coedited), and 60 book chapters.

Dr. McAlearney is currently principal investigator (PI) for a study funded by the Agency for Healthcare Research and Quality (AHRQ) that examines the implementation and use of an inpatient portal in an academic medical center. She is also PI of another AHRQ-funded study looking at patients' and providers' experiences with patient portals and is project director of an AHRQ-funded patient safety learning laboratory at the Ohio State University Wexner Medical Center. She recently completed work as PI of a study, funded by the Robert Wood Johnson Foundation, examining the impact of accountable care organizations and as the local PI for two additional studies, funded by the National Institutes of Health, attempting to improve breast cancer care using organizational and systems solutions to care delivery problems. Her general research interests also include primary care quality improvement, information technology innovations in healthcare, and organizational development.

Dr. McAlearney's book *Population Health Management: Strategies to Improve Outcomes* (2003) was published by Health Administration Press. She has held positions and had consulting arrangements with various organizations, including UniHealth; Monsanto Health Solutions; PacifiCare Health Systems; Merck & Co.; Massachusetts General Hospital; University of California, Los Angeles Medical Center; Arthur Young & Company; the Congressional Budget Office; and the World Health Organization. Dr. McAlearney received her bachelor of arts and sciences degree in English and biological sciences from Stanford University, her master of science degree in biological sciences from Stanford, and her doctor of science degree in health policy and management from Harvard University's School of Public Health.

**Anthony R. Kovner, PhD**, is professor at the Robert F. Wagner Graduate School of Public Service, New York University (NYU), and was director of the health policy and management program for 16 years. He was the fourth recipient of the Filerman Prize for Educational Leadership from the Association of University Programs of Health Administration. At NYU, he developed the health program Capstone course and the executive master of public administration program for nurse leaders. He has written or edited 11 books (mostly coedited) and more than 90 peer-reviewed articles, many of them case studies. Dr. Kovner has been a senior manager of two hospitals, a nursing home, a group practice, and a neighborhood health center, as well as a senior healthcare consultant for a large industrial union. He has been a leader in the evidence-based management movement and served as a founding member of the Academic Council of the Center for Evidence-Based Management.

# ABOUT THE CONTRIBUTORS

**Sofia Agoritsas, FACHE**, is a senior director in hospital operations at Northwell Health® Cohen Children's Medical Center. She previously served at Northwell Health® in a variety of departments and divisions.

**Alison M. Aldrich** is an academic medical research librarian at the Ohio State University. She holds a master of science in information degree from the University of Michigan and a master of public health degree from Wright State University.

**Emily Allinder** is the program director of strategic business development at Saint Luke's Hospital in Kansas City, Missouri.

**Barbara Barash, MD**, is a postdoctoral researcher in the Department of Family Medicine, College of Medicine, at the Ohio State University. She is also the medical director / quality improvement coordinator at Elite Home Health Care Services, LLC.

**Agnes Barden, DNP, RN, CPXP**, has worked in the Northwell Health® organization as a nurse educator, assistant director of nursing education and research, senior administrative director of patient and family-centered care, associate executive director, assistant vice president, and, currently, vice president in the Office of Patient and Customer Experience.

**Nathan Burt** is the system director of facilities management at Ohio Health in Columbus.

**Claudia Caine** is the executive vice president and hospital director / chief operating officer of Lutheran Medical Center in Brooklyn, New York.

**J. Mac Crawford, PhD**, is retired from the Ohio State University, where he taught environmental and occupational health in the Division of Environmental Health Sciences within the College of Public Health. His epidemiologic research focused on the health of first responders. He also worked with colleagues in the College of Engineering doing ergonomics research and intervention.

**Richard D'Aquila, FACHE**, is the president of Yale–New Haven Hospital and Yale–New Haven Health System in Connecticut. He received his graduate degree in hospital administration from the Yale University School of Medicine and his bachelor's degree in economics from Central Connecticut State University. He is a member of the lecturing faculty at the Robert F. Wagner Graduate School of Public Service at New York University and the Yale University School of Medicine's Department of Epidemiology and Public Health.

**Jason Dopoulos** is a managing director with Lancaster Pollard, a financial services firm based in Columbus, Ohio, that specializes in providing capital funding to the senior living, healthcare, and affordable housing sectors. He holds a master's degree in health administration from the Ohio State University College of Public Health in Columbus.

**James W. Ferguson, MD**, has been a solo family physician in East Islip, New York, for the past 30 years. He received an honorary doctorate from St. George Medical School in 2016.

**Peter Follows** cofounded Carpedia International Ltd., an implementation-based management consulting company. He is the CEO of Carpedia's group of companies: Carpedia International, Carpedia Hospitality, Carpedia Healthcare, and Carpedia Capital.

**Alice Gaughan** is a project manager in the Department of Family Medicine at the Ohio State University.

**Sven Gierlinger** is chief experience officer for Northwell Health®. He is responsible for building an engaging, innovative, and collaborative culture that drives organizational growth and customer loyalty through the customer experience. Previously, he served as vice president of hospitality and service culture at Henry Ford Health System and also played a critical role in the start-up and success of Henry Ford West Bloomfield Hospital.

**John R. Griffith, FACHE**, is professor emeritus in the Department of Health Management and Policy, School of Public Health, at the University of Michigan. His book *The Well-Managed Healthcare Organization*, now in the eighth edition with Kenneth R. White, has won several awards and is considered the "definitive resource" on the subject.

**Jennifer Lynn Hefner, PhD**, is an assistant professor in the Department of Family Medicine at the Ohio State University. She is interested in primary care and hospital care practice transformation to improve patient care and work satisfaction for providers.

**Adam Henick** is chief operating officer for AdvantageCare Physicians in New York. He received his MBA in accounting and business/management from Columbia Business School.

**Brian Hilligoss, PhD**, is an assistant professor in the Division of Health Services Management and Policy at the Ohio State University College of Public Health. He teaches courses in management and organizational behavior, leadership and organizational change, and quality and patient safety.

**Maria Jorina, PhD**, works as a survey methodologist at Boston Children's Hospital. She received her PhD in health services management and policy from the Ohio State University.

**David M. Kaplan** is the executive director, administration, at Northwell Health® Cancer Institute. He is an assistant professor at New York University, where he teaches the business aspects of medicine. Mr. Kaplan earned a master of public administration degree with a concentration in health policy and administration from the Robert F. Wagner School of Public Service at New York University.

**Kim Karels** is a clinical research assistant with the Department of Family Medicine at the Ohio State University. She has a professional background in program planning and project design, as well as monitoring and evaluation. She received her master's degree in intercultural service, leadership, and management from the School for International Training Graduate Institute.

**Barbara Langland-Orban, PhD**, is an associate professor and the master of health administration program director in the Department of Health Policy and Management at the College of Public Health, University of South Florida.

**Sara Little** holds a master of public administration degree from New York University's Robert F. Wagner School of Public Service. She presently works in London as senior manager in the National Health Service.

**Wilhelmina Manzano, RN, NEA-BC**, is senior vice president and chief nurse executive for the New York–Presbyterian enterprise, which consists of New York–Presbyterian Hospital and the Regional Hospital Network. Ms. Manzano has adjunct faculty appointments at the New York University (NYU) Robert F. Wagner School of Public Service, the NYU College of Nursing, the Columbia

University School of Nursing (CUSON), and the Frances Payne Bolton School of Nursing. She also serves as assistant dean for clinical affairs at CUSON.

**Terri Menser, PhD**, is a postdoctoral researcher in the Department of Family Medicine in the College of Medicine at the Ohio State University. Dr. Menser received her master of business administration degree from Florida State and her doctorate in health services research from Texas A&M University.

**Susan Moffatt-Bruce, MD, PhD**, is a tenured professor in surgery, molecular virology, immunology, and medical genetics and biomedical informatics at the Ohio State University. She was appointed associate dean of clinical affairs, quality, and patient safety in 2012.

**Arthur Mora, PhD**, is a clinical assistant professor in the Department of Global Health Management and Policy at the Tulane University School of Public Health and Tropical Medicine. He is a Certified Professional in Healthcare Quality and a Six Sigma green belt involved in numerous improvement projects.

**Duncan Neuhauser, PhD**, is the Charles Elton Blanchard MD Professor of Health Management Emeritus at Case Western Reserve University Medical School in Cleveland, Ohio. His interests include personal quality improvement, quality of care, and medical decision making.

**Zachary Pruitt, PhD**, is an assistant professor in the Department of Health Policy and Management, College of Public Health, at the University of South Florida.

**Ramya Rao, PMP, RHIA**, is a project manager at Swedish Covenant Medical Center in Chicago, Illinois.

**David Reisman, FACHE**, is the senior administrative director of the Department of Emergency Medicine and the associate director of the Center for Disaster Medicine at Massachusetts General Hospital. He holds a bachelor's degree in business administration from the University of Massachusetts at Amherst and a master's degree in healthcare administration from the Ohio State University. He is a Fellow of the American College of Healthcare Executives.

**Julie Robbins, PhD**, is the master of health administration (MHA) program director and an assistant clinical professor at the Ohio State University College of Public Health. She holds MHA and PhD degrees from Ohio State. Over the last 20 years, Dr. Robbins has held leadership roles and been responsible for strategy development in a variety of public- and private-sector healthcare organizations.

**Rebecca Schmale, PhD**, is vice president for learning and organizational development at Carolinas Healthcare System, headquartered in Charlotte, North Carolina. She previously served at Froedtert and the Medical College of Wisconsin, the University of Virginia Health System, and OhioHealth.

**Cynthia J. Sieck, PhD**, is an assistant professor in the Department of Family Medicine at the Ohio State University College of Medicine. Dr. Sieck received her PhD from the University of Michigan School of Public Health, Department of Health Behavior and Health Education, and her master of public health degree from the University of Pittsburgh College of Public Health, Division of Public and Community Health Services.

**Paula H. Song, PhD**, is an associate professor in the Department of Health Policy and Management in the Gillings School of Global Public Health at the University of North Carolina at Chapel Hill. Dr. Song received her PhD in health services organization and policy, as well as master's degrees in health services administration and applied economics, from the University of Michigan.

**Lindsey N. Sova, CHES**, is a senior research associate in the Department of Family Medicine, College of Medicine, at the Ohio State University. She holds a master of public health degree in health behavior and health promotion from the Ohio State University.

**Breanne Taylor** is a graduate of both Indiana University and the Ohio State University. She has been with Nationwide Children's Hospital in Columbus, Ohio, for ten years and is currently serving as the regional development manager.

**Jacob Victory** is currently chief operating officer for the New Jewish Home, one of the largest post-acute care systems in New York State. He has a master of public administration degree from New York University's Robert F. Wagner Graduate School of Public Service, where he currently serves as assistant professor of health policy and management, adjunct faculty.

**Erick Vidmar** is currently the administrative director of Cleveland Clinic Nevada, located in Las Vegas. He is a 2006 graduate of the Ohio State University, in the division of health services management and policy, and has worked for the Cleveland Clinic in both Abu Dhabi and Cleveland.

**Jason Waibel** is the director of therapy operations for HealthSouth Rehabilitation Hospital of Northern Virginia.

**Daniel Walker, PhD**, is an assistant professor in the Department of Family Medicine at the Ohio State University College of Medicine. He received his doctoral degree in global health management and policy from the Tulane University School of Public Health and Tropical Medicine, and he completed a postdoctoral fellowship in the Department of Family Medicine at the Ohio State University College of Medicine.

**Karen Schachter Weingrod** is manager of the Comprehensive Breast Care Program at Hartford Hospital, an 800-bed teaching hospital in Hartford, Connecticut.

**Michael J. Zaccagnino** is a consultant with more than 20 years of health system, medical group, hospital, and new ventures experience. He serves as the president of Lucania Partners and is the former managing director of Carpedia Healthcare. His areas of expertise include healthcare innovation, strategy formation and execution, health system development and organizational effectiveness, delivery system reform, patient experience, population health, and results-oriented performance improvement.